Projections 12

in the same series

PROJECTIONS 1
John Boorman fires the starting-gun for the series; includes interviews with Michael Mann, Gus Van Sant by River Phoenix and Demme on Demme

PROJECTIONS 2
Interviews with George Miller, Willem Dafoe, Jaco Van Dormael, as well as Altman on Altman

PROJECTIONS 3
The diaries of Francis Coppola, interviews with Quentin Tarantino, Chen Kaige, Sally Potter, as well as Kasdan on Kasdan

PROJECTIONS 4
James Toback's diary, an interview with Gene Kelly, Lindsay Anderson's tribute to John Ford, Walter Murch on sound design and Arthur Penn on Arthur Penn

PROJECTIONS 4½
What is your favourite film? Answered by Clint Eastwood, the Coens, Elia Kazan, Mike Leigh, Stephen Frears, Steven Soderbergh, among others

PROJECTIONS 5
Animation issue. Also includes Jamie Lee Curtis talking to her father Tony Curtis, Quentin Tarantino and Brian De Palma, and Jimmy Stewart's last interview

PROJECTIONS 6
Pieces by Mike Figgis, Eleanor Coppola, Tom DiCillo, Robert Towne and interviews with Vittorio Storaro and Stanley Donen

PROJECTIONS 7
Scorsese issue; also includes Jamie Lee Curtis talking to her mother, Janet Leigh, Willem Dafoe with Frances McDormand and an interview with Robert Mitchum

PROJECTIONS 8
International critics answer the question: Does film criticism have any value today? Also, Christopher Doyle's diary of his work with Wong Kar-Wai and interviews with Abbas Kiarostami and Abraham Polonsky

PROJECTIONS 9
The legacy of French cinema from Robert Bresson to Matthieu Kassovitz's *La Haine*

PROJECTIONS 10
The Hollywood issue. Mike Figgis explores the System in conversation with Mel Gibson, Salma Hayek, Paul Thomas Anderson and others

PROJECTIONS 11
The New York issue. A companion issue to the Hollywood one in which Spike Lee, Tim Robbins, Jim Jarmusch, David O. Russell and Wes Anderson provide an alternative to Hollywood film-making.

PROJECTIONS 12
Film-makers on Film Schools

Edited by John Boorman, Fraser MacDonald and Walter Donohue
Associate editor: Oren Moverman

faber and faber

First published in 2002
by Faber and Faber Limited
3 Queen Square London WC1N 3AU
Published in the United States by Faber and Faber Inc.
an affiliate of Farrar, Straus and Giroux LLC, New York

Typeset by Faber and Faber Ltd
Printed in England by Clays Ltd, St Ives plc

A CIP record for this book is available from the British Library

ISBN 0-571-20694-8

10 9 8 7 6 5 4 3 2 1

Contents

Introduction by John Boorman vii

UK AND EUROPEAN FILM SCHOOLS

1. Introduction by Fraser MacDonald 3
2. Roger Crittenden: Director of Curriculum, National Film and Television School 9
3. Damien O'Donnell: Director 23
4. Dick Ross: Tutor 39
5. Ben Gibson: Director, the London Film School 55
6. Michele Camarda: Producer 69
7. Simon Moore: Screenwriter 79
8. Kim Longinotto: Documentarian 91
9. Alwin Kuchler: Cinematographer; Jane Morton: Production Designer; Lynne Ramsay: Writer–Director; Lucia Zucchetti: Editor 101
10. *L'Année Dernière à Beaconsfield*: Diary of a final year at the National Film and Television School, by Fraser MacDonald 125

US FILM SCHOOLS

11. Introduction by Oren Moverman 171
12. Jay Rabinowitz: Editor 175
13. Lodge Kerrigan: Writer–Director 183
14. Dan Kleinman: Chair, Columbia University Graduate Program 189
15. Jessica Levin, Ayad Stehle-Akhtar and Claudia Myers: Students, Columbia University Graduate Program 197
16. Michael Spiller: Cinematographer; Oren Moverman: Screenwriter 211
17. Nicholas Ray: Director, Teacher/Master, Harpur College; Danny Fisher: Producer/Graduate, Harpur College 221

DIRECTORS

18. Walter Salles, by Peter Stephan Jungk 233
19. Pawel Pawlikowski, by Andrew Pulver 265
20. François Ozon, by Ryan Gilbey 283
21. Bruno Dumont on Bruno Dumont, by Kaleem Aftab 301

ACTORS

22. Days with the Maestro: My time with Michelangelo Antonioni and Italian Cinema in the making of *Beyond the Clouds*, by Peter Weller 315

23. Pissing in the Tall Grass with the Big Dogs. Fiction by Ethan Hawke 353

DIGITAL CINEMA

24. The New Frontier? Richard Linklater's *Waking Life* 361

IN MEMORIAM

25. A Tribute to Henri Alekan, by Wim Wenders 367

Introduction by John Boorman

The Hollywood studios developed extensive training schemes – everything from matte painting and wig making to teaching starlets deportment. Writers worked in cubicles like battery hens and were required to produce so-many pages per day. These were assessed, criticized and sent back to be re-written. It was a production line.

When the studio system collapsed, so did the training. What survived was apprenticeship. The clapper-loader became the operator, became the Director of Photography. Every cameraman could trace his provenance back to Billy Bitzer.

Under the Soviet system, film schools had been set up as part of an integrated industry. After training, the students were sent to a studio and were assigned to a movie as a director, cameraman or whatever. Employment was guaranteed. These schools, Poland's in particular, became the model for Western countries when they set about filling the gap. What they lacked was a direct connection to the industry – they could not guarantee a job, still can't. However, NYU and USC produced celebrity alumni – Scorsese, Coppola, Lucas – and soon students were beating down their doors.

Today there are thousands of courses offered in academe. There are virtual film schools on the internet where your mouse can take you through the process, show you how to break down a scene into set-ups or operate a steadicam. There is even an annual international festival for film schools.

A student will need $100,000 to get a Masters at a top American school, and not much less at the National Film School in England. For that money, he can make a full-length feature with a digital camera. What route should he take? Are film schools any good? What can they teach?

Veteran film student Fraser MacDonald poses these issues to teachers and to the taught. He is assisted in America by Oren Moverman, another film graduate. The concerns of film students are mostly practical ones: how to finance their courses, how to get the resources to make their films. Many covet the glittering prizes of the mainstream, but others are intent on subverting the system, seizing power by the daring and originality of their movies and wresting the audience away from the manipulative, mindless junk they are addicted to.

A fascinating venture is afoot that will try to connect film schools to industry. Simon Relph is trying to finance a kind of film factory, The Hothouse (email: info@greenpointfilms.co.uk), with experienced department heads supervising a continuous output of low-budget features by film school graduates and others. In a sense it is an alturistic version of Roger Corman's company where so many directors cut their teeth on his tightly controlled, but creatively free, B movies.

All across the world hundreds of thousands of students study film. They cannot all become practitioners, yet there is an impulse to learn the subtleties of film language. We take the movies for granted, but cinema, and its offspring television, have radically changed our perceptions. There is nothing we can experience that we have not already witnessed on film. The moving image has provided us with an alternative universe, a continuous metaphor for our own lives. As these images become more virtual, so this alternative way of being may well become dominant. Many of us moviemakers have intimations that film will grow into something else. Could it be that this impulse to study film is an evolutionary one, pressing to discover this alternative way of being?

John Boorman, 2001

UK AND EUROPEAN FILM SCHOOLS

Fraser MacDonald. © Zoë Norfolk

Introduction by Fraser MacDonald

Somebody once asked the great Akira Kurosawa when he would stop making films. 'When I learn how to do it,' was Kurosawa's reply. He was 80 years old at the time.

I turned 30 in the course of my graduating year (2000) at the National Film and Television School (NFTS) in Beaconsfield, England. By then I had been in institutional film education for most of the last decade; and as I neared the end of this self-imposed tenure, I found myself becoming more reflective about the decisions I had made, and the value of the schooling I received.

Ten years is a long time in film. While I was busy learning my craft, a so-called British Renaissance arose – and for the most part faded – in a blaze of National Lottery funding. Elsewhere in Europe, four mischievous Danish 'brothers' re-opened an old debate about aesthetics, and helped the ponderous question 'What is cinema?' to rear its ugly head once more. Meanwhile the inspirational young guns of the American independent movement seemed to get absorbed into the mainstream. Even the high priest himself, Tarantino, the self-taught *auteur* who gave so much hope to so many would-be directors, became a kind of modern-day Howard Hughes.

Speaking of Dogme 95, I too had once indulged in a small piece of *kino*-politics. Back in Scotland in the early 1990s, I flirted briefly with a movement known as 'Poor Cinema', a precursor to the Danish movement if ever there was one. Technically deficient, yet full of passion, I tried with gusto to find a personal cinema that *mattered*. (At least, that's how I remember things through the lens of hindsight.) My equipment may have been ramshackle, but I had a crew who believed in what I was trying to do. And what was that exactly? I was trying to discover something about myself. My identity.

It was during this period, while I was completing a degree in Film at Napier University, that one of my tutors, Amy Hardie, mooted the idea of my studying at the National Film and Television School. 'What?!' was my incredulous reply, 'Dae ye think I've got a rich faither?' I should explain that when discussing matters of social class, I often slip into the broadest Scots dialect; but that really was how I felt. My socio-political agit-prop ego told me that the NFTS was no place to make films. It was more like a finishing school for the sons of BBC governors who wanted to piss around for three years, secure in the knowledge that their school ties would gain them immediate entry into the profession. 'Oh no, not me,' I thought, 'for I am a grafter.' And for a west-coast Scottish Protestant, there is no such thing as an easy way.

But things change. My disgust gradually waned, to be replaced by a budding egotism. Maybe I *could* go down to London, I reasoned. I could always bring a bit of 'real life' down with me. And hey, it would be another three years of making films. Moreover I felt that I had burned my bridges with the film funding bodies in Scotland. (Here was another aspect of ego – I saw myself as a disfranchized political film-maker. Ah, the folly of youth . . .) So all roads were leading to London. I was further encouraged to meet Ian Sellar, the head of Fiction Direction at NFTS. (He hailed from Strathclyde, and I had liked his films *Venus Peter* and *Prague*.) I posted my application form, plus a show-reel and a cheque for £35, and waited for my interview. It came and went. I was cocky. 'Fuck it,' I thought. 'What happens, happens.' A month later I was back in Beaconsfield for a special two-week induction course, from which the School made its final selection. The Euro 96 football championship was in full throw, and I left Edinburgh the day after the English cuffed Scotland 2–0 at Wembley. I should have read this as an omen. But in fact I felt good. My graduation film from Napier had received a glowing review in the *Scotsman* two days previously, and my friends and peers were all behind me. 'Och, you'll walk it!'

Needless to say, I didn't. Only six people are admitted to the Fiction Department each year. There were 18 of us on that induction course, and my guess is that I was probably ninth on the list. I had failed. Meanwhile my partner Andrea applied for the NFTS Screen Design course. Two months after I came back with my tail between my legs, she was accepted. For about a fortnight after, I wandered round my flat looking for my ego. When I finally found it, it was a lot smaller than I remembered.

The New Year duly came, and with it the application deadline for the 1998 intake. I was spending more time in London to be with Andrea, and I was growing to like the place. Also I had been short-listed to make a film under the New Directors scheme at the British Film Institute (BFI), and the script development was ongoing throughout the spring months. Yet, the NFTS kept pulling at me. So I gave in and re-applied. Maybe the previous year just hadn't been my moment . . . I spoke at length to Ian Sellar who assured me it was the right thing to do. Cynically, I mulled over the prospect of handing over another £35 cheque. Was that how they made their money, I wondered?

I entered a now familiar routine. I waited. The BFI seemed to be pleased with the revised New Directors script, so that project carried onward to the next round. My interview for the NFTS came and went. Once again I felt slightly cocky, but I knew enough this time to keep my feet on the ground. Surprise-surprise, I was asked to attend the fortnight's induction course. But this time I had a nagging sense of dread that I might have over-played my hand. The BFI project was important to me, and the New Directors scheme was not open to fulltime film students. Becky Lloyd, the producer of the prospective BFI project, asked me what I would do if I got both. I hadn't thought of that.

Of course, I did indeed get both, and so at last understood my Gran's complaint about buses always arriving in pairs when it's sunny. I worked the predicament out thus: we received the BFI commission on Monday; the NFTS accepted me on Tuesday; so technically I wasn't a student when the BFI said 'yes' to me. Greedily, I said 'yes' to both invitations. Incredibly, the Lottery ticket I bought on the Wednesday turned out to be a dud. But otherwise it felt good to be alive . . .

All of that was three years ago. And now? Well, I am somewhat more tainted by experience. I have the feeling that in searching for something, I've also lost something. Whether this was the film school's fault or, as is more likely, my own doing, is the kind of question I now want to answer.

Film School is different things to different people. Some people enjoy their time there, and will later cite their school as the place where they 'became a film-maker'. Others struggle against a system that they see as intent on creating product rather than art. Even if you went to the best film school in the world (wherever that may be), there would still be something to complain about. But we can't deny the track record that the major film schools have established. The last 40 years of world cinema have been dominated by their graduates, from the Czech new wave to the American movie brats. Recently my own school's output has been further distinguished by the work of Lynne Ramsay and her collaborators. Yet, as cinema ages, it also evolves. Digital technology has made the 'Just Do It' mentality much easier to realize. And as the cost of further education mounts, the cost of equipment seems to go in the opposite direction. So can we really argue that film school is the right way to go for budding film-makers? Do we really need them?

If the following pages are an odyssey, then it's more *Candide* than *Ulysses*. But I hope that the questions asked, and the various attempts at answers, will be useful to others.

Acknowledgements

I would like to thank all the people who gave up their precious time to be badgered by a film student with a microphone. And my editor, Richard Kelly, for letting me complete this cathartic process, and keeping me from wandering too much.

After ten years of further education, I have been influenced by many people, all of whom I cannot possibly list, but I would like to single out some:

The crew that worked with me at the NFTS – Ali Reid, Gavin Struthers, Robert Bourke, Douglas M. Ray, Antonia Baldo, Jim McRoberts, Stephen Swain, Mel Byers, Ruben Koeing and Tara Crème.

Tutors – Ian Sellar, Dick Ross, Stephen Frears and Colin McLeod.

Friends – Luke Sutherland, Stevie Gilmour, Dave and Al Arrowsmith, Becky Lloyd and Lizzie Francke.

My Dad, Leslie Haswell, and my little brother, Grant MacDonald.

I would like to dedicate these pages to two women who have supported me throughout my education: my now wife, Andrea Matheson MacDonald, for a shoulder to cry on and for keeping my feet on the ground; and my mother, Cathy Haswell, who sadly did not see this book published. Thanks Mum for everything, I promise I will keep on trying.

Fraser MacDonald, September 2001

Roger Crittenden

Roger Crittenden: Director of Curriculum, National Film and Television School

Roger Crittenden has been at the NFTS since its inception in 1971. Over the years he has become a valuable source of knowledge for the students, a unique sounding board for ideas and frustrations, because he has seen and heard them all. Recently he became the school's Director of Curriculum, in charge of its development and its students.

The appointment came at a time of change: in 2000 the NFTS ceased to be a 3-year course, changing instead to a two-year diploma with an optional third year 'Advanced' course, which is also open to applicants from outside the school. The hope is to encourage artists, journalists, and other types of people not normally associated with film to study at NFTS, so enabling the school to produce a more eclectic range of work. I went to see Roger at Beaconsfield, to discuss these and other changes he has seen across his tenure.

Fraser MacDonald: What did you do before starting to teach at the NFTS?
Roger Crittenden: I was a film editor for ten years, largely at the BBC, until the school was started in 1971 and I joined as Head of Editing. Initially I came for just a year, with no idea how long I would last. Colleagues said to me, 'You must be mad, you're abandoning a promising career.' But for some reason I just felt it was important to be associated with the National Film School, as it was then. Really it was something of an embarrassment that one hadn't existed previously.

FM: So why do you think it was finally set up?
RC: Largely because of the initiative and energy of Jenny Lee*. I think that she saw – or was persuaded to see by others – that if we were serious about having our own film industry, then we needed proper training. This was within a climate where even the system of apprenticeship, of learning on the job, had broken down, because of another downturn in British film production. So I think that's why Jenny Lee took the initiative, in 1965, to set up the Lloyd Committee. They were given a very broad brief, but it included going to visit a number of what were then the leading film schools in both Europe and America, to see on what basis a school should be set up. Fortunately that committee

* Daughter of a Scottish coalminer, Labour MP for Lanark (1929), later for Cannock (1945). Appointed in 1964 as Arts minister by Prime Minister Harold Wilson; responsible for setting up Open University.

reported favourably in 1967, and for the first time all sides of the industry – unions, employers, leading directors and producers – agreed that we needed a film school, that it should be autonomous, and that it should be a partnership between government and industry. That was a fairly unusual conclusion, since all the film schools around the world prior to that, and indeed since, have either been publicly funded or industry-supported; or indeed, as in the US, part of the wider educational framework, with students paying huge tuition fees. But anyway, a bill went through Parliament in 1970, very much on the back of the Lloyd Committee's findings.

FM: Of those overseas schools that the committee visited, did they find any particular models for how they thought the NFS might work?
RC: Well, they went to Poland, Moscow, Hungary, and they also looked at France and Italy, because those schools were considered to be very effective, not only as trainers for business but also as conduits to it. The committee definitely felt Poland was a good model, and maybe that was one of the reasons they felt that the NFS should be a government-and-industry product. The industry's financial support at that time was based on money from the Eady Levy, which was drawn from box-office receipts. It was quasi-government money, from a circulated fund. But much of those receipts went back to the US, depending on how successful or unsuccessful an American movie was.

FM: So, in a sense, the school was to help bolster an ailing British cinema?
RC: Yeah. And I believe that the thinking among some of the committee, which included people like Karel Reisz, was that there was a talent pool in this country that just wasn't being tapped, despite the good quality training that the BBC had established, and later on ITV. But that training was in television, and cinema was being ignored. And although the film industry did begin to recruit from television, there was a feeling that cinema was something else, and needed its own form of education.

FM: This was during the golden era of British television, *Play for Today*, where you had people like Stephen Frears and Ken Loach working within the BBC. So you could say television was superseding British cinema at that point?
RC: There was a famous saying in the 1960s that British cinema was alive and well and living in television – which was a half-truth, in that British television was the least worst in the world (*laughs*), and I was glad to be part of it. But there still was a real separation. You were either cinema or TV, and not many people made the shift from one to the other. There was still a lot of nepotism – closed shop, if you will – in film. It was bloody hard to get into. So part of the motivation of the school was to find the talent and give it a chance, because part

of the graduation was a ticket, and that, to be frank, was the main reason why people wanted to come here.

FM: 'A ticket' being a union card?
RC: Yeah – and it was unrestricted too, meaning that you could even start in a certain position, for instance as a sound person, and if you got offered a job the next week as a director then you could take that too. Which was really quite exceptional.

FM: Did it cause a lot of ructions?
RC: It was challenged every year at the union conference, and fortunately every year the support was continued. In those first years, we had to fight really hard to sustain the school's support and to justify it. Colin Young's policy of keeping a low profile on what we were doing was to give us a chance to develop long enough and strong enough, to prove that we were producing results.

FM: A lot of the early NFS graduates are world-renowned now: Nick Broomfield*, Michael Radford†, Roger Deakins††. What was the ethos of the teaching back then?
RC: Because Colin was persuaded to come back from UCLA where he had been teaching, he was accordingly given a free hand to largely do it the way he felt was best. He could always describe it very briefly: 'Find the 25 most talented people who have applied, and give them a chance to develop in an open sand-pit.' Of course, the vast majority of those 25 wanted to be directors of fiction or documentary. In time, an animation course was added. But there was no curriculum, so it was very much, 'Here's the facility.' You had a stimulating peer group, and there was a very small core staff, plus some tutors who came and went. In fact, until the 1980s, there wasn't even specialization – you didn't have to elect to do anything. In spite of that, the camera department established a very high reputation early on, which has been sustained. And the character of the place remained like that, until finally we moved to specialization.

FM: Why did you make that move?
RC: There was pressure to do so. The industry felt that a so-called 'elitist'

---

* Documentarian whose often-controversial career includes films such as *Aileen Wuornos: The Selling of a Serial Killer* (1992), *Heidi Fleiss: Hollywood Madam* (1995) and *Kurt & Courtney* (1998).
† Writer–Director of *Another Time, Another Place* (1983), *Nineteen Eighty-Four* (1984), *White Mischief* (1987), *Il Postino* (1994) and *Dancing at the Blue Iguana* (2000).
†† Cinematographer on Radford's early features, and the Coen brothers' regular DoP since *Barton Fink* (1991). Also shot *The Shawshank Redemption* (1994), *Dead Man Walking* (1995) and *Kundun* (1997).

institution – and that's a label that has stuck in certain quarters to this day – should not be given a large amount of money from government and industry just to help 25 aspiring directors to 'play', if you like – 'to develop', we would say. But if you describe it as 'play', letting loose 25 more directors every year into a market that some people felt was already saturated, then it just wasn't a good use of public and industry money. In any case, there were other technical areas where people's needs were maybe greater at times.

FM: This was because of the breakdown of the apprentice system?
RC: Yes. There was little chance for people to learn unless they had connections, especially at the time when the industry was contracting. What hit us most was the terrible downfall of cinema attendance, which resulted in the abandonment of the Eady Levy. In that context the school had to make a different argument about its value. If you leave aside the level of investment, the stimulus for greater film production was only ever going to come from talent, pushing for the desire to make movies. Each generation of that talent had to be visible in order to regenerate the situation.

FM: So what was being taught at the school that made it different from a training course?
RC: It was felt that we shouldn't provide too narrow an education. Students did learn a hell of a lot of good craft, but through that they also gained a broader understanding of how the medium worked. So in that kind of open situation, someone like Mike Radford would shoot documentaries rather than just concentrating on his own fiction films. It was also a pretty good preparation for surviving beyond the school. In those early days, the idea grew that students should have a craft skill, not only to reinforce their ability to work with other people, but also to give them a means of survival in the industry, until other opportunities came along for them to do what they wanted to do. So the possibilities were healthy, though they did depend a great deal on the individual taking advantage of them. Of course, there were victims too, people who didn't get that broad education, or even the deep education in one area – maybe because of their own lack of energy or commitment. But it was certainly healthy for the majority.

FM: Do you think that the NFTS suffers from its relationship with the industry, in the sense of having to keep your sponsors happy? You could argue that it only became a film *and* television school to appease the industry's demands.
RC: But when I look at the lists of the current work of our graduates, which is printed here every week, I find that 70 per cent of the credits are television credits. The school has always supplied talent to television, and it was always going to be the case, no matter the aspirations of most students. As to satisfying

sponsors . . . in my mind it's very difficult to measure just what it is in an institution like this that encourages – rather than 'makes' – students conform to what they think the industry might expect of them. In the early days, in most intakes, I felt there was a core group of students who would go their own way and give each other strength and support to do quite extreme work. We knew that their experience at the school would at least give them a kind of 'Been there, done that' feeling that would enable them to go on and focus, and find their audience. And still, every year we see work that wouldn't fit the expectations of sponsors.

But one is always wishing there was more of that challenging stuff. It's very easy for me to sit here and say that, because I'm not at the sharp end of being a student who wants a career. But there is clearly a *zeitgeist* that affects people's attitudes to what they feel they can develop the courage to do. Quite frankly, what we noticed among the students in what have become known as The Thatcher Years was a narrowing of ambition and a growing of philistinism. I'm not talking about every student. But sometimes you got an overwhelming feeling that students were not willing to embrace the history of cinema, even if they knew it; or to use that history as a rock to stand on and say, 'Now what do we do with this medium?' That's been sad and I'm sure that we have done less than we should have done to fight against it, or to make the students feel comfortable enough to do that challenging work.

FM: Do you think that the school became a victim of its own success?
RC: In some ways, yes. I honestly don't think we have cracked the effect of specialization. And I don't think any other institution has either. Unless you are very careful, the trouble you find is that the demand of each area leads to a lowest-common-denominator result. You or I could choose any area to pick on, but one of the clearest is cinematography. Despite the wonderful success of the school in training cinematographers, I've often felt that their demands, put at their lowest – their show-reels – affect their desire to experiment and go out on a limb. That's why it's great to see that Alwin Kuchler has now shot a film for Michael Winterbottom (*The Claim*, 2000), because in his time here he was clearly someone who was not so concerned with going to Take 10 to get the perfect shot for his show-reel. He was far more long-sighted than some who will inhibit the director because they want the operating and the lighting to be perfect. In that case, if you're not careful, the story, the real nub of the film, comes second. I'm not blaming cinematography for everything; I just use it as an example of what happens when you have ten specializations. And in Fiction Direction you use six or seven of them on your films. Each person wants their bit of the cake to be the best, perfect in some sense. But it can sometimes downgrade the whole.

FM: There's a saying in Scotland, 'Fur coat and no knickers', which could be applied to a lot of work coming out of film schools: the films look beautiful and are well packaged, but the substance of the story gets lost. You often find that the students' second-year films were more interesting because there was less pressure.

RC: Whatever the gross disadvantages the East European system had, the students knew they were part of a whole system through which they progressed. They made a short that went into cinemas – that was almost guaranteed – and it was done under controlled conditions. And their scripts were vetted very thoroughly – they *had* to use metaphor and suchlike, as a way of making interesting work. And at least there wasn't that feeling of, 'Now it's the end of school, here is the industry I've got to get into, I must connect the two in order to get asked through a door to get my next film made.' In the early days of the school, after the first ten years or so, we could see that was a problem and we tried to build bridges. We were giving seed money to people after they left the school, and we appointed somebody to oversee that, but it was never entirely satisfactory. Most recently we have been trying to get this 'Jump Start' programme off the ground, which is a similar initiative. What about the first films of our graduates? Not that we would get involved in making them, but can we help to build a bridge to their development? Maybe the Advanced programme can work in that way. And perhaps our relationship with the Film Council can help too. Who knows? But it's the nub of the problem, and it forces students in all categories to think too narrowly about their work.

FM: Do you think that we concentrate too exclusively on the technique rather than the art of making films?

RC: I think technique has been exacerbated. The thing is that it's very easily definable – you learn another editing system because it's there, and it might be useful. Whereas learning to do something different with that editing system is harder to put your finger on. It's not the same as simply feeling that you're in control of one more piece of technology.

FM: How do you think the digital medium is going to change film education?

RC: My hope is that we will use it far more positively in education. When I first encountered Lightworks, which was designed by an ex-student of the school*, I thought, 'What an amazing educational tool!' rather than, 'What an amazing edit machine.' But he had thought of the process of editing when he designed it. And clearly there are ways in which you can use digital technology to incorporate the

---

* Paul Bamborough set up the Lightworks company. Rumour has it that the icons in the system's user interface were based on the buildings of the school. The notion that the 'shark' which enables editors to delete material bears any resemblance to an NFTS tutor is purely speculative.

kind of analysis of how cinema works, in ways that we could never imagined. I think we have only begun to nibble at it. Some of the exercises that we do are based on material from features; we should do a hell of a lot more of that, and partly looking at it from the point of view of editors. What you get to do as an editor on student films is a pretty narrow spectrum most of the time. You can get very good at editing student films, just as you can get very good at writing them. It's not necessarily the best preparation for that leap to the longer length, and to ideas and ambition that student short films just cannot contain. Take an editor who's faced for the first time with an action sequence; they have never tried to construct something like that as a student. Digital makes that breadth more possible.

But it's complicated – the advantages and disadvantages of technology. Walter Murch gave a wonderful talk here, and he mentioned that while he was doing the re-cut of *Touch of Evil*, he happened to meet Robert Wise, and he said, 'This is nice – the first of Welles's editors meets the last. Or at least, the latest.' But the two of them got to talking about some of the quasi-mysteries of editing, and they ending up deciding that the best way to cut was mute, with your eyes closed, and from the back of the film forward. All of which sounds crazy. And yet, those techniques *are* used by editors, albeit not necessarily combined together. The problem is that technology actually might get in the way of thinking like that, because somehow the machine is telling you not to worry because *it* can do it. It's almost sitting up and begging, 'Oh, do it again. It's okay if we have had fifteen cuts of this scene. Let's have another one.' I'm not arguing for a return to cement joins, but the mental process is obviously radically altered, and we have to be aware of that.

FM: Even though we are all learning on non-linear systems now, don't you think that for an editor and a director, cutting on film, there is a real decision to be made there, and a real discussion about what that cut means?
RC: As you know, we still have the resources to cut on film. Maybe there's an argument for an exercise that establishes just that discussion.

FM: I once spoke to someone who had graduated from NFTS without having touched a non-linear system, so he had to do a further course in order to get a job. Now you find that it's the other way around . . .
RC: Well, the editors still cut on film, but that's just an exercise for them. They don't cut a movie that way. I think we have to convince ourselves of the advantages of going through that experience, rather than just being seen as Luddites who don't appreciate the benefits of The New.

FM: The NFTS is involved in the Global Film School, which, along with UCLA (University of California, Los Angeles) and AFTRS (Australian Film Television

and Radio School, Sydney), aims to set up a film school on the Internet. I don't understand how this sort of school will teach. The one-to-one tutorials that you get at school are invaluable. How can you achieve that kind of teaching over the Net?

RC: I've not really been involved, except in the initial stages of the philosophy behind the venture. However, what we did say was that for many courses the one-to-one, face-to-face tuition is a value that you can never replace; even for subjects that seem like simple things to teach on the Net – production management, for instance. Because nothing can ever replace that first real experience of being in an isolated location, dealing with problems that can't be solved on paper. So, down the line, the suggestion is that whatever can be delivered, to any place in the world, has to be supported by an infrastructure – even locally. You can't have courses that originate in UCLA and everybody has to pop over to LA for the final week. Things have to be further networked, so that if you are in Manila and this course is being beamed to you, you actually have a tutor whom you can see if you get stuck. There is a hell of a lot you can deliver on-line without the cost involved in traditional schools. There are a hell of a lot of people around the world who have no access to training, and it's to be hoped that the Global Film School could deliver this to them. Some people might argue that this is better than no training at all. But one of the big problems for me is this process of the globalization of culture. I think that is a deep risk, one we have to be aware of.

FM: We'll all end up spelling the way Microsoft Word spells . . .
RC: And making movies the same way. Whereas the joy for me in cinema, what I see in a new Japanese movie or an old Polish movie, is such a special experience that I don't *want* to be comfortable about where I am in the world – the way you are if you're staying in a Novotel and you could be anywhere. It would be awfully sad if this initiative contributes to that process.

FM: You can make a feature film now on a camera that costs less than £2000. So film schools are seen almost as dinosaurs. Why should people go there, if they can learn while they're actually making a film? Shane Meadows is a perfect example.
RC: Well, as you probably know, Shane made something like 23 shorts, but he didn't work in total isolation – he did take some advantage of a workshop, so clearly some of the craft came out of working with other people. But you're right – it throws into sharp relief what is the actual, irreducible value of film schools. Stephen Bayly* said to the new students on their first day, 'Buy your "I-movie" kit and £1500 gets you the whole lot, plus a camera, for less than

* Head of NFTS since 1998. Ex-NFTS student, produced *Richard III* (1995) and *Mrs Dalloway* (1997).

half the fee to come to the school.' Now *that* does make you think very hard and long about the value of it. But it should be put in context and seen as a choice between values: the difference between making a movie with cheap digital equipment and your mates; or the value of film school, where you meet and are taught by talented people across a spectrum of jobs in our business.

A few years ago I read an interview with Paul Schrader, and he was asked, 'Where is the film talent coming from now?' He replied, 'Not from schools, but from the minorities. And that includes women, it includes blacks, it includes gays – it includes all those people who have an energy that comes from their situation in life.' I was moved by that, and I think he's right. So the task of film school now is to re-energize itself.

FM: I think digital film-making will help take away some of the mystique around technique.

RC: I don't feel any vested interest in film schools remaining a favoured route into the business. There are industrial and political structures that seem to want to encourage qualifications in order to get through the gate. But I would rather think of how Renoir started – because his girlfriend wanted to be in movies, so he got hold of the barest of equipment and made those remarkable early films. They weren't perfect, in fact there are terrible flaws in them, but they have so much life in them. Then I read somewhere recently, a successful young director saying he doesn't understand the reason for the second take. I mean, that kind of attitude is something film schools should try and avoid. It should be about the magic of making something every time you turn over the camera; it's a different shot, a different moment. Rather than the industrialization of the process, where you cover a scene with umpteen shots and umpteen takes of every shot, and so you have your conventional movie. As long as the movie retains that energy which is about continually thinking through the creative moment, then there is a future for it. Whether we have the structures that allow that kind of space . . .

You said the NFTS was maybe a victim of its own success. We started in 1971, but the first conversations I had with people from other film schools around the world weren't until three years later. They all welcomed us into the fraternity, but they also said 'Watch it. The arteries will harden. If you are not careful, the institution will create an environment that stultifies talent rather than encourages it.' So, in a way, the rise of the new technology and the way it gives people those choices is a good thing. Film school is no longer protected by uniqueness, or by access to technology that you can't get elsewhere.

FM: So do you think that the arteries have hardened?

RC: I think we are in danger of that all the time. This school has had a couple of quadruple bypasses already. (*Laughs.*) And the body hasn't necessarily emerged from it more vital. I think that being pushed to make sure the resources are available for us to continue is no bad thing. And I hope the school never feels complacent enough to feel that failure doesn't matter. We shall see. I think the next period is crucial, but then we've said that every year since we started.

FM: I looked up a Media Studies course-guide the other day. It gives a listing of all the media-related courses in Britain, and tells you the percentage of the course that is practical work. The NFTS got 70 per cent. Now when I was here, I always thought it was 100 per cent. And I only left in December.
RC: I used to argue it was 90 per cent – I thought that was fair. I don't know who has now decided 70 per cent. But maybe that protects us from students feeling that they will have access to cameras 100 per cent of the time.

FM: I think there are only two UK schools that can call themselves 'film schools': the NFTS and the LIFS. They stand alone, they're not attached to a university or to academia of any kind. Whereas in most courses, there is an obligation to do a dissertation, which means you might fail even if your craft, represented by the film you made, is a success. Now that the NFTS has taken on an academic dimension, what do you feel are the pros and cons?
RC: I think we still have to work it through, but actually I've been in favour of the idea for some time – in the sense that if the people to whom we are offering places and attempting to educate don't think deeply enough about cinema to articulate some ideas, then that is a problem. And I mean that across the board. So what we are attempting to do is to formalize some of the things that go on anyway. It's about taking the thought process that students ought to be engaged in – 'Why am I making movies? What sort of movies do I want to make?' – and giving it some sort of form. Also we've written up the dissertation in such a way that it allows students to do a practical exploration and simply add notes to it – rather than standing back and writing 10,000 words on some aspect of the business, which I personally am not interested in.

FM: When I was here, I felt that I learnt more from my fellow students, because they came from all over the globe. You could speak to someone from Denmark who'd say, 'Have you seen this director from Yugoslavia?', and I would mention one from China, and then you would swap ideas and argue. It felt fruitful. You won't necessarily agree with one another, but it was discourse none the less. But I remember being made to do a dissertation on my previous course. And that felt as if you had to answer the questions in a perceived way, and as long as you followed the rules or guidelines set down, then you would pass. It stifled creativity. I felt that if I wanted to be taken seriously as a film-maker then it was my film that mattered, not some 10,000 words that proved I could read books and watch certain kinds of films.

RC: You describe it almost as an isolated activity. Sounds dreadful, tearing your hair out and drinking enough coffee to keep going so it's delivered in the morning. It's funny, but we mentioned Paul Schrader earlier, and in *Schrader on Schrader* he talks about how he managed to get through UCLA without doing his dissertation*. I just hope and pray that we won't use it as a rod to beat students with, but actually give them an opportunity to express something. One of the other things we have said is that students can collaborate on projects, although we still have to judge the work of the individual student.

FM: There are certain schools that make you sit in a classroom for three years looking at every frame of *Citizen Kane*. Then they give you a camera and tell you to make a film. That was my main worry about academia getting its fingers into the practical world. You have to learn from your mistakes by being out there and making films.

RC: One of the things that I found encouraging in our discussions about the dissertation was the agreement that it should be embedded in the work the students are actually doing. It's not meant to be something that is separate from learning about the movies you want to make. A model I always thought was valuable was IDHEC in the 1960s, where every student had to do what they called a '*fiche*'. You had to take a film, approved by the tutors, either contemporary or a classic, and write up some aspect of it from a point of view. Some of these *fiches* are absolutely fascinating documents because they really are coherent analyses of what a film meant to an aspiring film-maker.

FM: What above all do you hope that your students will take with them from their experience here?

RC: It has to be a grasp of the creative process of making a movie, so that they know what it feels like. But also, a couple of years ago I heard Jean-Claude Carrière talking about the need to develop 'creative muscle'. There is that need, not to be over-confident but at least secure in some notion of how you might, given the opportunity, realize your or somebody else's ideas. Also to feel that you are ahead of the field in a sense – because of what you've shared with your peer group, what you've been through. Probably you've suffered abject failure most times you went out to bat, but therefore you've learned that you can come out and bat again. Even some of our most successful graduates have taken a while to find their feet. Some of those who seemed to be on top, within a couple of months have then floundered. Of course, the other thing is that you will continue to collaborate with some of your peers – the industry gives you that

* Increasingly busy as a critic but wishing nevertheless to graduate, Schrader made a deal with Colin Young to submit parts of the book he was then writing (*Transcendental Style in Film*) in lieu of a dissertation.

opportunity. Personally, I'd like to think that the European dimension will grow. It's a tough one to crack because of the language barrier, and nobody wants to see Euro-pudding films. But there are signs that the right kind of collaborations can produce some interesting work that isn't dependent on American money, or the film-makers having to go to the US to do it.

FM: This is a difficult question, but what would you say are some of the crowning moments in your 30 years of being here?
RC (*Head in hands*): Christ! I don't know . . . Moments? There are probably lots of them, but mostly it's the overwhelming feeling of the boy or girl 'done good!' Somehow, people do create a space for themselves, they make interesting work, and I feel that is worthy of respect. It's amazing how much of a kick you can get out of reflected glory – even from people who might never ever acknowledge that they got anything from studying here. And maybe they didn't. (*Laughs.*) But it's surprising how few one feels ashamed of, or feels that one should bear part of the shame for. Very, very few. Of course, some of that may be down to the half-decent selection process, whereby some of the people you chose are bound to be okay, and we just haven't spoilt them. Now, whether those people could have made their way without the film school . . . Who knows?

Damien O'Donnell

Damien O' Donnell: Director

Damien O'Donnell graduated from film school at the Dublin College of Commerce (now the Dublin Institute of Technology) in 1991. In 1992 he joined three of his classmates (Paul Fitzgerald, Harry Purdue and John Moore) in establishing a production company, Clingfilms. His 1995 short Thirty-Five A-Side *won numerous awards, including the BBC New Directors Competition. His first feature,* East is East *(1999), made for BBC Films and Film Four, was based on a prize-winning, semi-autobiographical play by Ayub Khan-Din about the ups and downs of a Pakistani family in 1970s Manchester. It won Best British Film of the Year at the* Evening Standard *Awards in 2000 and received six BAFTA nominations, winning the Alexander Korda Award for Outstanding British Film. Damien has since filmed Samuel Beckett's* What, Where *for Channel Four/RTE.*

I wanted to talk to Damien because his support for short films and their makers is well known, and though he may feel that his own film education was under-nourished, it is nevertheless typical of that offered to students by courses at less 'established' schools.

Fraser MacDonald: What was your route into film education?
Damien O'Donnell: Oh God . . . I was about 12 when I saw *Star Wars*, and by the time I went to second level school I was completely into film. It was a Catholic boys' school, so there wasn't much there to distract you. But they did have video cameras, and a Betamax machine and a VHS machine, and we were allowed to mess around with them. A bunch of about six of us got together in our second-last year and started making a monthly magazine programme for the school, where we did interviews, little documentaries and comedy sketches. It was called *The All-Electric Info Show*, and I think the graphics were done on a ZX Spectrum computer. But one of the guys working with us was a part-time DJ on a pirate radio station, so we got this really cool jazzy music. And we ended up making about seven of these monotonous, interminable programmes, basically cut together from Betamax to VHS machine – you know, real 'clunk' editing. But now I was hooked. So when I was 16, I went to night school to do a class in television production.

FM: And did you go straight to film school from secondary education?
DD: No, first I tried to get into a journalism course, because my career guidance

teacher told me there was no film industry in Ireland. He said, 'I know you want
to be the next Steven Spielberg, and I would *love* you to be the next Steven
Spielberg. But there is no film industry in Ireland, so you are not going to get a
job. How about being a journalist?' So I said, 'Okay', because I was easily
swayed, and I wrote for the school magazine and applied to a journalism course.
But they didn't accept me, so I sat around for a while until I thought, 'Fuck it.'
It's like that line from *The Commitments*: 'I'd rather be an unemployed musician than an unemployed pipe fitter.' I thought I'd rather be an unemployed film
director than an unemployed journalist.

I went to a Further Education College in Dublin called Colaiste Dhulaigh and
did a television and photography course that was almost entirely practical. That
was a great foundation for learning about film, because all the technical aspects
of stills photography apply to film – depth of field, lenses, shutter speeds, push
processing . . . The other plus about that course was that it was considered to be
a bit of a backdoor into film school: if you did it, then you were guaranteed an
interview for the film course at the Dublin College of Commerce. So I applied
there after my first year and got an interview, but they said, 'No. We don't like
you.' So I did a second year at Colaiste Dhulaigh, learned a bit more about television production, applied again to the Dublin College, and then I got in. By
which time I was about 20.

FM: What was the college like?
DD: It was the lesser of two film schools in Ireland at the time, the other being
Dun Laoghaire, which has evolved to the point that they actually make films
now, and the students graduate with a show. But the Dublin College had a
whole communications department, within which they taught Radio,
Advertising, Journalism, *et cetera*. I did three years on the film course, with
about 30 other people.

FM: And did you decide to become a director there?
DD: I always wanted to be a director, that was the whole reason I went there –
to learn about what a director is meant to do. But I doubt we learned anything
about directing. One or two of them came to visit us, but that was about it. I
don't think you ever know what a director really does until you do it yourself.
There's a Scottish writer who has a great line on this: 'A writer writes the film,
the actors act it, the cameraman films it, and the editor puts it altogether. What
does that leave? Fuck all, and that's what the director does.' It is a funny job,
you can do as little or as much as you want.

**FM: I was on a course similar to yours in Edinburgh before I went to the NFTS,
and the most valuable thing I took away with me was the saying, 'The art of**

good directing is letting other people think it was their idea.'

DD: Planting a seed and letting it flourish. It's true. As long as you get your own way in the end, it doesn't matter who wants to claim the idea later.

FM: Was your course very practical, or more theory-based?

DD: It became more theory-based because they decided that they wanted it to be an academic degree course, so they changed the curriculum to accommodate that, which I think was the ruin of it. I wanted it to be intensely practical – I wanted to make stuff. But that didn't happen. So I don't think it's a proper film school in the true sense of the word. I think the label misleads you.

FM: So how much practical experience did you manage to get?

DD: In the first year you were allowed to fiddle around with Super 8, which I thought was really useful. The real practical year was divided into three months of photography, three months of video production, and three months of radio, which was great because you don't often get the chance to concentrate on sound recording. The best part of the photography section was something they called a 'tape-slide project'. It was done with slide projectors plugged into a reel-to-reel, and you recorded a little sound piece to play alongside the images. There were pulse tracks on the tape that would cue the slides at the points you wanted.

FM: So it was a 'photo-roman', almost?

DD: Exactly. And I was really happy with mine because, even though it was all stills, you could cross-dissolve between them in a way that almost gave the impression of movement. Plus it was on 35mm, which was the last time I saw *that* size of film for many years, I can tell you. But that project was a great grounding, because we were dealing in shots and cuts. You had your soundtrack to help you tell your story, but mainly it was images. Mine was about my father going back to the house where he was born, which had been empty for about five years. He relives his childhood. I really like that piece, it's a memento of that time. It was probably the best thing that I did on that course.

FM: Why do you think that was?

DD: Because I had total control over it, I suppose. It was just me with a stills camera. When you're making films, you can have all this paraphernalia of crews, working with people you don't really like, making half-hearted attempts to create something that there's no budget for. But this tape-slide project was something pure and personal. Plus, there was also a great sense of competition among the students: you knew that everybody was doing this project, and I wanted mine to be up there with the best of them. Unfortunately, for the remainder of the course we were lumped into groups for our projects, groups that weren't of our choice. So I finished my final year with all these people I didn't know very well, and didn't really have a bond with.

FM: Were you each given a position in those groups?
DD: Yeah, and it would always be by default. For my graduation films, which I hope are never ever seen, I was producer on one of them and cameraman on another. It was a really weird process on how they decided what films got made. I wrote a script but it wasn't accepted. There was no budget for them either, and the films were really unremarkable, terrible . . .

FM: Why?
DD: The ideas weren't particularly good, and there was a laxness about the whole thing. None of us were inspired by our supervisors. We were more worried about the exams that were coming up. In Ireland at that time the economy wasn't so great –this was before the Celtic Tiger*. A lot of people were paranoid about what their careers would be, so they focused on keeping their heads down and doing well academically. Personally, I got more out of being involved in the college clubs and societies than I did from the course itself. And it's a shame, because film school is such an opportunity to do something really good. Nick Park is a great example of that, with *A Grand Day Out*.

FM: Which was years in the making.†
DD: Yeah, but it paid off . . . In fact, my second favourite piece of work there was an election video I made for my campaign to be student president. It was a self-parody campaign video, and I showed it in the canteen on the day of the election. It was about 15 minutes long, just a string of jokes about how obscure I was, the silly things I did. I could never show it now – I would be absolutely horrified by it.

FM: Did you win the election?
DD (*Laughs*): Yeah, by about 100 votes, which was the number of people who were in the canteen that afternoon. The other candidate was a business student, and there were about 2000 business students at the college compared to about 100 'art' students. So I would like to think that my film played a part in my victory.

---

* Jargon for Ireland's fast-growing economy since the 1990s, assisted by financial aid from the European Union and inward investment by hi-tech companies taking advantage of low rates of corporation tax.
† Nick Park entered the NFTS as an animator in 1980. *A Grand Day Out*, his graduation film which introduced the world to Wallace and Gromit, was begun in 1982 and completed in 1989.

FM: Did you consider continuing your film education after you left?

DD: No. And I really think I've already forgotten so much that I learned in my time there. On reflection, what I would have really liked to do was another kind of university course before doing film. There was so much that I was ignorant of that I am only starting to learn about now. If I had taken a course in English or Art, it would have given me a grounding. In fact, the Dublin College now does a Masters degree where you study pure film for a year, and I think that's a better approach – you can take another degree, then concentrate on film. I think I would have done as well taking just one intensive year, rather than three.

I was very uninformed when I went to the Dublin College. And yet somehow, when you're 18 years old, you are expecting to make films that tell stories that people are interested in. How can you do that if you haven't really lived a life? In fact, very few students actually made films about themselves, even when the project was an opportunity to do something personal. You know the old argument about writing a book, 'Write about what you know'? Well, the same can be said about film-making, particularly at film school level. If I was teaching, that's what I would say: 'Go and find a story from your own life. Be more personal.' But everyone was trying to make crowd-pleasing films. Very few experimental films were made, everything had to be narrative-driven. To be fair, before I arrived, the course had produced some radical students who made some weird, really personal stuff. But none of it saw the light of day, and because there wasn't a strong Irish film industry at that point, those people went off and did other things. By the time I graduated it was just the reverse, there was a strong industry, so I kept at it for a few years until finally things took off.

FM: How long did that take, though? It sounds like the school didn't really promote the idea of a career.

DD: Well, there wasn't really anywhere to go. None of us even knew of any potential for a job, be it a runner or a chief sandwich-maker in a post-production house. While you were studying you could get placements with various employers, but there wasn't that wide a pool. I ended up in a newspaper's photo-library, because I couldn't see anything better. I was offered placements in edit suites, but that didn't really appeal to me. When I left I thought about going back to photography, just because it seemed easier and you had more control. The thing is, at least at the NFTS you learn to be a director, or a cinematographer. I think our course should have been more tailored. Film and Communication is too broad a subject: all you can really do is skim, and get a taste. We needed to specialize a bit more.

FM: What was your attitude to institutions like the NFTS?

DD: From where we were, that felt like a *real* film school. There were people

who wanted to go on from our course to somewhere like that. Keiron J. Walsh*
went to the RCA after finishing school in Ireland, and he did some great films
there. But I had had my fill of institutions for a while, being at the college for
four years, one as student president and three as a student. I thought, 'It's time
to get out there and do some stuff.'

FM: Do you think film school helped you in any way?
DD: No! (*Laughs.*) No, it would be wrong of me to say it didn't help me. I did
learn quite a lot in that time, just not necessarily about film. Being 20-something,
getting involved in student politics. Bad flats, bad food . . . What is it about
college that you always have enough money to get drunk but never enough to
buy decent food? How does that happen? I think I just got very frustrated
because I didn't feel that I got the most out of my time. Whether that's my own
fault or the shortcomings of the course, I don't know. I think what I really needed was a benevolent dictator who would shout to me, to get me motivated.
Because it was so easy not to work there. There was one lecturer – Eoin
Harrison, he would argue with you and shout at you, so you would go out and
do the work. I needed that kind of dictatorial approach, rather than someone
saying 'Well, what do you want to do, guys?'

FM: With that in mind, would you ever want to do some teaching yourself?
DD: I would love to have a go at it. But I'd probably be a real bastard. (*Laughs.*)
I have this philosophy that teaching means being as brutal as possible, just
because that's what I needed myself.

**FM: There's that old adage that says, 'Those who can, do. Those who can't,
teach.' But in film school you really want to be taught by the people who can.**
DD: Sure, when we had guest lecturers, it was always great to hear from people
who were actually working in the industry. You respected them more. But then
there was also a certain arrogance we had as students. We thought that we could
do it all and didn't need to be taught anything. Then you go off and over-expose
a roll of film. (*Laughs.*)

FM: Or leave the camera running in the case . . .
DD: Has that happened to you?

**FM: Yeah. Shot a whole mag of the inside of the case. And we only had four rolls
to make a 15-minute film.**
DD: Jesus. That's horrible.

---

* Later to direct *When Brendan Met Trudy* (2000), written by Roddy Doyle.

FM: So did you manage to find directing work when you came out of college?

DD: No, I worked in a cinema for about nine months after I left. Now *that* gave me a whole different perspective on the film industry. Coming out of film school, all those highs, those heady days, I found myself cleaning puke off a toilet seat in a UCI in Dublin. I thought, 'Hmm . . . what am I doing with my life?'

FM: I heard you got sacked from there.

DD: I left of my own accord over a dispute with the management about the pick 'n' mix, but that's another story.

FM: At least you were working in film.

DD: I guess so. Delivering hot dogs, showing people to their seats. '24-C over there, sir.' Finally, I went off with these three guys from my year who had set up their own company called Clingfilms, because they didn't want to work for anyone else. They weren't interested in being runners, starting at the bottom and working their way up. I guess they had an arrogance, or a confidence, that they could do better than that. They could just go out and do their own stuff. And it worked, to a degree. At school they made some remarkable films. Their graduation film was 40 minutes long, called *Cold for June*. It was quite daring, unlike any other student film I ever saw. It was about a stale marriage, a couple just dying in this relationship, and how the wife stops another young couple from making the same mistakes as she has. They had this fantastically brave scene of a guy masturbating: the husband who rejects his wife's attentions and has a wank in the bathroom instead. It had real nerve, and it was funny too. Then they made another film straight after that, which won a prize at the Cork Film Festival. It was a real achievement, the budget was about £5000 and it was set in Ireland in the 1940s, but they managed to get all the period details right. While they were filming I was away in America taking advantage of my student visa, so when I finally saw it I thought, 'Fuck, I want to do stuff like that!' It just didn't turn out like that in my final year.

Anyway, I left to work with Clingfilms on a pop promo, a stop-frame animation. I just wanted to help out because I liked those guys, and I wanted to be part of the gang. Our philosophy was to make pop videos, corporate videos, whatever, but be paid to do it. Even though we would still be learning on the job, people would be paying us while we learned, rather than us having to pay someone else to teach us.

FM: Was *Thirty-Five A-Side* the first short film you did after you left?

DD: No. While I was working in the UCI there was a girl I knew at college in the year behind me. She was doing a filming exercise where you had to shoot something in one place. So I wrote this little script, secretly. She put her name to it because I had left. It was set in a photo booth, all one shot from the camera's point of view. They normally shot these exercises on reversal stock but I thought, 'If this works out we could have a little film out of this.' So we somehow managed to get a roll of negative and get it processed behind everyone's back. It meant that we only had two takes for everything. But it was five minutes long and it did really well: it won a prize at the Galway Film Festival. And there was outrage at the film school that we had underhandedly made a film. I mean, that was the kind of place it had become – they objected to you making a film! They got really uppity about it, it got to the silly stage where there was an exchange of letters between the Principal and myself. He demanded that I sign over all my rights to the script for a fee of £50 or the film would never see the light of day, because it had to be their property. It was just ridiculous, such a negative attitude, especially when the film was a real success.

FM: And it was good for the college.
DD: Oh yeah, it was great for everybody involved. They just objected to my involvement. It's funny. I'm now considered one of their most successful graduates, but I wouldn't even have got in if I had applied a year later than I did. They changed the admissions policy, made it more academically demanding, and they rejected people who were academically poor on the assumption that they wouldn't be good film-makers – which is a false assumption. But anyway, nowadays they ask me to come down and speak about the course and do newspaper interviews whenever they're launching some new aspect. I've even done lectures there.

FM: How do you feel when you go back there?
DD: Well, I've realized that one of the things we lacked was that we very rarely saw any short films. Which is very strange considering that short films are what you are actually supposed to make as part of the course. And it's very rare that you will go straight from school on to a feature. There is so much education and inspiration for students in just watching other people's shorts. But shorts are very hard to access, apart from in festivals, and then you may never see them again. Instead, all the schools show is feature films, John Ford westerns. Sure, everybody needs to see those films and learn about film history. But then what are they going to do when they actually have to go out and make a film? Where are they going to get a stagecoach from? So when I went back to the college, I showed short films, Peter Mullan's *Fridge* for example. I said, 'Look at these. This is what other people are doing for their first films, they're amazing and there is no reason why you shouldn't be doing the same thing. Take a chance.'

FM: You're quite vocal in your support for short films.
DD: Well, when you're going around festivals with a short of your own, you see a lot of other people's shorts, and that's when you see what's actually possible. I do feel that short films are worthy, they are worth making. Not just to learn about making films, although it is a great way to learn. I think short films are the purest form of film-making: there's no money involved in them, there's no pressure to find an audience. You just make it for its own sake. There are some great ideas out there that deserve to be filmed, but they don't necessarily deserve to be feature films. I would rather watch a short that is ten minutes of great film than sit through ten minutes of great film spread across 100 minutes in a feature. I'd rather sit through a bad short film programme than a bad feature.

FM: Do you see a difference between the short films of film students, and those by people who have never really studied?
DD: People who haven't studied seem to be much more individual. There's a passion there. Well, there has to be, if you're going to go out and make films off your own back, outside that comfortable and cosseted world of film school. Sometimes it's too easy to say, 'I'm at a film school, something interesting will happen if I just hang around with the right people, smoking marijuana and writing in classrooms. I'll have *something* worthwhile at the end of it . . .' (*Laughs.*)

FM: Sometimes I would like to talk to some 'failed' NFTS directors, people who left the college and took maybe four years before they even got anywhere. How did they survive? I mean, you weren't an overnight success, even though a lot of people seem to think you were.
DD: I haven't done a huge amount, and that's one thing to my shame. It's been ten years since I got out of film school. I've made four short films, a feature, various commercials and corporate things. I don't think I've done anything *bad*. Well, maybe a couple of dodgy adverts. (*Laughs.*)

FM: Unfortunately, there's so much hype surrounding the industry. A film-maker like Lynne Ramsay makes three brilliant shorts and then a feature and everybody focuses on that. But they ignore all the directors that were probably in Lynne's year. There is a corridor in the NFTS that has photographs of all the famous graduates, people like Danny Cannon, Michael Caton-Jones . . .
DD: Yeah, but where are all the other people?

FM: Exactly. Where have they gone?
DD: Well I hope they're all off living happy, successful lives . . .

FM: I think short films are important but there is a lot to be said for learning the longer form, especially with DV. Do you think film schools could encourage this?
DD: Sure, television is always looking for half-hour films or series. Bollocks to that, though. This whole digital revolution is fantastic, but it shouldn't eradicate the study of the process of film. My fear is that it will become irrelevant very soon. Film is such an imperfect process, all the way through. You never get exactly what you want. If digital helps you achieve a better vision and more control all the way through, then I suppose that's a good thing. But I feel a bit sad about the passing of the Steenbeck and the 16mm camera with a rattling old mag that scratches your film in the gate. Maybe I'm just being a sentimentalist . . .

FM: My feeling about digital is that it will produce great editors . . .
DD: Because everybody shoots such an amazing volume of stuff.

FM: And a really good editor will stand out. Otherwise, the amount of footage that you can and do shoot on DV leads to a kind of fascist cut, bang-bang-bang.
DD: Well, celluloid has that quality whereby you can actually watch a static wide shot for quite a long time. Video doesn't really have that. But it will change when the quality of the image reaches the level of film, or improves on it, as is alleged.

FM: With the DV culture that is growing every day, there is a feeling that you don't need to go to a film school now. You could take the money that would have paid your fees and just buy Final Cut Pro*. What's your view about that?
DD: It's true, there are film courses everywhere you look. And the amount of written material that's available means that you can learn all about film without going to film school. But there is something about being in a room with a bunch of people, bouncing ideas off one another, and then going out and making stuff, which can be quite motivating, much more so than just reading about it. The course I was doing was thirty-eight hours a week, and then some. You had classes and then you had to do your practical stuff round that, so it was quite intensive. I think it would be a mistake for film schools to stop doing what they do. It's just that the one I was in could have done it a lot better. (*Laughs.*)

FM: But then video seems to have invigorated the 'Just Do It' mentality that Robert Rodriguez and Quentin Tarantino embodied. That feeling that you can work in a video shop and then go out and make a feature.
DD: And regurgitate everything you ever saw . . . It should be about original ideas. There is that argument that anyone can pick up a pen and write a book. It's easy to do, but actually not a lot of people do it. The same can be said about

---

* State-of-the-art video-editing software for home computers from Apple.

film. I think the initial excitement about DV will pass over and then it will just be there for anybody to use at their leisure. The access to this cheap medium means that an awful lot of shit will get made. But I don't mind, I don't think that's a problem. There will still be the craftsmen, people who will do it exceptionally well, and they will always stand out. The one thing that film has over digital is that it imposes a discipline on the film-maker; and a good film school will do the same. It will make you appreciate the value of time and stock, and then once you've learned that, you can go off and break all the rules.

But being a good film-maker is not just about switching on the 'Record' button. You need an environment that's going to nurture and teach you. My ideal film school would have practising directors coming in – I think it's amazing that Stephen Frears comes back and lectures at the NFTS – but I'd also want a range of directors to come in. With directing, everyone has their own approach, everyone makes it up as they go along. There isn't an apprenticeship for directors as there is for editors or cinematographers. You just go out, do it, and learn from your mistakes.

FM: The trouble is that directors don't get enough chances to do that anymore. Whereas Hitchcock and Michael Powell learned their trade on the 'quota quickies'. And Frears, Alan Clarke, Ken Loach, all learned their craft on *Play for Today* – 26 hours of television drama a year, all new scripts . . .
DD: Well, I just had an amazing experience with Mike Figgis, shooting a documentary about his latest feature (*Hotel*) for his website. We put rules on ourselves – every day during the shoot we had to produce new material, shoot little dramas with the actors, edit it, and present it. There were 30 days where we had to go on air, so it was like a small television station, and that was great for just going out, shooting stuff, and then moving on. You can't get too precious about it. You need to go out and do it. And that is the problem with film schools. The amount of actual practical time you have on a film set is so small compared to what you have at film school. To go out and shoot six weeks solidly, that would be a great discipline to impose on students. Get out there and think about what you are shooting right now. Is it going to cut together? Will it work in an hour? It's all good practice. That's why I would have been happy to do something like *Ballykissangel**, had the opportunity come along after college – just to learn about directing. Unfortunately, or fortunately, *East is East* came along instead. And I'm sort of glad I didn't get to do *Ballykissangel*, because I'm sure I would have been sacked. (*Laughs.*) I would have been too slow or too argumentative; I wouldn't have lasted the pace.

* BBC-TV comedy-drama series about the escapades of an attractive young priest in a bucolic Irish town.

East is East: Chris Bisson, Archie Panjabi and Jimi Mistry. © Jaap Buitendijk

FM: I was asked in to a meeting about a new soap opera, and I was keen, because I had never worked in that environment before: an hour and a half of television each week. But the high-minded part of me is going, 'Yeah, but it's a fucking soap.' But then it's the question of 'What is cinema?' For better or worse we are influenced by television so much. The majority of our work will come from there. So when you are dealing with a full-frame cinema screen rather than a TV screen, how does the language differ? Or are the stories for television different than those for cinema?

DD: Most of the films you will ever see will be on television and there is that case where your perception of what a frame should be is different, you almost have to fight against that. If you look at films from the 1930s, before television, a lot of them were just these grand wide shots. Directors tended to relate to paintings and to theatre, so they would be thinking about these huge canvases. But they also had the confidence that, on the cinema screen, the audience would be able to see all of the details, in the actors' faces and so forth. But when you've grown up in a world of television, your automatic instinct is, 'Oh, I need to get a close-up.' So you film it, and it's usually too big, and it just looks ridiculous on the big screen.

FM: A lot of the symbolism has gone from modern cinema now as well.

DD: Yeah, television drama can be summed up by 'Wide establishing shot.

Track in. Close-up, shot-reverse-shot'. It's always a succession of close-ups, or a two-shot, just talking, talking, talking. But film is about images. A good script should be about description: this is what you see, this is what happens. This is what he does, not what he says. I prefer that, I like silent movies, animated cartoons, where it's not about the dialogue so much as telling the story visually.

FM: But *East is East* was based on a stage play, so there must have been a lot of dialogue there.
DD: We cut an awful lot out, through the development, even in the edit. You just don't need it on film, because you can say so much with a look. You can be on someone's face for fifteen seconds and just delete their monologue, because it's all there in their eyes. With television drama, though, there is a process, it's quite industrial. Doing an original TV drama is quite difficult, the path is so worn and rutted that if you're not careful, you end up going down that way. So you have to fight it. I would like to do television, it's such a powerful medium, and it would be nice to do something radical and original with it. But it's lost its punch now. There is no energy and no passion about having to say stuff. Just appealing to the lowest common denominator without offending anybody.

FM: Digital TV is not helping.
DD: No, it's terrible. There is a lot of great stuff in the archives, but it just never gets out. Can you imagine a Jim Allen* Night on UK Gold? I don't think so. When he died in 1999, the BBC showed *Spongers*, and when it reached its climax, where the mother poisons herself and her children, it suddenly came home to me that I had seen it when it was first aired back in 1978. I must have been about 10 or 11, and it really made an impression on me. You don't see stuff like that anymore. They just want to entertain you and I think that is bollocks. People should be confronted by film and by television.

FM: Now it's just a goggle-box.
DD: An opiate, a sedative. My dad always sits down and falls asleep in front of it within ten minutes. If he manages to stay awake for a whole film he will remark upon the fact.

FM: DVD gives the audience a narrative choice now. You don't have to watch the film in its chronological sequence. You can jump about. You have a choice . . .
DD: Yeah, but you can have too much choice. The thing about a story is that

* Jim Allen's scripts for Ken Loach included *The Big Flame* (1969), *The Rank and File* (1971), *Days of Hope* (1975), *Hidden Agenda* (1990), *Raining Stones* (1993) and *Land and Freedom* (1995). *Spongers* was a BBC *Play for Today* directed by Roland Joffe.

you want to be told it. A friend of mine was having a go at interactive storytelling, he thinks it goes against the whole nature of storytelling. You're there in
the audience. Do you want the director to suddenly ask you, 'What happens
next?' No, you fucking tell me. I paid my five pounds to get in here, you're
telling the story. You tell me what happens next! I don't want to fucking guess.

FM: Do you think there's not enough good storytelling anymore?
DD: The thing is, on a great night in the pub you hear some brilliant stories. But
I wouldn't necessarily pay five quid to see them in a cinema.

**FM: With TV though, there's the problem of attention-span. The buttons are
always there in front of you, and if you have 300 channels, you have to surf.**
DD: In theory, you flick from channel to channel to channel and that could be
your night's viewing. It would be quite funny to do a piece in which you assem-
bled the whole story just by changing the channels on a TV. I'm sure it's been
done, in a short film probably. Shorts are revolutionary in that way. A lot of the
ideas that you see in commercials, promos or features even, have already been
explored in short films. Whether they are experimental or narrative, it's always
cutting edge and always exciting. You see stuff where you think, 'I would like
the future of cinema to be like this.' When I was the judge of the short films in
Edinburgh, I found myself being drawn to the more radical pieces of work. Even
though there was some brilliant narrative shorts that were like scenes from feature films, beautifully constructed and well told, I found myself rebelling against
selecting a film like that as the winner. It's too easy to do a narrative film. I was
really keen to give the prize to people who were doing something dangerous and
interesting, because we don't award people like that at that level, and you want
them to have some acknowledgement. The vast majority of people don't see
short films, and yet if they did, you know that they would become addicted to
them. They are so fresh and rewarding and entertaining. And *short*.

**FM: The sad thing about short film programmes at festivals is that the majority
of the audience are the film-makers themselves, plus their mates.**
DD: Well, I think there is room for a short-film digital TV channel. Why not?
Why don't I make one? Who can I talk to about that?

FM: How about doing it on the web?
DD: No, websites are too slow and the quality is too bad. The whole technology of streaming video was something I found really annoying in doing that website for Mike Figgis. The compression process predicated a certain approach to
shooting – basically, keep the camera still and try to stay on close-ups. Because
if you panned the camera, the effect was like 15,000 butterflies had just taken

off and you thought, 'What the fuck was that?' Then the image would just turn to mush. So we found that locked-off shots and close-ups were the only way to go for web television. 'Radio with pictures' was how someone described it. Ultimately, you still want a big screen – that's what it's about. And a shared experience, sitting in a room with 500 people enjoying the same event. Video is a great place to watch a film again, to remind yourself of the original experience, but it's like taking photographs of your holiday: if all you have are the photographs and not the experience, you're not really getting the full event.

FM: Nobody does slide shows of their holidays anymore.
DD: No, and I don't think they should. But you see things like it on the web – people put photographs of their newborn kid up on a website. And instead of sending round the photos, they just send their friends emails inviting them to have a look at the site. I love that, it's fantastic. But you could have a holiday slide-show TV channel, where people send in their holiday slides with their own voiceover. 'This is the meal we had on the first night, this is my main course, this is my starter . . . Oh, I've got two of the starter . . . Oh no, that's your starter, Julia . . . You had the same starter as me, but without the cheese.'

FM: And then a naked photograph of Julia . . .
DD: 'Oh! I don't know how that got in there . . .' Actually I'm going to write this down – 'The Holiday Slide Show'. The problem is, though, that people will watch it . . .

Dick Ross

Dick Ross: Tutor

Born in New Zealand, Dick Ross got his professional start at the BBC in London. In 1980 he was appointed head of the Film diploma course at the Royal College of Art. He has subsequently taught at NFTS, New York University and the German Film and Television Academy in Munich, and has also been a visiting teacher in France, Holland, Belgium, Spain, Sweden, Finland, Norway, Italy, Turkey and Israel. So I was keen to get Dick's views on the similarities and differences between film academies across the globe.

(Interview begins mid-recording)
Dick Ross: . . . It's about giving students *space*. Ridley Scott said it was fabulous when he was at the Royal College of Art. All they had was a cupboard, and a Bolex with a door handle for a winding knob, and that was the film school. But he said, 'It gave me a chance to make mistakes, and a chance to stand on the corner and think.' Thinking is what was encouraged. He also said that what he finds sad about modern film schools is that thought isn't considered too important. Everybody is just getting through a programme. And a programme doesn't take any account of the individual development of an artist. You can't programme artistic development – you simply can't.

Fraser Macdonald: I was reading a statement on the Columbia University film school website, by the chairman Dan Kleinman, and he talks about 'grounding' or a 'cross-specialization', where everyone tries out each part of the film-making process. That's different from my experience at the NFTS, because I was concentrated on just one aspect, directing.
DR: In America, it's mix and match. On the first day of the opening semester, every professor or associate professor sits at a table with a little pile of handouts that describe their course, and they have to get between 16 and 30 students to sign up. So someone offers 'Film Editing for Directors', and someone else offers 'American Cinema of the 1950s', whatever. And if they don't get enough students signing up – if they don't get enough *money*, in other words – then the course isn't held, and they're gone. So the first thing the professors do is charm the students – tell them that they are going to do terribly well, that they are absolutely the type of student the professor is looking for, and just sign here please. I guess by now it must cost $2500 for a 13-week course, so then the

lecturer is in employment. It's also very important to give the student a good grade, because a bad grade means the student won't sign up for other courses, and can't borrow money. But all of that has nothing to do with the growth of a human being.

For me, the most exciting moment I had at the NFTS was when Lynne Ramsay came in with a grubby pile of 12 pages that had eight little stories on it. The school wouldn't allow her to make them. I read them and thought they were fabulous, because I knew the stories were *her*. That was the first thing I'd read, in the short time I'd been there, that was absolutely individual. I said to the school, 'We must make it.' They sneered and said, 'She's a cinematographer.' But what does that mean? What is the definition? So it was a great battle for Lynne to make *Small Deaths*, but it did very well. In the end we made three out of those eight stories. And now the school uses Lynne in its publicity, but at the time nobody liked *Small Deaths* at all. They hated it.

FM: One criticism of the NFTS is that we get spoiled rotten. At Napier, where I studied before the NFTS, my final-year film budget was £500, out of which £300 was to be paid to the insurance company so we could take the gear outside. In other words, when you went out to make your film, it was your own money that you were spending. So you had to be absolutely sure of your stories.
DR: That's true.

FM: But when you get given such a big budget to make your final-year film – you're almost dismissive of it. It's as if we have to do this, to fulfil the criteria.
DR: Yeah. The finance and the budgets, the ability of the school to be generous – it's good news and bad news, really. If you want to look at the appalling decline in German cinema, I think it's linked to the subsidy they receive. Each of the states in the FDR has a film fund: we're talking 160 million deutschmarks, a vast amount of money. They give money out to support young film-makers, emerging cinema. So they'll say, 'Okay, we can see the script's not there yet, but we'll give you the money. But you have to spend it before 31 July.' So the films go into production before the scripts are ready, and the film gets made, and they sell maybe a hundred tickets. Then eventually one of the television channels buys the film and screens it at 11 o'clock at night, so it just about breaks even. But we're talking about $1 million budgets. Hundreds of millions of deutschmarks are being thrown away on scripts that are not ready to shoot. Every student graduating in Germany is confident that they will be making a film within at least two years. I read their scripts and write back to them saying, 'Don't do it. Be brave. Say, "No. Can I put off getting the money for a year until I get the script right?"' But they tell me, 'Can't do that. Because next year there will be another bunch of new film-makers coming up.' So these films are getting

made. The film fund can be seen to be benevolent, supporting the film industry, supporting the culture. But they're making shit. I mean, have you ever seen a German road movie? *Kings of the Road* was the only good one. But Wim Wenders didn't do his nation any service by making it. Even his company's called Road Movies. A German road movie is the pastiche of all pastiches. They get a 1963 Cadillac – there's a company in Germany that hires them out – and they drive across Germany, wearing hand-tooled cowboy boots, carrying pearl-handled revolvers, but otherwise being totally German. These are the most lumpen movies you ever saw, and they're producing them in scores every year . . . But I'm famous for taking the piss out of the Germans. I'd rather watch a Godard movie than a German road movie, and that's saying something. You see (*laughs*), I'm a philistine.

FM: One of your big interests has always been the development of story. Do you think that development doesn't go on enough in film schools?
DR: No, and I think it's the wrong sort of development that does go on. What we do is develop student *ideas*. We say to the students, 'Come up with a treatment by 1 April.' They do that, and we work on it. But what we don't do is work on the student, so that when the idea comes up, it's fresh, it's intimate, it's small, it's painful, it's difficult. So that when the student finally gets to tell it, you watch them grow in front of you. Instead what we do is say, 'Well, this is a bit of Holly Hunter-meets-*Casablanca*-meets-Harrison Ford-meets-whatever the current British gangster movie is . . .' And I think that's tragic. The great experience of film school should be a private journey in a public place. But I can't find originality; I don't see enough of it.

I've just done a workshop for two months in Berlin with 11 students. Their student selection is brilliant there because of the guy who runs it. He'll take a homeless person and give them a grant. His reasoning is that he has to take the gamble that these people have something to say that nobody round us has said before. So you get this crazy class, which I took. I started by saying to them, 'I can't deal with sci-fi craziness, I'm not happy with drugs – you can do those stories if you want to, but you'll have to get someone else to work on them, because I'm not sympathetic towards them.' Then they started telling stories. We just sat around in class and drank wine and told stories for two weeks. I told stories too. And someone would say, 'Hey, once, when I was a girl, I got in a shower with my sister's boyfriend with all my clothes on, but he was naked.' I'd say, 'You've got to be joking. Why did you do that?' Well, at that point it's become a movie. That moment in the movie is maybe 20 seconds; but the girl who fights her sister by having sex with the boyfriend is completely fresh in my mind. I've never come across it before.

At the end of six weeks we had 11 first-draft movies, and when I say 'first draft' I mean virtually ready to shoot – they just needed another eye other than mine. The school has just read them, and they're knocked out. I did the same process in Helsinki, and five out of the six scripts are going to be filmed. What we did was stop talking about movies, and start talking about moments that we have had that were fun; or sad, disillusioning, whatever. You can't say, 'Tell me a disillusioning moment,' but you can steer the conversation around that way. And if you talk for long enough then you suddenly discover the student is beginning to hear the movie. Then you say, 'Okay, go away, and come back in a couple of days and tell your story to the class again.' Now, can you believe that these people will tell it over and over again for three weeks, the same story, five times – and in English? These are people who think in German, and can't write English very well. When the story is pure, as a piece of narration, like you'd tell it with friends, then I say, 'Okay, go and write it in German.' They say, 'You won't be able to read it!' But I don't need to read it. You know the movie already, because we've talked.

When we tell somebody a story, we tell it in a series of cuts. David Mamet writes about this in his book *On Directing Film*, which is a transcript of a masterclass he gave at Columbia. Basically he said, 'Film scripts have no direct lineage to theatre, they are not plays. They have a direct lineage to the oral tradition.' We talk in images. We try and make people see what has happened to us, and as we do it, we talk in little bursts, and each jump we make in our description is a cut . . . Mamet says it better. Paul Schrader has written about this too. I thought I'd invented it, so I was really pissed off when I found out all these people knew it already. (*Laughs.*)

The process of developing stories through a group of people learning to be comfortable with each other and then telling stories – it takes a while, but then there is a chance that you are going to get something original, instead of sitting looking at a blank computer screen. I've talked to Richard Price, William Goldman. And I asked them, 'When you sit down in front of a computer, do you ever write, 'Scene One. Exterior. Restaurant – Day'? And they say, 'Of course not.' I say, 'Do you know when you've got to the end of the "first act"?' They say, 'No.' I never met any professional writer who sits down and writes the 'first act' of a screenplay. They write a story. And later on, when they have written it and thought, 'That's pretty good', they then break it up. All this stuff, the three-act structure, Aristotle – it only comes into play after the story's told.

The tragedy of film schools is they don't care about the private story. What they care about, having got an idea out of the student, is turning it into a movie. I teach in a lot of schools, and the ones that are interesting will say, 'We'll have a psychologist come and talk to the students this week And we'll have a philosopher next week. Hey, there's a chess master in town, let's get him.' So the students are hammered not by film people, but by musicians, poets, whatever. Once a week they do a talk, and the students, being Europeans, do as they are told and they go along and they are stimulated to think for themselves. You think of the mammoth amount of time wasted in film schools on ideas that just aren't worth it. Then you think of the great, successful short films made by students, some of the best images I know . . . I mean, forget feature films, short film-making is far harder. You think of the really great short films, they're tiny moments, but they're examined in such a way that you know the film-maker was there, and they've done it.

Take your film *Simple Things*, about the son and his mother, which I showed in Berlin. (*FM gushes.*) They loved that film because they know what it's like to live in an inner city. All of them. They don't share flats, everybody has their own little cell and they have these private lives that I know nothing about. But every so often, a film like yours lifts the sticky lid a bit, like opening a yoghurt pot. And they related to it. It was a great experience.

FM: You weren't on the development board at the NFTS for that film, and we had to fight to make it, as you can well imagine. Everybody wanted to know what it was about. 'What happens in this film?' It got to the stage where I would say, 'It's about nothing. This film is about nothing.'
DR: That's a good answer. The students that I travel around talking to, I tell them, 'If something asks you what your film is "about", say "11 minutes".' Because you don't know until you've written it. Or even after the fact. But other people who see it will explore it, it will unlock the little cupboards in the heart. So the film becomes a key, and people will talk about it, about its sense of isolation or whatever. In Berlin there were two students who were so stimulated by your film that it transformed the stories that they were going to tell, which were otherwise totally different. But somehow one film gives another film-maker courage, and so on. This business of 'I don't get it!' – I hear tutors say this to students all the time, and I say, 'Maybe you don't know the student. Maybe you should go and have a beer with them, and talk a bit.'

FM: One of the criticisms, you could say, is that a lot of film schools concentrate on the craft rather than the art.
DR: Yes, I think that is true. (*Pause.*) I'm just doing one of those windscreen-wipers across the whole of Western Europe, thinking about it. It is true, and that creates a crisis. I used to edit the BBC *Nine O'Clock News*, and the idea at the time was that the programme had to be 24 minutes and 30 seconds long. We had a digital clock that counted backwards, and at the end of the perfect programme you'd have a row of what we called 'eggs' up there: zero-zero, zero-zero, zero-zero. That meant you'd hit 24:30:00 exactly – that was a mark of a

real professional. Now, my first day on the job was the dullest news day the world had seen for 20 years. Nothing happened. I spent the entire day inflating the importance of non-events. I had 144 people around me, and they were going, 'It's his first day, he's nervous, be nice to him.' And I *was* nervous. We went on-air, and sure enough, at the end of the programme I had a row of eggs on this digital clock. That was like snorting three lines of coke. I was over the moon. I came out, and the Managing Editor of BBC Current Affairs was standing in front of me. 'What about *that*?' I said, pointing at the clock. He said, 'Shit, but beautifully stacked.' So I say to my students, 'If you're worried about the *stacking*. . .' (*Shrugs.*) We should always buy champagne for the student who fucks up, because they made a great leap on our behalf, and everybody learns from them. To try something and fail is better than to deliver to Sir something that is perfectly light, perfectly sharp, but just crap in terms of content. That's just devouring celluloid, or whatever it's actually shot on.

FM: Part of me now, after graduating, feels that I want to forget everything I've learned. You start to understand a bit of what Picasso might have meant when he said he wanted to paint like a three-year-old.
DR: Well, you've probably said it better than I'm going to say, but there is something wonderful about innocence. And the great skill of Lynne Ramsay was in calling her first film *Small Deaths*. Every time a little innocence goes, it's a small death. My effort with students is to say to them, 'All right. You are now going to tell me another my-first-love story. I can see it in your eyes, I can see from your erection, that you are dying to tell me this story. And that's fine, as long as it contains at least one moment that I haven't heard from everybody already. And I don't want just any first-love story. Is it painful? Well, find me a metaphor for that pain. And if it's joyful and full of wonder, let me feel that wonder as well.'

I guess I've heard about five thousand first-love stories. That's a lot of first love. Then there's the 'I hate my father' stories, and the 'My father was never there when I needed him' stories, and 'The young guy with the oppressive mother' story, and so on. But every so often, a pure gem floats up, and you don't skim it off the surface, it just grows if you let it. Students so desperately want approval. *I* wanted approval, I still do, so I know about approval. When I was at the BBC, I wanted to make programmes my bosses liked. And what did my bosses like? They liked the programmes *they* made. And so we perpetuated that. This is what is going on in the cinema in Britain at the moment: *Lock, Stock and Two Smoking Barrels* . . . No, even further back. *Trainspotting*. 'That worked, so this will work.' I mean, *Trainspotting* is a great movie. But each imitation is a diminution, it's a weakening of the original.

FM: There is the attitude of 'If it ain't broke don't fix it!' What I think you're saying is that in Britain we should examine the things that are broken for a bit longer.
DR: Absolutely. Now, last year, I worked with students at film schools in Norway, Sweden, Helsinki, Berlin, Munich, Jerusalem, Amsterdam, and about three others. And we won 111 international awards.

FM: Do you think that you're happier working with the continental European sensibility; whereas in Britain we look to America more?
DR: Yeah. I mean, I was a disaster at the NFTS. It was my fault in many ways. I didn't do any teaching there, which is ridiculous because teaching is what I went there to do. So I was terribly frustrated to be side-tracked, to be the hit man for the management.

FM: But you were also at the Royal College of Art, and that film course obviously had an art school ethos. The young British film-makers whose stocks are now rising, directors like Jamie Thraves (*The Low Down*) and Ben Hopkins (*Simon Magus, The Nine Lives of Thomas Katz*), producers like Natasha Dack, were among the last generation of students to study there before the course closed. If you compare it to the NFTS, the RCA graduates appear to be making the more thought-provoking cinema, although in our market culture they're considered 'arty'.
DR: But there are surprises. When I was brought into the RCA film course, it was to close it down. I was meant to be disgusted at the waste and the pointlessness of it all. I had no intention of doing that. At my interview, once I was actually inside the school, I thought, 'Yes, they're quite right.' Huw Wheldon, David Puttnam, they said, 'We have assurances from the BBC that they will take you back within a year. If you find the place is unmanageable, you only have to say so.' God, I knew nothing about film education, I'd never had anything to do with fiction in my life. I knew nothing about film theory. But that's why I was taken on: I was expendable. If they have taken on an academic, that person would have known how to fight, academically. I didn't, and I wasn't interested.

Amongst the batch of incoming students, there were six who loved the cinema, and they were so proud to be at the Royal College. So I had to fight for them. I told them, 'In two years we will make this the best film school in Europe.' And a year and a half later we had won an award for the best film school in Europe. They told me what they needed. They wanted classes in spot meters and boring stuff like that. So I was running a film school for six people, who have dignified the world of film since. We arranged courses when the students were ready for them. The rest of the time we sat around and told stories. Somebody who graduated out of that first bunch said that I knew nothing about film education at all. They said, 'I suspect Dick isn't even interested. But what he

does know about is ethos. He created an environment in which we could grow.'
I am terribly proud of that. We took risks, and we did have champagne on many
days. I learned as well; I learned from my students as much, or more, than they
learned from me.

**FM: When my group started at the NFTS, Ian Sellar told us on the first day that
it's not that he knows more, it's just that he's been doing it longer.**
DR: That's a good point.

**FM: The ethos of that idea of growing mentally instead of technically – do you
think that is missing from a lot of film schools?**
DR: Yes I do. I'm very grateful that it is missing, I think it's fabulous, because it
keeps me in work. They can hire me for two weeks, and I go in when the students are fresh and innocent, and I get them fired up about story. That's not an
advertisement for myself, I'm just saying that a lot of schools realize that it's a
commodity that is really hard to find. There aren't many of us travelling around
teaching this stuff.

FM: You've taught at so many schools worldwide. Do you have a favourite?
DR: Well, I think that I can go round the schools of Europe and I can give you
the International League Table, and tell you why they are great. The best has to
be the Polish Film School in Lodz – nobody disputes that. Then I ask myself,
'Why is it so great? Is it because it has the old Soviet system?' Well, maybe. I
don't know. And interestingly enough, it's the one film school in Europe I've
never been to. They have some miraculous teachers there, and they are very
concerned about the story. They push the directors on why they care about the
story, its content. They're not interested whether you shoot it from one angle or
the other – that comes later.

FM: That's the silly stuff.
DR: Yeah, that's easy. What they then say to the director is, 'If you care that
much, how are you going to show it? How does your care become a compo-
nent?' The Polish Film School constantly amazes me because of the diversity of
the work produced – it has no house style. Everybody says, 'It's Eastern
European.' Well, it's not, it's Central European. But it's the quality of the
thought that marks it out as very individual. Then, close to the Polish School, in
some ways arguably better, is the Danish Film School in Copenhagen. In the last
six or seven years, they have produced the best European short films.

FM: You can certainly see the strength of story in the Dogme films.
DR: Yes, exactly, and they all came through the Danish School: Thomas

Vinterberg, who made *Festen* – his graduation film, which was called *Last Round*, was the beginning of it; and Lars von Trier, whose graduation film that he made in 1981, *Images of Liberation*, was so innovative, it was 15 years ahead of its time. Trier fought his way through the school in every sense of the word. But the Danish school has Mogens Rukov, who is the father-guru of the Dogme movement. Mogens is a passionate teacher. Just recently, I heard someone say that in Europe, there are six passionate film schoolteachers. And they mark out the school far more than the school's director, whoever that is. When it comes to passion, Mogens is right at the front of the queue. He and his students spend months and months in open forum, private sessions, group sessions, rewrite sessions – just working on the film script. Nine months to get a 25-minute script right. But the energy of the whole school is in that development. The actual shooting of it, they're not that concerned about that. But every year I sit on juries at film festivals, and every year the Danish work is dazzling. You can't get into the cinema – the Danish movies are packed out.

The next best, I suppose, is Jerusalem – the Sam Spiegel School. They have a lot of things going for them. They tell stories naturally, I think they are accustomed to stories, because of all the Rabbinical stories that have a point to them. Therefore, there's something satisfying and complete about their work. They make films of a maximum length of 16 or 17 minutes. Now, the NFTS has taken onboard the idea of working tighter rather than sprawling, as it's terribly hard to make a good 15-minute film. But then some of the greatest films I've seen have been that length. Jerusalem has this amazing concentration of story. And they also employ people like Mogens Rukov, myself, tutors from the Polish school and so on.

Then there are a lot of schools where concentration is on technique, and the leading one there is Munich. Munich student films are as perfectly made as you could imagine. I've taught there for ten years, but the power of technique is something I can't lick. They have enormous budgets, and they will go for 'the look', because their films are meal tickets. And indeed, the employment rate for their students is breathtaking.

FM: That's one of the criticisms I have about my own school. In the second year, when I did *Simple Things*, the pressure was off so there was an element of experimentation there. There was room for you to breathe as a director, writer, cinematographer, whatever. Come the third year, it changes because everybody is looking for the job they need to get after graduation. I've been guilty of that.
DR: I know. Do you know that the majority of really good short films out of European film schools are first films? By that I mean, after you have finished the exercise in year one, in the middle year you make a movie, and if you have a reasonable teacher to help you get the script together, then you make the movie you

want to make. Then you make your meal ticket. Graduation films are so often displays of skill. This is the sad marriage of a cinematographer and ambitious director. It's terrible . . . No, it's understandable. But it's really sad when you look back at the first film and you say, 'There's somebody who is comfortable with themselves.' Comfortable with their own pain, usually.

FM: It's shitty as well that the graduation film is the one that you are being judged on by the industry.
DR: That's the terrible thing: the people who judge. When the industry come to those screenings and they all stand around afterwards and you see the directors of the films standing there – it's like having meetings. 'I had 16 meetings this week, but nothing happened. What does that mean? And 16 people came up to me, and the neg cutter thought the film was wonderful. And Kodak spoke to me, Channel Four spoke to me, and they like my movie.' Then you have to say, 'What did they like?' They like the fact you might be employable. Ask them what the film was about and, well . . . (*Shrugs.*)

FM: We, as a class of directors, went to see a group of agents. And they were saying that at the graduation screenings, there will always be someone who's hot, and that's who everyone will run towards.
DR: Yeah. I remember watching that at the NFTS, and thinking, 'This is just so unfair . . .'

FM: Unfair for the other students.
DR: Yes, that's what I mean. I thought it was unfair because the energy was driving that way. I remember Jocelyn Stevens, when he was director of the RCA – how he was with the painters. He went around the hanging and said, 'I don't care about the name of the painting, what I want is a bigger price ticket beside it. Print it bigger.' It was like a market, and someone who could sell all their work would be taken up by Charles Saatchi or the like. Sure, that's the way the world works, I'm not objecting to that. But then you look at something and you say, 'To get that onto canvas wasn't easy. There's an awful lot of soul searching gone into that. What a shame no one is even looking at it.'

FM: How do you think Europe compares to America concerning education?
DR: Oh . . . I'd say European schools are 50 times better than the American ones.

FM: Mainland Europe rather than Britain? We seem to be more American-based.
DR: Yes, well it's become like that. Once the Royal College of Art course closed

down, then you could see that happening. Nobody really cared about that clo-sure . . . No, that's not true, Alan Parker cared, John Schlesinger cared, and a few others. But when they closed that course down, it meant a whole avenue was gone for people who would never be taken on at the NFTS. Colin Young and I used to compare our acceptance lists. He would say, 'This student applied to me and he applied to you, but we're not going to take him.' I would say, 'Really? He's top of my list.' But once they closed the RCA course, then that whole chunk of film-makers had nowhere to go. And I thought, 'What's left?' There's everybody hanging around the Fuji Scholarship area; there's Bournemouth and Poole, which is a great degree course, but essentially training people to make television – which is fine, they do it superbly well. And Leeds has stepped in and filled a terrific gap.

Years ago, 1982 I think, four guys from the Glasgow School of Art came down to the RCA to see if they could apply. They asked to see the storeroom. I showed them, and we had nine Arriflexes or whatever. And they just stood there. They said they had three Super-8 cameras. And they asked to see some of our students' work, so we put on a little screening, opened some beers, and the students who were in the building showed their films. Then we went round our cutting rooms. We had ten at that time, they had two in Glasgow. Then I said it was a shame they hadn't brought any of their own work. 'Oh we have,' they said, 'but it's on Super-8.' So we found a Super-8 projector and we showed their films. And my students sat silently, in envy, at what these guys had achieved. Their work was so much better than ours, because it was *desperate*. You know how Super-8 jumps every time there's a join and there's cement over the image? They didn't care about that. They could see their city as we couldn't see London, and they *used* their city. And it was wonderful.

FM: What happened to them?
DR: They never applied. They didn't apply, I think, because, inevitably, big insti-tutions intimidate people, which is terrible. I learned to go out and about to every film school I could, to look and find out who was interesting, and meet the students if I could. I very rarely took on people who just applied; I knew them before they came.

FM: When I was in Scotland, studying at Napier and getting involved in Poor Cinema, we felt it was Punk happening all over again. You didn't need big budg-ets or the finest stocks of film available. We plastered posters round the college saying, 'Here's a camera. Here's a videotape. Here's an actor. Now make a film!' We wanted to create debate. And people would write underneath, 'What about story? What about structure?' When I came to the NFTS I thought there might be more debate than there is. I've spoken to people from other film schools too, and it seems to be the case all round. Everybody's head goes down a bit. I was guilty of that too.

DR: The great thing about Britain was that education used to be free. Per year the NFTS had £48,000 unit cost per student. The RCA was the next richest with £9000. And from 1980 to 1989 we gave the NFTS a good run for its money, collecting a lot of awards along the way. But it's not about money, it shouldn't be.

I once talked to Suso Cecchi D'Amico about *The Bicycle Thieves*. I went to see her at her amazing apartment in Rome, and we had dinner. I asked her, 'How could you write that film? You're from a very distinguished, aristocratic family.' And she said, 'I love my city.' I asked her what she meant, and she said, 'I walk in Rome a lot, I listen and I look.' She told me, 'After the war, when we were rebuilding our film industry, we did things as a sort of collective. We used to bring our own chairs with us to dress the set. We would equip an office in one of our houses so that we could keep writing. With *Bicycle Thieves* there were five of us, because that's how we worked.' And, of course, that was what brought us neo-realism. And it's what Truffaut and the *nouvelle vague* had, too – this sort of collective energy through association with each other.

Now all that's gone. Nowadays, everybody is saying, 'I've got to get in, I've got to go through the process, leave the school with a good contact book, and get a job.' That's how the world has changed, and it doesn't do a lot for . . . well, the word 'art' is always very dangerous when used in relation to cinema, but if it's just 'training' then I think that's a shame, I really do.

While I was in New York, I had a theory that we could go out into the street and hand out 500 tickets to anybody, and ask them to come for an interview. And from that 500, we could pick 50 people – the same number of students we took in every year at NYU – and we would do just as well. In American education, you have to realize that universities are actually profit centres, and their principle activity is buying real estate. Columbia University owns most of Harlem; it owns most of the sub-standard city housing in New York. We had to make a profit; we had to generate hundreds of thousands of dollars each year. Although the money we took from the students was more than enough to educate them, it wasn't enough, because NYU had to make a profit. So you sell units of education for money, in order to buy real estate. If not real estate, then you invest in something else.

At the Tisch School of the Arts in NYU, the chairman, who was my boss, was reckoning from an undergraduate film department where there were 1200 students, 1200 wanna-be directors, plus 300 in the Graduate School. So if you have 1500 students being charged $18,000 apiece, the Tisch School was grossing about $17 million a year, and we were spending $7 million on their education;

so that made a $10 million profit. How do you make a profit? Well, the way you do it is you tell the students what they want to hear, give them an education which is so diverse, and introduce them to a few famous people each year, which their parents think is a good idea.

FM: At least their kids got to meet Milos Forman . . .
DR: In the year that I was there, Milos was co-chair at Columbia. He taught a workshop for six students and the competition to get on it was unbelievable. But Milos never appeared at department meetings, or helped with policy, *et cetera*. I did all the work and Milos came in for two hours a week for his one semester. In fact, the students had a life-sized photograph cut-out of Milos. It was absolutely brilliant. It was kept in one of the cutting rooms, and the students used to bring it out and get photographed beside it. With a bit of touching up, it did look like the student was standing with a smiling Milos. So they would send the photo home to their parents and tell them, 'This is me with Milos Forman.' Milos knew about it, but he didn't care.

Of course, some of these sorts of classes are legendary – like Richard Walters' course at UCLA on Advanced Screenwriting, and so on. These were miraculous courses, but for three hours a week for 13 weeks. The rest is people who have been teaching the same thing for 15 years because they have tenure. Once a professor in America has tenure, they can't be fired unless they commit a major misdemeanour.

FM: I've been lucky enough to have Stephen Frears in my cutting room for the last two weeks; and the majority of my school's staff *are* working film-makers. Yet there is the old adage, 'Those that can't do, teach' – which I disagree with, though some of the best teachers are—
DR: Failed film-makers. Yeah. Robert McKee wrote one episode of *Colombo*, as far as I can tell, but his book *Story* is probably the best insight to screenwriting that's around at the moment. I could never direct a film and the scripts I've written are . . . (*Shrugs.*) I mean, I had no qualifications to be head of a film school at all. They were desperate, that's why they took me. And they wanted someone who could fail, so people could say, 'Well, who was Dick Ross anyway?' It was great; I'm not embarrassed by that. I think that the problem is that most of the teachers in film schools *are* failed film-makers, and the trouble is that they remake their students' films and get the same sort of buzz as if they were making the movies themselves. If you knew the amount of war stories told by some tutors – it's just embarrassing. Teaching is a vocation; it's not a job. You have to believe in it. I look around and I divide the world up into the passionate and the rest, and I don't see a lot of good teaching, I have to say.

FM: So where do you see film schools going now? Do you think there's still a place for them?

DR: I think there is a tremendous place for those schools that look at the outside world, look at what's going on at other schools, and then modify and change. In other words, schools that are constantly reviewing what they are doing, offering students a curriculum that is written out, and saying to them, 'This is what we aim to be doing, whether we succeed or not.' I think there should always be national academies. Of course, the nature of film-making itself is changing rapidly. I got a really pathetic email the other day from the Georgia Film School, which used to be a great school. Now they have no film camera functioning, and they were asking if anyone had any damaged video equipment they could use. But still they believe that there is a national cinema of Georgia – there is a feeling there, there's a passion. I think to many people, though, teaching in film schools is a job. I think that they don't serve students well. And students are so hopeful, they are driven by hope, even though the statistics are stacked against them.

FM: Financially now, as well.

DR: Yes, totally. I remember when I heard the first suggestion that students should be fee-paying, around 1988. I said to my students, 'You have to march, and I march with you.' I have believed in free education all my life. I didn't go to public school; I went to state school, then to university, and I even got a grant to go. I said, 'If this happens now and we haven't protested, then we will never sleep.' It didn't work out, but then that's life . . .

The future of film schools will be increasingly involved in teaching complex skills, roles and functions. Post-Production Design will become an incredible part of film education because that's where the technology and need for training lie. My son graduated as an editor from the NFTS in 1995 and he had never touched an Avid; he had to do a short course to learn it. It's amazing to think that only five or six years ago there wasn't an Avid at the NFTS.

FM: Now, of course, nobody cuts on film.

DR: Sure, so my son was trained totally for a skill that even in 1995 was not relevant. Of course the grammar, the vocabulary of the image, he got all that, which was great and which stands him in great stead. I still think that image and sound acquisition, which is to say the work of the director, cinematographer, sound recordist – they are classic skills. I see post-production getting stronger. What is interesting is that in continental Europe, the swing is towards the triangle: the producer, the writer and the director. In Sweden, Helsinki, Berlin, all over the place, they are fostering this microcosm of the industry. But at the same time they're spending longer and longer in developing story and script. All of them have a special screenwriting department which is where the energy is compressed and where the visiting teachers are. It's all happening in 'Story'. The Berlin School has just moved and at the opening of their new building it was declared: 'This building is dedicated to *storytelling*.'

Ben Gibson

Ben Gibson: Director, the London Film School

Ben Gibson began his film career in 1981 with Metro Pictures, acquiring independent films for distribution and programming for the Metro Cinema in London's West End. In 1988 he joined the BFI as a staff producer, and was responsible for setting up the New Directors short film project. From 1990 to 1997 he was BFI Head of Production. His credits as Executive Producer in that period include Young Soul Rebels *(Isaac Julien, 1991),* The Long Day Closes *(Terence Davies, 1992),* Wittgenstein *(Derek Jarman, 1992),* London *(Patrick Keiller, 1994),* Madagascar Skin *(Chris Newby, 1996),* Gallivant *(Andrew Kötting, 1996),* Under the Skin *(Carine Adler, 1997),* Love is the Devil *(John Maybury, 1998) and* Beautiful People *(Jasmin Dizdar, 1999).*

In 2000 Ben was appointed Director of the London International Film School (LIFS). Originally based in Brixton (as the London School of Film Technique), the school moved in 1966 to a deserted six-floor Covent Garden warehouse, once used as a ripening store for bananas. It offers a two-year, full-time, intensively practical diploma course with a very structured curriculum. Its famous alumni include directors such as Michael Mann, Mike Leigh and Les Blair, as well as a significant number of leading DoPs: Roger Pratt (Batman), *Tak Fujimoto* (The Silence of the Lambs), *Geoffrey Simpson* (Shine) *and Ueli Steiger* (Godzilla).

Ben was one of my executive producers when I made a short for the BFI. Always outspoken about the state of British film, he surprised me by his decision to take over the running of a film school, as his attitude seemed to be the complete antithesis of that found in traditional film education. So I went to see him in Covent Garden, two months into his tenure.

Fraser MacDonald: How do you think your background in film production prepared you for now running a film school?
Ben Gibson: Well, I think the principle purpose of film schools is so that people can find their voices, and have the support to do so. And as a producer, I was always trying to find the right place for films within the market, so that people could respond to talent. But funnily enough, when we were running New Directors at the BFI there was a lot of emphasis on selecting people who *didn't* go to film school. These would be people who had achieved something in another domain, for whom film school was maybe not an appropriate lifestyle choice for that moment in their lives, or who simply didn't want to work in that

environment. And it's true that there are a lot of places other than film schools where you can now learn to be a film-maker. Think of Shane Meadows, for instance. What concerns me, as someone who didn't go to film school and now finds himself taking one over, is that there is a sub-culture in film schools wherein the people who run them and turn them into departmental structures would like to think of them as classic American 1940s-style studios. That has a lot of side-effects that are very damaging.

FM: Such as?
BG: I think the principal one is that the director of the school becomes this kind of Irving Thalberg figure at the head of a fictional, controlled command-economy. A regime is created, where the school has one person who is responsible for 'Script', and that person convenes everybody else who deals with script, and tells them how writing will be taught and what the key principles will be. I think that's completely irrelevant. If you look at the sharp areas where art and craft combine – let's say screenwriting, direction, music – what you can take out of them as a craft element is very, very small. You could be totally sceptical about the possibility of actually teaching them. But what you might be able to do is provide a kind of art school environment, where people can teach themselves – a space where adults moderate and coordinate their own education through lots of coherent arguments with people who might disagree with them totally, but who are working in the same practice.

But if you put students in a situation where they just have to argue individually with their teacher, then you are perpetuating a model that is not out there in the real world.

This notion of solid people who are always employed in some BBC department or studio set-up – it's not a good model of how directors will operate after they graduate. In the real world, those kinds of production units are put together only to be taken apart. As a director you have to survive in the independent sector, roaming up and down Old Compton Street, alongside lots of other directors with their own strengths and weaknesses. I think one of the reasons film schools become out of date is because they are more attuned to how things are done in Los Angeles or Shepherds Bush than they are to independent film-making practice. Whereas, if you look at how we actually make films now, we are all really in New York, or London, or Copenhagen . . .

FM: It sounds like you're really arguing against a structured curriculum. When Colin Young set up at UCLA and the NFTS, he wanted it to be more of a *conservatoire* of ideas. So nobody was really enrolled as 'a director', for example.
BG: I think that's right. You should create a balance. At the extreme end you have IDHEC in France, a kind of playground where there's a lot of equipment,

and full-time film-makers coming in to talk to the students, but there's no permanent teaching staff. I'm not sure that would work so well for us, though there are a lot of attractive things about it. The question is what the balance is between those professionals who come in and assist this *conservatoire* notion, and how you can support and consolidate the energies of tutors who go for long periods of time teaching film without making any films themselves. One thing that is very easy for me to support here, which is most traditional about the LIFS, is that people only learn about film by *making* films. They really don't do anything else.

FM: Your idea seems to be at odds with the old BBC mentality of 'training for the industry', which film schools like the NFTS probably grew up with.
BG: I think people get trapped in this idea of 'the industry'. It traps politicians, bureaucrats, everybody. The truth is that in Britain there is a very big, well-connected and viable television industry, and now there is going to be a narrow-casting Internet industry tied to it, as well as various links to publishing *et cetera*. If you think about the gap between the Soho-based independent sector and the people who are working in Pinewood and Shepperton, they are really two different cultures. They're not really an industry, they are two separate areas of supply.

It's because of the dominant economic power of the British broadcasting industry that the NFTS has to call itself 'The National Film *and Television* School' and offer courses in three-camera studio direction. What it can't do, educationally, is tell the truth – which is that, a) the best place to learn three-camera studio directing is within television itself, so television should undertake its own training. (I mean, Skillset* recognizes that somebody has to be doing a job professionally if they are to assess whether or not somebody else can do it.) And, b) nobody can make a really powerful argument that the grammar of television drama or documentary is somehow different than that for film. The LIFS is very badly supported, so we don't have to tell the lie – we just call ourselves 'The London Film School', and there is no chance we'll insert the word 'Television' in there, even if they do give us money, because I don't think it helps television to think of themselves as a different domain of artistic practice.

FM: So you are really arguing against industry funding?
BG: I really am. One of the paradoxes in the UK is that the people with political influence who are charged with finding the right recipe for building a British film industry are in fact the people who are most conservative about innovation, and the creation of new markets for new ideas. It's the independent sector,

---

* National Training Organization for Broadcast, Film, Video and Interactive Media.

which is by definition privately funded, that is most forward-looking in that respect. I had a conversation with Chris Smith* about cultural policy, which the government likes to lay out as a way of controlling people. He talked about 'access' and 'excellence', which was the philosophy behind the Millennium Dome. But the people who designed the Dome's content turned out to be like commissioning editors in broadcasting, who decided what tone was needed and then hired a crew to reflect that tone; so that they became the creators. I asked him, 'Is there going to be debate in politics about whether this paradox can be properly resolved, after a year of the Dome in which the idea of "access" completely overtook any notion of "excellence", at least in the public's mind?'

The situation in British film is even more complex. After all these years of Lottery-funded films, one real lesson worth learning is that in France, they like British films. They think it's a productive and stimulating area of work. But then the British films that are considered crap are not distributed in France, because they don't have to be. Yet the government says that you must have access to everything that the government funded. So then Alexander Walker† goes to a public screening and says, 'It's bullshit.' And at that point you have destroyed the value of the brand that you are trying to promote to the local audience, by having a political obsession with everyone getting a comprehensive look at it. So it would be a good public policy to say, 'We'll only show good British films, and call the rest the devil's share that would probably have gone wrong in any case.'

FM: Do you think there is a complacency about film education in this country?
BG: There's still the same old problem in Britain, which is the idea that you create academies and institutions in order to say to people, 'Remember you cannot do that in the real world. The real world is not about your voice or your imagination. It is about having a view of an audience wider than your auntie and your best friend and the three people that you were at school with.' So you have a tabloid newspaper idea of cultural production, with the audience as this generalized mush of people about whom, in general, you have to be quite condescending. In reality, what you want is for students to look their lecturers in the eye when they talk about 'the real world', and say, 'Yeah, you would be out there all the time if you were so right.'

You do find students who don't believe that finding future audiences is about second-guessing the audiences of the past and just delivering the milk to them. For them, the process is more like inventing a product. They bring energy to form rather than condescending toward it. That energy is the energy that will allow them to work in film. Or if they chose to make three-camera television

---

* Then Secretary of State for Culture in the Labour Government; author of *Creative Britain* (Faber, 1998).
† Film critic of the *London Evening Standard*, and outspoken ex-governor of the BFI.

drama, they are going to transform that as well. And it's as true of sound recordists as it is of directors – they are going to be the greatest sound designers in the future. It's not just about *auteurs* who sit at the back being strange and moody and magnificent.

FM: My training at the NFTS has been anti-auteurship, partly because of the curriculum and partly because of the industry. The attitude is, 'Your career will take a certain path. Maybe a few episodes of TV drama. Then, hopefully, a feature.' It's industry training, it might even be realistic training. But it can stifle creativity.

BG: Yeah. That's why you have to only hire teachers who can really project themselves into the excitement of another person's success. Otherwise, you may see a culture of envy, an older generation of teachers who are like non-commissioned training officers, as in say *An Officer and a Gentleman*, wanting to break the ambitions of world domination of younger film-makers. I think there are obligations. If you are in charge of a school and you are going to spend the government's money on somebody whom you believe will be a significant creator of something or other, then there is a pressure on you to let that person create. That way, that person then has an obligation to surprise us, the audience. Television editors go into work every morning and check their diaries, and what they want is someone to come in and surprise them. It doesn't matter if they are commissioning soaps or drama serials, they are not interested in meeting people who just have craft training and low expectations of the environment they will be working in. Of course, if you go to a soap and start talking about your Bresson influences when you should be delivering seven and a half minutes a day, that will have to be overcome.

FM: When you were head of BFI Production, it was in the nature of that institution to take risks. It seems that you want to carry on this with your tenure at LIFS.

BG: Maybe. I mean, whatever institution I go to, I'll try and carry out the same thing. For me to go from commissioning – largely of first films and low-budget work – into a film school environment seemed possible for one important reason. One of the imaginary boundaries is gone. There is no such thing as an 'amateur film'. There are only films. That should free up everybody. In fact, the only people who define what is a professional film and what is amateur are music publishers. If they define a production as 'non-commercial exploitation', they mean it. And they have a lot of lawyers. So if we are going to do deals with Internet companies to put our short films on the web, I have to make contact with a large amount of original composers, so that students don't spend all six terms using their record collections to score their films.

A big problem for producers is that they don't get much money making short films in the professional sector, be they funded or not. They need new kinds of support, within experimental houses or bases where innovation is a part of the agenda, where you create mixed economies – like film schools. The lines need to be blurred. In this post-industrial world, you need to be able to create centres where innovation is at the top of the agenda. There is good reason to suppose that down the line we will be bidding to house producers who are working in the professional sector, who need some infrastructure support to help them develop that kind of innovation.

The LIFS is now instigating a programme called CNC – Centre for New Cinema – because we want to put full-time students in the middle of an environment of synergy. We want to have a centre that can take in fulltime students, transfer students, or just people who want to attend a series of evenings where some iconoclastic film-maker will show them a different way to look at their work. In three years' time I hope I can walk down the corridor and see one person who's on the two-year course; another who's on an intense six-week transfer course from producing to directing; someone else who's working on something like the new Mike Figgis–Don Boyd digital video experiment which has been funded by a group of media partners. And the key thing is that I hope I don't know which one is which. Then you have a centre in which there is a culture of experiment, excitement and innovation. Then you may have found what the film school of the twenty-first century needs to be.

FM: You mention new digital technology and with the explosion of the Internet, there is now a proliferation of virtual film schools, where people can sign up for classes, receive notes on film-making, even post their work up for critique. Do you think that this will pose any danger to the traditional way of teaching film?
BG: Not really. I think you have to remember what are the limitations, for the moment, of the form. I was one of those people who was quite slow to get on the Internet, because I already had a reference library. But if you see the Net as a library resource, then a 'virtual film school' is a very valid way of using it, while you are busy making films, to develop a critical vocabulary with living and dead film-makers around the world, and a sense of looking in parallel through lots of different visions of the same situation. James Monaco's *How to Read Film* has now been turned into an on-line book, in which you can see a Steadicam demonstration by pressing a button. I think that's wonderful. But if you then say that everyone should learn to be a film-maker in an isolated way, where they don't collaborate, then I would say it doesn't work. My anxiety about on-line film schools is that the generations of people who can use that new equipment in the most innovative way are the students, not the faculties. If the faculties get together and create something, it is going to be limited by their

understanding of what the technology should be used to do – which is essentially an extension of the kind of computer file exchanging that's been going on in offices for many years.

What does interest me is ways of getting on to virtual communities and networks. We have students who come to us from all over the world, and if they want to shoot a documentary in Colombia, they can get in touch with people in fulltime education in Colombia, and crew up half of their documentary shoot using local students. The other thing that interests me is that we could create a virtual network of short films, through which people could also pick up screenplays. This would enable students from all round the globe to work on different projects, and so work the network themselves. I'm sure in five years' time everybody in film education will have a unique password that allows them into certain spaces where they can collaborate, and so make film school a global community rather than a single institution. We'll see what happens with the Global Film School, and I wish it well. But I think to have a correspondence course, rather than a fulltime 'face to face' course with different classes of emphasis, articulation and value, is potentially dangerous. It means you create a *declassé* film-maker, somebody who hasn't met anybody. They've just been sitting in their room, smoking too much with the window closed, thinking about film-making.

FM: Mike Figgis has said that for him the most exciting thing about digital film-making is that you don't have to answer to or place your trust in anybody bar yourself. You can shoot your film, take it home, edit it on your home computer, then distribute it on the Net. But that scares me – because it cuts out the nature of interaction. In a sense, that attitude sounds the death knell for film schools.
BG: It does in some ways, but in other ways it's useful. In the early 1960s the British film industry was re-capitalized by the American studios, which meant that we went from being a European production base into a very rigorously American one. The knock-on effect is that it is very hard to make a film for Film Four costing £1.5 million without having a catering bus. That's because you have 35 people who have to be there on set, even if it's just a dialogue scene between two actors on location. You can't really do low-budget film-making with all of its insurance costs without having an awful lot of people thinking that the film has great market value ahead of time. And that breaks down any aspiration of the democratization of film-making. It also has the effect of creating a system where people think that they have to have a three-year training in a single craft area, rather than a general education and a sense of enthusiasm for an area. Fetishizing the technology means that it creates ghettos and ghettos create exclusion. I think that is quite dangerous and it's something that digital film-making can break down.

One of the most interesting things, industrially, about the French *nouvelle vague* and the Eastern European waves of that time is that very often you'd see a person directing a film one day, then writing or producing someone else's film the next. The independent sector in the US has seen something similar. If you look across the most interesting careers, you find collaborative groups, people working in different specializations for one another, creating some kind of stimulation by moving about. Without that, you can't have an independent sector; and that's why I think specialization can be a very dangerous thing. What we need is to find the right articulation of it. One of the best traditions of the LIFS is that it graduates film-makers rather than directors, writers, cinematographers, even if the students think of themselves as writer–directors when they come out. For a lot of them, that is very relevant, especially if they are going to graduate into working in Mexico where all those industrial demarcations are much looser than they are here.

FM: In a way the NFTS curriculum backfires a wee bit, because the majority of the alumni who are successful directors actually entered the school as something other: Pete Hewitt* was an editor, Mark Herman† was an animator . . .
BG: What we don't have is the problem that arises when all the students walk into the coffee bar on the first day of the course, and the ones who have long speeches to make and wear rather interesting scarves become the directors. And the wallflowers who need to think before they talk all suddenly become sound recordists, just because that's the way the industry operates in terms of personal style and its articulation. I think that's very backward, and it made for some bad publicity for the *conservatoire* of Colin Young, for example. It was built on that idea of picking winners. If you think of Terence Davies sitting at the back of the class, not wearing cowboy boots, not having as many girlfriends as Michael Caton-Jones – by a long way. Carine Adler is publicized in the new NFTS prospectus, and she is a film-maker at some long way apart from those of her generation who went straight into television. But now she's being advertised as a distinctive, individual film-maker. There are all kinds of problems in the idea of, 'Let's have directors, writers, producers and so on,' and they are expressed by the careers of these people. Take Lynne Ramsay – she is a really interesting cinematographer. She's suffocated within that structure, because she is also probably one of the most interesting and instinctive writer–directors to have emerged in the UK over the last decade. But it is important to say that she graduated from the NFTS as a cinematographer.

* Director of *Bill and Ted's Bogus Journey* (1991), *The Borrowers* (1997) and *Thunderpants* (2001).
† Director of *Brassed Off* (1996), *Little Voice* (1998) and *Purely Belter* (2000).

FM: There is a view that a director should have an encompassing knowledge of all aspects of film production.

BG: I think courses that engage students with all of the different departments have an advantage to them. It means that people can spend time working in film when they are not directing. In the second year, we try and work out what people can do because it's the real world. A lot of people who leave the LIFS will work as First ADs or other such jobs, without worrying that there is something degrading about their position having graduated, in their own minds, as writer–directors. They will know the basics of those jobs having done them at film school in a comprehensive way. Certainly they can't graduate from the LIFS unless they have edited a film, camera-operated a film, built a set, produced and written and directed a film. Now, it means that some of them are terrible cinematographers. Put a light meter in their hand and they get nervous. That's inevitable.

There are a *lot* of film-makers in Britain. And when you look at the less interesting output of British cinema, you realize there are a lot of directors who think it's their job to have their lives saved by heads of department who have a technical understanding of the cinema. So the directors will turn up and stand by the catering truck eating a bacon roll, and the cinematographer will tell them what the effect will be if they use this or that lens, or shoot different coverage. It's as if the directors had never been to film school at all. They never sat and made plasticine models of their actors and so on, because it was outside their experience. They just want to spend all the time in the caravan with the actors. I don't think that's a very appropriate way of looking at the form.

But if you look at the people who go onto set in an ambitious way – like Orson Welles, the number of times he and Greg Toland watched *Stagecoach*. Or Sam Mendes, the way he has described working with Conrad Hall on *American Beauty*. These are people who want to be able to understand enough of the craft to communicate with people from other departments. Sam Mendes is a good example of someone who came from nowhere near cinema in terms of his background training; but he knows the address of the National Film Theatre, and he has some critical vocabulary to talk about cinema. Therefore, in a real collaboration, he will command the respect of people around him.

I made films with Derek Jarman, and Derek used to make a speech on the first day of shooting. He'd say, 'I can't believe I'm this lucky, because here you all are working on my film. I couldn't have replaced any of you. You are my dream and I want you to show off as much as possible all the time, to show me how brilliant you are.' So it was like conducting the *1812 Overture*. But in a quiet way Derek understood everything that was going on. I believe that's the way Stephen Frears works as well. He speaks as a total amateur, but he understands the craft very intimately. In order to do that, you have to have a core belief in your whole understanding of the whole craft. So if you have a curriculum, and you should have some kind of curriculum, that's what it should deliver.

FM: A lot of film students feel that they walk out of film school tainted by the experience of having been there. Sometimes it can take three or four years to actually pick up a camera again. How do you think that you can solve that problem?
BG: I don't think that courses should be too long. It can make for a problem with people graduating. You know, in folklore people graduated in medicine from Trinity College ten years after they signed up. I'm glad that the NFTS has sorted that out to some significant degree. Because there is going to come a moment when the film-maker has to get out there in the world, and it is going to be a frightening place. They have got to get through that as quickly as they can, but preparing for that moment has got to start as early as it can. Otherwise, you will have people who are hanging around, experiencing the comfort of film school for too long, and I think that's bad.

FM: I think the LIFS and the NFTS are the only two film schools in Britain that aren't attached to a university. In some ways, that lightens the load for the practical work. But it can equally be criticized for not having enough academic discourse. Discourse amongst students always happens – at the NFTS we argued constantly about the Dogme 95 manifesto. Yet some students complain about there not being enough studying and tutor-led discussion of films.
BG: You can't legislate for it. There will be people who have a very low level of ability for getting into debates about whether Bresson was a better film-maker than Godard. Generally speaking, I think that a lot of people in Britain have spent a lot of energy making sure that cinema is not considered an area of culture on a critical level within our society. The paradox these people have to live with is that this campaign has actually taken them out of the leading edge of world cinema innovation, which now seems to happen in Denmark and New York, but not in London. There are not many instances here where we say, 'Here's a new Bill Douglas', or 'Here's a new Terence Davies'. I think there is an incredible lack of tolerance for a little bit of pretension, a little bit of over-ambition.

Now, I can't set up the LIFS as a national institution. We are trying to make our ties within the UK much stronger, and to democratize UK access to the course. That is a very high priority, in the short term. But in parallel with that, LIFS is an international institution that doesn't get involved in parochial debates about what should happen in our local cinema. Independent cinema is an international form, and the financing of it is tied up in local politics. I don't think that 'national cinema' is a very useful category for anyone working outside the critical framework, which is why we spend all our time talking about the Dogme movement and suchlike.

So I think the role of film institutions within that is to be as unparochial and as international as possible about the development of a clinical discourse about film. At LIFS we have a lot of discussions and screenings and try and build up a framework for people to talk about film-making historically. Barry Salt teaches here and he is a world leader on the development of film grammar, and a lot of people find his lectures fascinating and engaging, although they don't all want to go into the level of detail that he is into. Viewing films is very important. I was told, and I'm sure it's a myth, that at the NFTS they would screen a film like *Wild Strawberries*, and the students would be lost in admiration of Bergman until a tutor would say, 'But remember, they have film subsidy in Sweden, so this has got nothing to do with *your* practice. We don't want you aspiring to make these types of films, because it's just not practical in your case.' Now I think to get money from the government to educate people, and then to squash their ambition like that, is a crime against nature.

FM: I can't verify that story. But in some ways there is a more industry-orientated ethos at the NFTS. I also think that since the Royal College of Art closed its film department, we've since seen a new generation of British film-makers who studied there, and their work is coming from the left field.
BG: At the BFI when we were allotting the New Directors funding, the RCA supplied five directors for every one coming out of the NFTS. It was a fantastically significant place. All kinds of people came out of it and experimented with the form, before turning to a more narrative bent. Yet the industry very much discounted that direction, and that's why the BFI had to create that avenue. It's interesting that people like Carine Adler and Lynne Ramsay are top of the list with leading agencies, having gone through an experience with the BFI making a low-budget movie, whereas before they couldn't have got themselves arrested. What it means is lots of people have been bashed into submission by the industry by making soaps or television drama, and in the meantime the industry is still hankering after some surprises.

What worries me is that the Film Council want to create a 'tone' for the films they support, rather like magazine editors in that respect. 'Hip-hop films', by certain kinds of young people from certain regions, with a lot of energized camera movement, that will look like this and sound like that. Whereas curatorial programmes, where you hope to be encouraging the art of surprise, have to be about responding to real talent that's there and keeping faith with it. So it becomes necessary for institutions like film schools to be wary of setting up agendas of what is new or trendy, which will be immediately out of date in any case. They need to be more like art schools, allowing these voices to come through. Here we take the view that the art school tradition, which works well in architecture and design, where people try and find a very distinctive voice for themselves, should be a significant part of training for the screen arts. Though it's a strange combination of cultures we have, because it was members of ACTT* who set up the London International Film School because they wanted to establish an ACTT-recognized course. So the camera department is the school's strongest because of that. Most of the people who apply see the advert in *American Cinematographer*.

So, in a way, this is a very pro-industry place, but on top of that we place the freedom that students can make any film they want to make. Half the films are made by writer–directors. Then the question is to find out if they can work with another writer to see what that then brings to the process. Otherwise, you have *auteur* films made by people with Hollywood running in their head, which makes for a climate of fear that you need to bar when running a film school. That's why people like Mike Figgis are becoming very important figures for the future of British film. What Mike is fighting in everything he says about creativity is that climate of fear. That has been the downside of the Puttnam–Parker 'Let's get serious' period that we have had for the last twenty years. They have tried to instil fear in people, and I don't think that is a way of making good films.

FM: When I first started making films in Scotland, there was a movement up there called 'Poor Cinema' – championed by Colin McArthur – which was almost a precursor to Dogme 95.
BG: Yeah, I know it. There have been so many movements of frustrated people inside the UK, and I was a great believer in Colin McArthur's campaign. In a small place like Scotland, where everybody knows everybody else and they are all making arguments about resources all the time, it was very difficult for him to pursue that. One of the things that excited me about seeing Lynne Ramsay's work and then working on a short with her was that, for me, in a way, it was worth Bill Douglas having lived and died.

For years at BFI Production, we made films that were very ambitious, but not very successful for their audiences, in terms of emotion or performance or whatever – because they were being created by a disenfranchized bunch of people who had the critical vocabulary, but not the craft skill. Then, by the time we had made films like *Love is the Devil* or *Under the Skin*, you suddenly realize that these films make all of your arguments for you. You don't need to argue any longer, because they are cheap enough, and they will make their money back over ten years, and they profile, and they cost the same amount as a film that's written off in a fortnight.

* Trade union: the Association of Cinematograph and Television Technicians.

Everybody always thought that if you had less money, you had more freedom. But it wasn't an argument about culture and commerce so much as a case of everything having its price. And that's an incredibly liberating way to think. Lars von Trier thought, 'I'll publicize one movie this way', and that has now turned into a way of publicizing and financing a lot of movies. But it's been coming for the last twenty years. If you think about Badly Drawn Boy or Tracy Emin or Will Self, the way in which they reach our consciousness costs so little in terms of materials – they have the freedom to surprise us. Giving the freedom to people to surprise us should be the number one target of the Film Council if they are really committed to the idea of having a local audience, and dealing with British culture and identity by having a cinema here. It's exactly the same thing as building a market.

FM: So how do you feel about the current attitudes against film school? Many people are now taking up the banner of Robert Rodriguez's 'Ten-Minute Film School'.
BG: Everybody needs to do it in his or her own way. At any one time, 70 to 80 per cent of those people who are talented and interesting and will make a contribution to the moving image are not going to be people who can take three years off to go to film school. It's important for us to cater for this new generation, as we hope to do at the LIFS with the Centre for New Cinema. The thing about New York and Copenhagen is that they have a cultural advantage over us, because they have fewer demons to fight. They say, 'If you can make a small film interesting, there is commerce in that. We will find the commerce in it.' In this country we are always trying to separate culture and commerce, which means we are all tied up in these mad ideological arguments. Perhaps that is the British tragedy, that it is so polarized. Film schools should be working out how you combine those things.

Michele Camarda

Michele Camarda: Producer

US-born producer Michele Camarda is at the forefront of the 'renaissance' of British film. Her credits include Photographing Fairies *(dir. Nick Willing, 1997), two comedies by David Kane,* This Year's Love *(1999) and* Born Romantic *(2000), and Michael Winterbottom's* Wonderland *(1999). Her time at the NFTS was, by anyone's standards, incredibly successful – she managed to graduate with the Oscar for best student film. It is her attitude to development that sets her apart from the average, run-of-the-mill producer. She believes in getting the film right on paper first.*

Fraser MacDonald: What did you do before you went to film school, Michele?
Michele Camarda: I went to university in Boston and did a Bachelor of Science degree in Broadcasting and Film. It was very liberal arts-orientated, and in the last two years we studied a lot of film and broadcast history. There wasn't much production – it was more to do with theory, criticism and aesthetics. So it wasn't until the last term that we actually got cameras in our hands and made films.

FM: And what was your film like?
MC: Well . . . it was called *Super 8 1/2*, and it was very arty and black-and-white. I was a big Fellini fan at the time. (*Smiles.*) After that, I planned on going to New York and getting a job as a runner in TV or film. I had all my entry-level interviews set up, but then I just suddenly freaked out. Back then the yuppie thing was starting, all the girls were wearing sneakers with their dresses. I thought to myself, 'I'm 21 and I'm running round Manhattan like a crazy person.' In the US the idea is that you graduate, you get a job, and by the time you're 30 you should be a millionaire – this weird work ethic. I was too much of a hippie for that. I had some friends in Europe, so I decided just to hang out in London for the summer, then go back to New York and restart my life six months later.

FM: How did you end up at the NFTS?
MC: The first week I was in London, I fell into a job as a runner on music videos, and I ended up with a company called MGMM. It was the mid-1980s and they were making big promos for the likes of David Bowie and Diana Ross, for ridiculous amounts of money. And I found that a lot of the cameramen and

art directors I was working with on these promos had gone to the National Film School, as had my boyfriend at the time – now my husband – Nick Willing. He had studied animation – in fact, he was the youngest student ever admitted, just 17 at the time, and now he was working in special effects for commercials. So everyone I spoke to about this school just raved about it. It was clear that it was unlike masters degrees in the US – it was about taking people who were mature and knew exactly what they wanted to do.

So I spent three years in London on visitors' visas, and I worked my way up from runner to PA. Eventually I started producing commercials and music videos. But after about a year of that, I was tired of it – it was rock 'n' roll, and I really wanted to do drama and make movies. But the crossover between music videos and commercials into features was difficult. It still is – they are two different worlds. I would go round to meet feature film producers, but because I was still in the promo world they seemed really alien to me. So that was what really drew me to the NFTS. David Puttnam had just become chairman, so they were really focusing on the producer's course. Previously it had been mainly about production management, but now it was about encouraging the producers to be much more creatively involved, and I was really impressed by the sound of that. So I applied, was accepted, and it was the best thing I could have done. I spent three and a half years there, but what I gained was equal to ten years' worth of experience if I had tried to take the route from music video.

FM: A lot of people don't see a film school as the way to learn producing. They think you should be walking the streets of Soho or wherever. So why do you think that this course was so good for you?
MC: I think I was lucky. I met a director who was open to collaboration. There were six directors in my year, John Roberts was one of them, and we just clicked over the kind of material we were attracted to. So we started working together from day one. I produced his first-year exercise. We were given poems that we had to interpret on film, and John and I developed a script. He involved me as a creative producer, so that every decision that we made was collaborative, which was very rewarding. The film was called *The Soul Food Shack*. It's a lovely ten-minute film, and it still stands up – I watched it again just recently. It's got Ainsley Harriott* in it – he plays Marvin Gaye. (*Laughs.*) And it has some really good soul music, which we actually cleared the rights for. I mean, for a ten-minute exercise, it was quite ambitious. It ended up getting a television broadcast, and going to the New York Film Festival and opening in front of the film of David Hare's *Plenty*. It was weird standing there in the Lincoln Center, getting a standing ovation after going up the red carpet in evening dress. It was

* Now a household name as the host of the BBC daytime TV show *Ready Steady Cook*.

like a taste of things to come. I thought, 'This is good. I'll have a bit of this.' (*Laughs.*)

FM: Not bad for your first-year film!
MC: Yeah. So the following year John and I worked together on our intermediate film, and I found a short story by Kurt Vonnegut from his collection *Welcome to the Monkey House*. I gave it to John to read, and he loved it. It was set in America, but we co-adapted it, which again was really rewarding, working together to get the script right. That one ended up winning the BAFTA for best short that year. (*Michele turns round and points at a framed letter.*) In fact, that letter came from Vonnegut after we sent him a tape of the finished film. He had given us the rights beforehand anyway, but after seeing the film he wrote to say, 'It's all yours!', which was really sweet of him. That film went to loads of festivals too.

So then it was graduation film time. We were feeling a little bit on our high horse, thinking, 'Okay, we've won a BAFTA, we've been to festivals.' We developed a film called *This Boy's Story*. And I remember walking into Colin Young's office with the first draft, thinking we were the bees' knees and we were going to get our green light to go off and make this hugely ambitious film. He just said, 'The script's not ready, I know you can do better', and he threw us out of the office. We were absolutely gutted. But because of that we spent another three months developing the script, getting it into shape, talking to people in the industry about it. The script tutors at the school, Cary Crabbe and Jan Fleischer, were very helpful too.

FM: I think that because you get given a budget on the producer's course at the NFTS, you tend to concentrate on story and script development. Was that the same for you?
MC: On *This Boy's Story*, definitely. I feel I know an awful lot about development now having done those three films at the school. When it became clear that it needed more work, they were quite tough on us, which was the best thing that could have happened. It gave us the discipline to go away and work on it. In the end we got the script right. Then we drew up a budget and it was about £100,000. I managed to pull about half of that within the film school, then I went out and raised the rest. The script was set in the 1960s, it was about two little boys who run away from home to meet George Best*. So I went to Companies House and looked up Manchester United Football Club, and then I wrote off to all their big shareholders. I got loads of cheques back, for £500, £600, from these wealthy people living in Cheshire. We had done a brochure

* Widely idolized Northern Irish member of Manchester United's 1968 European Cup-winning side.

and a pitch – I mean, it was very similar to what we do now to try and raise money for features. I went to Joe Bloggs* in Manchester, which was a new company at that time, and they loved the idea and gave us something like £25,000. Then I went to LA, because a friend of mine was working at a studio and she managed to sneak me some home addresses of some very powerful people from her bosses' Rolodex – about a dozen of the big players in Hollywood. Then one day I remember Richard Jenkins† came into my office and said, 'We have just received a cheque from the "Californian Community Foundation" for $20,000, and it's written out to be used only for *This Boy's Story*. The donor wishes to remain anonymous.' (*Laughs.*) I mean, we were surely blessed on this film.

FM: Sometimes it's said that your grasp should always extend your reach. Did the school encourage you to do that, or did they try and hold you back a bit?
MC: On one hand, I think they were slapping my wrists, and with the other they were patting me on the back. It was mixed, because everybody genuinely thought the script was good, everybody genuinely believed in John Roberts as a new star director. We had made two films that had shown our potential, and they liked the idea that we were developing as a team. In other words, the producing course seemed to be working in the sense that there was a real collaboration going on. So I did have their support. But they did have to be restrained because they couldn't allow this to be happening to all the films . . .

I found out when raising the money for *This Boy's Story* that there was a government grant that would match any money raised for a film from outside the industry. So they matched our money from Joe Bloggs, pound for pound. So suddenly I had the £100,000 we needed, and then we were making this film on 35mm. It was 55 minutes long, a huge production – we had cranes, and we filled up the Anfield Kop†† with extras dressed in 1960s gear. And it went on to win the Oscar for Best Student Film. That was in the last year that Colin Young was at the school, and it was a real thrill for him.

FM: Once you finished your graduation film, that's you in the industry. How much was the NFTS a help to you in that environment? I ask because you talked about the school being a fast track into the industry . . .
MC: I think it was the films that we made at the school, and the fact that winning the BAFTA created a buzz – and we worked that buzz. Then getting *This Boy's Story* out and winning the Oscar. So I took the print and set up screenings for people in the industry. John and I left the school with an idea for a feature film, we were graduating as a team. Unfortunately – well, fortunately for him –

* Fashionable clothing company founded by young entrepreneur Shami Ahmed.
† Studio Manager of the NFTS, also takes care of the budgets for the graduation film.
†† Area of fanatical support behind the goal at Anfield, home of Liverpool FC.

John went on to do a feature with David Puttnam (*War of the Buttons*, 1994), which is the sweet irony of the situation. So, in a way David was encouraging myself and John to graduate as a team, because he was the chairman of the school, but . . . (*Shrugs.*) Still, he was very supportive of me while that was happening, so I'm grateful to him for that. Making those three films at the school enabled me to have the courage and the confidence to then say, 'Okay, I am now a producer. I'm not going to be an assistant to a working producer, I'm going to do this!' I set up my office and worked from my front room, found a project that I was passionate about, developed it, and just did what I had been doing at film school, only on a bigger level. And I raised the money and got the film made. It took me three years, sure, but I wouldn't have had the confidence to do that if I hadn't been through the school.

FM: And that film was *Photographing Fairies*?
MC: Yes. Nick Willing directed it, so it was his first feature as well. I simply found the book and worked on it with him and another writer, Chris Harrald, until it was ready. Also, Simon Perry at British Screen was very supportive of us because he had seen *This Boy's Story*. In fact, I set up a screening for Simon and sort of barged my way in there and set up a few projects in development, because I had his support. He really supported *Photographing Fairies* and helped me along the way with the co-financing with Polygram. He was sort of the godfather to me through my first feature.

FM: Were a lot of the crew on *Photographing Fairies* film school graduates?
MC: Well, apart from Nick and myself there was the production designer, Laurence Dorman, who designed *This Boy's Story*.

FM: The NFTS tries to set itself against '*auteurship*', and the idea of film as a collaborative medium seems to be something that you obviously want to continue in your own work. Do you believe in that way forward within the industry?
MC: I suppose so. I've worked with Nick, with David Kane, and with Michael Winterbottom, and they were all very different. David was a first-time director, so that was a challenge. But he was very open to collaborating, he is not an *auteur* in that sense. Neither was Michael, he was very open too. That was an unusual situation, working with Michael on *Wonderland*, because he has his own production company, which has its own producer. But I had a script that I had developed, and I took it to him. He responded to it and we developed it together, his company and mine. And that was a massively collaborative effort, just to get that movie made.

Wonderland: Gina McKee as Nadia.

FM: But it was one of the most successful British films in recent years.
MC: *Critically* successful . . . It should have made more money. (*Laughs*.)

FM: The thing I liked about *Wonderland* was that it looked at the details: small things suddenly became epic. It harks back to the 'know thyself' way of writing, which is something that is taught at Film School. Laurence Coriat [the writer of *Wonderland*] didn't study at the NFTS, did she?
MC: No, I came across her writing because after *Photographing Fairies* I was on a panel for British Screen and I was fortunate enough to see a lot of new writing coming through. I was really impressed by her writing samples, so we started working together on a few things. And she had this idea of a *Short Cuts* type of story set in London, which really appealed to me. We developed it through British Screen and spent about a year and a half getting the script really right. Michael Winterbottom was our first-choice director, so we were really lucky there.

FM: It feels like there was a real student ethos in the shooting of *Wonderland* – the use of natural light, the small crew . . .
MC: Yeah, it was very liberating, after making films with the whole circus and all that goes with it. The actors just loved it because it felt so pure to them. It was really about the performances. We tried to keep as little as possible between the actors and Michael, and I think that comes through.

FM: That brings us to the idea of digital film-making and how that will affect film schools. Do you think that the wide availability of digital cameras and editing programmes on personal computers will stop people going to film schools?

MC: It's true that anyone can now pick up a camera and make a movie. But certainly, looking back on my three years, you wouldn't now have had the opportunity to see all the films that we saw. We had this thing whereby we could request two films a year, and the BFI would get that print. You could request the most obscure masterpiece from Russia at the turn of the century, and the National Film Archive would try and get it for you. Not only that, but you would also have a tutor 'debrief' the film, and we would all talk about it and discuss it. That was huge for us, having the visiting tutors. Istvan Szabo came over, Stephen Frears came in. It was absolutely priceless. But there are a lot of young guns out there now who are just not that film-literate, and it's sad. You can talk to them about film history, and a lot of them don't even know the 1960s movements like the Czech New Wave.

FM: When I was there, most of the discourse happened on the bus going into school, or in the canteen – mainly between the students, in other words. And you learned a lot from the people you were studying with. Was that the same for you? Or were you told, 'These are the films you should watch'?

MC: Not at all. We were just presented with a wealth of different types of film movements and film-makers. And you could respond to them or be influenced by them if you liked. It was clear that certain people were influenced by certain masterpieces, and would discuss those films and relate them to their workshops. But that was sparky, it was a very exciting thing – we were watching films and talking about them a lot at the same time as making them. That was huge, huge.

FM: Do you think that mentality still exists with you today?

MC: Absolutely. There is this tremendous feeling within the industry at the moment that we must make commercial films. It was Colin Young who said, 'Everybody is talking about making commercial films, and it's like we only just got this idea, when really this is something that we have all been trying to do. But we mustn't lose sight of the fact that we need to be making *good* films.' I think it is very important to know your place in the history of cinema. A lot of British young-gun directors may not know who Powell and Pressburger were, or who Lindsay Anderson was. I think that's a crime. You must know your craft – and not just technically. As a producer, I think it is really important.

FM: Looking back at the NFTS and seeing the students that are graduating these days, do you think that its ethos has changed any from when you were there?

MC: I think recent graduates have been influenced by film-makers like Tarantino. He's had a huge influence in the last five to seven years. And that's fine. But it would be nice to see films that are perhaps more surprising. I've noticed that there is a huge inclination to be commercial, to be slick. And I think that it might be nice just to go back to basics and tell a story visually, and focus on character. That's what film school should be about – you can get all the rest of it later.

FM: So what's your advice for graduating film students?
MC: Find a project that you are passionate about . . . a *story* that you are passionate about telling. Do whatever you need to do to tell it in your own personal way. And work with a good team.

Simon Moore

Simon Moore: Screenwriter

There is one myth above all that permeates film schools, and it concerns the student who went straight to Hollywood with the first script they wrote after graduation. Simon Moore is the NFTS's embodiment of that myth. On spec he wrote a Western called The Quick and the Dead, *which duly became a vehicle for Sharon Stone, directed by Sam Rami. It all sounds like the romantic notion of overnight success, but then Simon Moore's story confirms that there is no such thing. I met with him just after the Oscar nominations for 2000 had been announced and Stephen Gaghan's screenplay for* Traffic *was up in the 'Best Adapted' category – adapted, that is, from the Channel 4 TV series* Traffik, *which Simon wrote back in 1988. He has also written the TV series* Dinotopia *(2002) and* The 10th Kingdom *(2000) and directed* Up on the Roof *(1992) and* Under Suspicion *(1997).*

Fraser MacDonald: So when did you go to the NFTS?
Simon Moore: From 1979 to 1982. I had previously done a degree in Drama at Hull University, and I was very wary of just doing another three years of further education. At that time, the school had a very relaxed regime, so you could stay for as long as you were able to finance yourself and finish your films. I kind of made an agreement with myself that I would leave three years *to the day* from when I started; and that by the time I left, I would have some work outside to go to. So while I was there, in addition to making films, I really did try very hard to write scripts that I could send out, and try to sell.

FM: Did you apply to the school as a writer?
SM: I did. I really wanted to be a writer–director, but not exclusively. In truth, I wouldn't have got in as a director, because the two films I directed beforehand were crap, really. But the school was very much looking for writers, and I had written a lot of stuff – I was like Ernie Wise*, I would turn out a play every five minutes. The writing department there was quite a new thing, and they were

* One half of the famed British comedy duo, Morecambe and Wise. Every episode of their BBC series would include a sketch about Ernie's playwriting abilities, much derided by Eric Morecambe. Ernie could turn out a play in an afternoon, often pastiches of classic texts, and would cast the notable actors making guest appearances on the show. Needless to say, the plays weren't very good, but hey – that's comedy.

starting to realize that they had to address the fact that New Cinema wasn't just going to come from a group of directors getting round together and having an attitude. The key to it, which I think is still a big problem in this country, is moving writers away from the so-called 'literary' and 'theatrical' traditions, and thinking in a more visual way.

I had a fantastic teacher at the NFTS, John Bryce, who was very confrontational and radical. Before I got to him, I was very pleased with myself, because the school only took 20 students a year, so it was really tough to get in. They used to tell us, 'Next to fighter pilots, yours is the most expensive training in the country.' So I thought, 'I've got on to this really difficult course, and I'm a big star, and this is fucking great.' Then for the next nine months, John Bryce pretty much rejected everything that I wrote. He just put red lines through it and said, 'This is rubbish. It's theatrical, it's not visual, you're just writing dialogue.' So I tried to turn it round, and it was mainly my determination that saw me through, because I thought, 'I can't have come here only to discover that I can't write at all.' John did a couple of exercises with us that I thought were great. One of them was to write a naturalistic film with no dialogue, and in the process of doing that, it was kind of like a door opening for me. I thought, 'Oh, I see. It's not like writing a play with instructions, it's something else.'

FM: Of course, there is an opinion that you can't actually teach writing for the screen.
SM: I think there is a stage where everybody makes these pronouncements. It's true insofar that I could practise running from now until doomsday, but I'm never going to be a professional athlete, or even get in the top ten. So you have to make the assumption that you are dealing with people who have some talent to begin with. And I think that is a *huge* assumption – because writing for the screen is something that not a lot of people can do really well, or have the stamina to survive the world that they are going into. Nevertheless, if you are dealing with people who have the talent but not the experience then, of course, you can teach it. There are so many quick-fix courses, you know – 'Learn how to be a film director in 48 hours'. I have no problem with that, but it's a bit like jump-starting a car. It doesn't solve the problem while the car is broken down, it's just a sort of energy-boost. And I think that a lot of taught courses about writing are crap.

FM: Everybody gets Syd Field-itis*.
SM: Yeah. At the same time, I think that if you are serious about writing then you should try and embrace all that stuff. I've gone and done those courses, and

---

* Syd Field's books, *Screenplay* and *The Screenwriter's Workbook*, have established themselves as bibles for would-be screenwriters.

found them very interesting. But they don't tell you how to write a good script. They just remind you about things, and point you in the direction of certain classical structures. It's difficult to teach writing; and when it comes to film schools, you have to be careful about being taught by people who haven't been all that successful professionally.

FM: That's often the case with 'gurus' like Robert McKee or Dov S. S. Simmons.
SM: Exactly. You often want to stick up your hand and say, 'Hey, Robert, show us a list of your screen credits.' But on the other hand, that's a kind of prejudice. It doesn't follow that people who are very good screenwriters are very good teachers. One of the best things for me while I was at the NFTS was that Colin Young had the great idea of keeping the permanent staff as small as possible, and basically putting the power in the hands of the students. If more than six people wanted to organize a workshop on some topic, they could do so. There is no question for me that I learned the most from visiting professionals, rather than from the resident teachers there.

FM: While you were there, did you primarily write for other directors?
SM: No, I only really wrote for myself. It wasn't particularly through choice. When I first got to the school I did think that I would be writing for a lot of other directors, but actually I found that directors were pretty much concerned with making their own things.

FM: So how many scripts of yours were actually shot at the school?
SM: I wrote and directed two films when I was there, and I worked on a couple of other things for people.

FM: One criticism of film schools is that they pander to directors. Did you feel that was the case?
SM: My professional experiences as a writer, as much as I resist it, have cruelly reminded me that you only have power before you have handed over the rights to something. That's your only moment when you are in demand. After that, there is this ridiculous idea that films are only made by directors. History teaches us that there have been past periods of film-making when studios were in charge, or producers were in charge. Nowadays a lot of American TV writers are in charge of what they do. To me, it's such an absurd argument. I am very happy to get on the bandwagon that says, 'Film is a collaborative medium,' but that has to start with the serious dismantling of the vanity parades, 'A Film By', which are the bane of my life. I have had projects where you deliver a script to somebody and get a whole lot of notes where they are very open, and even visceral, about the script. And then I would get a phone call ten minutes later

where they would apologize for the notes, because they didn't realize I was directing the film too. (*Laughs.*) That really is so fucking insulting.

In Hollywood, the difference between when I walk in the door as the writer–director and when I walk in as solely the writer is a world apart. So there's a lot of work to do there, and I think that film schools should absolutely face up to the responsibility of that. If you don't set out with people taking an interest in scriptwriters creating things, and truly having a respect for their work, then you are not going to get anywhere. What I encounter a lot of the time is when somebody says, 'Oh, you've written this film script about the Nativity! I've *always* wanted to do a script about the Nativity.' Then you realize their enthusiasm is not for your script but for *a* script, so let's have a go and start writing it, shall we? The cult of the director has hurt writers massively, but it's hurt directors too. If you gave a director a choice between shooting one script every four or five years – which is what they do now – or going back to an earlier system where they make at least one film a year, but they aren't expected to be in charge of all the 'child-rearing' that goes with it . . . then I think a lot of them would chose the latter course. Because it would be more fun, and more interesting.

FM: You could almost blame film schools for creating that cult as well. In America the studio system was broken around the same time that the 'Movie Brats' were coming out of film schools in New York and Los Angeles.
SM: Of course, these things are never as simple as they seem. It's not just a case of, 'Isn't this bad?' A lot of good things happened. Steven Soderbergh operated the camera himself on his film version of *Traffik*, but he wasn't allowed to take an operator's credit. As cameras get increasingly lightweight, film schools are surely going to be about people walking round with cameras, and not the traditional breakdown of camera jobs. When I went to NFTS, getting an ACTT ticket was one of the main points of going there, because you couldn't work in the industry without one. And by the time I'd left, Thatcher had dismantled the unions to such an extent that the card wasn't worth anything anymore.

The technology cannot be ignored; it will probably be the key factor that will change film-making, much more so than any symposium or decisions by directors. The pressure to replace film with video is immense. And film has always been such an expensive medium, which has prohibited the freedom of entry. If you look at what has happened in music in the last ten years, the big recording studios are struggling because young artists don't need to book them. In the same way, a bit of me feels that I would love to see this change happen so that people could make films that went directly into the market place, that didn't cost a lot of money, and that didn't have a lot of people around them. And I think, in a way, that this change will ultimately resolve, or shift, the question of,

'What is a writer and what is a director?' Because writers will start to pick up cameras too.

FM: In his book about Richard Lester, Steven Soderbergh talks about the making of his own film *Schizopolis*, how he shot it, acted in it, did sound in some instances. In fact, most of the actors doubled as the crew. It seemed to be a revolt for him against the Hollywood studio system; almost a return to the film school/ low budget mentality. And it seemed to give him a new lease of life too, because he regained control, in a sense.

SM: Yes. Also, I think that what constitutes an acceptable image is changing now. People are more receptive to video images than they used to be. You have to understand, though, that this is an argument where lots of different things are happening. It's not about just having an attitude of, 'This is important, and things must change' – you're kind of missing the point if you do that. When I was a film student 20 years ago, film schools were rare and exotic things. You met someone from the Moscow Film School, UCLA, whatever, and this was a person who was doing a rare course. Now there are a lot more people who are routinely thinking, 'Oh, I'll just make films.' When I directed my first feature, there were 27 films made in Britain that year. It was easier to get into the England football team than it was to make a proper theatrical feature film. Now there are – what? 200, 250 British features a year? And most of them don't get released; 70 per cent don't even get into the cinemas.

FM: It comes back to an idea that digital equipment has made the tools of film-making available to everybody, but then the actual core of a film is story. And some people criticize film schools for not teaching the art of storytelling. Do you think that was the case with yourself?

SM: One thing I think about making films – rather than videos – is that if you are going to be a concert pianist, you can tell by the time you're seven years old whether or not you have any aptitude, because you've been playing since you were four or five. Whereas, going to film school, I realized that I went, and everybody else went, having done virtually nothing beforehand. It wasn't as if I'd been making films since I was ten years old. That just didn't happen. So there was this curious situation where you had a set of mature adults – and there were a lot of people in their thirties who had done things like stills photography previously – but they knew nothing about film. Therefore, I think it's natural that the thing that preoccupies you most at film school is this immense technical world: 'Oh fuck, I don't know how this works. And what's this film stock? And how do I process this?' The concentration on the technical is inevitable.

I'd also make the point that short films bear very little resemblance to feature films so, whether or not you can introduce epic storytelling or a three-act structure into a film that might last eight and a half minutes, I'm not so sure. I only started to learn about narrative and storytelling once I began to tackle ninety-minute scripts or six-hour mini-series. You can largely make short films about some sort of novelty item, and the short that pretends to be a feature film doesn't work anyway, so I think that may be the reason why you don't get a lot of storytelling at film schools. But it's all down to the teachers, really. I would love to see a proper writing of the history of film-making in the twentieth century that concentrates on writers and storytellers. It's interesting how the pool of commercial film-making is always being fed from a different source. For a while, in the 1980s, it was advert-makers and promo-makers. Now a lot of people are coming up from the video underground. Most of those people don't crack it because they have been working in short form, and they don't really know why it doesn't work when you make a two-hour film that looks like an advert. I think there is an understanding now that storytelling is the heart of any kind of drama.

FM: What was your first job after leaving film school?
SM: Well, I did a cinema short while I was still there, which was a sort of transition for me from being at the school to making something real. Then I got a six-part drama series for the BBC called *Inside Out* which was about two women who come out of prison and set up an employment agency for ex-cons. The great thing was that the series only happened because another series had folded, and I'd only written about one and a half episodes of this before it went into production. So all the things that people had told me about television, 'You've got to serve an apprenticeship writing episodes of soaps to learn your craft' – I didn't have to do any of that. The first thing I wrote was six hours of original television, plus they sort of had to film whatever I wrote. The bike really was waiting at the door, because they had all their facilities and all their resources set up, and they had to shoot *something*. That was fantastic for me.

And then the first thing I directed was a feature film. So I've always said to people, 'Don't believe that you have to do any of this stuff that is deemed to be "The Process".' I'm not suggesting that it is easy to do that. You have to cope with an enormous amount of rejection. But I never wanted to be a jobbing writer – I'm not saying that from some grand point of view, it just didn't interest me. I had a couple of opportunities early on to write episodes of things that were already on television, but my heart wasn't it, so I just didn't do it. As a result, I've always said to people, 'Don't write commissions, write original work. It's more risky, but if you get it right, you have more power, you also earn more money, so that you can keep yourself going longer.'

Traffik: Jack Lithgow (Bill Paterson) is offered opium by his Pathan guide (Tariq Rahmin).

FM: How did you come to write the original *Traffik* series for Channel Four?
SM: *Traffik* came about because a producer friend of mine, Brian Eastman, who I've worked with a lot, came up to me and said those wonderful words, 'What would you like to do a series on?' I'd always felt that drugs were treated stupidly on film. It's always about drugs busts and getting the smack off the streets, *et cetera*. I had a couple of ideas, one being that I wanted to start a series with the big drugs bust. The other was to be completely non-judgemental, so that you became increasingly lost as to who was to blame, and therefore one could look at the drug trade in a different way. Again, that was a fantastic thing for me to do, the first drama series that Channel Four had completely financed themselves. And it was quite a big risk because I was going in saying to them that it was going to have subtitles and 200 characters – you know, 'It's not going to be conventional.' That sort of set the tone for me: it was exactly the kind of project I wanted to be doing.

The Quick and the Dead: Sharon Stone as Ellen.

FM: It was also one of the first British drama series to have multi-layered stories going through it.

SM: I don't know if I could claim that or not, but the inspiration there really came from cinema. I was thinking of *Prince of the City* and *Serpico*. They were looking at police corruption, but they were looking at it through 200 characters, and that just changes everything. I write a lot of fantasy, so it was fun for me to do something that was all based on reality. Pretty much everything that happened in *Traffik* was based on newspaper articles and research that I did. I knew I wanted to have quite a melodramatic thriller at the heart of it, that was my promise to Channel Four. 'If you let me do this difficult thing, I promise you that the subtitles won't last more than a minute in the whole series, and it will be fast-paced and it will have a clear story so you can follow it.' I love those combinations. That is exactly what I am interested in delivering – something that is accessible, but also a bit darker. Unresolved, and reflective of a complex situation.

FM: What about *The Quick and the Dead*? How did that happen?
SM: It was a spec script that I wrote. Back then, every time I went to America I was being advised by people, 'You cannot expect to sit in London and think that you can write a studio script and expect them to make it!' So when it happened,

I was like, 'Yes I fucking can!' (*Laughs.*) You've got to remind yourself that these things happen about once in a millennium. But that was very exciting, because I was writing spec scripts back to back at the time. And if you write too many of those and don't sell them, you get poor and you start to undermine yourself.

FM: By selling that script to Hollywood, you were really bucking the trend of how it tends to go for graduates of British and European film schools.
SM: Well, the problem for me wasn't just that there weren't that many British films being made, but that the ones that *were* being made were not appealing to me at all. The one genre that I have never gone near is the period piece, the heritage drama. It wasn't a question of me being ambitious to go to Hollywood to make Hollywood films, so much as just feeling that if you wanted to make a lot of different films in this country, people just looked at you blankly. I had always loved westerns, particularly the spaghetti Westerns – I love the world that they inhabit. In fact I wrote *The Quick and the Dead* intending that I would direct it myself as a low-budget film in Italy or Spain . . .

FM: Since there are so many film schools now, do you think it's harder to graduate from film school straight into the industry?
SM: I think it's less special. After I graduated, when I was directing my first feature film, you'd sit in the pub at lunchtime with the British crew and there was a lot of, 'Oh you guys just come out of film school and you expect to do it all when you're young.' So there was a lot more friction then. But at the same time it was still more unusual to be a film school graduate. Whereas now, you think, 'Oh yeah, there's hundreds of people graduating every year.' So it has changed – in a way, it's both easier and harder to make a film. There are far more films being made now, but as a result far fewer of them are being distributed. So instead of it being very hard to get to a point where you have a film that will get some sort of promotion, it's much easier to make the film. But you realize that people are now making a whole load of films for $1.5– 2 million dollars on the basis of, 'Let's just wait and eventually we will get a *Full Monty.*' Meanwhile, the distributors are deciding whether films have an audience or not.

It's my belief that the percentage of people who are very talented all-round filmmakers doesn't vary that much. There are certain circumstances that you could create whereby you give them a better chance of success and a better chance for self-expression. But I don't believe that if we had the best film schools in the world then we would suddenly discover 100,000 amazing writers. The trouble is that if you multiply the number of film schools, you would think that there'd be a wholesale increase in the talent pool. But there may not be. In which case you're just letting more people into the group. You only have to look at auditions – you maybe see a hundred actors for one small part, and if they were electricians half of them couldn't wire a plug. All you are seeing are people who want to act – you're not seeing people who have the skills to be actors. And there is a danger that if you give a video camera to everybody, then everybody can make a film. Whereas in the past, the attitude was more like, *'Don't touch the lens!'*

FM: But then Coppola did once express the hope that some kid in Indiana would make a masterpiece on their father's camcorder . . . With hindsight, would you still have gone to film school?
SM: I think it was absolutely necessary for me. If you asked me, 'How long do you think it takes someone to be a good and competent writer?' I would say, 'At least ten years.' So the opportunity to have three years of those in a sheltered environment, with exposure to lots of films and lots of ideas, was just fantastic for me. I suppose the only thing I'm nostalgic about was the incredibly open environment. After the first two terms, we were told that if we were going to succeed in the film business it would be by our own enterprise. Therefore, nothing else was compulsory: we could do what we wanted, we could leave when we wanted, and the object was to go to various departments and convince them to make a film with you. And you were given access to £10,000, which in those days was more like £100,000. Over the course of three years I got to make one 30-minute film and one 45-minute film. You're not going to hear me complain about that.

FM: And you got the chance to make mistakes as well.
SM: Yes, and that's very important. As I said, it's not like you've been doing it since you were seven years old. I always say to young writers, 'Be prepared to write a million words of crap, because if you do it all the time and you keep learning from it, then at some point you get into a different sort of groove.' It's about being relaxed but also concentrated – that's what I yearn to be. It has to do with an application of experience, and when you start out it's just inevitable that you will be trying too hard to do something. That's a very difficult thing to try and dissect in a script course. What you really want to say about a student's script is, 'Fine. Put it away, write another one, and then put that away. And somewhere down the line you will settle into that groove.'

   No, I'm a big fan of the film school, it really did provide me with a great opportunity. And I'm a big fan of Colin Young really, I thought he was the most amazing teacher I had ever met – because he never seemed to be doing any teaching. He just swanned around Europe on these freebies. He was never fucking *there*, which I thought was a brilliant way of running a film school. (*Laughs.*)

FM: Do you think that film schools are still relevant in this day and age?

SM: Yes, absolutely. But we have to accept that things are changing now. It's always worth looking at another medium for comparison, and I think it's very interesting what is happening to music. You can buy programmes that enable you to record very sophisticated sounds for next to no money, and then post them on the Internet, so that these minority things can enjoy a worldwide access. I see exactly the same thing happening with film, through desktop editing programmes and the like. That is going to be a challenge to film schools. But just giving people a studio doesn't make them into film-makers. If I were teaching now, I would challenge those students who imagine that drama automatically starts just by turning the video camera on. One of the great things about film, however frustrating, is that it is expensive. You don't just turn the camera on and see what happens over the course of a day, then try to make a drama out of it. With film, every time you turn over, you watch the money going through the gate – so you have to be sure of what you are doing. I love that, and I think it's a good discipline to learn.

Kim Longinotto

Kim Longinotto: Documentarian

Kim Longinotto studied Camera and Directing at the NFS, where she made Pride of Place, *a critical look at her boarding school, and* Theatre Girls, *about a hostel for homeless women in Soho. In 1986, she formed the production company Twentieth Century Vixen with Claire Hunt. Together they made* Fireraiser, *about Sir Arthur 'Bomber' Harris;* Eat the Kimono, *about the Japanese feminist performer Hanayagi Genshu;* Hidden Faces, *about Egyptian women; and* The Good Wife of Tokyo, *about love and marriage in Japanese society. With Jano Williams, Longinotto directed* Dream Girls, *about Japan's spectacular musical theatre company, The Takarazuka Revue; and* Shinjuku Boys, *about three Tokyo women living as men. Her most recent films are* Gaea Girls, *about female wrestlers, and* Divorce, Iranian Style *and* Runaway, *both of these made in Iran and co-directed with Ziba Mir-Hosseini.*

I first came across Kim's work when she did a talk at the film school. She seemed to exemplify the ethos of the documentary department at the NFTS: a prominence of good storytelling and strong characters.

Fraser MacDonald: How long was the school's documentary course when you studied?
Kim Longinotto: It was three years, though a lot of people stayed for longer. I went in 1976, when Colin Young was in charge. Before that I had done a basic one-year audio-visual course in Bristol. You know the type – you do a bit of everything there, and you can work out what it is you most want to do. Before that, I went to university. And before that, I was homeless.

FM: So you didn't wake up one morning aged four and decide you wanted to be a film-maker?
KL: No, I went to university wanting to be a writer. While I was there I used to do storytelling for Lambeth Council. I'd go round the public parks with a microphone and tell local stories to kids, and tell them what libraries to go to. They all loved hearing the stories, but nobody went to the library! At that time too I was thinking about doing a Ph.D. on 'The Modern Novel' – I had got a grant. But I just thought, 'Either I want to write a novel or do something else entirely.' And I didn't think I could do writing. I didn't like doing stuff on my own, I wanted to work with other people. I was friends with Nick Broomfield,

and he said, 'Why don't you go to the National Film School?'

FM: Did you decide it was documentary that you wanted to do when you went?
KL: Yeah, though there wasn't even a documentary department at the time. But I went there knowing what film I wanted to make. And what was nice about the school was that you could work out your film by yourself. There was a lot of freedom. I remember one time I was worried about how to light one of the studios there. My tutor Ernie Vinze just came down and showed me how. So you could get support whenever you wanted it, but nobody told you what to do. You could spend as long in the edit as you wanted. So I think if you went to school knowing what you wanted to do, then it was wonderful, like being in heaven. (*Laughs.*)

FM: And that film you wanted to make was *Pride of Place*?
KL: Yes. It was about my boarding school, and it was a revenge film, really. Plus the boarding school was very near the Film School. I made it with a woman called Dorothea Gazidis – I shot it and produced it. Dorothea edited the film and she was quite bossy, but I learned from watching her do it. And I knew then that I wanted to edit my second one, which was *Theatre Girls*.

FM: So you only made two films over the three years there?
KL: Yeah. Does that seem strange?

FM: No, but the course is quite structured now, so you tend to make more films, though they're often seen primarily as exercises. What interests me about the documentary course is that you get this overall grounding in skills like camera and editing. Whereas I studied Fiction Direction, and I didn't really move out of that single discipline.
KL: I think it's going to change. I remember when I was teaching back at the NFTS a couple of years ago, and one of my students wanted to use a musician from another year, but Henning Camre* said that they couldn't work together. I was upset on behalf of the student, because it seemed an unnecessary rigidity. Film-making is about finding people you can work with and making really nice teams, so that you keep on working with them. That's half the battle. But Henning wouldn't let this student of mine do that, just because of some ridiculous rule . . . (*Fraser's mobile phone rings.*)

FM: Sorry . . . (*Switches the phone off.*)
KL: Who was it?

---

* Ran the NFTS 1993–98, now Head of the Danish Film Institute.

FM: The editor of my graduation film.

KL (*Laughs*): That's ironic.

FM: I'm probably in trouble. Sorry, you were saying?

KL: No, it's not so much about finding people there whom you'll go on to work with. It's more generally about learning *how* to work with people, to trust and respect them. Colin Young wasn't really into structure, and I think that was important. When I first started, I could get a camera out of stores and spend a week learning how to use it, how to pan and focus and so on. There was space to do that, and it gave me time to work out what I wanted to do and how I wanted to do it. But some people found a lack of structure difficult, because they didn't know that we could just go and ask for things, like when Ernie helped me rig the lights. Whereas I suppose that because my own life had been so unstructured, it just fitted. Recently I took part in the induction workshops for the new students, and what we were looking for were people who were quite sure in themselves, not needing to ask what to do every five minutes. You know what I mean by that?

FM: People who had come with something to say, rather than just going to school to be there?

KL: Exactly. I think film-makers are people who want to find something out. It's about being curious all the time. In Colin's time there was a structure in a way, because there was a very strong ethos about 'observational'* work. You let the material speak for itself and you didn't impose a heavy hand on it. You just had to be self-sufficient and have a passion to say something.

FM: Colin Young was very pro-storytelling, wasn't he?

KL: That's what I absolutely loved. What I had to find out was how I could tell stories, and you can't do that with a rigid course. Nobody can teach you how to tell stories. You can only do it through experience, using your imagination and taking risks, learning how to find a story, and how to let that story reveal itself to you.

FM: That's still the film school mentality: 'Don't impose your own ideas on the film, let the film work that out for you.'

KL: The nice thing about film school is that you can do that because you don't have the pressure. Whereas if you're working on a commission, it can be quite scary. The last film I made was a five-week shoot in Iran, and in that situation you have to be pretty sure about what you want to do.

---

* As Dean of Arts at UCLA in the mid-1960s, Young played a key role in setting up a 'Film and Anthropology' program, so signalling his career-long interest in an ethnographic or 'observational' style of documentary.

FM: A lot of former NFTS students go back and teach there. Have you noticed many differences in the school since you were there?

KL: I've liked teaching there. I especially like taking classes alongside somebody else, showing the students how you work as a team – because it's not just me. What I find when I work in a team is that the film is very much a reflection of the team. For example, if your sound recordist isn't very good, you just don't get the same film. I haven't been back to the school since Stephen Bayly took over, but when Henning was there I was disappointed by the rigidity. What is really good about the school is that you have two or three years to meet people, explore, take risks, make mistakes. But I went to a meeting there recently and there were a lot of people saying, 'What is the point of a film school? Why don't people just join the industry and make it that way?' Well, for me the point is to use your imagination and break rules. That's what the school did for me. I took a lot of risks and I wouldn't have dared do that if I was working in the industry. I mean, I wouldn't even have got the opportunity – some idiot who hadn't really done much, looking for money to make a film about their boarding school, or homeless women. Nobody would have been interested in doing that, not then. You wouldn't get the chance to sleep in a hostel for three months, as we did before we made *Theatre Girls*.

FM: Looking back on it, is there anything you would have changed about your education?

KL: I think I wish I could have met more people who I could have worked with! There weren't very many people in my year who I hit it off with. All the people I really liked were doing other things. Maggie Brooks, who I really liked, was a fiction person. Dorothea, who was in my year, was a bit controlling. On *Theatre Girls* I worked with someone from outside the school, and it was a bit difficult. I wish I hadn't done that, actually. It would have been much better if it had been another student.

FM: Did you feel you had to find someone with the same mentality as yourself?

KL: Usually students find their teams and go off together and get on well, and that's nice. It was only because of the type of film I wanted to make that I couldn't do it like that. I wanted to make a film about homeless people, but it wasn't the kind of thing anybody in my year wanted to do. It was such a long project that people felt they couldn't commit that amount of time. I knew it had to be a woman and I knew they had to be prepared to sleep in this hostel for three months. For me, having been homeless myself for quite a while, the film school was like luxury, because you got a grant and so on. But the hostel was a tough place, it was dirty, it was violent. That's why I had to choose someone from the outside. And I couldn't pay them.

FM: Were you fully supported by the school for *Theatre Girls*?

KL: They just let me do it. Brian Winston* was really supportive. The film was shot observationally, so there was a lot of material, 70 to 80 rolls of film, and Brian helped me to sort it all out and edit it. He was always there when I needed him.

FM: Did you do much film study and theory on the course?

KL: Yeah, we watched a load of films and thought about how they were put together, and why they worked or didn't. That was another nice thing – everybody wanted to talk about films, after screenings and in the canteen.

FM: We had a bus that took the students into school, and that's where most of the arguing happened. That's where I learned a lot about cinema, through my fellow students.

KL: Yeah, we had the bus too. Except at 8.30 in the morning you don't really want to go into semiotics or something. (*Laughs.*)

FM: Yet now the NFTS is becoming an MA course, so that some of your work has to be written, or a dissertation.

KL: Oh I would have hated to have done that. For me, the whole point of making films was to get away from academia. What is really good about the film school is that people can come from all different areas, without having been to university or knowing much about writing essays.

FM: The practical approach is more agit-prop. You can tell your essay through a camera.

KL: Yeah, and that's why you should be going there.

FM: It is positively encouraged that you have some life-experience before you apply to the NFTS, and it seems that the students who get the most out of it are people who come from a background other than film.

KL: I think having had a bit of a struggle in life can be useful. Not that I want anyone to suffer. But sometimes if you've had a hard time, it makes you a better film-maker, because usually you're *filming* people who've had a hard time. The people I'm interested in are people on the edge of society. They haven't had it too easy. Sometimes it helps if you can empathize with them.

FM: What do you think was the most important thing you learned at film school?

* Renowned film scholar, author, documentary-maker and teacher. (See Jay Rabinowitz interview, pp. 177–8.) Currently Head of the School of Communication, Design and Media at the University of Westminster.

KL: Confidence. I was really unconfident before I went. But I did *Theatre Girls* with a woman who was working as a secretary, and she was fed up. Together we got the confidence that we could do a whole film – she could do sound and I could do camera. When I left film school, everybody said, 'You've got to go and work for television.' I knew I couldn't do that. I didn't want to make structured films with lots of voiceover. I didn't want to work with a big crew; I knew I wasn't the kind of person who could tell people what to do, like, 'Walk left to right across the screen.' I didn't want to be a director, I wanted to be a *film-maker*. Do you see what I mean? And at the school they told me how to achieve that.

FM: Do you think *Theatre Girls* gave you a 'calling card' after you'd left?
KL: Not really. It's a strange film. (*Laughs.*) But it gave me a kind of knowledge about how I wanted to work and what I wanted to do, to get me through all the years when I didn't have work. It was hard after I left, and I think that's something the school is more aware of now – following up with people who've graduated. I didn't think that I could go back there and ask for help, which I think people wouldn't be so bitter about doing now.

FM: Thanks to the Graduate Network*.
KL: Yeah, and the 'foster parent' scheme they run. That's brilliant, I didn't have that.

FM: So what exactly did you do once you graduated?
KL: It was difficult. I did camerawork for people, then I went to a Channel Four workshop when they were just setting up the Independent Film and Video department†. And that was the right situation for me. I worked recently for Anglia†† and I just did it as if I was at film school. I worked with two women, one on sound, the other asking the questions, and I did camera. It's getting more like that now with DV cameras anyway, which I think are great, because you can get that informality and that smallness.

FM: At the same time, it's also stopping people from more advanced technical learning.
KL: Yeah, there are two sides to it. The good side of it is that ordinary people can make films as well, without all the paraphernalia, in the culture that I come

---

* The NFTS alumni, a graduate support network involving regular meetings and newsletters.
† Channel Four began transmitting in 1982. The Independent Film and Video department's remit was for more experimental, cutting-edge work. Directors such as Chris Newbury and Derek Jarman were funded in this way. The department ceased to be in 1999, and its remit was inherited by FilmLab.
†† Regional television channel in England.

from: no big crews, nobody shouting action, no fuss, nobody bossing anybody around – almost looking like you're not filming. I worked on camera for a lot of people and I am really shocked when you are trying to get a sensitive scene and someone bellows 'Action' . . .

FM: What? During a documentary shoot?
KL: Oh yeah, it happens all the time, and you think, 'What the hell?' You say to them, 'Just tell me what you want me to do. You don't need to yell "Action".'

FM: The NFTS emphasis is on story – it doesn't matter so much what it looks like, just get the story told, and tell it well. Sometimes from other schools and on television you see documentaries that are more flashy and slick, though they don't necessarily add up to much.
KL: I would do anything to get the story. But it's on the big screen so I want to do it on film, and I do care how it looks. I support DV, but people say of it that you can get more intimacy with a DV camera than you can with an Aaton. I don't agree. It's about you, it's not about the size of the camera. After five minutes, if your subject gets on with you, the fact the camera is bigger doesn't make any difference. And if you have a good lens and you know what you are doing with it, the film will look nicer.

FM: I think people confuse intimacy with the fact that you can stick the camera in a smaller place or get in to somebody's nostril if you wish. Agnes Varda shot her film *Les Glaneurs et la Glaneuse* on DV, and she said the most interesting thing was that she could turn the camera on herself and still operate it. But apart from that, she felt it was just another tool.
KL: I suppose so. I don't feel excited by equipment. Sometimes I speak to people who do camera and they ask what lens I use. And I can't remember the number of it.

FM: Do you think there is still a place for film schools?
KL: They are absolutely essential. If people only learn how to make films by going into the industry – or what they call 'the industry', meaning television – what often happens is that people make what they think people want them to make, particularly if they're young and trying to work your way up. So you get a TV commissioning editor saying, 'Can you do this?' Whereas Film School allows you to do something that is completely different and experimental. Otherwise, we would just be churning out the same films over and over again.

FM: I remember a woman who applied to the Television course at NFTS a couple of years ago. She wanted to make documentaries, and she complained that

she wasn't getting taught that. She was asked why she hadn't just applied to the Documentary course, and she said it was because all the documentaries she had seen were on television. That's kind of telling about the way documentaries are seen. But film schools teach cinema, and that includes, I think, the documentary form.

KL: Absolutely. I totally believe that documentaries should be on the big screen, because I love the thing of it being a shared experience – particularly if the film is something quite strong.

FM: Your son is at the school now, doing Documentary, isn't he?

KL: Yeah. Strange, isn't it? He's not there because of me. He did all sorts of other stuff before applying, an engineering course and so on.

FM: If you were 20 years younger, would you still go to film school?

KL: Oh definitely. It was the best thing that happened to me. It changed my life. I was ready for them and they were right for me. I don't know *what* would have happened to me if I hadn't have gone to film school.

Jane Morton and Alwin Kuchler

Alwin Kuchler: Cinematographer
Jane Morton: Production Designer
Lynne Ramsay: Writer–Director
Lucia Zucchetti: Editor

Writer–director Lynne Ramsay established herself on the international stage in 1999 when her debut feature Ratcatcher *premiered in official selection at Cannes. Though Lynne has been widely acclaimed for her individual gifts, she has always stressed that she works closely with a regular team of collaborators: cinematographer Alwin Kuchler, production designer Jane Morton and editor Lucia Zucchetti. They all met at NFTS in the mid-1990s, Lynne having previously studied Photography at Napier University; and together they were responsible for some of the most innovative short films to come out of the UK in years.* Small Deaths *(1995) earned the Jury Prize at Cannes in 1996.* Kill the Day *followed that same year, and their third collaboration* Gasman *won the Premier Prix du Jury at Cannes in 1998. Alwin, Lucia and Jane have also worked separately on various other projects including* The Claim *(dir. Michael Winterbottom, 2000),* The Low Down *(dir. Jamie Thraves, 2000) and* Come Together *(dir. Graham Theakston, 2001). I interviewed the quartet in pairs, just as they were finishing principal photography on their second feature together, an adaptation of Alan Warner's novel* Morvern Callar.

JANE MORTON AND ALWIN KUCHLER

Fraser MacDonald: So why did you decide to go to film school?
Jane Morton: I had been studying Sculpture and Fine Art, but I was also doing outdoor pyrotechnics for theatre productions, which meant performing with fireworks. And I think there were two things that made me quit. For one, I got fed up with the lack of script. It was like 'There's the beast. Now let's kill it', whereas I wanted to work on something that had more content. And I also thought that I might get blown up.
Alwin Kulcher: Were you really worried?
JM: Oh yeah, I was nearly blown up a couple of times. A friend of mine died pretty recently because he was dealing in pyrotechnics. And they won't insure you for it – not that it makes any difference if you do get blown up. So, in the end, I thought that perhaps I should be doing something a bit less dangerous.
AK: And then you find out that it isn't . . .

FM: How about you Alwin? Why film school?

AK: I was doing stills photography before, but I felt I had to move on because I didn't much like the world I was in. I found fashion photography to be the most crazy fun, but I just couldn't stand the people – all that kissing and eating good food. Advertising was kind of anal, you know – once I saw a client placing breadcrumbs in a certain way inside a breadbasket. Then a friend of mine who was studying at the Munich Film School asked me if I wanted to shoot an exercise for him. I did it, and I thought, 'That's terrible, so many set-ups in a day!' But when he showed me the cut I thought it was really powerful, and I was intrigued by the mechanism of how it was done. That's when I started to take an interest in film. I heard about the NFTS, and there was no equivalent training in Germany to become a cinematographer. So I came to London and looked around for a job as a photographer's assistant, and at the same time I applied to NFTS. I knew the traditional route to being a camera-man, from clapper loader to assistant and so on, but I couldn't see myself doing that, maybe because I had already done an apprenticeship and worked for a year as a freelance assistant.

FM: Jane, did you consider trying to go straight into the industry?

JM: I never even thought about it. I think that was because I was coming from a fine art background. And, in fact, I was sort of drifting towards theatre design at that point.

AK: You didn't want to work as an assistant?

JM: No, because I couldn't draft then, so I needed a full training. And when you go to the film school as a production designer, you really are being trained to enter the industry in that area.

FM: Was the NFTS everything you thought it was going to be?

JM: I think my first thought was, 'Finally I'm going to get a sensible job!' (*Laughs.*) I had been a fine artist for years, and now I was retraining, and a job would be created, slightly different in terms of content but offering almost a regular income. I thought I might change a lot by being at the school, but I don't think I did. I was always into low-key design. I didn't want to do period drama or the like. I was much more interested in film-makers like Scorsese and films like *Raging Bull* that designers wouldn't be obviously attracted to. When I was interviewed, I didn't name all the films that designers are supposed to like – Peter Greenaway, or sci-fi. I always remember *Rumblefish* – the clock clicking on the wall, and Tom Waits saying, 'You've got 35 summers.' Things like that stuck in my mind, rather than the idea of building a Victorian house or whatever.

FM: How was it for you, Alwin?
AK: I enjoyed the experimentation. I mean, if you don't know that much technically, then you don't know how you can fuck up. That's especially true for cinematographers. Traditionally cinematographers are really conservative – they're just meant to get the rushes right and so on. But I think film schools have made a big change, because there you're allowed to really fuck up, and to learn from that; or to fuck up accidentally, and maybe find that it worked really well.
JM: I was surprised by the range of people I met there. At a fine art school, everybody is fine art-oriented. But when you get to film school, you are all under the same umbrella even though your tastes in film can be so widely different.
AK: That's really important. You know when you were at school, and maybe there were 35 people in your class, and you were the one who was really good at drawing or photography, so your work stood out? Well then, suddenly you come to film school. And for the first time in my life I felt, 'The people here are so bloody talented, and they're all at the same stage as me.' It was really inspiring, the first time I felt that I had to do my absolute best to be able to compete. In my year we had one student from Mongolia, one from Turkey, and a documentary student from Japan, so the cross-cultural aspect was really good. I thought the Mongolian student was an outstanding talent, but she had real language difficulties. There were some people who were genuinely interested in what she would do and so wanted to work with her, but there were others who thought, 'Well there's no point, because she's not going to have a career here.' So you did meet a lot of people who were thinking about what happens after film school.
JM: You became very quickly aware that there were different types of people there, with different agendas. Some people had already worked in the industry, certain producers wanted to do very commercial film-making. By the second day I was talking to Lynne, because neither of us had ever been on a film set. We both came from a fine art background, so it was almost like arriving in the wrong place. We were both freaked out for the first few weeks thinking, 'Do we belong?' And I remember Lynne just clocked me immediately, she homed in and asked me, 'Do you feel uncomfortable here?' It was quite scary at first, to suddenly be around these people, knowing that you were going to be working creatively together, and thinking, 'How am I going to relate to them?'

FM: The producers are always looking for the best director ...
JM: Yeah. Maybe they're looking to make the next *Notting Hill*, or the next *Jurassic Park*, or the next *Nil by Mouth*. And even as a mature student, you're still trying to find your own feet. I knew where I was coming from, but I also knew I still had a hell of a lot to learn. But then what's great about film is that I've learned so much since, even about fine art, photography, just because working in film makes you do so much research.

FM: It's true, Alwin, that variety can be seen as a good thing, but it can also breed competition, especially amongst directors. And that can be quite detrimental to the films.

AK: I think that probably affected this Mongolian student. If she had found a producer who helped her more in terms of overcoming her language problems, then she might have got more out of it. But then maybe she wanted to go back to Mongolia anyway.

JM: There is that paranoia and we definitely felt it. Say you have 25 people, five in each discipline, five designers, five directors. It's a strange situation when you know you have to team up. 'Which director am I likely to end up with?' It creates pressure, because everybody wants to work with that director or that designer. Then you think, 'God, what if I make a mistake?' I know there's room to experiment financially, but initially I did sometimes feel like, 'If I make a mistake nobody will work with me!'

AK: I didn't feel the competition was a hindrance, it was something I genuinely enjoyed. But there were certain students, directing students, who would try to create competition to get more out of people.

JM: You were always off in your own creative tract, which I understand after the fact. You had already graduated when we met. But I was paranoid because I felt that if you weren't 'the best', you wouldn't get to work with who you wanted to. It sounds horrible. But if there are only 25 people and you know the kind of films you want to work on, you need to suss out who is going to write those scripts, *et cetera*. It's quite unnerving at first. But after a while you do tend to find your own level. There was a small pool of people I connected to creatively, and that was when I started to branch out.

AK: True. Once you find one or two directors you really click with, you create an atmosphere where it's more important to try something together than to be afraid of fucking up technically. If everybody around me had given me the impression that I was making technical mistakes all the time, that would have had a terrible effect on me.

FM: You shot a feature [*Welcome II the Terrordome,* 1995] while you were at the school, didn't you?
AK: Yeah, well . . . (*Raises an eyebrow, laughs.*)
JM: Unofficially!

FM: Is it true you shot the film during the school's set exercises?
JM (*laughs*): I think Ngozi* should be here to defend this.
AK: Well, there's nothing to defend. She had already worked in television and

---

* Ngozi Onwurah, Alwin's wife, director of *Welcome II the Terrordome.*

she could have carried on working in the industry, but instead she went to the NFTS. And she definitely came in with an agenda of 'I'm here to push myself, to experiment'. So the first exercise we ever did, she wrote it with the thought of extending it. And when we did the second exercise it just happened to be an extended version of the first exercise, and then came the third exercise, and so on. The funny thing is that *Welcome II the Terrordome* was shot over three and a half years, with kids who were always growing, whereas the action was meant to happen over one night . . .

FM: So was that production frowned upon by the school?
AK: I think Colin Young had certain people he really liked, and Ngozi was somebody who could really argue strongly for something. She never had problems with Colin. That's why people really came on under him, though it may be that some other people suffered.

FM: Jane, how long would you say it took you to feel comfortable about what you were doing at the school?
JM: By the end of my first year I had art-directed a graduation film, a big studio build. I really found my feet doing that build, and from then on I basically kept doing graduation films, because there was such a backlog of them. The school was trying to stop that happening, because you were supposed to stay within your own year. But they also knew they had to clear the backlog. And from the second year onwards I just worked on one film after the other.

FM: Which is the point of going to film school, surely? You learn by making films.
JM: Yeah, and I definitely had that, but by default. It wasn't where the school wanted things to go, and I did have to argue on a couple of occasions when they decided that I should be doing a workshop instead of a film. It's a difficult argument, because you do need to learn to do specific things, like lens projections or architectural drawing. But we had done a hell of a lot of that in our first year. And even when I was working on graduation films, I made a point of still going to workshops, even if they were for the year below me, so that I would get a bit better at doing certain things and that would feed into a production. It was a difficult way for the school to work, but I felt like I had got the best of both worlds, coming from a hands-on sculpture background, responding to real situations rather than theoretical ones. Going from film to film you are in real situations, talking to directors who say, 'Yeah, but I thought we were going to shoot in this style, so I need a big space, otherwise I'm going to use wide lenses.' Even now I can't design a set without those discussions going on, pushing me further.
AK: These are the things you can't be taught. When I left the NFTS and did my

first short film, the only thing I thought that counted was that I should make it look as good as I possibly could. I didn't have any concerns about how much it would cost or how long it would take. And for a year and a half after that, I suffered the reputation of being really expensive and really slow. Now I only suffer from the latter. (*Laughs.*) But that's something I never completely learned at film school – how people prepare for when they get out, the psychology, the etiquette of it. What kind of jobs are you going to be offered, and why are you being offered them? What should be your priorities? Those are things you learn the hard way once you leave.

JM: Knowing that things are going to cost a little bit more because of a schedule change. Knowing that you have to go back to the line producer immediately, rather than thinking, 'I'd better just sort it.' You don't learn that at school.

FM: You know that the NFTS promotes Lynne, Lucia and the two of you as a team that was created at the school?

JM: It's nothing to do with what the school said. That connection was already there, one way or another. You just kind of know when that happens with people – you get excited about similar things, similar films, a particular artist's work.

AK: We clicked, we enjoyed working together. I remember doing the first film with Lynne, *Small Deaths*. We just did whatever we thought felt good. Especially Lynne, that's what I thought was really great about her, she didn't care about failure. She just did what she felt was interesting or right. How she was going to put it together was a secondary thing. The first time we sent off the rushes, we got these reports from the tutors saying that they were never ever going to cut. (*Laughs.*)

JM: We were all sat in a bus in the absolute peeing rain when that phone call came through, thinking, 'Oh my God!'

FM: Do you think that sense of overcoming adversity is why you stuck together?

AK: It's a bit like *Living in Oblivion*. So many directors come out of school and get the chance to shoot a commercial or something, then they come back to you and say, 'I really have no influence on who is going to shoot this or who is going to cut it.' You never knew how much truth there was in that, or whether they actually wanted to try working with someone more experienced. So you have to have respect for Lynne, because with her it was always non-negotiable, whatever she did.

JM: That's true. There was always pressure on her to use more 'experienced' people.

AK: A lot of pressure on *Gasman*.

JM: And *Ratcatcher* too. It's that whole thing about getting the film bonded. The companies that insure films do look at CVs to decide whether this person will be able to carry it. I was quite amazed. But you have to have done it before they let you do it, you have to have made X amount of shorts, then a half-hour drama, so that you've built up your CV and the budgets you've worked with.

FM: They always seem to give first-time directors an experienced cinematographer.
AK: It doesn't make sense. It's like saying to a director, 'We want something really new and fresh', then pairing them with a cinematographer who sits down and says, 'Well, we can't do that. Not in my experience . . .'
JM: 'And I've been doing this for 30 years. You can't give it that colour.'

FM: Both of you have worked with film-makers who didn't go to film school. Within the industry, do you think there's a resentment of film students among people who learned their craft inside the industry and worked their way up?
JM: It's down to the individual. You will get that 'industry standard' thing off some people, if you try to experiment with the film stock or something.
AK: I definitely encountered some resentment, but it was partly deserved. You graduate film school, you do your first short film, and you go on a film set really believing that people are there for the love of film-making. Then you learn that some people are there just to make a living, and they want to go home at a decent hour. When I was at NFTS and met Ngozi and started to go out with her, it was like three years of 18-hour days talking about films. You're so passionate about what you're doing that you lose any boundaries. But there's a point where you just have to switch off.
JM: You're still quite an obsessive, though. I've never known you to 'job it'.
AK: There are times you just run into a wall because you want to do things differently, and then you learn painfully why certain conventions are in place, so you take them on board. It must be quite painful for a gaffer who has worked with 20 different DoPs, then I come in saying, 'I want to do it like this.' Fifty per cent of the time he might be right, and 50 per cent of the time you really care about pushing through a new idea. But every time you work with very challenging people it is tiring, because they always push it to the absolute limits. Lynne is one, Michael Winterbottom is another.
JM: And you are another.

FM: What was it like for you both after you graduated?
AK: The first two years I found very depressing. I was shocked by how long it takes you to get a job. You start with such high hopes: I thought I was going to get pop promos and stuff, only to find out that I was really crap at selling

Ratcatcher: William Eadie as James.

myself. Then over the course of a year, you suddenly think, 'God I'd better do something!' You start doing corporate films or whatever, thinking at the time that it's beneath you. And when you look at directors, it's even harder isn't it? Four or five years, trying to develop projects . . .

JM: I didn't work for ages. In all honesty, when I first graduated I wasn't sure what I wanted to do. I was quite scared of the industry, and I was also interested in writing, so I kind of backed away for a bit. I was doing Lynne's films, and that was it. So for a while I was quite hesitant to go full pitch as a designer. I must admit *Ratcatcher* was a baptism of fire, a real leap in terms of the scale of things that I had dealt with. '*Ben Hur* on a *Blue Peter** budget' was how the location manager referred to it.

AK: There was a lot of pressure on us, because we were all first-time heads of department: Jane, first-time designer; me, first-time cinematographer; Lynne, first-time-bonded director. And Gavin Emerson was a first-time producer. It seemed to me that everything was really being watched: a lot of psychological pressure because of that.

---

* Much-loved BBC-TV children's programme, specializing in handicraft tips for kids and their long-suffering parents.

JM: I think somebody actually congratulated Lynne on surviving it. Not about whether it was good or not, just because she managed to complete her first feature.

AK: When we finished there was this weight just lifted off my chest. It was the prettiest feeling, it really was.

FM: Do you still get that feeling?

AK: When the responsibility is lifted, yes. Not waking up waiting for the rushes report, or all the other things that could go wrong. You never relax while you are on production.

JM: You feel like you have to be accessible 24 hours a day. I do, anyway. Even if the crew are on night shoots and you are prepping ahead, you never know when you're going to get a phone call saying they suddenly need you on set. During filming you never feel that you have a day off, even if one is provided for you. You always have your mobile phone on, just in case somebody has an idea.

FM: Now that DV is so accessible and you can have non-linear edit suites on your home computer, do you think people actually need to go to film school anymore?

JM: I think it's horses for courses. Tarantino didn't go to film school, did he?

FM: No, but he did attend courses like the Sundance Institute.

AK: You can turn round the argument. You can borrow a DV while you're at film school, and get the best of both worlds.

JM: Despite what we said about it being competitive, there is something special about being around like-minded people. If you meet a brilliant tutor like Moira Tait – Head of Production Design at NFTS, and I love her dearly – then you learn a lot.

AK: The thing with DV is that if you're into 'authorship', there are less people who have to be involved in the process, it is more personal. So if you're a director and you want to be as close to 'art' as possible, and you're absolutely sure of what you're being driven by, then . . . But if you're not really sure where you want to go, then you can just drift around film school and meet people who trigger you off, and so you find something out about yourself. I wasn't one of these freaks who had a Super-8 camera when they were 12, I didn't know about all these film theorists. I just fell into it, and I was really interested in finding more out about it while I was there.

JM: In my discipline, I would definitely say you are making it incredibly tough for yourself if you don't go through film school to get up that ladder. It does seem to be the fastest route into an art department. I work with a lot of art directors and assistants coming out of NFTS, and you know that they have a solid training behind them. They are visually aware, they know how to draft, they've been on film sets. There are other people who I take on board as assistants, who are visually strong and really brilliant people, but they can't draft. And that's really hard for me. Even if they work with me a few times, I can't give them that promotion, because they are sometimes lacking in the main skills. And there are certain things that they really need to know how to do.

AK: Meeting people in the industry, one thing I've felt is that at film school you learn to communicate between the departments: the director, the production designer and the DoP. You have more time than you get doing a TV shoot, where it's very clear how you communicate to the cameraman, and the cameraman wouldn't think twice about challenging the director or suggesting an idea. Film school gives you the time to think how you might do it differently. People who only know the industry are not used to that way of working.

JM: True. Working with Alwin and Lynne, I learned so much about lighting and film stock, just by having those conversations about whether it's going to be soft light or hard light, what size is the space, *et cetera*. I learned from Lynne when she was a DoP and she would say, 'I think that colour would work really well if we used this grainy stock. Would you do that to this?'

AK: What do you think as a director, Fraser? What did you feel you would get out of a DoP or a production designer at the school?

FM: The film I felt was the best, where the crew felt like a unit going for one thing and achieving it, was my second-year film *Simple Things*. With my graduation film, it slowly felt that as problems with the script got more and more prevalent, people started to build wee walls around their departments: 'This is my graduation film so it has to look bloody brilliant, it doesn't matter what the story is about.'

JM: You don't think that was in the nature of designers only getting one chance to do a build at the film school? Some people in our year did have that attitude once we reached graduation. I didn't, because I was always saying, 'I don't want to build.' But then I did end up building because I was the only designer left at the time.

FM: I remember it all coming to a head in one production meeting. I said that I was going to write a new script: one character, in a white room with no windows and no doors, all shot in black and white. And they all looked at me like . . .

AK: 'Run!'

JM: That was almost the same as when I did an advert at the school. First I put forward the idea that I was going to build the back of a terraced building. Then, as it developed, I thought, 'Sod this, I just want to make it all in camera and play around with opticals.' In the end I didn't build anything other than a flat wall with a line coming out at an angle, so it looked like the character was walking towards camera. To me, it was very designed. But it certainly wasn't a pretty back of a terraced house. And the head of department – not Moira – was really disappointed that I wasn't making a really big build. But sometimes there is that tendency to say, 'This is my opportunity to do a massive build!' My argument is, 'If you can find it on location, bloody well shoot it on location.' If you're spending all your energy trying make it look real when you can actually do it for real . . . But I know that not everyone agrees with that. And there is a *lot* of pressure for designers to do a build in their last year.

LYNNE RAMSAY AND LUCIA ZUCCHETTI

Fraser MacDonald: Lynne, why did you decide to go to film school?
Lynne Ramsay: It was a total fluke. I was going out with this guy, and he had always wanted to go to film school. At Napier there was a notice up on the board for the NFTS, and for me it was just a whim: 'That sounds interesting, I'll send in some of my pictures.' (*Laughs.*) I had really expected that I would go to the Royal College of Art to do an MA in Photography, but I didn't get in there, I got into the film school instead. So it was chance, really. I had never done film before, I didn't know anything about it. But I saw one film at Napier, *Meshes of the Afternoon**, which they showed to us with sound and then without. That was really powerful, and it had quite a big impact on me, made me think, 'I'm really interested in this.' Then I wavered between applying for Documentary or for Cinematography at the NFTS, because I didn't think I would be accepted as a director. But I was interested in fiction: my photographs were partly documentary, and partly set up. So I looked at the choice from a photographer's point of view, and I chose Cinematography, which was the wrong thing to do. In fact, at my interview Henning Camre kept saying, 'It sounds that you really want to be a director.' It was like, 'You can't say that, this is a Cinematography interview.' But I didn't know what a director meant; I didn't have that wide overview, coming from my arts background.

And once I got to the school, I realized I'd made a big mistake – I should have applied for Documentary. It seemed more my cup of tea, because you shot stuff and you edited it in teams of two. It seemed really intimate and interesting. After the first week I realized that I was on the wrong course, went to see the Head of Documentary to see if I should reapply, and he told me I was mad and persuaded me to stay. I still tried to get into the documentary department several times after. (*Laughs.*) But they never entertained the idea. You were really stuck in your discipline, though later on I was glad of that. But looking back, I think it

* Made in 1943, a classic of the US avant-garde co-directed by Maya Deren and Alexander Hammid.

Lynne Ramsay

Lucia Zucchetti

would have been better for me if I'd taken some kind of foundation course first, instead of going straight into a post-grad in film, not really knowing anything.

FM: What about you, Lucia?
Lucia Zucchetti: My film education started a long time ago, when I was in Italy doing the equivalent of A-levels – I was studying film even then, probably as a consequence of spending my childhood playing and performing, setting up theatres and all sorts. Eventually, I came to England to do a film degree, and then straight to the NFTS to specialize in editing. So if I count them up, I've studied film for quite a number of years – first in a playful way, then more theory-based, and then practically.

FM: You didn't want to go straight into the film industry?
LZ: I didn't think it was possible. In Italy it all felt quite nepotistic, whereas I didn't really know anyone, and anyway that wasn't how I would have liked to enter the industry. I felt that if I wanted to move into higher film education, then my country didn't have much to offer. So I ended up here, by chance, really. I felt that as a foreigner I had to start somewhere, and the easiest place to start was in an institution, getting to know people and finding out how it worked over here.

FM: Was the NFTS everything that you thought it was going to be?
LZ: I don't think so. But then again, if you ask me what I thought it would be, I would struggle to answer . . .
LR: I think my initial conception of film school was that we would all sit around smoking spliffs into the night, discussing film and wearing avant-garde black shirts. So I was really shocked to get there, because everyone wore Timberlands. (*Laughs.*) I thought it would be a really subversive place and it wasn't. So I decided I should wear high-heeled boots with my 35mm camera, just to be subversive . . . But for me, it was all connected to making the move from Scotland to London. If there had been a film school in Scotland, I would have applied there. The NFTS was like going to public school. Being Glaswegian, I felt very aware of where I came from, and really lucky to be there. If it hadn't been for the grant, there is no way I would have been able to go. There were maybe certain other students there who had connections in the industry, but the grant gave the possibility for someone like me – you too, Fraser – to go there.

Coming from more of an art school background, I found the NFTS quite a shock – maybe because I was doing Cinematography, which was such a technical course. There were some brilliant tutors, but the place did feel industry-orientated. There was quite a lot of pressure for graduation films to be of a certain ilk, quite slick. I remember going to see the RCA graduate films and finding them more interesting.

But then I think it also has a lot to do with the time that we were there. There wasn't anything happening in the British film industry, it was nigh on impossible to think that you could make a feature within the first couple of years of leaving. So the school was more orientated to your making something that could get you into television: an end product to show the industry. That felt quite oppressive to me, because I felt that you went to a school to experiment and take all the risks that you might not get the chance to do again. But I think the students played a part in that too, it wasn't just the style of teaching.

LZ: We did start there at a time of change. Colin Young had just left, the school was going through a massive transformation, and I think we suffered the consequences of that. They were really trying to impose rules, be really strict, and you could feel the pressure of this new regime. It was like, 'Don't think you are going to come out and make feature films because you won't. You'd better just get used to that now and start thinking commercially. Do your TV workshop and learn how to use multi-camera.'

LR: Man, I hated that workshop. Nothing against TV – I mean, you get a massive audience, more people will see your work there than in the cinema, nothing against that. But this workshop was just the old-style multi-cam, and you felt like, 'Fuck it, why are we doing this?' I didn't go to film school to learn that, I really didn't. I felt that I was a photography student, coming in from a fine arts background, to study Cinematography – not to shoot stuff on a multi-cam set wearing wee headphones.

FM: When I did that workshop I got told off, because my framing was too cinematic. I was sticking everybody to the edge of the frame when they should have been nearer the centre.

LR: But then I always felt that I was good in places where I had something to fight against, and things like the workshop brought that out in me. So, in a way, it was productive.

LZ: Looking back, what I think those exercises were good for was in bringing the right people together and uniting them. There were students who enjoyed them and got into them and bonded with each other through them – and others who didn't. In fact, me, Lynne and Jane ended up finding each other in the context of those experiences, because we realized that we had something in common.

LR: Yeah, it was very much like that. Wee groups. I had a terrible first year because of the first two pieces I shot. I had never shot film before, so I framed like a photographer. I didn't know how to do a tracking shot – I mean, it was a total mess. I remember going away for a week for my birthday, and when I came back nobody at the school was talking to me. I was like the total outcast, shunned: 'You'll never shoot anything again!' It was very competitive in that way. Nobody was saying, 'Oh, you've just never really done any film before, this is what you do.' It was all just assumed, because a lot of people had been to film school before and the levels of attainment were so different. But for me, the first year was like playing catch-up. I remember thinking almost every day that I wanted to leave.

FM: Didn't a tutor say to you that you would never be a cinematographer because you were too small to carry a camera?
LR: Och, this always gets bandied about. Put it this way, I wasn't getting on with the cinematography tutor. He used to make snide BBC jokes about blondes and redheads, and it just got really boring. You know, 'What the fuck am I doing here?' It wasn't just that I was too small – he admitted that he wouldn't have chosen me to be on the course. It was Walter Lassally* who chose my work to get me into the school, and I was really proud of that. But this other tutor came from telly, and it was just a different kind of vibe altogether. I didn't agree with the ethos that was being taught, so I really rebelled against it, to the point where it got pretty impossible for me to talk to him.

FM: Jane mentioned not fitting in too. So that's how you got together . . .
LR: We were all losers. (*Laughs.*)

FM: And now the school promotes you as a team that was created there.
LR: Ironically, I think they promoted a lot of stuff about collaboration and yet everybody was fighting with each other. And you were 'in' if you were considered 'good'. It was like primary school, only really heightened. But yes, we ended up working quite collaboratively, which is something the school really promoted.
LZ: I have to say, I didn't feel that they promoted collaboration *at all*.
LR: Well, they purported to. It was shouted out, but never followed through.
LZ: The competitiveness was always there, even between heads of departments. But again, we were there at a time of crisis. People were leaving because they didn't agree with the new regime and the new rules, so there were some brilliant people who had put their life and soul into the school who now were going. They seemed to be instating managers more than anything else, and I think we suffered because of that.
LR: It was a shame. There were a lot of fantastic tutors, and when they left it felt like a different school. There was a certain degree of 'Let's get rid of the people who have worked here for 20 years.' Those were people who really wanted to

* German-born cinematographer, whose credits include *A Taste of Honey* (1961), *The Loneliness of the Long Distance Runner* (1962), *Tom Jones* (1963) and *Zorba the Greek* (1964), for which he won an Oscar.

teach, who were very much icons there. But for me, by default, it ended up being a good experience. It taught me what I didn't want to do, and that's always a valuable lesson.

FM: Do you think that's why you ended up directing?
LR: Kind of. I feel like I only discovered what it was to be a director outside, when I left the film school. But I was glad that I had done cinematography, and photography before that – it brought that knowledge to my work. I feel like quite a visual film-maker, so it was all an influence on what I'm doing now. It was so good and valuable to know how to shoot something, from working on documentaries and working with other directors, experimenting. There was one film that I shot where the director appeared in it, so a lot was left up to me. I would shoot a whole film using wide shots and nothing else. So I was really learning about the form.
LZ: You were taught the rules on how to do stuff, but then we also learned how to break the rules. It made us think, 'Do we really need to follow the conventions?'
LR: Funnily enough, the people whom I considered to be the best directors there at the time have ended up not directing. They all had trouble in the directing department. This director, Ashley Irving, was very talented and a real rebel, and in the end she was very much sidelined. But to me her work was the most interesting. I seriously think that I would have been chucked out of cinematography if the directing department hadn't liked my work. But I established a lot of relationships with people who I still work with. In fact, Alwin was on my interview panel. I think he really liked my work, and he was always a support, even though he was a few years ahead of me. Then I met other interesting DoPs like Peter Thwaites*, who influenced and helped me. I met Jane because I was a DoP, and Lucia through working with Ashley. So there was a bit of a team developing . . .

FM: And it just felt logical to carry on working with each other?
LR: It was also a kind of support network. But we did form this sort of aesthetic together.
LZ: The fact that we all worked with each other on equal footing as heads of departments for another director is probably one of the reasons why we work so well now. We bonded over that.
LR: Then I wrote these short stories, stuff that was rubbish at first. But I showed them to Lucia rather than a tutor, and she said, 'These are really good, why don't you make them?' So that gave me the confidence to approach the direction

* Subsequently the DoP on *Appetite* and *The Tichborne Claimant* (both 1998).

department and say, 'I really want to make these.' I don't think I had that support elsewhere at the school.

FM: Dick Ross was also quite influential, wasn't he?
LR: He was. He liked what I'd written and he did help to get it made. I do think it started with me pushing right from the first year, saying 'I want to make a film, I want to make a film!' for three years. But Dick Ross was one of the people who supported that.
LZ: He saw the potential in Lynne's writing. In fact, I just discovered that I have all those original stories that she wrote. I'm the only one who still has copies. I kept saying, 'One day these will be worth something!' (*Laughs.*)

FM: Was it quite hard for you to convince the school that you should direct?
LR: I think they were beyond irritation – because I just kept asking and pushing.
LZ: You constantly wanted to leave. I remember two or three times I had to convince her to stay. It was probably selfish on my part, because I couldn't bear losing a friend more than anything else. 'If she goes I'm going to be so lonely!' But seriously, you did think, 'I can't stand this any longer. I just don't fit in and I want to go!'
LR: I did. But that fight to make a film ended up being quite a good thing in a way, because the constant pushing just toughens you up. At times, I felt that it was a very unfair place, and that it was fairer on certain others. There was really a big anger in me about that. The school promotes itself as a very diplomatic place, but it wasn't.
LZ: There was a constant feeling that there were people who fitted in and there were people who didn't. Somehow, all the people who fitted belonged to the same category . . .
LR: They perhaps found it easier to do whatever they wanted.

FM: But what were their films like?
LZ: Exactly.
LR: I don't think we should go into that. (*Laughs.*) It came to a big crux, and there was a producer called Jane Pugh who ended up helping me. I got her in at the very last meeting about *Small Deaths*. By then I had the whole crew up in Scotland and yet we were still having this meeting about the budget and whether we were actually going to get to make it. It was really scary being in that position. But I was really determined, after three years that had sometimes been hell.
LZ: Somehow the rules they had set ended up working against them. They said that somebody who works in another department is not allowed to direct a film; and yet every student is entitled to graduate with a film. And circumstances just made it so Lynne didn't have a film to graduate on, because her collaboration

with a particular director didn't work out, and so they felt forced into sponsoring Lynne's first film as a director, as a duty to her. So *Small Deaths* kind of officially fitted into the graduation films, but it was a bit of a one-off really.

LR: I had actually shot a documentary, but with DoPs it was the norm that you graduated on a fiction piece.

LZ: Now I think they realize that it was the best possible move that they ever did. Because they use *Small Deaths* to —

FM: Death?

LZ: In many ways, yes. (*Laughs.*)

LR: I remember coming out of this weird meeting, having dragged Jane Pugh into it and going through the grill about how much money a day people were getting to eat, which was about 50 pence each. It was really ridiculous. I wasn't getting the full budget that a director would get, it was about half of that. And afterwards one of the tutors – name no names – turned round to me and said, 'You were always going to get the money.' But I went through this horrible meeting thinking, 'I'm not going to make my film, there's people up in Scotland, what am I going to do?' And they just put me through this! Maybe it was one of the lessons you have to learn at film school. But I remember feeling really angry, because it just felt so unnecessary.

FM: Jane mentioned that when you sent your rushes down, you had people telling you they would never cut.

LR: Yeah, I had tutors on the phone saying that. Some people took an interest, and others really distanced themselves. During the editing there weren't people coming in and looking at it, or asking me about it. I didn't really have anything to lose.

FM: Which is a good way to be, though?

LZ: We were left alone, did pretty much what we wanted, and it just worked out really well for us in the end. But it was painful at times.

LR: I had such a great time on that shoot though – the greatest time I've ever had on a shoot, I think. It was like utter rebellion, because by that time everybody was so fucked off by it all. Ordinarily, it's very stressful doing your graduation film but I felt a real sense of liberation, like 'I don't give a shit, I'm just going to make this and have a really good time.' It made the whole three years add up and seem worthwhile. We felt like we'd ram-raided the school's camera and run away to make a film for ten days, and maybe we might never come back. I got one phone call saying, 'We are going to pull the shoot. The camera is meant to be back here!' Normally, I would have felt really threatened by that, but instead I just put the phone down and burst out laughing. I'd had enough, and I really just felt this freedom.

LZ: Meanwhile I was back at the film school waiting for the rushes and getting so frustrated, thinking they were never coming back. (*Laughs.*) I kept telling the tutors the rushes weren't ready yet. And I wished I was up there with them.

FM: So when do you think that the 'administration' came on to your side? Was it before or after the film's success at Cannes?
LZ: After, definitely. Once *Small Deaths* got official recognition . . .
LR: But there were NFTS people who liked it, so we can't take that away. Ian Sellar liked it pretty early on. It got a good response at the graduation screenings. Gavin Emerson* saw it there and bought it from the school. They didn't know what to do with it, they just weren't interested in it – maybe they regret it now, I don't know. But it was like, 'Let's just get rid of this thing.' It was Gavin who decided to send it to Cannes, and when I heard that, I was like, 'Yeah *right*. That will never happen.' But it did, and it was fantastic – just such a buzz. It didn't really have an impact at the school until after Cannes, I would say.
LZ: And now they sometimes use it as an example. Yet at the time there was that feeling of 'This is a bunch of nutty women who just went off with a camera . . .'
LR: Not just women.
LZ: True, but Alwin was not officially a student at the time, so it was very much us. We were not considered as people who were making anything worthwhile. It was more like, 'They're off doing their own thing, good luck to them.' Then later on you realize that actually it's something worth looking at . . .
LR: It feels like a bit of an achievement. It was the best thing I did there, and I'm glad it took a lot of fighting against that system. If I had said, 'Okay then, I'll just graduate with a documentary,' then I wouldn't be in the position I'm in today.
LZ: I don't know if I should say this but one of the tutors – name no fucking names – thought the segment in the film called 'Holy Cow' was about menstruation. That just says it all. It just goes to say what they thought of us, a bunch of nutty women.
LR: I remember being told by a tutor, 'Don't you think that the girl should nurse the cow back to life?' I was like, 'You just don't get this story at all. That would have been so cheesy.' You think to yourself, 'I don't think I'll be coming back here for any more of *your* advice.' (*Laughs.*)

FM: I want to ask you about DV, because Stephen Bayly recently said to the first-years, 'Why are you coming to film school when your fees will buy Final Cut Pro and a DV camera?' Why should people still go to film schools? Are they still important?
LR: I still wonder that myself. (*Laughs.*) It's really retrospective for me, because

* Subsequently the producer of *Gasman* and *Ratcatcher*.

at the time I didn't enjoy myself, I was always on the brink of leaving. But later on I felt that it was a totally invaluable experience. How many people, even as camera students, get the chance to shoot really expensive tests, and experiment like we did?

LZ: Film school means having the opportunity to meet and collaborate with other people, which you probably wouldn't get with DV. Some people have got the ability to go off on their own with a DV camera and just do fantastic stuff, but I would say it's probably one out of one hundred.

FM: So you would say film school is mainly a place for meeting and exchanging ideas?

LR: It also gives you an overview of what's going on. At the time, the school was like, 'This is all the British film industry has to offer.' And we thought, 'Is that it?' But within that kind of system or network, it's much easier to have a feeling about what's going on and what's out there for you afterwards. No way do I think that it's necessary to go, because there are some tremendous film-makers who never went to film school. But nor do I believe that anyone can pick up a camera and make a brilliant film; I think that's absolute bullshit. I do see new technology as really positive, it's a way that you can move forward. But I'm happy that we did a training that was in some ways quite traditional, doing it the hard way on a Steenbeck.

FM: I think DV will bring out really good editors. Some people will shoot till the cows come home . . .

LZ: But I find when I talk to people that anyone who goes out and shoots miles and miles of footage on DV has a real problem, because they don't know how they are going to cut it down and they need help. Often there might be incredible footage in there, but it never ends up anywhere because they have such difficulties putting it together.

LR: With DV, anybody who is an outsider in terms of class or culture, they will have the access to cameras and that's going to bring up something good. It's like when I applied to the NFTS to be a DoP – 'Oh we'd better get more women on board, positive discrimination.' I think that went a long way towards getting me in there, because I'd never shot anything before. But with DV you maybe won't see the true results of it right away. Perhaps it's a generational thing. There are now these things like the Lego animation kit*. Kids are much more aware about films and what goes into making them, just from watching a lot of TV. And once you get a DV camera for kids . . .

* The Lego & Steven Spielberg MovieMaker Set, a package that allows kids (and indeed grown-ups) to create stop-motion animation films on a PC. It contains Lego pieces, a USB camera with built-in mike and an explanatory CD-Rom.

FM: There was Pixelvision*.
LR: True. But anyway, it's not going to happen overnight. It's not like we'll find there are a million great directors out there because of DV cameras.

FM: After all, it took 20 or 30 years before cinema really became an art form.
LR: Yeah, and you have to find a slightly different language for DV. I think you have to test out any new form. It's like Cinemascope. Something implicitly changes in the language, in the way you shoot it. Some people shoot on DV because it's a cheap medium and they don't have a choice. That's fine if you've got a really good idea. But if you have a choice, some things work well on DV and some things work better on film.

FM: So are you saying that the success of a film comes down to the story?
LR: For me, the films that have worked really well on DV are things like *The Idiots*, even more so than *Festen*. *Festen* was a really good script, the performances were fantastic, and having DV probably helped them shoot it in the way they did. But *The Idiots* was really shot with the right kind of film language. It felt like quite an experimental and subversive idea; it was a pseudo-documentary in a way. And I thought it really embraced the form and the medium, rather than saying, 'We don't have any money so we're going to make it on DV.' I have nothing against that. But *Festen* would have worked on film; whereas *The Idiots* really works on DV, but I don't think it would work on film. So for me DV films that really work are ones that have the right language for that format. It's not just a case of cheap film-making. But the whole Dogme thing was a fantastic idea, a really good gimmick.

FM: It set up a lot of good arguments as well.
LR: Yeah – 'We can make films in this way, we don't need to go through all this bullshit to get money.' Of the Ten Commandments, I'd say five of them were jokes. It was a laugh, you know? But picking on things from the *nouvelle vague*, that was interesting too. There's nothing so new in shooting handheld and not using music and being purist. But Dogme was something that was really necessary now, because before it just seemed like you needed a hell of a lot of money to go out and make a film. And that means less control with your first feature. Here, it's really expensive to make your first feature. In America if you are doing an indie film it's much cheaper, not so much set down in the rules that we have here.

---

* Brand name of the PXL-2000 camcorder, made by Fisher Price in the 1980s and marketed unsuccessfully as a kids' toy. Named for its highly pixelated monochrome image, it acquired a cult following and was used in Richard Linklater's *Slacker* (1992) and Michael Almereyda's *Another Girl Another Planet* (1992) and *Nadja* (1996).

FM: That's something the film school can't really teach you about – working in the outside world. You could say film school is technically a driving test. Then once you've passed, you go out and really learn how to drive.

LR: I found things less conservative outside film school. I was quite surprised because we were braced for this attitude of 'Oh my God, if you don't prepare your treatment like this, then you won't get anywhere'. But then I did go to the BFI for my first funded short, which is a bit different. I just wrote a wee story, there was no format. I thought, 'This works well and gives a sense of the atmosphere, I'll put that in.'

LZ: But if it wasn't for *Small Deaths* going somewhere, I don't know what would have happened.

LR: I remember being really, really depressed the first six months after film school. We left in October 1995. I sent *Small Deaths* to a lot of TV channels asking what they thought of it and got letters back saying, 'We don't take experimental films, don't call us, we'll call you.' So it was the Cannes confirmation that really helped.

FM: It only takes one person to take notice before everybody else follows.

LR: Yeah, and especially if it's an international forum. People need that confirmation – that's a shame, but it's the truth. I know that I got a really lucky break

LZ: And as a consequence, we all did.

FM: What would you say was the most valuable thing you got out of NFTS?

LZ: What I valued most was that I had the opportunity to work on loads of stuff. At the time there was a big backlog of projects needing to be cut.

LR: I shot a graduation film in my second year, which was just fantastic to do.

LZ: But I guess the most valuable thing was that we met each other there.

LR: Yeah. Alwin shot the last part of *Small Deaths* and that established another relationship. He was there for me with advice and we liked the same things creatively, we got a bit of a bond going. And you know, if it ain't broke don't fix it. We can all work with other people, but the combination of the four of us, which was formed about eight years ago – we complement each other.

LZ: Is it that long?

FM: Would you still go to film school, knowing what you know now?

LR: It's a different climate, so it's hard to say.

LZ: At the time we went, the NFTS was the second richest educational institution in the country, after the fucking airline academy. We were privileged students and we didn't have to pay to be there, with amazing people coming to teach us. I'm sure it was the same for you, Fraser. But the only difference was that you had to pay.

FM: Okay, would you recommend film school to other people then?

LR: It depends on what you want to do. I think if you want to be a cinematographer, an editor, a designer, it can be a really invaluable experience, because you are jumping the industry. You are not going to be a focus-puller for ten years.

LZ: I have recommended it to some people, because it worked for me, as someone in a so-called technician's role. If I had gone down another route, I might have started off as an assistant, and might still be an assistant now. But I came out of NFTS and started editing straight away.

LR: For directors, I would say it's up to the person in question. I don't think you have to go to film school to be a director. That's why I'm glad I went as a cinematographer because I learned a lot that's relevant to what I'm doing now. Whereas on the fiction direction course, there seemed to be a lot of pressure to reach this standard that was seen as 'professional', and I don't think I wanted to be 'professional'. (*Laughs.*) But I would recommend the school for a director in the sense that you can meet really interesting people who you might want to work with. Films are not made by committee, but they are definitely made in collaboration, and you want to be working with people who have the same attitude as yourself, because it makes your life a hell of a lot easier. One brilliant experience I had at film school was meeting Derek Jarman, who came in to do a talk. He just said, 'I always work with my mates. Why give yourself the pain?'

LZ: Exactly.

LR: Why have terrible relationships and people hating everything they do? It can be such a bitchy, horrific industry and people can really be nasty to each other. I really took that to heart. So I work with my mates, but all my mates are good film-makers. And I met these people at film school.

Fraser MacDonald (right) takes cover with DoP Gavin Struthers. © Zoë Norfolk, 2000

L'Année Dernière à Beaconsfield: Diary of a final year at the National Film and Television School by Fraser Macdonald

Saturday, 1 January 2000. Glasgow

A New Year, a new millennium, and all the chintz that goes with it. Last night, caught up in the excitement of it all, I proposed to Andrea ('Andi') Matheson, my partner of eight years; and as the fireworks flew over the south side of Glasgow, she said 'Yes'. We tell our mates, who pour champagne and flat lager over our heads. Phone calls are made to parents and absent friends before drunken stupor descends upon us. This year has started well – long may it continue so.

Monday, 3 January 2000. London

Back home to Peckham, SE15. Andi starts work today as stand-by art director on a TV drama, and I return to my part-time job as a projectionist at the Gate cinema, Notting Hill. But within two hours, I get a call from Doug Ray, the producer of my final-year film. Our writer Antonia ('Toni') Baldo has completed a first draft of her script and e-mailed it to us from Australia. Toni actually graduated from NFTS in 1999, albeit in unconventional circumstances: originally she had to leave the course, not being able to cover the fees, but she ended up writing three of the year's six graduation films, so the school made her an 'honorary' graduate.

'Have you read it yet?' Doug asks. I haven't, and I can tell by his tone that he's not confident.

'By the way Doug,' I say, 'Andi and I got engaged . . .'

'Really? That's good. So, about this script . . .'

Later, in bed, Andi asks me what I want to do in my final year. I look at her blankly, and tell her that I just want to make a film that I'm happy with. 'That's not enough,' she replies. What can I say? All I know is that the same team who worked with me on my second-year film, *Simple Things*, have decided to work on the graduation film (bar the writer and the composer, both of whom have since graduated). That must show they have some confidence in me as a director; and if you have the backing of people you trust, then you should be able to achieve anything. I just don't want to be caught up in the usual graduation madness, where people worry that the film they're working on will make or break them, and so care only about their own contribution. (I.e. 'Even if the film's crap, I'll make sure that I come up smelling of roses.')

'Why don't you write something yourself?' Andi asks. But I haven't written a script in two years, not since I worked on a feature in my first year and got done over by a production company. I was writing a treatment of a book I was adapting, getting paid absolutely nothing for it, until finally a contract for development came through and – hey ho what do you know? – my services were no longer required. It was my first taste of the business, and I haven't really felt confident about writing since.

Besides, I came to film school to learn how to work with writers, however painful that process can be.

Thursday, 6 January 2000. Soho

Meet Doug in a web café on Wardour Street to discuss the script. (We're not yet at the stage of lunchtime meetings in exclusive media clubs.) It's not what I hoped for, but then it's only a first draft. Doug seems more worried. Toni won't be back from Australia for a couple of weeks, so everything is being done through e-mail. I tell Doug that I will send Toni my reactions and comments. 'Is it definitely a script that you want to make?' asks Doug. Well . . .

The original idea was about a young guy called Archie Hams who lives in the vicinity of Green Lanes, a long road that runs for several miles through north London and has a strong Turkish immigrant population. Archie wants to break free of his family home so that he can spend more time with his girlfriend, Lizzie. So he applies for a council house, but is turned down. After some advice from his elder brother, he pretends to be mentally ill in the hope that as a 'special case' he will be given a house. But instead he becomes genuinely unstable.

The idea was to show the naivete of our main character slowly disappearing, affected by the narrow views and bigotry of some of his friends. London is a melting point of different cultures that try to co-habit. Often there is resentment of the more successful of the 'in-comers', mainly because of the hardship felt by the self-proclaimed Anglo-Saxons who imagine that the empire still exists, Britannia still rules the waves, *et cetera*. Both Doug and I feel that Toni's script doesn't yet capture the essence of that. But I think there's good stuff in there, and Toni will work on it some more. So we have another coffee and watch the British film industry scurrying about outside. In another year's time, will I be doing the same scurrying? Or even worse, still watching and waiting?

Wednesday, 26 January 2000. Beaconsfield

Back to school. The NFTS is in Beaconsfield, 27 miles west of London, but the school lays on a free bus from town, leaving at 8.30am and returning at 5.30pm. I've done this for the last two years but this will be my final journey, as the school has now given us all train passes. I board the bus outside the Allsop Arms pub off the Marylebone Road. Taking up my usual seat (top deck, just before the stairs . . . don't ask me why), I meet up with my fellow third-years, and the talk is all of graduation films. We scan the bus for the new year's intake. They seem to huddle together, reading *Sight and Sound* or *American Cinematographer*, trying hard not to look or sound pretentious. I listen out for any Scots accents, but there are none to be heard.

I try to sleep through the hour's journey into Beaconsfield. It's a strange town, the closest I've seen to the Tory Party vision of heaven: large houses, public schools, cars that probably cost more than my three years' fees at NFTS. The school itself is actually an old studio; they shot a lot of the Norman Wisdom* films there in the 1950s and 1960s. I liken the place to a holiday camp that time forgot: white-washed walls and prefab extensions, but no clowns (though some might dispute that . . .).

I spend most of the day in the edit suite with Alastair ('Ali') Reid. He cut my second-year film *Simple Things*, and is now working on an improvised piece that I shot before Christmas. We watch the rushes. They're not good. There isn't much of a story in there, apart from one monologue, so we decide to concentrate on that. We've got a week and I hope we'll finish on time – I hate long edits. Various members of the crew drop in: Rob Bourke, our soundman; Gavin Struthers, the cinematographer; and Stephen Swain, the set designer. They all enquire about Toni's script. I tell them it's coming along fine, and I'll show it to them when I think it's ready to be seen. Toni has requested that this be the case, and I don't blame her. It's bad enough having one person closely scrutinizing your work, never mind six. Also, if truth be told, I don't want them to see it. I have this hunch that they might not like it.

Thursday, 3 February 2000. Beaconsfield

Stephen corners me in the library. He wants to see a script as soon as possible. He (rightly) feels that it's time for him to start preparing drawings, mood boards† – basically, all of his research. More worryingly, he tells me that he isn't really 'into' the story. 'It sounds like we're going over the same ground again. Can't we try something more ambitious?' It's funny he brings this up, because his tutor said the same to me earlier. ('Can't we do something more interesting for Stephen? He's already designed a council flat . . .') I try and calm Stephen down, but I'm also starting to feel angry about his attitude. Sure, I know that he wants to challenge himself here and push his own boundaries, but it feels like he's dismissing the script before he's even read it. Later I talk to Andi and she tells me that, from a designer's perspective, she can see Stephen's point. So I

---

* An English slapstick comic whose likeable 'salt of the earth' characters were always getting into scrapes with members of the upper classes. He's still alive and, famously, still very big in Albania.
† Mood boards show images that relate to the atmosphere and colour of scenes within the script. They are not drawings as such, more conceptual references that the designer has in mind.

Gavin Struthers and Stephen Swain (right). © Zoë Norfolk, 2000

decide to let things lie for now. But it's only a week into term and already people seem to be getting The Fear. That goes for me too, however I may seem on the outside. My feeling is that there has to be a certain amount of trust when you're making films. I trust Toni; therefore the crew should trust me. Isn't that how it works?

Thursday, 10 February 2000. Beaconsfield

Script meeting with Ann Skinner, head of the Producing department, and Ian Sellar, my Direction tutor. Toni's new draft has appeared, but it still needs more work. I chat to Ian about it beforehand. He thinks there are some strong points, notably the treatment of racism. In the meeting, he asks me why I want to tell this particular story. I go round the houses with reasons, but none of them sound right. Ann then throws the killer punch:

'What film do *you* want to make, Fraser?'

Abruptly winded, I start talking about approaching a subject head-on, trying to tackle difficult issues but, in a way, showing all sides of the argument, blah blah blah . . .

'You mean,' says Ann, fixing my gaze, smiling slightly, 'you want to make an Alan Clarke film?'

And with that, she has me totally sussed. I stammer to no avail.

'It's good to aspire, Fraser,' Ann tells me. 'But you are not Alan Clarke.'

I excuse myself from the meeting and go to the toilet. Looking at myself in the mirror, I reckon she's right. I take off the flat cap and drop the faux-Scouse accent. We all need heroes, but should you always try to emulate them?

Ian stops me later in the canteen, and asks if I have any other script ideas. I tell him about one, all to do with my childhood. He shakes his head. 'Too easy. You already know how to make it, how it would look. Would that be a challenge?' I suppose not. 'This year is about pushing yourself, Fraser. Making choices and sticking by them – not producing a film that everybody loves. I mean, if that happens, more the better. But it shouldn't be the main objective.' It makes total sense to me, but try telling the crew that: 'Sorry guys, but I'm going out on a limb here. Perhaps it won't work, and you'll have to be associated with something that you think is a piece of shit . . .' That attitude sounds selfish to me. Sure, the nature of being a director is to push the boat forward, captain the crew – all those clichés. But I empathize with all the crew. We all want to make a good film. The only trouble is that maybe my definitions of 'good' and 'bad' are different from theirs.

Tuesday, 15 February 2000. Beaconsfield

Paul, one of my fellow directing students of my year, tells me about the ambitious idea for his graduation film. It involves a hell of a lot of blue-screen work. He doesn't have a script yet, but he knows how he wants the finished film to look. The school is being funny with him, maybe because of the absence of a script, or maybe because of the scale of the project. But Paul is determined that he'll do it, and on video if needs be.

Toni is back from Australia with a new draft of the script. I ask her if the crew can now get a read of it. She is reticent. I want to appease her, but I know I need to show the boys something, even if it's just an indication of the idea. So Doug and I photocopy and distribute the script, and wait. In due course Stephen comes to find me in the library. His feedback isn't good – to the point where he says he doesn't want to work on the film. All I can offer in response is that the script is still a work in progress, and any feedback he can give now will be helpful. He goes off to re-read it and make some design notes. But I get the feeling that his reservations are more to do with the small, contained scope of the story, rather than how it's all going to be realized on screen.

I work my way around Ali, Gav, Rob. Their reactions are much the same: 'We no like. We want something different.' But on the upside, they are all willing to wait for the next draft. I phone Toni, who is upset to hear that I distributed the script. I apologize and try to explain my reasons, which now sound false, I should have waited until she felt that the script was ready to show. I think Toni feels a bit naked with this draft and the confidence that the crew may have in her could be severely eroded. She asks about their feedback, and my silence speaks volumes. Later Doug and I have a chat. 'We can ditch this script now if you want,' he tells me. 'Nothing is set in stone.' But I like to think I have some high morals about loyalty; and I asked Toni to do this in the first place. Somehow, it's the sense of the pressure on me that makes me say, 'No. Let's go with it.' Doug nods his agreement. Plough on we will.

Sunday, 20 February 2000. Beaconsfield
Script meeting with Toni. It's beginning to dawn on us that our original premise is not going to work in 17 minutes. We just can't do justice to the story in that amount of screen time. So we look to focus on the areas that interest us both: the diversity of the area, and how the different communities deal with each other. Doug turns up, and seems to agree with us – but mainly he wants to know when the next draft will appear. 'Ten days,' offers Toni. Doug writes this down – I think that makes it official.

Thursday, 24 February 2000. Leicester Square, London WC2
Tonight there's a screening of all our second-year films, set up by some of the producing students. They felt that these films ought to be shown outside the school, since everybody (especially the non-NFTS runners, gaffers, clapper-loaders *et al*) put so much hard work and effort into them. The venue is a dance hall behind Leicester Square. The floor is sprung, so every time somebody walks past the video projector, the picture bounces. You can hear the chatter and laughter from the bar, and the sound can't be pushed any higher. But it's brilliant – everybody cheers and claps at the end of each film. Towards the end of the show Toni approaches me, looking worried. She feels she can't meet her deadline. I tell her to take her time, that there's no pressure. But I think both of us know that's not true. Earlier Gav had cornered her to ask some questions about the script, and set out what he thought its faults were, something that may have panicked her yet further.

Wednesday, 1 March 2000. Beaconsfield
Since the graduation film is my only project this year, I find I do a lot of hanging around. I could go up to Green Lanes and look for locations, but I'd rather have the script in my hand first. So instead I go into school to catch up on my film history. One of the best things about the NFTS is its extensive video library. Noel, the librarian, has been collecting films on VHS ever since the format became standard. Now he has almost 20 years' worth of tapes in there, and he reckons the collection runs to 6000 films, both features and shorts. You feel like a kid in a sweet shop who's been given too much pocket money – you just can't make up your mind what it is you want. I often play safe and re-watch the old classics:

Boys from the Blackstuff and *Blue Remembered Hills*, early BBC plays by Alan Bleasdale and Dennis Potter that I remember from when I was a kid, glued to the goggle box instead of playing outside and smashing telephone boxes.

Wednesday, 8 March 2000. Beaconsfield

Toni's new draft has appeared and I have a script meeting with some of the tutors. She has concentrated the action between young Archie, our main character, and his best friend, Hashmet, a second-generation Turk. Archie still wants to get a flat, and finds it harder than he imagined. Racist undertones now play a big part in the story: Archie is told that if he were Turkish, he would find his flat-hunting just that much easier, and he starts to believe it. Doug is a little worried by this angle: he suspects we could be in danger of being seen as racist ourselves. I vaguely agree with him; and yet in terms of the drama, it definitely feels like there's something working now. It's a story I want to tell. The tutors have the same fears as Doug. I can't really argue with them yet, as I don't feel I have a strong enough response. I spend the remainder of the day in one-to-one tutorials with Jan and Rob (writing department) and Ian and Ann. I'd like Toni to be here too, but she's trying to find work in that big world outside the school gates. So I try to speak for us both, though really I should be speaking for myself.

We gave the crew a copy of the new draft first thing this morning. At the end of the day I seek them out and solicit their opinions. Rob and Ali both see improvements. So does Gav, but he still has a lot of questions. Stephen hasn't read it yet: it sits on his drawing board as we talk.

Tuesday, 14 March 2000. Beaconsfield

Crew meeting about the script: time to get everything out in the open. Stephen sits across from me. He doesn't like it. I ask if he thinks it's at least going in the right direction? He just shrugs – he doesn't like the story, so it doesn't much matter what direction it goes in. I respect his honesty. Gav, despite some reservations, feels that it's getting much better. But Stephen wants to know if we are going to stick with this idea. The shooting dates have been allocated, and we start on 22 May. I tell Stephen that even though the script we have is not quite there yet, it's closer than anything else we could get at this short notice. He nods but says nothing more. Afterwards Doug introduces me to his friend Miles Wilkes, who will be our production manager on the shoot. I welcome him on board, and ask if he's remembered his life jacket.

Thursday, 16 March 2000. Peckham

Doug calls me at home. Stephen has left the crew. I get angry. This early stage in the game, and already we have pressure when there needn't be. Fuck him, I say.

Doug laughs nervously down the phone, and tells me that's not in his job description.

Saturday, 18 March 2000. Beaconsfield

I've been keeping out of Stephen's way for the last two days, mainly because I don't want to say something I'll later regret. I spoke to the rest of the crew and asked if they too wanted to find another project. 'No', came the answer. But they're all worried about the strength of this one. 'Just give us time,' I plead. I'm saying this partly to myself. It feels like the more resistance there is towards the script, the harder it is for me to back it up. Maybe it's because I'm beginning to have my own doubts about the story line. I don't feel I know these characters well enough yet, and I can't yet see the film. Still, when I listen to people whom I trust, expressing reservations about the script, I take this as a personal slight and use attack as the best form of defence, but only because I can't articulate an argument in rebuttal. This, I suspect, is why Stephen left us. He wanted to be convinced, and I couldn't do it. Or perhaps he was just being selfish and wanting more design opportunities than the script permitted. Who knows?

Tuesday, 21 March 2000. Beaconsfield

The trouble with NFTS is that it's a small place where rumours spread like wildfire, and that's what is happening to our production. People always want to know the gossip, so as to gauge whether their production is going better than everyone else's. At least Stephen's departure has freed us up a little more, in that we're no longer committed to a set build, thus saving a sizeable chunk of the budget. That's the positive spin on the situation. The negative aspect is that I've lost a crew member whom I trusted and respected, and all as a consequence of my decision to stick with a script. But Stephen is in a good position. There are only three designers for six graduation films, so he has options. Mine are starting to look increasingly limited.

Monday, 27 March 2000. Notting Hill

A new draft is here. Well, actually, a new ending, but it's really strong. Archie basically becomes a racist, and we lose all sympathy for him. It's a brutal ending, perhaps one that the audience doesn't deserve. But Ali doesn't share my doubts. For him, the end is powerful: a killer punch. I don't think it sits with the rest of the film, but I can see that it's progressing along the right lines. Toni and I meet later. She throws me a look that says, 'Please don't ask me to do more work on this!' So we sit in silence, trying to work out what to do with this story. 'Maybe,' I suggest, 'we should give each of the crew five blank pages and get them to write something.' Toni laughs. But at the moment, that doesn't seem such a bad idea.

Wednesday, 29 March 2000. Peckham

Doug calls me at home, where I'm wrestling with the script. School has too many distractions and the production office is starting to get a little crowded. All the producers share the same room, talking in hushed tones down the phone, hoping that no one will overhear the deals they're making or the problems they're trying to solve. But Doug has some good news. He's found a designer. 'Really? Who?' 'Well, he seems very keen on the project after reading the new script a couple of times. And you do like his work.' Now I can hear Doug smiling down the phone. 'It's Stephen. He wants back on.' I laugh. Part of me wants to say no, but I know that I'd be shooting myself in the foot. What's changed his mind, I wonder? Doug laughs as he hands the phone over to Stephen. As I welcome him back on board I try my best not to sound snide or gloating.

Monday, 3 April 2000. Soho

Industry screenings of the second-year films, again set up by the producers, this time in a plush Soho theatre. Lizzie Francke, director of the Edinburgh Film Festival, is there. I've worked at the festival for the last eight years and feel lucky that I can count on her as a friend. She enjoys *Simple Things* and tells me she wants to show it at the festival this year. Hey! Things are looking up. Channel Four has just acquired the film to show it in their shorts strand. Still, part of me thinks that Lizzie only likes the film because we are friends. She tells me to shut up.

Friday, 7 April 2000. Beaconsfield

Somebody once told me this story. A film director was picking his way through a war-torn landscape, looking for possible locations, when a local townsman came up and grabbed his arm. 'Please,' said the man, gasping back his tears, 'my home is destroyed and I have lost my family. I don't know whether they are alive or dead. My life has gone. Please help me.' The director takes his arm and looks into the man's eyes. 'You have nothing to worry about,' he says. 'Look at me. I start shooting in six weeks and I haven't even started casting.'

This is my ninth short film, my last at NFTS, and you'd think it would get easier. But no. We're now in pre-production: the scary time, the time I hate the most. Each department is bristling with questions. Design wants to know what to build, Camera wants to know the colours, Production wants to know the frame-rate. Everybody wants an answer from you, while you're still thinking up questions yourself. But answers are things that just come to you: when you're on the train, or brushing your teeth, or staring into space while your girlfriend's talking to you . . . Unfortunately, the decisions you take now will affect the whole shoot, and thus the finished film. An offhand remark is taken literally, and later when you ask why a certain department has done the things they've done, they refer you back to a brief conversation over a shared cigarette, and how you mentioned you didn't like the colour blue. Pre-production – it's like the first meal with your girlfriend's parents. Watch your words closely.

We're now on our seventh draft of the script, and I do feel it's still getting better. But meanwhile, events in the outside world can't be ignored. Two Leeds United football fans were stabbed to death in Turkey before the club's UEFA Cup tie with Galatasaray. Our film concerns the co-existence of Turkish and English communities in Green Lanes. Now the script may take on new and unexpected meanings. Under the circumstances, we will have to be clear about our standpoint and how it might be interpreted.

Monday, 10 April 2000. Beaconsfield

The school production office has now become a war zone, everybody fighting over computers, each deeming their task to be of greater worth than anybody else's. We have another new addition to our team, Alice Bell. Doug has brought her on board as a production assistant, and she's as keen as mustard. Together we go through the script, looking to anticipate possible location problems: she photocopies the London A–Z and marks out the area where we plan to shoot.

Monday, 17 April 2000. Green Lanes

Research trip: Toni has arranged for Doug and I to meet some local Turkish people she knows. We go to a snooker hall to watch the return leg of the Leeds v. Galatasaray tie. I am the only 'British' person there. Since the deaths of those two Leeds fans, the tabloid press has been making a big deal about this match: rampant xenophobia and blind fury are the order of the day. So it's hard for me not to feel slightly uneasy in this situation. But I needn't have worried: everybody is just there to watch the match. I chat with our guide about the local area. He tells me a bit about Turkish history, the struggle of the people in this area. Looking me in the eye, he asks me to be honest in making this film and treat people as I see them. 'Do not be so politically correct about everything. That is more offensive than honesty.'

Friday, 21 April 2000. Peckham

Today I turned 30. I started my education in film ten years ago. I had left school when I was 17, to work in a supermarket. After two months I knew I hated it, but it still took me two years to leave. In my spare time I played bass in a band in the small town where I lived. Eventually I applied to do Sound Engineering at the Perth Further Education College – it was an escape, and it beat getting into fights every Saturday night. Only I walked through the wrong door and ended up in a Media Studies class. The first real lesson was about video production, and, always having been interested in films, I thought, 'What the hell . . .' So, a decade later, here I am. Making my graduation film at the Best Film School in Britain (a distinction that could, of course, be disputed). As Vito Corleone says, 'How did things ever get so far?'

Right now there's pressure. The script still doesn't seem to be working. A month away from the shoot, the crew are tetchy. This is their graduation piece too, and the 'This is my career here' mentality is coming to the fore. It's up to me to allay their fears, but I'm starting to feel that they forget that this is my final piece as well. Meanwhile Andi leaves for Scotland tomorrow to work until the end of July. I'm proud of her, but selfishly I want her to stay here, so that I have someone to hug when my shoot falls apart.

Monday, 1 May 2000. Peckham

Toni comes over for one last (!?) script meeting. Both of us know this isn't going to be fun. For the last three days, I've been secretly rewriting her script. I feel bad about it; but my problem was that I still couldn't 'see' the film, and I thought that taking a bash at a rewrite might help me to find out what's really important to me in the story. So, after half an hour of carefully skirting around the subject, I show Toni what I've done. She looks hurt – then starts to read, shaking her head and roughly flipping the pages. 'Why did you write this? Why did you change this scene?' She defends certain scenes passionately, and we get to work together on the computer. After a while I feel like we've started to work on the real crux of the story. At the end of two hours, we have 14 strong pages, and we're friends again. We both agree that, come hell or high water, this script is locked. (Give or take a few small changes . . .)

Thursday, 4 May 2000. Soho

Doug has arranged a meeting with casting agent Sookie McShane. I never used casting agents before the NFTS. Scotland is quite small, and most of the actors I used were people I knew anyway. But casting is probably the most important set of decisions I will make on this film: the audience has to believe and like the characters from the word go. Thankfully Sookie likes the script – in fact, she seems to understand its meaning and subtext better than me. We talk through some suggestions, to help her envisage the type of actors we're looking for; and I start to feel like I'm in a scene from *The Player*. 'Well, I see Ray Winstone in this role . . .' She's brought along CVs of various actors, so Doug and I hum and ha over the 10 x 8" photos. Sookie suspects our choices could be limited, especially with the Turkish element to our script. Originally, I had hoped to cast non-professionals from the local community – I thought it would be a good challenge for me. But time is now against us, and anyway I'd like to make it a bit easier on myself. As the old adage goes, 'Ninety-nine per cent of good directing is good casting.'

Wednesday, 10 May 2000. Piccadilly, London W1

For our casting Miles has managed to get hold of a room at BAFTA headquarters, a rather plush location for our purposes. He sits and studies his schedule beneath an imposing photograph of Sir Richard Attenborough, while Toni, Doug and myself wait for the actors to appear. We are seeing about 16 people today, and we know we don't have time for recalls. I don't envy actors. This is only a small film, and yet still they turn up, all smiles, and are put on show for 15–20 minutes. I always try to be as courteous to them as I can. But at the end of the day it's about who I feel I can work with.

The morning doesn't bode well. We see nine or so people, but nobody seems to fit. Over lunch we look back over their photos, placing them in different combinations, asking the needful questions. 'Can these two look like a couple? Do you think you could get a performance out of this one?' *Et cetera* . . . Luckily the first candidate of the afternoon session is Nitzan Sharron. He reads really well, and he listens to Toni and I very intently as we talk about the character of Hashmet, offering his own suggestions along the way. I place a big red tick beside his name. Toni isn't so sure: Nitzan isn't Turkish. But she agrees that he's the best we have seen.

We manage to agree on the next two parts too. Emily Hillier gives a great reading for the part of Lizzie, Archie's girlfriend. And Vic Tablian blows in like a hurricane, regaling us with tales of working with Alan Parker (*Midnight Express*) and Steven Spielberg (*Raiders of the Lost Ark*). He says he'll take the part of Mr Talek, Hashmet's dad. Looking me straight in the eye, he says he does everything in one take. My feeling is that he could be hard work, but that it could be well worth it. After that, our main worry is that we still don't have an Archie. Until, that is, we see the last actor of the day. Roland Manookian walks in, head held high, and gives a great reading. He's seen the script, and he talks in depth about the story. As he closes the door behind him, we kneel on the floor and bow in his general direction.

Friday, 12 May 2000. Piccadilly

The last day of casting, so I gave myself a treat. Today we met Tony Selby, an actor who has worked with all my heroes: Alan Clarke (*The Gentleman Caller*), Ken Loach (*Up the Junction*), Lindsay Anderson at the Royal Court. We talked about the script for an hour, then he fed me some stories of 'Clarkey' and 'Ken'. By now he'd already agreed to be in our short and I didn't want the meeting to end. Later we stood at the BAFTA bar, watching him re-enact a number from *Oklahoma*. I had to laugh at the surrealism of it all.

Roland Manookian (Archie). © Zoë Norfolk, 2000

After he left, I gave Doug a big smile, and he told me it was the first time I'd done that in weeks.

Friday, 19 May 2000. Green Lanes

The second day of rehearsal. Yesterday Roland, Nitzan and myself went up to Green Lanes and sat in a pub for most of the day, just talking and finding out about each other. I always spend the first day of rehearsal like that. The first time I tried out this method, I had no intention of drinking myself: I thought I would sit back and let the actors slowly get to know and 'reveal' each other. Unfortunately, they were a lot cleverer than that, and by the end of the night it was them pouring me into a taxi and making sure I got home all right. So I don't know how beneficial it is, but I do think it creates a bond between the actors and myself. As for today, we read through the scenes and talked about the relationship between Archie and Hashmet. Great. Now all that's left is to shoot it.

Saturday, 20 May 2000. Green Lanes
Scouting for locations with Vita Gottlieb, the AD. I try to tell her what kind of shots we hope to achieve, but then the shot list isn't finalized yet, and truthfully my heart isn't in it. I still can't see the film yet, so it's hard for me to imagine how I'll be blocking the actors. Gav has begun work on a rough storyboard, and I keep calling him up during the recce to ask his opinion on the questions that Vita continually asks me. A recent NFTS graduate I know is having a barbecue in the neighbouring vicinity, so as soon as we're finished I head off to that. Various people I haven't seen since they left school are there, all wanting to know how the graduation film is going. I rely on the stock answers. ('Oh, getting there. Should be fun . . .') When I tell them I start shooting in two days, their jaws drop. 'What are you doing here? Shouldn't you be at home sweating?' No, I tell them. If I'm not prepared now, then I never will be. This probably comes over as supreme confidence. And the truth? I'm not prepared now, and I never will be.

Sunday, 21 May 2000. Beaconsfield
I take the train to school, laden down with bags of clean clothes. I plan to stay at the school for the next three days. There's a caravan in the car park, nicknamed 'Rosebud Cottage', and mostly used by editors and sound people. Two rooms with three beds in each, linen not supplied. The set is a hive of activity. In the two rooms that Stephen has built, people I've never seen before are feverishly painting, peeling, or smoking. Things are looking good – except that they're not finished. The main set, the Taleks' kitchen and living room, hasn't even been dressed yet. Gav is angry because he wanted to pre-light. This rubs off on me, so I start to raise my voice at Doug. I don't think even he believes his own reassurances. I enquire about progress on the third set, and Doug tells me it hasn't even been thought of yet. I'm about to say something harsh when I notice that he is covered in paint and has a brush in hand. I storm off and find Rob, beaming with pride as he wanders around the grounds pushing his sound trolley. I have to laugh. The thing is covered in equipment: boom poles protrude from the front like some medieval torture device. I challenge him to a race round the college.

Later I eat with Gav and Doug. Doug berates me for failing to thank everybody who helped out on the set. I have no answer to that. Meanwhile Gav adds his voice to the complaints about the unfinished sets. Twelve hours before turnover and already there's tension in the air. Some people thrive on it. Not me.

Monday, 22 May 2000. Beaconsfield

Two scenes to shoot today, both of them set in a bedroom that Archie shares with his older brother Gary (Perry Blanks). The first will go near the beginning of the film: Archie and Lizzie are 'getting it on' only to be disturbed by Gary. It's a scene that establishes the frustration of Archie's domestic set-up, why he wants to move out. The second scene is near the end: Archie has broken up with Lizzie, and his anger boils over in a clash with his brother, in which he comes off second best. All nice and easy on paper – except that I decide to throw the storyboards out of the window. Sod it – everybody else is trying out new things, why not me? Rob's got his trolley, his radio mikes, *et cetera*. Gav has employed a camera operator. So where's my fun? (Oh I forgot – I'm the director.) Probably not the best timing for this decision, but when I watched the action through, it just felt like the camera was in the wrong place. So we moved it.

All in all, a good day. Ali shows up on set, probably to make sure we aren't getting carried away with ourselves. Roland and Emily play off each other nicely – a little too nicely, maybe. I ask Roland how much acting went into their screen kisses. He just smiles and winks. An hour after we wrap, Stephen is still working on the main set. I nearly offer to help, but decide that it's his responsibility – too many cooks, and all that. I feel resentful towards him, maybe unfairly. I do offer to buy him a pub lunch but he declines. 'Too much work to do!' I nod, a bit too readily.

Later on in the caravan, Gav wants a quiet word. He is worried about the working dynamic between him, me and Richard Stoddard the operator. Apparently I wasn't including Gav in decisions about the shots. In my defence, I've never worked with both an operator and a DoP before, so my instinct is to turn to the person behind the camera: in this case, Richard. Gav understands this – he just wants to be more involved in the shot choices. So, another note to myself. Around midnight I pop off to the bathroom. There is still light coming from the main stage – Stephen rearranging furniture around the set. It still doesn't look finished. Watching him work towards an unachievable deadline, I feel bad for being so short with him earlier on. Though my sympathy stops at the point where I ought to go and help him.

Tuesday, 23 May 2000. Beaconsfield

Today's plan is to shoot a four-page scene, a bitter altercation between Archie and Hashmet in front of Mr Talek. It's basically the turning point of the whole film, and it's meant to happen on the set that Stephen hasn't finished yet. An 8am call for turnover at 9, and everybody arrives on time, including the actors, Nitzan, Roland and Vic Tablian. But I ask costume and make-up to take their time with them while I try to find out what is happening on set. Stephen needs

Nightmare on Day 2: from left, Julian White (gaffer), Nitzan Sharron (Hashmet), Gavin Struthers, FM and Vic Tablian (Mr Talek). © Zoë Norfolk, 2000

at least another half an hour to dress it, and Gav is eager to get on with lighting. Vita and I try and work out a shot list, but it's hard because I haven't seen the action yet. The sparks and the art department are tripping over each other, and tempers are getting frayed, so I ask them to leave the set temporarily while we figure out a revised schedule. Then I call in the actors, and we block the scene roughly, trying out some basic movements for the fight.

I had wanted to set aside a whole day for this tough scene, so as to take things nice and easy. Now we have about four hours to nail it. We make the shots wide, to take in as much of the action as possible. I try to pull back so that the need for focus-marks is kept to a minimum. It starts to feel more staged than I had hoped for. We decide to shoot all the angles looking down the set first, and then do the reverses. This means I have to ensure the actors keep their motivation up from the first slate to the last. I opt to start with a long track that will establish the location, bring Roland into the scene, and get him sat at the Taleks' kitchen table. That shot alone will cover most of the first half of the scene. The only problem is that it's probably the most difficult shot of the day, and I've now decided to do it first.

By now we're an hour and a half past the point when we were supposed to turn over; and still at least another hour away from being ready. I run away from the chaos on set, and sit with the actors in make-up. Ali pops in with yesterday's rushes. We have two 'soft' shots. Gav and I watch the tapes to gauge just how bad these are. It's not good – the scene was one continuous handheld shot, yet the suspect moments are on a stationary close-up of Roland. The focus is right on the edge: none of us can tell how this will be affected in the blow-up from Super-16 to 35mm. Doug comes and has a look. We work out a strategy for a re-shoot tomorrow, our last day on the stage. I think I can pick up a close-up, because there's a cutting point in the hand-held stuff. Yet this will break the continuity of the shot. Doug smiles: problem solved. Except, I point out, that we haven't started turning over today.

Finally at 12.30 we're ready to go for a run through in front of camera. The atmosphere is fraught. Everybody is looking for someone to blame. We turn over, and eight takes later the gate is checked. This actually feels terrible. Vic tries to leaven the mood with his Spielberg and Parker stories– not really what I want to hear at the moment. We call 'Lunch!' and I disappear into Ali's edit suite to look at yesterday's rushes. He seems happy, having cut a rough assembly of the two scenes. Watching them cheers me up – Roland and Emily have great screen presence together, and each scene seems to achieve what I set out to do. So far, so good.

After lunch, though, we're back to struggling up the hill. The crew have lost any momentum they had. I start discarding shots, and get the list down to just eight set-ups. The atmosphere starts to affect the actors, which means that we shoot more takes and so lose the time we thought we had saved. I find myself thinking of ways to just cover the action and get the scene in the can. (Only the second day, and I'm already acting like a jobbing director . . .) Toni is here, watching the afternoon's progress silently, and I feel guilty for fucking up this scene. But after we wrap, she gives me a sympathetic hug. Then Gav convenes a meeting of all main crew members, to establish exactly what happened today. I see Vita making herself smaller in the corner. She blames herself, offers to quit. I stick by her and try to cheer her up. Besides, where am I going to get another AD at this short notice? (This raises a smile at least.) Rob hands me a Mars bar, and I realize I haven't eaten all day. I ask him how he guessed, and he tells me he could hear my stomach rumbling through his headphones. In fact, he recorded it.

I resolve not to make a repeat of today's events. Whatever problems arise, the focal point for the crew is me, so I must have focus – even if I have to fake it.

Wednesday, 24 May 2000. Beaconsfield

This morning we duly re-shoot those 'soft' shots of Roland. I stand in for Perry, and the shot is framed over my shoulder. That takes all of 30 minutes. Then we hang around, waiting for Stephen to finish today's set – a housing office where Archie is interviewed about his application for council tenancy. Stephen has

Day 3, and bad news of ratio trouble: FM with Alastair ('Ali') Reid.
© Zoë Norfolk, 2000

commandeered an office space in the school's administration block. He is busy constructing the false walls when he's stopped by a staff member, demanding to know who gave him permission to build in here. They're upset about all the drilling and hammering going on. Doug and I try to reassure them that the work will only take an hour or two to finish, and Stephen presses on regardless.

Just before lunch, Ali and Gav approach me. There seems to be a 'slight' problem with the rushes. We're meant to be shooting at 1:1:85, but boom poles and ceiling pieces are clearly visible in shot. Richard is adamant that he framed correctly. I agree with him: the image looked fine on the video-assist. The rushes must have been transferred at the wrong ratio. Ali phones the labs to check.

The set is finished before lunch and we do a quick run through. Gav and I decide the shots: 12 in all, more than we did yesterday, but at least they're all locked off. As soon as we start turning over, the atmosphere feels good. Vita is smiling again and the crew seems to be working as a unit. We cover the whole scene in every shot, playing around with the focal lengths. Stephen's set looks great – it's the simplest one he's made, yet it feels like the most dynamic. (Funny, that . . .) We wrap after three hours, and everybody seems to know it's been a good day.

Tomorrow we go on location for the rest of the shoot, so we start packing the vans for the move. Then Ali comes to see us. There's a problem. A big one. It turns out that the masking plate in the camera's eyepiece is wrong. The lab have been transferring the rushes at 1:1:85. But that's not what we've been shooting. Using the masking on the Avid, Ali works out that we are shooting at a ratio of 1:2:47 a ratio that doesn't exist, basically. If we decide to carry on shooting at this ratio, we might not be able to get a print. But if we switch back to 1:1:85, that means re-shooting all of the last three days – everything that has been shot on set, a set which has to be pulled down tonight, as another graduation project starts building on the stage tomorrow. Selfishly, I don't want to go through the nightmare of yesterday again. But in fact we don't really have a choice anyway. We will have to carry on shooting with our newly invented ratio. A mask will have to be made in the printing so as to make our frame. All of this will cost money that we don't really have, by Doug's estimate. So Stephen begins dismantling the main set, and I try to help him – only I use my feet instead of a hammer.

Ali drives me back to London and we get something to eat. The rushes are good, he's been having fun with them, but the fight scene we shot on Tuesday could prove to be a problem. I hope I covered it well enough to tell the story, but will that be enough? My mobile rings. It's Gav, and he's not happy. He has just arrived at the unit base in Green Lanes and there's no electricity. Unfortunately, two of his crew are meant to be staying there for the duration of the shoot. Gav blames Doug and threatens to walk from the production. I then phone Doug, who loses his temper with me, and we have a half-hour shouting match down

Doug ('I want this done yesterday') Ray, producer. © Zoë Norfolk, 2000

our cell phones. Nothing is resolved. It feels that this is more between Doug and Gav, producer and cinematographer; and the politics of the shoot mean that I'm getting dragged into this petty rivalry. I tell Doug I want a meeting with him and Gav first thing tomorrow. This can't go on. I sit on the number 12 bus home, fuming. It's crowded, but nobody sits next to me.

Thursday, 25 May 2000. Green Lanes

I get up around 6.30am and leave for the location. Travelling from Peckham in SE15 to the other side of London means an hour of buses and tubes. So I sit staring at adverts, still angry about last night. By the time I get to Green Lanes, the sun is out and the air is beginning to warm up. Neither Gav nor Doug are at the production base, so I buy coffee for Julian and Steve, the two guys who had to stay the night without electricity. It seems that the house is on a card meter. You just buy a fixed amount of electricity, slot in the card, and hey presto – light and hot water. But nobody told Doug: a simple mistake blown out of all proportions.

Gav duly turns up, all smiles. It seems he and Doug sorted it out. I'm still not happy about getting dragged into it, but I let it pass. Sometimes I think I give up too soon, because I dislike confrontation. Is it best to stamp your feet on set and act the mini-dictator? No matter how much you do that, you can't get away from the fact that this is a student shoot. Yes, we all try to work as professionally as we can, but we're not professionals – we're not getting paid for this.

The pub scene: Nitzan Sharron, Roland Manookian and Andy Dennehey.
© Zoë Norfolk, 2000

Antonia ('Toni') Baldo, writer. © Zoë Norfolk, 2000

Because of that, I think we tend to overcompensate. How many times on a student shoot do you hear the argument that starts 'Yes, but in the real world . . .'?

The day's work goes well: a bar scene with a few dozen extras and three characters, Roland, Nitzan and Andy Dennehy, who plays 'Fat Pat'. A Londoner with racist views, 'Pat' believes the Turks have no right to be here, and that they bend the system to accommodate their own needs, so making it difficult for 'proper Londoners'.

I learn that there were some scratches on the rushes from yesterday. That makes three things gone wrong in the first three days. It's good to be consistent.

Friday, 26 May 2000. Green Lanes

I wake up to find that my mobile has been cut off. My holiday pay from the cinema has been and gone. I have no money until 1 June when my bursary comes in. So it's official – I am poor.

Two scenes today: one in a Turkish restaurant, the other in Finsbury Park at night. The restaurant proves simple. We lay a long track down the middle of the floor and join Archie and Hashmet halfway through their conversation. Then I just pick up the rest of the scene in singles. Again I make sure that the actors play out the entire scene in each take. Film stock is only film stock: and I'm after the best performances I can get.

Over lunch I go through tonight's business with Gav and Julian the gaffer. It's a massive lighting set-up, and Julian has managed to wangle a 50kW generator. They will need about three hours to set up, and another hour for tweaking after it gets dark. So that leaves me about an hour and a half to get the scene. 'How many shots?' asks Vita. Six – maybe seven? Tight.

Afterwards, I repair to the base to rehearse the park scene with Roland and Emily. The action is clear: Archie tries to initiate sex with Lizzie, *al fresco*, as it were; she is upset, and they break up. But we want to show something deeper. Having just heard Mr Talek promise to help Hashmet find a place to live, Archie has started to believe the racist views of others around him, and his desperation is coming to a head. He wants to get closer to Lizzie, but he makes all the wrong decisions, not just in what he says, but where he puts his hands – his forceful nature.

As rain starts to fall hard outside, we try out some improvisation and various costumes. Eventually I lose track of time, and try to call the crew. But nobody seems to be answering at the location, which is a mile and a half away. We sit tight. Roland treats Emily to some energetic impressions of what's been going on with the shoot in her absence, most of which is news to me. (Caught up in my own wee world . . .) Soon it's 10.55pm. Finally Miles turns up outside in the people carrier. We drive to Finsbury Park in the rain, Miles' walkie-talkie intermittently crackling with anxious voices. As we round the last corner we see

Panic in Finsbury Park: FM, Vita Gottlieb (AD) and Richard Stoddard (camera operator). © Zoë Norfolk, 2000

Emily Hillier (Lizzie). © Zoë Norfolk, 2000

the trees and pavilion lit up like Christmas. From the combined effect of the car, the walkies and the waiting crew, I get a slight buzz. Is this what it's like? Images of Winnebagos and personal assistants enter my head. Walking up the red carpet at Grauman's Chinese Theater under the pencil beam of a spotlight . . .

'So – what's the shot?' asks Gav. And in an instant I'm back to a rainy Friday in north London with a pissed-off crew who have been working in the wet for the last two hours. A group of local spectators has formed, attracted by the big lights. I overhear them 'ooh' and 'ah'. 'Which one is the director?' they ask Julian. 'Him over there, with the dry clothes!' he replies. And with that I fling myself into the scene.

Saturday, 27 May 2000. Green Lanes

We wrapped around 1am last night, so it's a late call today. We've managed to blag a crane for the sake of a single shot to use in the film's opening. The camera starts high above the houses and swoops down to ground level, as our heroes run towards us down the lane and turn into an alleyway. It's complicated so we do numerous run-throughs, with various crew members standing in, just to see how fit we really are. (If we were racehorses, most of us would probably be shot.) Eventually Gav thinks he has got the pace of the actors' run matched to his grasp of the hothead controls and we go for a take.

Six takes later, we still haven't got it, and Roland is nearly sick in the alley. We break for ten minutes to let the actors catch their breath – and then the heavens open. Hail descends on us, and I run to the car while the crew cover the equipment with whatever they have to hand. The shower lasts for ten minutes, but any chance of further shooting is gone. The ground is soaked, so the continuity will be wrong. Besides, after that hailstorm we're all expecting further showers of frogs and locusts. Somebody definitely does not want this film made. So with the afternoon off, I go and watch some football with friends I haven't seen since all of this started. Making films is fun. Spending time away from them is, at the moment, absolute bliss.

Monday, 29 May 2000. Green Lanes

After a day and a half off, everybody seems fairly refreshed. Or maybe it's because the end is now in sight. The good thing about our schedule is that we're never in the same place twice, so new locations each day present new challenges. Today we're in a fruit-seller's shop for three scenes, mainly between Roland and Tony Selby. Stephen pops by to check the location. It's his last day on the shoot, as he's about to go work on the Harry Potter film, and wants some time off beforehand. We say our goodbyes. I'm not sure there's any love lost between us. Good on him, though. He's managed to get what he wants, and I wish him well.

Craning on Green Lanes, before the heavens opened. © Zoë Norfolk, 2000

It's funny that the disciplines that create the most 'hassle' during pre-production are probably the ones that offer the best chance of postgraduate employment. Within the art departments of movies there are so many positions that need filling: art director, stand-by, assistant. It may not be designing *per se*, but it's a start. But directors and writers are really only trained for one job. Sure, you might find work as an assistant or a script reader, but is that really putting your training to the test? If I'm honest, it's not why I spent the last ten years in education. Even now I'm not sure I could cut it as an AD. For one thing, I'm not the world's best-organized person. And for another, well . . . there is a wee bit of pride left in me.

Tuesday, 30 May 2000. Green Lanes

Today we get our first look at the Steadicam. I'm in awe of this fabled contraption, partly for its futuristic look, but mainly for how it will allow our actors to move about without fear of marks and focus. As Richard straps it to his breastplate, we enthuse about some of the great Steadicam operators in cinema and their best-known shots, from *Goodfellas* to *The Shining*. I ask Richard if he has seen Alan Clarke's *Road*, and he appreciates the reference. I hand him a T-shirt that Andrea got from her last job: a gift from Roger Tooley, probably the best Steadicam operator in Britain at the moment. Richard's eyes light up. I tell him he has to wear it every time we use the Steadicam, and he readily agrees.

On Green Lanes. (Johnny English's first name isn't 'Johnny', nor is his surname 'English'. Makes you think . . .) © Zoë Norfolk, 2000

Tony Selby (Archie's dad). © Zoë Norfolk, 2000

We're shooting the very opening of the film: no dialogue, just the two boys running down the street. Ali calls. He has seen the last two days' rushes, including the crane, and he reckons everything should be okay. Luckily, the continuity of the weather seems to be holding, so the crane shot looks like it's in after all, which delights Gav. 'That shot is just pure cinema!' he tells me. This is Gav's scene, really. My job here is just to tell the actors to run faster or slower, turn right past camera, *et cetera*; with one eye on how it will all cut together. I have a tune running through my head for this sequence: 'Teenage Kicks' by The Undertones. It just seems to fit . . .

The video assist has broken down, and there's no way of looking through the eyepiece as Richard is running backwards at full speed in front of Roland and Nitzan. We shoot from about eight angles, the camera constantly moving. At one point the Steadicam is in the people carrier, looking out of an open side door. As Green Lanes is a major thoroughfare, this proves to be a logistical nightmare and we are hostage to the sequence of traffic lights and the build-up of traffic. At least the locals seemed to be used to us by now. A couple of them stand in as extras to help with the continuity of the cutting points. They laugh and smile after I thank them for their time. 'It's gonna be on telly, yeah?' they ask. Doug quickly answers, 'Yes' and they walk away happy. The promise of a blink-and-you'll-miss-it TV appearance seems to make their day.

After lunch we move to shoot the next scene on Pemberton Road, a residential street just off the main drag. Curtains twitch and front doors open. A lovely old Greek lady comes out and starts talking to Vic. I tell her about our film, and she clucks her tongue every time I mention the Turkish element. 'It used to be Greek, you know. But everyone moved out just as soon as the bloody Turks came in.' I smile and nod as best I can. So much tension in this area, among young and old alike. I try and concentrate on the scene, but by the end of the third take the Lovely Old Lady is bringing out coffee and biscuits for everyone. For the crew, that means Down Tools. 'Well,' they argue, 'you've got to keep the locals happy.'

I have a sudden flashback to my schooldays. One day our class, having just read about the Russian Revolution in History and got ourselves totally hyped up about the power of the people, went into a Maths class and refused to take any part whatsoever in a lesson about algebra. The teacher, after 20 minutes of trying to stamp her authority on us, ran off in tears. Now, at this moment, funny though it is, I understand how she must have felt about that loss of control and, more importantly, respect. I received 12 lashes of the belt for my part in that insurrection. Today I just sit down by the kerbside and pray the light doesn't go.

Wednesday, 31 May 2000. Green Lanes

The last day of the shoot, and it's a big one: three scenes, all exteriors. The first is probably the hardest: Roland has to break down and cry convincingly, having been hit by Hashmet in the previous scene after spouting forth racist views ('I'm not a fucking Turk like your old man, no-one's looking out for me'). This scene is important because we have to regain some sympathy for Roland. Some people think scenes like these are a test of a director's mettle. Can she/ he delve into an actor's emotions and bring out all the hurt that's been bubbling down beneath the surface? I've heard of sadistic directors who have verbally abused actors to get the desired results; I've even read of directors getting physical, Sidney Lumet, for instance, something they have later regretted. I can't see myself deriding Roland in public, slapping his face, kicking his shins. (Certainly not on the money we're paying him.) Yes, you want it to be believable. But actors have their own techniques for this stuff. As a director you just hope that the character arc has been sufficiently built up so that the actor knows instinctively how much emotion to unleash.

So I ask the crew just to give Roland his space, lay off the jokes, and let him be for a while. He and I sit and talk about nothing in particular until I find myself being more and more detached from him. So I leave him to sit on his own for five or ten minutes. Then we call for a take, no rehearsal. Roland runs down the alley and hits his mark. He stops, kicks the wall, and slumps to the ground, tears flowing from his eyes. I quietly ask the camera to cut, and we move in for a close up. Roland curls up, sobbing louder. Rob gestures frantically, to indicate that we can't go for a take. But I don't want to stop Roland so I decide to shoot him mute for a minute – one that seems to go on for ever. Then I ask the camera team to check the gate. Roland, still crying, walks with me away from the crew. We sit down at the other end of the alleyway and share a cigarette. Wiping the tears from his eyes he beams and says, 'Thanks Fraser, I needed that.'

Afterwards I ask Rob what the sound problem was, and he points down to his trolley. One of the wheels is flat – he couldn't move it close enough to Roland to get a mike in. I try not to laugh, because I don't think Rob finds it funny. Switching my mobile phone back on, I see that I've missed a call from my dad. When I call him back, he tells me that Mum has gone into hospital. I look up at the crew, preparing for lunch, and realize that I don't want to be here. But I know that I can't leave. I tell Dad I can be in Scotland first thing tomorrow. 'No need,' he says, 'it could just be routine . . .' But I was planning to see Andrea in Edinburgh for the weekend in any case, so we agree I will see them then.

After lunch we shoot what will be the last scene of the film, a kind of uneasy reconciliation between Archie and Hashmet. Toni and I have never managed to get this quite right on paper, and now the dialogue (though minimal) is not the same as when we rehearsed. Roland is upset. He doesn't think that this ending does justice to the film, mainly because he feels Archie's lines ('We've lived in Green Lanes all our life, ever since it's been green') are both lame and weighty, placing too much emphasis on something that isn't really there. Trouble is, Roland can't think what should be there instead. I secretly agree with him. Toni is on set and tries to explain to Roland what she was getting at, but he still doesn't agree. The crew waits for us to make a decision. Ian Sellar is here to watch, and I ask his advice, but he's as stumped as me. So we shoot, and I ask Nitzan and Roland to elongate their pauses and bring some awkwardness to it, knowing that if I can capture looks and glances then I can manage without the dialogue. We manage to get the scene before the light disappears. But I feel thrown off by the events of today. I'm starting to think that I've failed – that the story, and hence the film, just doesn't work. Fine acting, yes. Well shot, yes. But what else?

The very last scene to shoot is a long two-minute Steadicam sequence with about a page and a half of dialogue, set on the main drag of Green Lanes just as the pubs are coming out. Cars pass by tooting their horns, people offer us fights, and we struggle to cover the scene. Vic Tablian has to contend with the sound of hardcore techno beating out of the pub next door to the location. I get aggressive with drunken onlookers who shout during takes. In fact, my eye is so completely off the ball, I'm not even in the stadium. Once I hear the gate is clear, I walk away, not wanting to speak to anyone. Nobody cheers. There is just a sense of relief that this whole thing is over.

Back at the production base Doug has bought a crate of beer, but nobody really wants to drink. He comes up to me, all smiles. 'That's that, then.' For you maybe, I think. But I've got to live with this for the next four months, watching it daily with Ali, trying to explain what went wrong. Slowly everyone heads home, after agreeing to meet up for a wrap party tomorrow night.

Thursday, 1 June 2000. Beaconsfield

Back to school to view last night's rushes. The first person I meet is Ian Sellar, who has seen them already and sounds upbeat. Somehow I don't believe him. In the editing corridor I run into a fellow director. He was shooting about the same time as me, and we compare horror stories of our experiences, each trying to outdo the other, both of us thinking, 'Hope my film is better than yours!'

Ali shows me what he's cut together so far. Then, as we watch yesterday's rushes, I tell him about the nightmare experience I felt I'd had. He keeps his eye on the screen, pausing the Avid every now and then to look for cutting points. 'Should be all right,' he says. Our first real worry is with some of the acting, which seems inconsistent with the rest of the film.

Ali feels that the opening of the film should definitely be cut to music, and advises that I get Tara Crème, the composer, to come in and have a look. We spend the rest of the day watching the tapes and doing a paper edit. Every time something bad comes up on screen, I remember exactly why it happened, and wonder why I let it happen. Ali is only working on the film for the next two days, then he goes off for a month to cut a documentary. He asks me if I want to take VHS tapes of the rushes home with me? I shake my head – I don't want to see the mistakes over and over again. We leave for the wrap party in a crowded bar in Soho. Most of the crew turns up and, since I got my bursary this morning, I buy a round and then nearly have a heart attack at the price the barman quotes me.

Friday, 2 June 2000. Edinburgh
It feels good to be back in Scotland. Andi meets me at the train station, looking radiant. I'm looking forward to seeing my family, my friends, and my old home-town. For the moment at least, Green Lanes feels like a thousand miles away.

Wednesday, 7 June 2000. Edinburgh
Once again I have no money. I've paid my bills and had two nights out, and that's it, bursary gone. Not that Edinburgh is a bad place to be broke – I spent eight years here in a similar situation. But one day I hope to make a film and still have a little money to spend at the end of it. It gets to you after a while, being poor. Sometimes there seems no end to the tunnel. And of course the bank isn't as understanding as they make out in their adverts.

I didn't set out making films because I wanted to be rich. I wanted to say things, comment on life. The biggest budget I've ever had was £50,000, and I felt guilty about that – it was twice my father's salary at the time. How many student teachers, nurses or doctors could that money have helped? And yet I reasoned to myself that the film was important, because it was commenting on an aspect of society. My payment out of that budget was less than 2 per cent, but it was a lot to me at the time, and it still is. Now I feel like I would do anything for the cash, and I hate myself for feeling that way. Has film school done this to me? Or is it just the properly realistic point of view?

I believe that education is a right: one of the last-surviving socialist ethics, albeit one that has been steadily eroded by right-leaning governments, with courses in the arts suffering more than most. I also believe that education should be free. Tuition fees were introduced at the NFTS over the last four years. However dis-tasteful, it was deemed necessary for the school to survive. Luckily my fees have been sponsored by Canal Plus, though I've still managed to rack up a medium-sized debt, even though I work part-time. I understand that my chosen vocation is an elite form of education, and that the rewards upon graduation can be quite high. The trouble is that the NFTS, and many other film courses, demand a level of financial investment that can deter the poorer prospective students. So you get a domino effect – the film school graduates of the future are liable to have experienced less struggle and hardship through their backgrounds. Surely this will affect the kinds of stories they want to tell?

Monday, 19 June 2000. Beaconsfield

Back into the edit suite. Ali is on a health kick, so he sets some ground rules. No smoking in the suite. No pub lunches. No chocolate bars and other such confectionery, especially when the cut is going badly. I draw the line at his suggestion of a five-mile run; but we go to the local supermarket to buy healthy food for lunch. There's a set of scales at the entrance, and I challenge Ali to see who is heavier. I come in at 18 stone, which beggars belief. Yes, I've got a beer belly. But 18 stone? Twenty minutes later I realize that Ali had his foot on the bottom of the scales. And so we begin. The good news about Ali is that he's a friend: I can be honest with him. The trouble is that I don't yet feel sufficiently distanced from the shoot. Every time I look at a take I see the problems that we encountered. There's an old saying, 'Live with it, make it better', but right now I'm not hearing it.

Thursday, 22 June 2000. Beaconsfield

We've managed to get an assembly together, running at about 17 minutes. Now for the real work. Ali and I have to start trimming and refining individual scenes. We need to put music down over the opening of Roland and Nitzan diving about the streets; and since we're both going through a retro-punk phase we try everything from The Clash to The Selector. Then I mention to Ali about 'Teenage Kicks' and we try that for size. It works – too well, in fact. Ali shakes his head. 'We can't use this. It would cost us a bomb.' Various people come in to have a look, and all have the same response: 'Looks great. But you're not going to use that music, are you?' Still, we leave it on the soundtrack for the time being, just because it cheers us up. Then David Mingay, the Head of Editing, drops by. He's bringing in a professional editor to help oversee all the graduation productions. Sure, the more the merrier. We play him the opening and he smirks. 'You're not going to use "Teenage Kicks" are you?'

Sunday, 2 July 2000. Beaconsfield

The novelty of 'Teenage Kicks' wore off about three days ago. We took it off the soundtrack, and I realized that I hate the film. There's no emotion in it whatsoever. I resent myself for not being bold enough during the development and shooting. It feels like we just went through the mechanics of storytelling without adding any dressing. Now all my ideas seem tame and groundless. I think it's become a chore for Ali too. Our laughter of ten days ago has dwindled down into snide remarks and sarcastic comments. I keep feeling that he has better things to do, and wants to get on to them a.s.a.p. George Akers is in helping us most days. He's an experienced editor (from *Caravaggio* to *Carrington* and many others) but while some of his suggestions are helpful, Ali seems to think that I listen to George more than to him. Truth is, I would listen to anyone at the moment to make this film work. I don't believe in it anymore. The worst thing for me is to be writing this down, and yet still be unable to do anything about it. I don't see anything of myself in the film. But clearly it's because of me that it doesn't work. I decide to take a couple of days away from the edit to try and clear my head.

Thursday, 20 July 2000. Green Lanes

Well, here I am again with Gav and Roland. Two days ago we looked at the cut, and after much discussion it was felt that we needed a couple of extra scenes to plaster over the cracks. We're shooting Roland on his own, hence the skeleton crew. Roland asks me about the progress of the edit, and I assure him it's going okay. But somehow I think he sees through the bullshit. These scenes are just to add some breathing space to the film, to help some of the emotion of Roland's character come through. They're slightly cheesy, a bit clichéd, but if I have to hit the nail on the head to make the film better, then needs must. Later, back at Gav's flat, he asks me if we got all we needed. I just shrug, and that pisses him off. I guess what he wants is a firm answer. When I'm so obviously down on the film then it's bound to rub off on the crew, and they probably resent me for that. 'I think we've made a good film, Fraser,' says Gav as he shows me to the door. 'I just don't think we've found it yet.'

Wednesday, 26 July 2000. Beaconsfield

Andi drove back from Scotland last night and arrived in London around 3.30am. I reluctantly got out of bed to go to school. It's the last day of the summer term, and we're supposed to have a locked-off cut. The extra scenes are now in the film, and their main effect has been to make it longer. Ali and I sit watching the cut with Ian Sellar, Rob Ritchie and David Mingay, plus Gav, Doug and Rob. When it's over, there is that awful silence. Lips are pursed, chins are stroked. I swear I can see tumbleweed drifting between us. The consensus is that it's a film, but . . .

But what? There's no answer to that, so we walk out at the end still unsure whether or not the picture is locked. Later that night I get a phone call from Ian. He thinks it can get better. 'Can you tell me how, Ian?' I ask. We agree to leave it for a month, until school restarts. Maybe the solution will become apparent to fresh pairs of eyes.

Wednesday, 2 August 2000. Rhodes, Greece

Andrea decided that we needed a holiday. I don't have any money, but she determinedly offered to pay for me. We had to move fast, as the Edinburgh Film Festival starts in week. I've worked there for the last eight years and have an unnatural loyalty to the event. This year, Lizzie Francke wants me to chair some Q&A sessions with directors, and generally hang about a bit more. 'It's important for you, Fraser,' she chides me. 'And we are playing your film.' But first, to Greece. I resolve to relax, and bring some Faber and Faber film books out with me in the hope of inspiration: Christopher Frayling's weighty tome *Sergio Leone*, Milos Forman's autobiography *Turnaround*. Andrea takes *Harry Potter* and I spend most of the week reading that, much to her annoyance. At night, we eat out and talk about the future, me toasting Andrea's success, and she promising that mine will appear soon. This sentiment helps me to forget about the recent letters from my bank, which I've decided to ignore anyway.

Saturday, 12 August 2000. Edinburgh

In the bar of Edinburgh's Filmhouse, I get a phone call from my friend Sigvaldi Karrson, who's arriving in two days' time. 'Ziggy' was my editor in first year at NFTS. Back then he was asked to cut two features at home in Iceland: *Angels of the Universe* and *101 Reykjavik*. Now they're both playing at Edinburgh. My chest swells with pride. In the meantime I have agreed for the duration of the Festival to act as Lizzie's PA (or as I quickly become known, her 'bitch'). I know it's going to be a rough fortnight. But at least Damien O'Donnell, director of *East is East*, has shown up. We got close last year through some shared bouts of drinking. I persuade him to stay for the entire fortnight (not a hard job, I might add), so that he can judge the Short Film Award.

Monday, 14 August 2000. Edinburgh

The Festival is taking its toll. Despite my penury, the temptation to drink and be merry is too great. I had my first altercation with a film-maker today – a short film-maker, I might add (that is, a maker of short films). He complained that his film wasn't getting enough coverage, and that the colours didn't look right. I've had enough Festival experience in varying capacities to know that the people who complain the most are always the short film-makers. I have long promised myself not to treat people with contempt, to try and understand every problem. But, truth be told, most of the time the ones who complain the loudest have made the worst films.

Saturday, 19 August 2000. Edinburgh

I am introduced to the assistant Head of Drama at Channel Four. She seems quite keen to meet me, as they have 4 x 30-minute scripts for which they need to find directors. Would I be interested? My mind conjures images of bears, woods and toilet paper.

'Do you have an agent?' she asks. I shake my head. Is that a problem? No. She gives me a card and makes me promise to phone her when I get back to London. Cool. A job. I start to fantasize about the pay cheque. Unfortunately the face of my bank manager keeps intruding upon my happy reverie.

Tuesday, 22 August 2000. Edinburgh
Simple Things has its public screening in a programme of shorts. The cinema is full. Ali and Paul Rattray, the main actor, are on hand to watch. Our film is on first, and I manage to sleep through most of it. I'm told the audience reaction is mixed. But Jim McRoberts, the writer of the film, appears. It's good to see him, because we fell out just after filming finished last year. But he enjoyed the final product, and lets me know as much. A certain warmth fills me. This is what it's about – showing your film. It doesn't matter what strife arose in the process. The audience doesn't care. All they see is what is on the screen. Which, in turn, is ideally what the director saw on paper when she/he first read the script.

Friday, 25 August 2000. Edinburgh
I take part in a panel discussion on the topic of 'Innovation in Film'. I'm included partly because I'm writing this book, and partly because I'm a film student. The other panellists are Robin Gutch from Filmlab, Liz Rosenthal from Next Wave Films, Tom Morgan from Madstone Films, and the writer–director Lynne Ramsay (*Ratcatcher*). Ben Gibson chairs the discussion. I feel that I've been set up as a bit of a dinosaur: somebody who is studying in an institution rather than grabbing the new technology and going out to make a film for the cost of a tin of beans and a parking fine. In some ways, I can't argue with that. Some of the short film work I'm seeing at the moment is quite brilliant in its poverty. Watching it, I feel like a kid who's been given too many toys at Christmas and doesn't know which one to play with first, so that they all just lie there unused. I'm aware that we are a little bit spoiled at the NFTS – I was told as much last night by a tutor from another British film school. She also claimed to be striking a blow for feminism by not enrolling male students. By her reckoning, we turn out work that is condescending to its audience. In the end I had to walk away, because there was no arguing with her. In fact, part of me did sympathize. And yet, surprisingly, in the discussion there is still a lot of interest in the NFTS, especially from other students. I try and act as the good ambassador, fielding questions at the end . . . like I have any knowledge to impart whatsoever.

Monday, 4 September 2000. Peckham
Andi meets me off the train, and it's good to see her again. She has started work

on another TV two-parter, thankfully based in Camden. Then Ali calls. He wants me in tomorrow to go through the latest cut with Ian Sellar and listen to his worries. He'll pick me up at 9am.

Tuesday, 5 September 2000. Beaconsfield

Silence. We've just watched the cut, and people are trying to find things to say. Rob Ritchie, the writing tutor, feels that the location isn't used as well as it should be. He doesn't get a sense of the minority communities in the area. The aspect of racism seems mishandled, the subtext lost. Ian nods, and before I know it, I'm agreeing to do more pick-ups. Ali is worried about time. Our track-lay and mixing dates are looming at the end of the month, and he has two other projects still to finish. But we arrange to go out next week and shoot some documentary footage to slot into the film – just general views of the area, and the locals going about their daily business. Gav and I discuss what we're going to shoot. 'Shop signs,' I suddenly say. 'We should get some moving shots of street signs and stuff.' 'Can we storyboard them this time?' he asks. I shrug. 'Whatever.' As you can tell, I'm clutching at straws now, so I head to the 'table tennis' area. Over the summer, some of the animators nailed together an old dinner table, a large bit of plywood, and an upright skirting board down the middle. Hey presto, Film School Ping-Pong. The table is hogged by third-year editors and sound designers, all trying to ignore their impending deadlines. I get beaten every time I play, so much so that it becomes a running joke.

Thursday, 7 September 2000. Green Lanes

And I thought I would never see this place again. We're in a van, Gav hiding in the back, the tailgate opened just enough for the lens to fit through. Echoes of *The Conversation*. I talk to Doug about the Channel Four offer. He tells me flatly to give that commissioning editor a call; he even dials the number for me. I disappear round a corner to speak to her.

'Is that traffic in the background?' she asks.

'Yeah, I'm doing some pick-ups for my graduation film . . .' As soon as I say that, I feel like a failure. I shouldn't be telling her this.

'Oh! Sounds like fun.' She actually sounds like she means it. She asks me to send her a show-reel, which I promise to do.

Thursday, 14 September 2000. Beaconsfield

We finished a cut with the new footage. I can't tell whether it's good or bad. Ali is the same. I'm sure I haven't been much help to him in the editing. We show the cut to the rest of the crew: a few nods, but overall silence. Rob has begun the track laying, and we go into the mix next week. We have to lock this cut off. The pressure of time demands it. Now we all start making excuses for the film. I feel

I let down the crew by not being sufficiently assertive or focused. I don't know what feels worse – making a bad film, or losing the respect of my friends in the process. But at least we are on schedule; and that, at the moment, feels like the most important thing. I've sort of resigned myself to making the best of a bad job. Doesn't mean I've got to like it, though.

Thursday, 21 September 2000. Beaconsfield
The music is recorded; Tara manages to polish off four cues in one afternoon. I sit with the musicians and chat about guitars and amps, something I haven't done for years. I wonder what would have happened had I stuck with playing in a band. The rewards are definitely more immediate. But I wouldn't ever want to have missed out on all the people I've met and worked with through film.

Monday, 25 September 2000. Peckham
I didn't get the Channel Four job. A letter came in the post today, apologizing for not being in touch sooner. It seems that my show-reel 'was not suited to the scripts they are filming'. Hmm, how short-sighted of them. I pin the rejection to the inside of the toilet door, and resolve to do likewise with all future letters of dismissal. It stays there for a couple of hours until Andi tears it down, saying that it depresses her. I actually see the rejection as a compliment of sorts. Well, at least I see it that way after Ali tells me that I have a particular style and voice, meaning that Channel Four don't see me as a jobbing director. The money would have been nice, though. And the experience – a week to shoot a half-hour drama on DV. I really want to get behind a camera again, and see how much I've learned from my recent mistakes.

Sunday, 8 October 2000. The Empire, Leicester Square
Hereby known as Andrea's Day. This morning there is a cast and crew screening of *The Man Who Cried*, a feature by Sally Potter that Andi worked on just before Christmas 1999. Then in the evening, there's a broadcast of *Tough Love*, the TV drama she did immediately afterwards. Today, I bask in her reflected glory and am introduced to people as 'Fraser, Andrea's partner'. She squeezes my hand, whispering that soon it will be me introducing her.

Wednesday, 11 October 2000. Beaconsfield
For the last week I've sat behind Rob as he mixes the film. Sometimes I've slept on the couch, sometimes I've ordered pizza – like tonight, because we are going to be here until the early hours. I bought Ali and Rob each a bottle of whisky today, just to say 'Thanks' and 'Sorry'. Rob's bottle was cracked open about half an hour ago, as we thought that we were nearing the final pass of the mix.

Then the desk crashed, and we lost most of the night's work. So it's back to square one.

Earlier today, Stephen Frears came in to watch the rough final mix of the film. Recently he decided to take a year out of film-making to come and teach at the school. We met briefly last year: I showed him *Simple Things* and we talked about it. At the end of our affable conversation he stood up and announced, 'Of course, you know your film makes no sense and you will have to re-cut it.' I argued against that for a while. But I did submit to an overdub of dialogue to help appease the situation, and it did actually improve the film, narrative-wise.

So today, flanked by Ian Sellar and David Mingay, Stephen watched *Green Green Lanes*. I sat at the desk with Rob while they all lounged on the sofa behind us. When we brought the lights up at the end, there was the usual moment's silence. Ian suggested a few changes in the sound, seconded by David. Then we all turned to Stephen, awaiting his comments. 'Could I see it again?' he asked. Rob raised his eyebrows at me. When the film had run its second course, Stephen peppered me with questions. 'Is this how you intended the finished film to be?' 'Do you believe your main character?' And, most perplexing of all – 'How much do you think you have pulled back from the original intention of the script?'

I answer as best I can, and Stephen nods. 'Well, if you set out to show confusion in a young man, then you have achieved it.' Shortly after that comment, he takes his leave of us. But at least he watched it twice. Later in the morning Ali joins us, and we tell him about Stephen's request to see the film a second time. Ali smirks. 'You know he fell asleep the first time.' Shared realization dawns on Rob and I, and we laugh. That is exactly what happened.

Wednesday, 25 October 2000. Beaconsfield

Technically speaking, I have finished school. The mix is done, the picture is locked. All that remains is the paper work and the blow-up, which is entirely out of my hands. But I still find myself waking up and coming into school, and it just depresses me more. I've watched the final cut a few times now, and any initial enthusiasm has waned to an extreme hatred. I have fucked up my final year and I can do nothing to fix it. The cat is well and truly out of the bag.

I've just done a phone interview for a magazine wanting to speak to new graduates from various establishments. Glossing over my graduation film, I talked mainly about the need for a new approach to drama (which, in fact, is actually an old approach – the one where you concentrate on character and story, not how fast you can spin the camera).

I think I started questioning my own ability soon after I arrived here. I always felt it wasn't enough to just 'make films' – you had to find reasons why. I thought that my politics and my self-confidence would carry me through. But that confidence soon started to erode, especially when I found out I knew less than I thought I did. My visual sense seemed limp next to the camera gymnastics of some of my fellow students. And my storytelling was forceful, almost soapbox stuff – an approach that I now believe is a no-no. Slowly I became aware of the camera in a different way, but I maybe over-compensated – worrying excessively about the angles, 'Does this shot look dynamic?' *et cetera*. Basically, I started working more with my head, and ignoring my heart and my gut. Needless to say, the work I produced was completely unsatisfying.

But that was a good lesson, one that I must have been conscious of when I threw the storyboards out the window back in May. It's not about the shot, it's about the scene: the shot is just one element in that construction. And that's the problem with *Green Green Lanes*. It's a succession of shots that tell a story, and that is it. I didn't listen to my gut and heart, I tried to please many people, and wound up pissing all of them (and myself) off. The idea that it's all about making mistakes and learning from them is not much solace to me now.

Graffiti spotted in one of the toilets at school: 'Me make film, Mum very proud!'

Monday, 30 October 2000. Beaconsfield

Stephen Frears stops me in the canteen. 'When are you and me going to have a chat?' I'm caught off guard. 'This afternoon?' I suggest. He nods, and we fix to meet. Later in the Fiction office, the answer machine has about ten messages on it, all for Stephen. As I wait for him to appear, the phone rings and another urgent voice leaves him another urgent message. He enters as this voice rings off. 'Hmm . . . Hollywood!' he mutters as he sits down.

'What can I do for you?' Stephen asks. I look confused. 'It's just I see you walking around the school with a scowl on your face, and I'd like to know if we can remedy the problem.' I start to tell him of the angst I have over my film. He nods. 'It might not be the case that it doesn't work. It just might be that you haven't made the right decisions. What if we go back to the rushes and have another look?' I must seem doubtful, because he adds, 'You have nothing to lose, do you?' I stutter. What about Ali? I don't think he'd want to open the wound again. But it transpires that Stephen has already spoken to him and explained what he wants to do. The London Film Festival starts soon, so the school more or less shuts down. It's agreed that we will spend a couple of days on it then. Stephen nods and shoos me out of the room. He has phone calls to make and sleep to catch up on.

Sunday, 5 November 2000. Beaconsfield

Stephen goes through my rushes scene by scene, stopping every now and then to ask why the hell I called 'Cut' here, why I didn't pick up another shot there.

I offer excuses, but they sound oddly shallow now. 'Look after the master shots,' he tells me. 'Get them right, and the close-ups look after themselves.' He doesn't want to see any of the pick-ups or additional scenes, just the footage from the original shoot. I start to gain more confidence about the material. All the things that I was worried about and tried to cut around, Stephen puts back in. He doesn't seem to share the worries Ali and I had about bad acting. He asks if we have any other music for the opening. Tara composed a powerful, slow fusion of Western and Turkish instruments. Stephen suggests that it gives the game away too quickly, that the images are fighting with the sound. It's not that the music is bad, anything but; it's just the wrong decision. I mention 'Teenage Kicks' and we show him an earlier cut with that song. He nods and smiles. 'Of course I know nothing about modern music.' Yeah, right. This from the man who just directed *High Fidelity*.

What's becoming apparent is that there is another film in there, one so simple that it better shows the complexities of the argument we wanted to make. Once Stephen has left the room, Ali asks if I'm planning on re-opening the cut. If we can find a better film in there, I think we should. Ali understands this, but he finds the idea painful. 'Stephen only did this to make you feel better about yourself as a director, not to find a better film.' But surely it's the same thing? I know that Ali has been worked to the bone, cutting a still-unfinished documentary from over 60 hours of footage. And he still has an animated film to do. A re-cut will affect Rob too: he's under the cosh to get work completed and the dubbing theatre is booked solid. Moreover, there's the psychological effect of finishing something then finding out that you haven't – like approaching the tape after a 16-mile run, only to be told you have to go on and finish the full marathon. I ask Ali for another week of his time, so that we can carry on from where Stephen has left off. We will show the two cuts together and make a decision on the strength of the comparison. And it should be our decision, the crew's – nobody else's. Ali agrees, albeit with some trepidation.

Tuesday, 14 November 2000. Beaconsfield

The school rumour mill has been working overtime, and my name is now a by-word for 're-cuts': 'Better make sure of your editing decisions! You don't want to come back in two months' time and do a Fraser, now do you?' Ali and I have made a new cut. We adapted some of Stephen's suggestions and reintroduced some of our own ideas. We went back to paper and worked out the rough 'acts', deciding where we wanted to be at which points, both in the narrative and the emotion, then using the footage that best achieved that. But the situation has become a little bit political now. The sound department is saying, quite rightly, that their resources are over-stretched. I'm less sympathetic when someone tells me that the graduation film is like an exam, and sometimes you fail. I retaliate with the argument that you also get a chance to re-sit. So I take my case to Roger Crittenden, the Director of the school, and Richard Jenkins, the studio manager who oversees the budget and progress of the films. Richard asks me what I feel is the difference in the new cut? For me, the first one was about a locale in which two characters lived. The second is about those two characters. That makes all the difference. The conflict is stronger, and the ending, though not fully resolved, is more satisfying. My biggest concern is Rob. He doesn't feel that he has the time to commit to another mix. I appreciate that, but I'm feeling a bit selfish at the moment. I like the film now. It's starting to achieve what I set out to do.

Wednesday, 29 November 2000. Beaconsfield

The sound department has relented, conceding that the second cut should be mixed, but that it can't be done until after Christmas. Fair enough, but we're now on a tight schedule to be ready for the graduation screenings in February. Moreover, after the euphoria of finally 'finding' my film, the future is now looming nearer, and I'm starting to get the fear. The fluffy blanket of film school is about to be wrenched away, along with the security of my monthly bursary. Previously when I've graduated, there was always another level to try and attain educationally. Now, that level is to be a professional director, where your mistakes could cost you your reputation. Already my classmates are gearing up to look for work, compiling show-reels and talking about meetings and pitches. I look through the hard drive of my computer, blowing off the digital dust from several half-finished scripts and lazy ideas.

Tuesday, 5 December 2000. Covent Garden, London WC2

The fiction department has arranged a meeting with a respected company of agents for all graduating Fiction Direction students. I dutifully make my way to their offices, and mistakenly arrive half an hour early. I sit in the front offices feeling like an arse. There's only so long you can fake interest in back issues of *Campaign and Screen International* without looking like you're not meant to be there. Eventually the others arrive, and we are taken to a meeting room with a huge glass table and several assistants fussing round. Three agents appear. For their privacy, and also because I'll probably be approaching them in due course, I shall describe them as such:

– Mr Seen-it-all-before-so-I'll-stay-quiet
– Mr Public-school-but-I'll-be-honest-with-you
– Mr Hey-I'm-the-same-age-as-you-guys-so-I-know-what-it's-like.

We listen to this trio for the next hour. They each have different opinions, but the one word I keep hearing is 'fun':

'If a short is fun then we'd be interested.'

'We should have fun with our clients.' And so on.

'Fun' isn't something I'm attuned to right now. Financial insecurity? Yes. Creative bankruptcy? Right there with you, sparky. But 'fun'? At the moment, it's just a three-letter word. Increasingly, I'm realizing that the film business is all product. Everything is speculative. Nobody knows whether I have it in me to make a great feature. But is it fair to make an opinion on the basis of my graduation film? 'This is my life,' I want to say. 'I can't do anything else.'

At the end of the meeting, business cards are produced and handed round. I only get one given to me instead of three, and I take this as a personal slight. I look at the agent who gave the card and think, 'Are you really that desperate?' We repair to a local pub to review the last hour's proceedings over beer and whisky. Slowly my fellow classmates dissipate until it's just Paul and me. He already has an agent, so all is fine in the world with him.

Thursday, 7 December 2000. Beaconsfield

Review Day. This is when you present your finished film to the tutors, and any interested students. Afterwards you are required to walk down to the front and sit facing everybody while they tell you what you should have done instead. Beforehand, Mr Frears stops me in the corridor and tells me he will not be taking part. 'Cutting the umbilical cord, eh Stephen?' I ask. He grunts an affirmative and turns away, as if to say 'You're on your own now'.

I hate these things. It's a valuable experience but it always seems so false. Nobody walks away from a review saying, 'I really enjoyed that.' Everybody has to find fault. And, needless to say, I suspect that we are in for a kicking.

In fact, it doesn't turn out so bad. It's good to watch the film with an audience, and Doug takes control of the proceedings afterward. I describe our various problems, and try not to be too hard on myself, though Gavin points out that I seem to blame myself a lot. Later there's a Christmas meal in the canteen and Stephen pulls me over to ask how it went. 'Good,' I reply, 'I think everybody feels we've done the right thing. Even the sound department agrees. Now we've just got to work out how to mix it.'

'Well,' says Stephen, 'you've got to be nice to people.'

'Stephen! I'm always nice.'

He looks me in the eye. 'That's not what I've heard.'

I spend the rest of the day apologizing to anybody who will listen to me.

Monday, 11 December 2000. Beaconsfield

I had my end-of-year assessment today. Only for me it's now the end of three years, and I'm feeling a little low, tearful even, reassessing my time here. An old joke is running rife around the school. 'What do you say to a graduate of the National Film School?' 'Can I get fries with that?' It would be funnier if I hadn't heard it from a member of staff.

I hang around the table tennis area, waiting to be seen. I slump to four straight defeats, and regret not working on my backhand. Three-thirty rolls around and I'm in the Camelot Room (so called because of its small round table). Roger Crittenden and Ian Sellar look concerned. They must know how I feel, but now they want me to verbalize it. Still, I feel strangely relaxed as I describe my mistakes. Last night I looked back over my journal and realized that if mistakes were made, then it was because they could be. This is an education. You don't get it right all the time.

When I stop talking, Ian hands me his assessment. I pass. His tutor's statement reads:

'The thing is – it doesn't stop. The education is incomplete. You've achieved a great deal, progressed, very palpably, made one film you rightly seem proud of and another that has been nothing but trouble for you. The thing is not to be distracted by either of the above. You clearly have an understanding of each element of screen language; you need now to develop ways of playing them relative to each other. If I have a criticism, it is that the element of circus, putting on a show, you've let slip. That element in the past was attached to a particular self-view. As your self-view has developed so you need to reform the circus. The achievement is the development; the circus is the easy bit. Don't underestimate the value of what you have achieved; it's a great deal, and it's taken you to the edge. That's when it gets exciting. I look forward to seeing your next films. All of them.'

I take the school bus back to London. Most of my fellow passengers are first years, just finished shooting their last exercise of term. Chatter about rushes fills the air. Their enthusiasm annoys me. That air of cockiness they have. It's a state of confidence that will surely be questioned, but (with luck) never lost.

And for me?

Over and over in my head I keep repeating:

'Do you want fries with that?'

Afterword

In Scotland there used to be this five-minute television programme called *Late Call*. It came on just after the late-night local news, and consisted of a minister or quasi-religious figure leaving you with a final 'thought for the day'. This often involved a parable relating to some difficult aspect of modern life. ('The other day I was at the Old Firm match with my ten-year-old son, and he asked me, "Daddy, did Jesus play football?" And you know, in a funny way, he did . . .') This, in a funny way, is my own *Late Call* moment: a few final thoughts on my last year at film school.

Green Green Lanes was finished in time for the graduation show in February 2001, and screened at the National Film Theatre on 35mm in full Dolby Digital

Surround. At the party afterwards, hands were shaken, phone numbers exchanged, meetings arranged. Everything seemed as it should. There I was, a graduate of the National Film and Television School: world, come and get me. The film enjoyed a good reception – at least, I think it did; my bullshit detector isn't quite as finely tuned as others. But I repaired into the London night with my crew, drunk on euphoria and the completion of the course.

Now, let's pretend this is a DVD and skip forward a few scenes. Walking round Soho, I bump into no fewer than six former classmates from NFTS. We're all doing the same thing: going to meetings, exchanging phone numbers, shaking hands. Over the cheapest beverages we can buy, we all talk about the short-term future. Each one of us is worried about going under. We all complain about the bank manager we happen to share, we all hope to land that one big job so that we can tell him where to stuff his loan. Then I ask the question, 'Do you think it was worth it? Film School?' Silence falls and brows are furrowed as an answer is tossed around. Nobody answers in the negative. Though certain things, it's agreed, could have been better. Hell, that's just human nature.

I used to play a game in Soho: 'Spot the actor'. Now I play 'Spot the film school graduate'. They sit beside the windows of coffee shops, nursing luke-warm cappuccinos, copies of *Screen International* in front of them, open at the Production pages. They scan the columns for a name they might recognize, dismayed when it's a former colleague, because those columns are the antithesis of the newspaper obituaries: you really want to be in there.

Meanwhile, I have joined the 'No-use-crying-over-spilt-milk' contingent. Film school was my decision and I stick by it. To say I didn't learn anything would be a lie. To say I didn't achieve anything would be an injustice to myself. Personal growth, mental development – sure, these things don't pay the bills, but they are steps in the right direction. If I have one piece of advice to impart then it's this, which was told to me at the first college I attended. A person with no talent but determination will go as far as they can. A person who is all talent and no determination will be left behind. Film school is a tool: it helps you achieve what you are determined to achieve, nothing more, nothing less. It's up to you why you chose it, and how you use it. Just remember this – always check the equipment as soon as you get it out of stores.

US FILM SCHOOLS

Oren Moverman

The Dream Factory:
The American Film School Experience, East Coast
Introduction by Oren Moverman

It is often forgotten, perhaps conveniently, that the American cinema, much like the American union, was born on the East Coast. The industry's migration to the West followed subsequently as a highly pragmatic step, and with it the American cinema came to be forever defined by Hollywood. There, in Los Angeles, California, the biggest film-training academy in history was established under the banner of the studio system; a vocational school for technicians, actors, directors, and virtually every other production, post-production, distribution and exhibition position, the system established well-defined career paths. Film labourers were trained by *doing*, doing led to earning, and earning led to advancement for those ambitious enough to desire the betterment of their position within the Hollywood machine. The disintegration of the studio system therefore not only signified a historic and dramatic alteration in the economic structure of moviemaking, but also created a climate in which a previously scorned career choice came to be prominent in American production training: the film school.

They were always there: New York University's and Columbia's film programs date back to the 1940s; UCLA's program started in 1947; the USC film program was already up and running in the 1950s. But it would take Baby Boom luminaries of the late 1960s such as Francis Ford Coppola and Martin Scorsese to legitimize film schools as practical training grounds for accomplished film-makers. The rest is history – and also myth. Film schools have become a huge business in the United States, and programs are offered at hundreds of colleges and universities under the auspices of Film Production, Film Studies, Media Studies, Communication, Visual Arts and more. According to the *US News and World Report*, an overwhelming majority of first-time feature-film directors are film school graduates, not withstanding the Quentin Tarantinos of the world. But very few graduates are able to construct successful directing careers similar to those of such film school alumni and graduate school poster-boys as Spike Lee, Jim Jarmusch or Oliver Stone. The exact official number of film students in America is hard to tally since thousands of students throughout the country are making thousands of films of various lengths in various mediums, all regarding themselves as emerging film-makers. It is also hard to quantify just how many film students end up working anywhere within the film industry, regardless of their directing ambitions. Suffice it to say, film school education has now become an official, accepted exploit by which film-makers can enter the American film industry.

Currently, with new advances in film-making technologies such as digital video, the rising costs of education in the US (an average graduate Directing student at Columbia University or NYU, for example, is expected to spend around $100,000 to earn a Masters degree), and with the fierce competition to get into the 'better' film schools, both undergraduate and graduate – one cannot avoid reverting to the past and doubting the necessity and validity of the film school experience. The more popular they get, the less film schools seem to be about filling the film-training gap brought on by the collapse of the studio system, and more about the dreams of a generation. Hence the inevitable question: are they worth it? Or more specifically: why not just make a film, rather than spend the money on studying film-making in a competitive academic setting? And since it is impossible for so many students trying to become feature film directors to achieve any kind of real success in the business, are film schools selling their students an illusion at an absurdly high price?

And so I set out to chat with a few friends about their views on, and personal experience at, film schools of one kind or another. Concentrating on the East Coast, I was not just attempting to bring it all back home, as it were, but to focus more specifically on the New York indie sensibility, the 'alternative' American cinema, where big budgets and common-denominator entertainment values appear to be, at least on the surface, of less importance than artistic vision and serious content. In no way do these interviews attempt to paint an authoritative picture of the film school experience. They are subjective snap shots, but they reveal personal stories that reflect a certain truth about college experience in general, where young men and women, acting upon a typically middle class ethos, attempt to venture into the world and mature into productive beings. Ultimately, experiences in the world of higher learning are about finding paths; these interviews happen to be about film paths.

Oren Moverman, New York, July 2001

Jay Rabinowitz (left) with longtime collaborator Jim Jarmusch.

Jay Rabinowitz: Editor
Graduate of NYU Undergraduate Program

Jay Rabinowitz has worked as an editor on Darren Aronofsky's Requiem for a Dream *(2000)*, Jim Jarmusch's Ghost Dog: The Way of the Samurai *(1999)*, Year of the Horse *(1997)*, Dead Man *(1995) and* Night On Earth *(1991)*, Paul Schrader's Affliction *(1997)*, Lodge Kerrigan's Clean, Shaven *(1995) and many more.*

Oren Moverman: When I first asked you about your film school experience, you said that you didn't go to film school. But you graduated from the NYU undergraduate film program. So I sense a bit of confusion around the term 'film school'.

Jay Rabinowitz: There was a lot of discussion about film schools when people like Jim Jarmusch and Spike Lee and a whole wave of directors were coming out of film programs. But they were actually coming out of *graduate* school. So when people generically asked me, 'Did you go to film school?', for a while I thought they really meant, 'Did you go to graduate school for film?', because that's where all the famous people were coming from. I think a lot of people really associate the term 'film school' with a masters program, whereas there are obviously many, many undergraduate programs throughout the country that are basically schools with film programs or media programs, communications, whatever they call it.

OM: When you go to film school as an undergraduate, there are a lot of other courses in other disciplines you have to take. It usually isn't exclusively about film, unless you go to places like the School of Visual Arts.

JR: That's it. Most of the undergraduate film programs also provide you with a pretty broad liberal arts education where the focus is on film. At NYU we had a cinema studies program and a film production program. So there are more choices and tracks. I thought I was taking a joint major, so I was taking courses in both departments. But then I realized the courses were not lined up like that credits-wise. So I ended up with a bachelor's degree in Cinema Studies where I knew I was going into production.

OM: Was production your plan all along?

JR: Not really. But I was very anxious to get out of high school; I did all my twelfth-grade work in eleventh grade and got out a year early. And at college I was in a bit of a rush to get to work, so I took summer courses and saved half a year there. I wasn't a fanatical film buff, but I liked films and I liked music quite a bit and I wanted my studies to be over fast. I don't know why I chose Film as a viable course of study. Now the choice seems kind of magical to me. I wouldn't say it was a whim, but it simply seemed like an interesting idea. It was once I immersed myself in film that I became a fanatic.

OM: In that respect film school at undergraduate level is essentially a degree, getting an education, because you think it's needed, or because your parents insist on it, *et cetera*.
JR: Yeah, so you come out with a degree and hopefully a broad liberal arts education. That's the thing about film, and it may have to do with why I chose it as well – it encompasses so many areas: psychology, religion, the arts, literature, music. Broad studies and a range of ideas make film-makers interesting artists. But studies aren't everything. All kinds of great film-makers were obsessed with watching and studying films – Scorsese is an obvious example. But some of the film school directors seem like they have way less life experience than the old-school directors, like a John Huston or a Sam Fuller, people who have had these tremendous life stories – as opposed to high school and college filled just with films and nothing but. The life experiences of many film-makers nowadays seem to be defined through films themselves. A broad education, broader than film, was, and is still, important for me.

OM: So you were satisfied with your film school experience also because it wasn't only about film?
JR: Yes, and you only appreciate that a while after you've gone to film school. I knew I wanted to be an editor when I graduated and started getting internships. At that point I felt I shouldn't have gone to film school, I thought I should have started working four years earlier, by which time I would have been an established assistant editor, rather than an unpaid intern! I felt I wasted my time. It wasn't until much later that I appreciated it for the broader education and the fascinating Cinema Studies classes that I took. Having this basis and appreciation for film history helps when you are working on shaping a film with a director.

OM: People often overlook the value of a background in Cinema Studies. It carries the stigma of 'theory', which is far from appealing to those wanting to work in production.
JR: I think it's true that for kids going into college, the production classes are the more exciting alternative. I enjoyed the production classes and took the famous NYU Sight and Sound class, with Professor Brian Winston, who was also my

academic adviser. It was in that class that I realized I could edit. Editing was the language in which I could communicate. But at the same time I had great Cinema Studies classes. One was called 'Hitchcock and Buñuel', and the teacher was trying to find the common ground between them, and it was fascinating. Then I had a fascinating class with the great animator John Canemaker*. And of course the French new wave classes and Italian neo-realism classes. That was happening at a time when I was devouring and loving films. I had a film history class with Robert Sklar, and his assistant really opened my eyes to ways of reading films, how layered and textured films can be. And some great things have come out of that in projects I've worked on. Working with Paul Schrader was amazing because of his knowledge of film history. He is one of the most interesting directors I have ever worked with – he conceives scenes, sequences and a whole film in relation to cinema history. He has a brilliant mind. But it is much more extreme in his case, not having seen films at all in his childhood and then devouring them. While my childhood wasn't as sheltered as his, I felt a kinship. I liked experiencing the degree to which films could blow your mind as you discover more and more about them. That hunger has kept me going all these years.

OM: You mentioned the famous Sight and Sound class?
JR: Yeah. I took it as a summer session: a six-week class where we met for five days a week, eight hours a day. So making films fulltime was very exciting. I believe it hasn't changed over the years, I still see the kids in Washington Square Park today. The class would split up into groups of four, and rotate jobs. You would shoot one film, direct one film. You would go through the different tasks, which was a great way to learn and work together. You would help someone pursue their vision, and then pursue your own vision utilizing the help of others. You got a sense of the collaborative process of making films. Nobody makes films by themselves, and it's important to learn that and appreciate it. That's what Sight and Sound establishes. I think it's a really good way to help students understand what it might be like on a much broader level.

OM: What was the relationship between the students?
JR: It was already known as a very popular program. But because I was there during the summer, lots of the students weren't pursuing degrees. There were students there from all over the world. They were taking the famous class, trying it on for size, and because it was at the undergraduate level I didn't find it

---

* Internationally recognized animator and historian of animation. Directed the short *Bottom's Dream* (1984) and has provided animation for films as diverse as the Oscar-winning documentary *You Don't Have to Die* (1988) and George Roy Hill's *The World According to Garp* (1982).

terribly competitive. Of course, people got pretty focused on their projects and sometimes got consumed, but not so much in a competitive way. At the graduate level people really know what they want to do with their lives, and have ambitions. But some of the kids with me were simply getting a taste of film education.

OM: Did any of your classmates at NYU end up in film-making?
JR: It's an interesting question, but I really don't know. I haven't run into anyone I knew at NYU in the film business.

OM: It's unusual you came out of the undergraduate program knowing you wanted to be an editor.
JR: For me it came out of Sight and Sound. We had a series of exercises to do as well as the short film. In doing them and sitting down at the flatbed with the 16mm film, physically cutting it and working with sound, I realized I loved it and I really felt like I could communicate with this language of editing, as opposed to other languages I have been less successful in learning. Editing felt natural. I also got some good feedback from my teacher, Brian Winston. We would show the projects in class and talk about them and when the lights came up after my piece he said, 'Well, you can see the guy could edit.' It made a real impact, because I already felt it, but to hear somebody say it made an impression. After Sight and Sound I really started to think about how films were put together in my Cinema Studies classes. There was an overlap.

OM: What did you do once you graduated?
JR: First of all, I started canvassing post-production facilities with my résumé, just walking around day after day until people noticed. But that wasn't leading anywhere.

Then I got a job from a posting at NYU with a dancer called Amy Greenfield, who was pioneering a genre called Film Dance. She was making a feature-length dance film of Sophocles' *Antigone*. I was working at the liquor store throughout my days at NYU, and I would work a few afternoons a week with her. And I learned a lot. At the same time I continued canvassing facilities like Sound One, and had this cover letter that in retrospect was really goofy. It looked like an ad for a film, and it said something like, 'Coming Soon. The Editor's Apprentice, starring YOU as The Editor.' And then I even had a pull quote. Amy Greenfield had written me a letter of recommendation and had written something nice about working with me, so I quoted her and put it on the ad: 'Amy Greenfield says Jay is a pleasure to be with.'

Also, at one point the great cinematographer Nestor Almendros – who, by the way, studied at the famous City College Film Department in the 1950s – came to the NYU bookstore to sign his book, *A Man with a Movie Camera*. And I got to the front of the line and he asked me, 'Where in film does your interest lie?' I told him I was going to be an editor, so he inscribed in the book, 'Without proper editing our images don't have a meaning,' and he signed it and dated it. It really meant a lot to me, because his images were so amazing and the fact that he thought it took proficient editing for them to really do their job meant a lot to me. So I also put that quote on my résumé.

OM: So your résumé was a diploma and some nice quotes fashioned as advertisement?

JR: As I said, pretty goofy, but that's what I came up with. Then one day I slipped my résumé under the door of an office in the Brill Building on the sixth floor, and started walking away, and then somebody opened the door and called me back. He sat me down and he said, 'I see from your résumé you went to NYU.' And I said yes. Then he said, 'Well, we're preparing a new film here and our director went to NYU and our editor went to NYU and we need an intern for the editing room. There's no pay involved, but if you like I'll pass your résumé along to them.' I said 'Sure' and asked what the film was, but he didn't want to tell me. He just said that if they were interested they would call and tell me. All my pals at the liquor store where I worked said it was going to be some schlock horror or ridiculous porn movie, but the next day I got a call from Melody London. She was going to be cutting the new Jim Jarmusch film *Down By Law* and she wanted me to come down for an interview. By that time *Stranger Than Paradise* had come out and had blown many people away, including me. It was just so exciting to get that call. That was in the fall of 1985, and I've been working with Jim to this day. So in a way, NYU had a lot to do with it.

OM: Do you now see film school as a necessary step?

JR: I'm not sure it's necessary. I think it's a very viable way of receiving an education in film. Obviously, a lot of people are doing it and a lot of people are coming out of schools, some are becoming film-makers, some are working in the film business. But I think it would be quite fascinating to find someone who came out of some other endeavour into films, the way it had been done in the past. It seems unlikely for people to take an alternative route now. Film schools seem to be an established entry into the business. But necessary? I'm not so sure.

OM: Are they selling entry into the film world as a dream? There are more students now than ever.

JR: It does seem like the sheer numbers of students and graduates are daunting. The industry can't grow that fast, there's no way. So there's going to be a certain percentage of people who graduate from film programs but find their careers elsewhere. Film school has no guarantees. It's not false advertising, there's just nothing they can do about it. And there is a distinction between undergraduate and graduate – I think you are more likely to end up in the film business with a masters degree, because you're invested in it in a deeper way, and there are less graduate students than undergraduate students. Now, it doesn't mean you are going to be a director, but you may end up in film. School is a launching pad: the nature of working in film can't be taught or even tasted in film schools. When I was done, the feeling I had from the school was basically, 'Thank you very much and have a nice day.' I moved on.

Lodge Kerrigan and daughter Serena

Lodge Kerrigan: Writer–Director
Graduate of NYU Graduate Program

Lodge Kerrigan wrote and directed Clean, Shaven *(1995) and* Claire Dolan *(1998). His new film is entitled* In God's Hands.

Oren Moverman: You are an independent film-maker and a photographer who teaches periodically. How do you structure your teaching around your creative work?
Lodge Kerrigan: I try to teach, for a semester or so, after I complete a film.

OM: What's the significance of teaching to you?
LK: Teaching helps me focus on my work. I tend to write my own material, and it can be an isolating experience: one spends an enormous amount of time alone working the film out. So I benefit from interacting with students and having to articulate my ideas and beliefs about film-making. It helps me define what I'm doing as a film-maker. I also learn a lot from the students. They're full of ideas. They're enthusiastic and energetic, they haven't been through the grind of actually making a picture and they still have a somewhat naive but incredibly fresh and positive can-do attitude, which inspires me.

OM: Where have you taught?
LK: On the undergraduate level, I've taught Cinematography at SUNY Purchase, narrative film-making at Brown, and on the graduate level, I've taught Directing and Film Production at NYU and Columbia.

OM: You also went through the NYU graduate school yourself. You probably have a good perspective on East Coast film schools. From your experience, how do they differ?
LK: Actually, that's a difficult question for me to answer. As a visiting professor, I have the liberty to focus on what I want to teach within the parameters of the school's curriculum. So my perspective tends to be shaped by the students rather than the institutions and the students vary tremendously year to year, even within a given program.

OM: You studied political philosophy at Columbia before going to the graduate program at NYU.

LK: Yeah, I had never taken a film class or studied film-making. I never had an uncle who gave me a Super-8 camera when I was a kid; no romantic notions about the film-maker. At the time that I applied to NYU, I was also considering becoming a journalist, but I mistakenly thought that fiction was more interesting and had more possibilities than real life.

OM: And film school helped you sort that out?
LK (*Laughs*): Yeah, now I wish I were a photojournalist.

OM: Was film school a good choice for you at the time?
LK: Well, I wanted to be a film-maker and I thought that to become a director you needed to go to school. In retrospect, even though I question that belief now, I think there are benefits to film schools. You get an overall perspective on how a film is made. If you don't go to school you may get track-oriented, start as an apprentice and work your way up in the industry. So it could take years before you get an overall view of how a film is made. For all the limitations of film schools, you learn how the film is put together. For the most part film schools and the film industry are two totally separate entities. They have little connection and the crossover is limited.

OM: So if you want to learn how to make a film, film school is not a bad move?
LK: It's one way, if you can afford it.

OM: There are State schools and City universities throughout the country that are much more affordable than Ivy League, NYU and the rest of the 'prestige' schools. Are they less of a choice?
LK: No matter where you go it's about what you make of the opportunity and what you do afterwards. Get the education and move on.

OM: What are some of the problems you've noticed as a teacher?
LK: One of the problems of film school is the pressure to get a portfolio, a reel. Students are told that if they make a good short film they'll be able to direct features. The schools' portfolio building is wrong, because the experience should be about making errors and learning from the process. You shouldn't have to make work that can stand on its own in film school, it's too early. You have to learn film-making as a craft first, rather than a revelation of some talent that the students are encouraged to think they have. Also, I don't think short films necessarily lead to film-making careers. Everyone in the industry is looking for material, not shorts. Everyone in film schools is making shorts. Thousands of them a year. The odds are next to nothing that you will direct a great short film, have it shown at major festivals and then get some deal to direct a feature film

based on someone else's great script for a few million dollars. From my experience, shorts are not enough. Consistently writing material, day in and day out, is crucial.

OM: How do students react to the pressure of building a portfolio?
LK: Some students develop an arrogance born out of fear. They reject the school, reject the teachers, reject narrative, reject everything except their vision. I had a student tell me, 'I don't want to learn, I want to paint in images.' And I have no response to that. A student who takes that view disregards the development of tools, and the fact that school is simply an opportunity. Some students focus on the politics of the school, how to make it better, when they should first focus on their work. Students need to accept they may not become the great film-makers they think they can be right out of the gate. It sounds so basic, but there is a learning curve. It's the repetition of work, doing more and more of it, that allows one to learn and grow. Talent, vision, art are all part of it, but that tends to be personal. You can only teach craft, and you have to embrace that as a student. You have to treat school as an opportunity to learn.

OM: Do you get a different kind of respect from film students because you are a working film-maker?
LK: You shouldn't be on any pedestal as a working film-maker. Film-makers are not necessarily the best teachers; it's a different craft in itself. Hopefully they can provide more insight, but students have to be open to gaining from that. Most students learn the hard way. They go into the world, try to make features and realize they have been in a bubble all this time.

OM: What sort of teacher did you respect as a student?
LK: From my experience, the best teachers are those who strike you as intelligent, serious and open. It's not about them; they are there for the students. They never try to prove how great they are, or follow a rigid agenda; they try to help students see their work clearly. And they try to help students overcome certain obstacles that either they, or production, or the university puts in their path. I think great teachers are personally invested in their students' work, where they develop strategies and find ways to help individuals achieve the goals that they set for themselves. In the same way, as a film-maker you try to surround yourself with people who help you see the film itself in a clearer way, while you have different ways of dealing with different crew members so they perform their individual task. At the end of the day, you should be professional: do your job, show you care about individuals and their needs, and then go home and leave it behind you, knowing you've done your best.

OM: Do you think it's difficult to be a production teacher and not be making films?

LK: I don't know how that's possible. How can you communicate what to do if you don't do it? It must be so hard. You have to rely on some textbook approach that may not be relevant anymore. I feel that I have only just scratched the surface as a film-maker; I'm at the tip of the iceberg. What I have to teach is based on experience, limited as it may be. I can't imagine how you could teach narrative, documentary or experimental film, without making them.

OM: You teach it as theory.

LK: Perhaps. But then it's just theory for you as a teacher. You don't know about its implementation. Film-making is not a theory, it's a creative process carried out within an industry, a business.

OM: Do you find an industry consciousness amongst the students?

LK: I recently met somebody, a former classmate from my film school, who had spent six years writing a screenplay for herself with a budget range of $30 to $70 million. I really feel for people who put these kinds of obstacles in their own way. I don't know if it's lack of knowledge of where they stand in the industry, or ambivalence, or they don't really want to make a film. A school that has a working faculty like Columbia is naturally much more in tune with the way the industry works than a school where a guy who made a film 20 years ago is teaching the only production class. It's basic Darwinism, but the students are more conscious of the industry where the teachers are able to instil that consciousness. Your awareness as a student is always going to be limited until you start operating in the professional world. And this is where it gets cruel. In America, you want to be a lawyer, you go to law school, you pass the bar, congratulations – you're a lawyer. You want to be a film-maker, you go to film school, make shorts, you graduate, congratulations – you went to film school.

OM: Most people tend to think of themselves as directors or screenwriters after school, both undergraduate and graduate.

LK: Film schools do not produce film-makers; film-makers go to film school. I don't think film-makers get their creative ambition from film school. To go from a place of nothing, no contacts in the industry, no money, to making a feature film usually takes an enormous amount of endurance and drive. That drive is not imparted to students by an academic institution. If the most important thing for a graduate coming out of film school is to make a film, as opposed to being seen as a film-maker or to having a career, money or fame, there is very little that could stop him or her from becoming a film-maker.

OM: That's a very optimistic attitude.

LK: Like everyone in life, you tend to believe in the path that has worked for you. So I tend to believe in the practical, no-budget route for emerging film-makers more than the route of trying to get a 'professional' budget with a 'professional' crew. And that's where the people you meet in film school can really play a key role. They can be your production crew and there can be this creative spirit of making a film with people you've grown to trust over the years. I've worked with the cinematographer Teo Maniaci on two features. He was a classmate and I knew that I could trust him because we were both on the same level at the same time. I knew his loyalties were always going to be to the film. In the professional world, some people have other agendas, other loyalties that don't always serve the film, and that's natural. This is just my personal opinion; I'm not saying this is the right way for everyone to make a film. At the end of the day, there is no blueprint to how to get a film made. You just find a way, or you don't make films.

Dan Kleinman

Dan Kleinman: Chair, Columbia University Graduate Program

Dan Kleinman is an Assistant Professor and chairperson of the MFA program at Columbia and a former Associate chair of the Graduate Film Program at NYU. He has written a number of screenplays, including Rage *(1972) and* Welcome to Oblivion *(1992).*

Oren Moverman: What is the Columbia graduate film program philosophy?
Dan Kleinman: We're story-centred. Our emphasis is on story first and foremost, which doesn't mean we only train screenwriters. But we start with dialogue straight away and have a lot of emphasis on working with actors. We put forward how to project the story as the first thing. If that means we have to catch up on the visual and the technical side later on, we do that. We are also different from most other schools in the US, where everyone starts off by choosing a concentration. At Columbia, everyone takes the same courses in the first year before deciding on a speciality. This means we have a unified faculty encompassing writing, directing, producing, history and theory all in one, which, I think, is a good thing. There are schools where if you concentrate on screenwriting, you get off on the fourth floor, and directing is on the tenth. Here, the faculties overlap. It's a two-year, fulltime program, plus one to three years to finish your thesis work.

OM: Does everyone make a thesis film?
DK: No, we have three concentrations: writing, producing and directing. Directors have to make two films: a pre-thesis film and a thesis film. The writers write two feature screenplays, minimum; and producers graduate mostly by producing a director's thesis project. You also have to produce other short films at Columbia. You could also do a virtual feature – you produce the feature on paper, so you don't have to raise the money and make the movie. If you do that you can get credit.

OM: When you say you're first and foremost story-driven, philosophically, and technically oriented only afterwards, what does that entail?
DK: One thing it means is that we work in video for the first two years. There is some shooting on film for a few students, especially students taking cinematography with something else as a dual concentration. Most students do not take

cinematography as a separate course in the first year. In fact, most don't take it as a second course at all. Everyone takes the following courses in the first year: Directing, Screenwriting, Directing Actors, Elements of Narrative (story), a course in Short Films, some general lectures on Directing for all students. Then Introduction to Film Theory, unless they have already done it as undergraduates. Ninety per cent of students also take a producing course called 'The Business of Film', and that's the first year. In the second year, the producers have their required courses as well as the writers and the directors. The requirements are not so extensive that you can't take the requirements for two concentrations and most people who concentrate on directing also take the second-year screenwriting course. So, this is one of the best places to come if you want to come out of school with a short film and a feature film screenplay, because you can get good training in both.

OM: How big is the program?
DK: We take about 65 students each year. The fulltime population is 130. Then there are the students in research arts, as we call it, who haven't yet graduated. The population of matriculated students at any one time is close to 300.

OM: How many applications do you get?
DK: About 500. It's going up though.

OM: Do you have any idea why it's going up everywhere?
DK: I don't know. I assumed because people are recognizing how good we are, but you've just dashed that theory. Maybe it's because everyone is applying to film school? It's become the thing to do.

OM: At Columbia a student pays very high tuition and makes a short film that is self-financed. Isn't a student better off taking the tuition money and making a film outside a school program?
DK: When you say go to film school or make a film, keep in mind the average person is not trying to decide whether to go to film school or make a feature film. Our students, with very few exceptions, make shorts. I've been here five years and we've had two features made – one is in pre-production now. In general, however, a student's situation doesn't lead to a very good feature. Let's say you want to be a director – you could spend $100,000 at Columbia on making your two films, plus tuition. Certainly you're going to be spending $60,000–$70,000. Are you better off taking that money and making a DV feature film, for example? That depends on the situation. Some people have made rock-bottom-budget features that have done very well. Most people want the atmosphere and encouragement and nurturing they can get here. They want to meet

the people who do what they aspire to do, they want to make the connections, gain a shared experience and some added benefits. And they want to get their film education in a carefully laid-out and systematic way.

OM: What about working your way up in the business?
DK: Apprenticing is harder to do than it was 50 or 60 years ago when there were studios and you could see an upward path. But if somebody came to me and said, 'I have a script, enough contacts and enough money to make the film, should I make the film or spend the money coming to your school?' I would never tell them flat-out to come to Columbia. I would tell them the advantages. If I really wanted to advise them carefully, I would read their script!

OM: Was it a very conscious decision to put together a staff mostly composed of working professionals?
DK: That pre-dates my arrival here. We have always sought working faculties. We have the advantage of being a small program. The precedent has been set that enough good people want to teach here, and so we keep hiring in that fashion. I think the industry people know the program is small, they know the people here are good – students and faculty – and I guess they like our approach. We've hired some very good people since I have been here and we have two job searches on now for which the candidates are very strong. The finalists are all in the industry.

OM: Most schools say that it is hard to find quality people who work in the industry because it's hard for professionals to juggle a fixed teaching schedule with film work.
DK: We are flexible. If someone has a picture and leaves on fairly short notice, they take a semester off and we say, 'Go for it!' That's all there is to it.

OM: How did you become a film professor?
DK: I graduated from NYU in the 1960s with an MFA, and then I started writing screenplays. Shortly after my first film was made, I was asked to come back and teach screenwriting at NYU and I took to it. Before that, my only teaching experience was when an Ivy League school with camera equipment asked me to do an extra-curricular course. So I had a little experience when I got to NYU and started teaching professionally. I loved it! I kept doing it!

OM: You were basically part of the famous first generation of film-makers coming out of film school as opposed to the studio system. How are the students different today?
DK: I went off to NYU to study film-making in their graduate program and we

were the largest class they'd ever taken by a factor of three. There were 35 of us. The only requirement we needed to get in was a BA degree with a B average in anything. You didn't need an artistic portfolio or anything. I was a Math major as an undergraduate and I fell in love with film in the first year of college and was quite surprised at that development in my life. So I've observed the steady climb of film student enrolment from the mid-60s to today. The rise in interest has not abated. If there is a difference in the quality of students, it doesn't feel like it. I started teaching at NYU in 1974. So I have been teaching at serious and top-rated film schools for a long time and I'm not sure I've seen any significant difference in students over the years. But I do notice that in the late 60s and early 70s, which is really the period between my student days and the beginning of my teaching days, a lot of the best-known NYU graduates came out of the program. The percentage of people who had successful careers as directors was much higher because NYU was smaller then. And my theory about that is that there was no particular cachet to film school in those days; you really had to have a personal interest in it because it was a surprising discipline to pursue.

My impression is that majoring in Film in the 50s as an undergraduate was like majoring in Radio today. It had no respectability, and that's not true anymore. Also, the 50s and early 60s were the tail end of the long period when people who had artistic aspirations wanted to write the Great American Novel. You don't hear about that much anymore. But people want to make films and our students are very serious about it. Other people may be caught up in the glamour of making films. Our students aren't like that, but I do think there are more people who want to make films because it is what one does, than there were when I started as a student or even when I started teaching. The best students are similar and have been for the last 30 to 40 years. There are more stories of people having careers out of film school. I was still at school when Coppola made *You're a Big Boy Now*, which was said to be his thesis project at USC. He was dubbed as the first film student to get a deal with a studio – it was a big deal for all of us. There was no history. Now there is, and everyone knows famous people who went to various film schools.

OM: So while students are basically still students in your view, the industry has changed, the expectations are different?
DK: Certainly students today are more industry-savvy than we were at NYU back then, or even in the 70s. But the whole world is more movie-industry-savvy. You read about the inside workings of the film business in the popular press. That wasn't true back then. Everyone wants to feel that they know about the mechanics of the movie business and entertainment in general – it's part of our current celebrity culture.

OM: **Film professors have yet to enjoy celebrity status in our culture.**
DK: And that's a good thing. Professors are about their students. A good film professor helps the student make the student's film, rather than steer the student towards making the professor's film – that's essential. The qualities of a good film instructor are that of any teacher: understanding the subject matter, understanding the way in which people absorb information. One of the keys to teaching film is knowing how much information to give and knowing when to allow students to go out and make mistakes. Film-making is very complicated and you have to know a lot of things to get it right. There is always a temptation in teaching to try to give a student all he needs to know. It is the same as with any skill. But it is usually better to show them something and let them make mistakes, thereby making them ready to learn the next thing. A professor needs to ration the information around an assignment, a curriculum. There is an expression they use at USC, 'the teachable moment', which I like. And I have had the experience at NYU where I developed some lectures on where to put the camera. I gave them to the third-year students and they loved them. I was then encouraged to design a whole course, but we gave the course to the second-year students and the same lectures didn't go over well at all because they hadn't made their second-year films yet. They haven't made the mistakes that helped them know what they needed to learn. And there were third-year students auditing then and they were the ones who appreciated the class. But that is true within a course and a curriculum – you need to figure out how much to give the students and get them going. And the students have to want to know, then they can go out and try it with varying degrees of success. And that is a good reason to be in a school because you learn from your mistakes and successes and everyone else's too, not just one example which is your own. It can be intimidating to only look at polished and finished professional work, never see the mistakes in the process, because it is easier to see what the skills are when you can see where they are misapplied and wrong.

OM: **What about the criticism of film schools? Some say the famous ones are absurdly expensive and growing bigger to capitalize on the profit margin, using their famous alumni as myths. And professors can't give bad grades to students because it isn't good for the school's reputation and its ability to attract more students . . . There are all these commercial considerations that seem to dominate film programs and are about the industry of teaching rather than teaching.**
DK: Look, we are a graduate program and our courses are pass/fail. The undergraduate situation is different. With only a few exceptions I know of in this country, undergraduate programs are part of the general education. They are not conservatories and they have the problems that undergraduate grading systems have. In our program we will put a student on probation if he is not

performing well; we want to let the student know that we think the work is not up to what it ought to be. But we don't usually fail people unless they are blatantly not doing anything. We did create this grade, low pass, to indicate that we could get some degree of differentiation recognition. If someone is doing outstandingly well, we let them know by giving him or her honours on the course. The question is whether we feel impelled to keep a student for financial reasons, and the answer is no. We get a very good crop of students; our dropout rate is extremely low. I could imagine schools in which professors are reluctant to fail students and I have seen it occur to a certain extent elsewhere, I won't deny it.

OM: The ideal would be a faculty that feels no financial pressure because their tenure is guaranteed, their salary is guaranteed, and therefore they can speak their minds freely and evaluate students freely.
DK: The disadvantage to that is that you don't get much new blood in your faculty if everyone is guaranteed their position. Knowing that nothing can shake them from their position, faculty can get more and more set in their ways and indifferent to the needs of their students. The biggest difference as I understand between European schools and US schools is that we take more students. That has its pluses and minuses too. Frankly, in our experience of evaluating who gets in and who doesn't, we've learned you can't be that accurate. Last spring I spoke with a young French film-maker who had made a fabulous short film and came here to show it. He had tried to get in FEMIS and failed, and he explained to me the application process, which is quite lengthy. He felt that, in the end, the decisions on acceptance of students were fairly arbitrary, and I agreed. There's a big argument right there: is it better to have an arbitrary selection of a few students and leave many others out, or give more people a chance? When I started in the graduate program at NYU in 1980, they had a major fellowship that gave students a year's full tuition. That was a three-year program; I taught in the third year so all the students I got to know were third year. The fellowship was awarded to two students at the end of the first year. So there were two people who were chosen as the outstanding students by their faculty after a full year in their class. And I found, over ten years, that only one of those students was ever top of the class when they got to me in the third year. If it is that difficult to evaluate a student after having him for an entire year, then it is bound to be difficult to draw fine distinctions between young students when they are applying. That's a major downside to the process.

OM: I was wondering if you could explain another commercial aspect of film programs like Columbia. There seems to be some overlap between the corporate world and the academic world. Your festival is actually called the Polo Ralph

Lauren Columbia film festival. Why is there a need for sponsor relationships for such an expensive school that is a lucrative business in itself?

DK: Our festival is sponsored by Polo Ralph Lauren and New Line Cinema and we have had significant support from Lifetime television. They don't meddle in our curriculum. Ralph Lauren likes their association with us because they know we do good work. It reflects well on them and they have a certain amount of philanthropy as certain corporations do. I believe that *New York* magazine sponsors the NYU festival. Lifetime donated a large sum to renovate our screening room, which is now the Lifetime Screening Room, and it looks beautiful and their motives were similar. But they don't affect our curriculum. It's true that we do have needs for private funds. I have never taught in a state-funded institution in this country or elsewhere. I am just guessing that the need to please the people who decide how much money you are going to get would be greater in the government-funded institution than it is here.

OM: The question I guess is why is it really necessary to have that corporate involvement in schools that take such high tuition?

DK: Let's take the two cases separately. I mentioned the screening room. Our screening room had fallen into disrepair and we needed several hundred thousand dollars to repair it and make it into a top-flight academic facility. Well, that is a straightforward academic need and we had no obvious ways to get those funds, so we got sponsorship. Maybe I'm completely ignorant of the British system, but are there no big donors there who get buildings named after them? The film festival arose as our student production got better and increased in quantity, but the pedagogical need is to show student work to the public. I feel that that is the final step of a student's work in film. You can't simply show the films to the faculty, talk about whether they're good or not and leave it at that. You owe the student a public forum. Like any training in the arts, a film festival well presented in a good venue costs a little money. So we formed a relationship with Polo Ralph Lauren and they help us present it, but they are helping us to meet an already defined academic need. I see nothing wrong with that. Our students benefit from it.

Jessica Levin

Ayad Stehle-Akhtar

Claudia Myers (centre)

Jessica Levin, Ayad Stehle-Akhtar and Claudia Myers: Students, Columbia University Graduate Program

Jessica Levin is the Production and Development Manager for Madstone Films, a New York-based digital film company. She has produced numerous short films including Gina, An Actress, Age 29 *(Jury Prize for Best Short Film, 2001 Sundance Film Festival).*

Ayad Stehle-Akhtar is completing his MFA at Columbia this year. He is currently working on two projects with fellow graduate Tom Glynn: American Stranger, *a feature-length film, and* At Play in the Fields of the World, *a documentary about sports and American culture. Ayad and Tom are recipients of a 'Young Documentary Film-makers of the Year' award from the New York Documentary Centre.*

Claudia Myers attends Columbia University's graduate film program as a writer/ director. Her non-thesis short, Buddy & Grace, *shared the Best Film Award at this year's Columbia Film Festival, in addition to winning the National Board of Review Award (Second Place) and the Lifetime Student Film-maker Award. She also received a Nickelodeon Screenwriting Award in 2001 for her romantic comedy* Kettle of Fish, *and is currently writing a second feature,* Clinical.

Oren Moverman: I'd like to start with the road to graduate film school.
Jessica Levin: I did an undergraduate BA in Modern Culture and Media, formerly known as the famous Brown Semiotics Program, and I went to Columbia to do the producing program.

OM: So you came in knowing you wanted to produce rather than direct or write?
JL: Yes.
Ayad Stehle-Akhtar: I also went to Brown where I studied Theatre. I never entered the halls of the modern media department.
JL: We wouldn't let you – you were too sincere.
ASA: Now I'm at Columbia directing.
Claudia Myers: I graduated from Yale with a BA in Comparative Literature – a very useful and a very valuable degree!
JL: I actually tell people that my degree in Film Theory is immensely valuable. And they believe me.

CM: A degree in Comp Lit is more useful than I thought, actually, because it's really about stories. So I have now, three years into film school, discovered that a non-film degree was actually somewhat useful. I came to film school really wanting to be a director and now I'm split between writing and directing.

OM: Why did you decide to go and pursue a master's degree in film-making as opposed to pursuing a career in the industry after undergraduate school?
JL: I had worked a bit in the New York independent film world before going to Columbia. Among other things, I worked as a research assistant to a director, and beyond that I did some post-production work and some set work for companies like Good Machine and Killer Films. I knew that working my way up through production was one way to go, but not one that would teach me really how to work with writers and directors. I knew I wanted to be a producer and working through production was going to be a hard way to pursue that. A more academic context was necessary for me in developing material with writers and directors. I knew Columbia, as opposed to NYU, had a great producing faculty, there are a lot of good New York independent producers around there, and since a structured program already existed for producers, I thought it was right for me.

OM: Basically, you were very targeted. You knew you wanted to go to Columbia, you knew you wanted to produce. That's not always the case with film students. Directing is usually the thing.
ASA: In my case it was about directing and it was very different, I guess, because I came from a different background. I worked in the theatre for quite a while. I had a very long apprenticeship with a couple of very good figures in the theatre, Andre Gregory and Jerzy Grotowski. For me, going to Columbia is intertwined with my personal life: I got married and I started to ask the question, 'Do I really want to be doing theatre?' I guess I realized that I never read the reviews of plays, I never went to plays, the only thing that really interested me was film. I'd open the *New Yorker* and read the film reviews every week. I wanted to work in a dramatic something-or-other, and film seemed appropriate because it was already a theme in my life and the thought of doing film seemed suddenly very exciting. But it took me a long time to realize that was what I wanted to do. And then I thought, 'Well, what's the best way?' I tend to be methodical in the same time as I remain open, and the methodical aspect of my personality said, 'How are you going to achieve this? You can go into production, you can learn how to make a movie, or you can go to film school.' I come from a bourgeois background, and film school is obviously the more comfortable choice. But at the same time, I think I realized that to learn how to make a film was not necessarily to learn production-wise, but to learn to speak a language that I didn't know

how to speak. The best way to learn how to speak a language is to go to a community of speakers. And that was really my intention – aside from hiding from the world for another four or five years, frankly.

CM: I was really very passive after college. Basically, I waited for the careers fairs to come to campus, and I was hired by a law firm as a paralegal. I came to the States from France with the intention of going to college. I was going to go to law school and then return to France to a law firm and sort of mirror what my father had done. And I thought working as a paralegal made the most sense because of the whole myth about being a paralegal as a way to learn a bit about what it's going to be like to be a lawyer. Well, it didn't do that at all, I hated it! I got carpal tunnel syndrome, I was bordering on depression and I quit, and I started working for a couple of independent producers who did both theatre and film. It was just the ideal job. It was fun, it was a completely different field, it was creative, it went in a million different directions; everything about it appealed to me. It was the first time I felt really passionate about something. I worked as a development person and then I realized I really wanted to start working on my own things. I wrote a really bad script, I took a couple of classes, I worked on some shoots and I felt that I was outgrowing my position. I was facing the choice of staying in the industry or moving somewhere else. I was trying to find out whether I wanted to work my way up as an executive, or go the creative route. It's funny, because in my family going to film school is very bohemian while going to law school is very safe. But to me, it actually felt that if I could get into a good program, it would give me some skills that I just didn't feel I had. And the irony is that the skills I thought I needed most, the technical skills, were the only things I really didn't get from Columbia. I still don't know a whole lot about how to operate a camera. Not a DV camera, I'm talking shooting 35mm, it is still a mystery to me. Working on the Avid I can do, but it's not like I'm a wiz. The things I thought were important were not really important. What film school gave me, basically, was time to explore my own ideas. As corny as it sounds, it allows you to find your own voice, to figure out what is a story worth telling in film, what makes a great character; and just taking that time and nurturing what it is about you that is going to be interesting to other people.

OM: Ayad also called it a place to hide for a while from the particular struggles of the film world.

CM: The only thing I would say instinctively about that is that no one is quitting a director track when they leave the industry and go to film school. It's because you're on the administrative/executive side of things or you are working your way through a long chain of hurdles. What you are doing in film school is in some way trying to take a short cut to doing exactly what you want to do.

You want to get out of film school and be a screenwriter, and not be some assistant writer on someone's staff by being a reader first. In a way, it's to better yourself so you can go into the world on a higher level.

JL: I think that's true. One thing I was trying to do by going to school is reconcile my rigorous academic/theoretical undergraduate background with finding new innovative ways to actually bring those formal ideas back into production.

ASA: Jess and I were at Columbia together for a couple of years and watching her go through it, it seemed like it was a really great thing for her. So I don't know about the 'hiding' element in her case. I mean, Jess, you were really engaging those theoretical questions and really pursuing what you were interested in, on a truly fundamental level, and always trying to find creative practical ways to implement your ideas with people in class or in school or in films. It seemed like a very rich process for you. So I wouldn't call it hiding. I speak of hiding for myself because I've always been obsessed with being a great artist or something like that. And so I have always devoted myself a little slavishly to the process. I guess I've always shied away somewhat from criticism that would put my sense of self in jeopardy. At the same time, criticism is essential because without it I can't grow. So it's a fine line. Maybe I went to school in the hope that I was going to begin to be able to find some kind of back and forth, that I was going to be able to tolerate the criticism and be allowed to grow. I don't know that I have a strong enough constitution to throw myself into the world with my vision and say, 'Okay, I'm going to get this done come hell or high water.' I don't know if I have that constitution, for me it's been a much longer process and will continue to be.

CM: I tend to think the distance from the industry that school allows is also really productive on a critical level. It allows you both proximity and a distance that you can't have when you are in it. Whether it is about hiding, I'm not really sure. For me it was about giving myself distance to focus on personal development. When you are outside of the industry it's easier to look in and say, 'Well, that aspect of film-making is interesting to me,' as opposed to, 'That looks like my next pay cheque, I hope to work on that film.'

OM: In that sense you are all saying that film school can actually be a very practical choice as opposed to what some people would call a huge waste of money.

JL: At the same time I think you are talking about a certain select group of people who go to graduate film school as a trade school with certain professional expectations that they are going to come out with a degree and a portfolio and be able to work in the industry. But then look at the tuition and how outrageous it is that there are actually enough students to support these graduate programs like Columbia, NYU and the ones in California! Everyone is paying $100,000 for a degree that will most likely be worth very little. I don't want to say I know the percentages, but I would guess that if you look at any given graduating class, there will be about two people who will ever work in the film business, let alone write or direct.

CM: Oh, come on, it's not that bad. I think two people will actually write and direct for a living.

JL: The others will find low-level jobs they could have got without going to film school.

CM: Maybe. I'm not sure. But let's be honest here, first of all film school is a luxury. We are basically all buying ourselves, at a very high price, the luxury of focusing on our own work for four or five years or however long it takes. That isn't afforded to everyone. So I don't know how practical it is in terms of the tuition investment and what the future holds. I actually never thought about school as hiding or not hiding from the industry. If you are going to a program you are satisfied with, you're kind of ensuring that among your teachers you are going to have people who really respond to your work and challenge you in a way so you can improve yourself. And I think that's really the whole point of the exercise. It's the process of trusting that some people will teach you things and make you better and encourage you to do better work.

ASA: I think that there is an aspect of hiding which is essential, if there is a process under way. Organically speaking, there is a time when an organism, like a butterfly, is not exposed to light, and is allowed to remain unto itself in order to grow. I think that echoes something that Claudia was talking about – you grow in your own work. Film school is a shelter that can be very positive. I think a lot of people, and I am not excluding myself from that group, use it as a crutch. And I'm not even sure I do that, I include myself in that just to say I'm always suspicious of myself. I think there can be something positive about it as well. Hiding doesn't have to be pejorative.

CM: I think the nourishing environment/shelter analogy is really tired after your second year because you have been in class fulltime. You haven't had time to do anything except go to classes and do your assignments and then suddenly you've got this desert of three years with one class a year. People say, 'I don't really have the time to worry about getting a job,' but they do after the first year. And so you should worry about getting a job or use the time to nurture your wonderful screenplays. I think a really interesting part of the program is this freedom you have to develop your crowned jewel – your thesis film or your thesis script. We are going through that now.

ASA: My approach to that has been very different. I work with another guy, Tom, up at the school. We make our films together. And as soon as we finished classes, he and I sat down and we asked ourselves: fulfilling requirements is going to get us what? It's going to get us a degree. So what? We came here to learn, at least *I* came here to learn, a language. And now I have to put that language to use and ultimately use the time that lies ahead after the first year to do something which would further me on my so-called artistic quest in the world. In fact, much to my shame, Claudia is a third year and she finished her second-year film, and I am in my fourth year and still haven't finished my second-year film. I have been doing some work for hire outside, and have been sort of working on what I and Tom think is going to get us into the world as opposed to making a short film, which I have never felt would get me anywhere. Frankly, I have no desire anymore to work in the short form – it just felt like a waste of time after a certain point. But that's obviously a very different approach to the one you have taken, Claudia. You seem to have thrown yourself into doing.

JL: As a producer, my path was somewhat different. There were things that were valuable about having to do the same coursework as writers and directors in the first year, mostly because the classes put me together with people I wanted to be working with. But I don't think producers should have to go through things like Directing Actors classes – that was a total waste of my time. I felt I was very focused on what I was going to do and those classes for me were not directly on course with producing. I fought it kicking and screaming.

OM: Isn't it essential for you as a producer to understand what directors are up against?

JL: Yes, I understand the pedagogical impulse to say, 'Even producers must learn what it's like to talk to actors.' But I think you get that working with directors as a producer; they express that to you. The producer does not work with actors, it's a fact! I was producing a lot of student films – altogether I think between eight to ten of them – and I felt I didn't need to be at Columbia anymore. Creatively, I didn't feel like I needed more time in the institution. After my second year, I produced four serious short films and then I was running the film festival. I felt that was all I really needed to do in school, but the faculty still tries to tell me, 'But there are still requirements . . .' And so I haven't graduated. Other than producing a lot of short films and developing feature products with a couple of writer–directors at Columbia, I feel I was ready to get outside the academic structure that allowed me the freedom from other work for a while. It was almost like a neurotic impulse to get back into a more professional context. But at the same time, I wonder if in three years' time I'll get the urge for an academic getaway somewhere, so that I can get back that distance from the professional world. It wouldn't be at Columbia, but like an imaginary conservatory somewhere I could go teach. I can see why academic institutions have appeal, for that critical distance they allow.

ASA: That's an interesting point because that makes me think that this whole question of artistic development is something that is not necessarily aided by the presence of teachers or mentors. There can be instructive guidelines in school that are helpful. And if you find some teacher you really have a connection with, who understands what you're up to and what you're up *against*, then that's great. But I have not necessarily found that. I know that what I'm saying is contradictory, talking about hiding in school and then not wanting to have anything to do with school. But there is room and a time for both. I haven't had much to do with school recently, and that's been essential because I'm developing my own work. So I haven't had anyone tell me, 'This works, this doesn't work. This is what audiences like, this is what they don't.' I'm working on a strange documentary at the moment, which I really enjoy, and I also see some of the work people are doing in the editing room, and much of it looks very good, but they all look like 'a Columbia film'.

OM: What makes a short film 'a Columbia film'?
JL: Studied mediocrity.
ASA: Perfectly put. You know the first shot and you know the close-up is coming and you know that the next shot is going to communicate the information that we need to get the story moving. So that we have the expectations that are going to be fulfilled by so many number of shots . . . To me it just seems a little practised. But maybe that practice is essential.
CM: I disagree. I was speaking with someone yesterday about the perception of NYU, and they were saying that Columbia films are actually much fresher in general. But I was truly impressed with the students I entered the program with. I feel like there are a lot of talented people in my class in very, very different ways and I appreciate that.
ASA: I certainly think that our class had many vibrant personalities, but my criticism is of the school, of the programmatic attitude. There are people of great potential, I think, but they are filling school requirements with every shot.
JL: I think you have to admit that Columbia doesn't put a lot of weight on innovation. It's very much about teaching traditional practices and classical techniques, and innovation is rarely valued. There are a couple of amazing members of the faculty from whom I have benefited tremendously, but for the most part the general aesthetic underpinning the program is quite out of touch with the more interesting things happening out there. Which is about taste.
ASA: Maybe it's an interesting fight to be in when you are at school, I don't know. This whole idea of learning the rules so you can break them may actually work. But I don't see the results of that in many of the student films.
CM: I have a different take on it. My school experience was in France and it couldn't have been more rigorous. I did a baccalaureate and I was a very good student, I liked learning. And in terms of film I think it was very helpful for me to understand the basics of what drives a story, what is action. Yes, Aristotle and all of them were on to it way before any of us, but I don't think that's actually

such a bad thing to learn. I had no film theory training; I did one class. But theory really doesn't interest me; I like films because I respond to them emotionally, and somewhat intellectually also. Maybe that's the kind of film I'm drawn to, which doesn't mean 'Hollywood blockbuster', it just means communicating on a visceral level where I have to know the basic rules.

ASA: In my opinion the most interesting people working in cinema today are Hou Hsiao-Hsien, Todd Haynes and Abbas Kiarostami. And I don't think that these kinds of directors correspond to the rules and regulations learned at film school.

CM: But how do you teach that? You can't teach that kind of artistic vision. I think the shortcoming of the program is that there isn't enough room for more experimental work. There used to be a teacher at Columbia, Larry Engel, who had a more open experimental approach, encouraging students to play with screen time, play with screen direction, play with all the conventions like the 180-degree rule. So, definitely the program can use more of that, but what appears to be the slightly more formulaic approach is also the easier and more logical way to teach.

JL: Also, when you look at the demographic that's recruited for these schools, you see it is fairly homogeneous. People come from a certain class, a certain education level. It's mostly upper-middle-class kids.

ASA: *Upper*-upper middle class.

OM: Is it a playground for the rich?

JL: Sure.

ASA: But hasn't art, for the most part, always been the playground of the rich?

JL: Absolutely. But interesting work can be created at this moment when technology is changing and media doesn't have to be the terrain of the rich. When tuition is so insanely high, it attracts certain types of people who can afford to pay that kind of money and they tend to contribute to a generally lethargic, unstimulating film culture that is also perpetuated by the faculty. Aside from the very few visionary people I was impressed with at Columbia, most of the students did not come from interesting worlds and did not have much to say as people. Again, it's that studied mediocrity: most students are not interested in saying new things in new ways, so all the craft training in the world won't provoke them to create interesting work, at Columbia, NYU or any other expensive program.

OM: Why did you choose Columbia?

ASA: In true bourgeois fashion – there's that word again – I looked at the university rankings as compiled by *US News and World Report*, and applied to three of the best six schools, UCLA, USC and Columbia. Very methodical. I

didn't send anything to NYU because I've never taken a photograph in my life and they wanted to see some sort of photographic portfolio. UCLA was my first choice because it was a very small program. I had an interview there and I ended up arguing with this woman about the importance of thinking in pictures. They wanted me to pitch them a story based on the assumption that I would get 20 million dollars tomorrow. I told her I submitted a story in my application, but she insisted that I think of a situation where Twentieth Century Fox gave me all this money to make a film. So I started pitching her a story I was thinking about that day. I was trying to describe a scene, going through the psychological motivation of the characters, and she said, 'I'm not *seeing* what you're describing, I want to see it.' By that point I was perplexed. I started talking about Ingmar Bergman and Sven Nykvist and their relationship, where seeing and speaking are interwoven, and how there are other kinds of films, and film-makers like Rohmer, where the films could be about other things than seeing. Anyway, I didn't get in. I got into Columbia, which was my second choice and that was it. I can't imagine what would have happened if I got into UCLA. To be so close to the Hollywood studio world, I'm sure I would have been out of my mind in no time. It was a misguided idea, and I'm now relieved I ended up on the East Coast.
CM: That's a glamorous story compared to mine. I applied to NYU and Columbia, didn't get into NYU.
JL: For me New York was a determining factor. I only applied to Columbia. But it would never even occur to me to study or work in film on the other coast.

OM: Is there an anti-Hollywood feeling at Columbia?
ASA: *Faux* anti-Hollywood. Very polished. I think they are into the kind of new indie movement that dominates now – smaller than Hollywood, maybe somewhat smarter, but still accessible. So many of the teachers are invoking the classical language of Hollywood films and are extolling the virtues of the ideal Hollywood film: engaging, moving, thought-provoking entertainment. And there's nothing wrong with that. It's perhaps misguided to think you are going to film school to learn how to be an artist. You may be on that path, but that's not what you should expect to learn there.
JL: I found a basic illiteracy in the program. A lot of the faculty were well versed in classic texts, but ignorant of most of the small, contemporary films coming out, which I think is strange, since a lot of the students could look to these films as production models for the kind of films they would want to make as their first features. I'm not sure if it's still true, but people didn't seem to be paying attention to the more daring films.
CM: I wouldn't say that the faculty members are completely in touch with everything that's going on, but I don't get a feeling of isolation from the small art-house film world.

ASA: We need to make a distinction. Jess and I had some of the same teachers and I think there is a faction of people that corresponds with what Jess is describing, but there is another group that does go to see those films.

JL: I think it's because I come from the undergraduate tradition of cinephilia, where students were rigorous moviegoers. We'd go to see everything. I was puzzled to find a lack of dedication to art-house film culture in New York.

CM: Maybe because many of these teachers juggle teaching with working in the industry, so they don't have the time.

JL: But that's the point – it's their business to see movies.

ASA: There is a stodginess around the university. Maybe it's the Ivy League cachet, maybe it's the whole academic setting, but there is definitely a stodginess to the place.

JL: That's right. And my problem with the students and faculty may have to do with the university as a whole. It's a school in New York that seems to have very little to do with the more vibrant parts of the urban cultures around it. It may be larger than the film department. It's an isolated university in many ways.

OM: Within this so-called isolation you have many working professionals, directors, producers, writers of some fame and acclaim, who teach some of your classes. Is there a difference between the teaching film-makers and the fulltime professors?

CM: There is and there isn't. But I think it adds something to have a faculty that is also active in the industry.

JL: There seems to be greater dedication amongst faculty members who don't have such active careers. They simply have more time to devote to the students. And that can be a good thing, it can also be difficult – it depends on the quality of the teacher. And some of the more inspiring teachers can be so precisely through their work. There is no across-the-board distinction between working faculty and 'professional' instructors, it varies from class to class. Some classes you get a lot from, some very little.

OM: What classes did you get least from?

CM: Strangely enough, the directing classes – because there are four classes over two years, and we all feel that it's too much, that by the end of the first year you got the point. There is only so much we can do in terms of taking scenes as directing exercises. I remember when I started the program I felt, 'There is not going to be enough time for me to catch up and fill the gaps in my knowledge of film theory and practice, and all these directing classes are going to be essential.' Then I realized that many of the students came from undergraduate film programs, and I thought to myself, 'Why have they come here, to get more of the same?' I felt I needed the training because I had none, but undergraduate film students were supposed to have that already. Anyway, by the second year, no matter where you came from, you felt overfed with the directing classes.

JL: I think the undergraduate production programs in the US tend to be more experimental or theoretical. I know the NYU undergraduate program is narrative-based, but compared to the kind of dramatic development work that is expected of students in graduate programs like Columbia or NYU, it is much less sophisticated and rigorous, and much more technical.

ASA: I think a lot of people come into the graduate program – and I certainly can't except myself from this – expecting, or hoping, to find someone who, like a parent, is going to see them and recognize their value and their worth. It may be an important process psychologically for the growth of the individual, a maturation that is essential in their lives that has more to do with who they are than with film. And, in my experience, faculty members at Columbia are relatively good at saying, 'Listen, I'm not here to be your mom or dad, I'm here to teach you.'

JL: 'I'm not here to love you. I'm here to oversee your development.'

ASA: Exactly.

JL: There might be a need for mentoring that is pursued through that, but that's often substituted by finding a community of collaborators who provide that kind of support. It would have been nice to find a producing mentor at Columbia, more like this great mentor I had at undergraduate level, but then you tend to find those people as you enter the professional world. I must say that probably the best class I had at Columbia wasn't actually a class but an independent study group I put together with another friend from Brown. There were five or six of us, and we got together once a week and pitched each other stories and work-shopped them. They were probably the most rigorous and productive sessions I had at Columbia, without any faculty supervision, just a self-selected group of fantastic people. So it was the other students who ended up pushing me and inspiring me.

ASA: The most important experience I had at Columbia was to meet my collaborator, Tom. In the first year I really thought I had found the community of speakers I was looking for. It was very cohesive. But after the first year, there were scholarships given out, Jess received one, I did, along with a few others in our class, and there seemed to be an abrupt disintegration of any cohesion in the class.

CM: It's true. I wasn't in their class, but we had a similar experience. The first year was like day camp. You were finally with a group of people who loved films as much as you did, wanted to talk about film as much as you did. We used to go out every night and be excited about talking to each other. But after the first year, clusters were forming and people started seeing less and less of each other after class. Part of the reason is money, but also people get more nervous as time goes by, about producing something, creating contacts, moving on. You can go into film school as a group, but you certainly emerge as individuals. And it is part of feeling more professionally motivated as you go through the years. You start to feel that there is more at stake.

ASA: In the first year people were genuinely excited about the possibilities of each other's work. But as time went on, people got less excited and were getting really annoyed with having to read each other's work. It was very clear in their criticisms.

JL: I think it's part of learning a new language. Those group critiques were practice grounds for the skills you'd just been taught in the first year. People are practising their vocabulary as they learn it and that comes off as enthusiasm, but it's not about the work, it's about discovering the tools of a critical language. After a while people start evaluating how the work is living up to what they've learned, and that's where the annoyance may come in.

CM: It's true that as the program moves on there is a strange atmosphere of insecurity, where people are over-critical of each other's work.

ASA: I don't think it's overly critical, I think it's unconsciously destructive.

CM: I've seen people trying to do something a little different, and there would be this gleeful criticism session where they get slammed. I think it comes from insecurity and the pressures of creativity.

ASA: But it also ties in with this studied mediocrity we spoke about. A Columbia film is typically agreed upon by everyone as 'good' if it falls on the right side of the axis.

JL: There are basic skills being taught and the films tend to be attempts to show how well you've learned those skills. It's about a celebration of mastery of basic skills. And I would hope that a program of creative people would be about something a bit more exciting, a bit more worthy.

OM: So, $100,000 or so later, was it worth it?

JL: Given that the majority of those who graduate as screenwriters or directors will not write screenplays or direct feature films for a living, I don't quite know what they're thinking spending that kind of money. It may be a thing to do in this generation, to go to film school. But it baffles me that people should graduate as directors and then not attempt to direct. As a producer, I knew I had very few job-tracks, and I certainly wasn't paying this kind of money, because as a producing student you don't need to spend money on making a film, you just need tuition and living expenses for the two years you're there. And I feel I can evaluate what I paid for and say that it was the right choice for me. But I don't know how directors can evaluate that.

CM: Well, I don't think I could have done the short film I have just directed without having gone to the school, so at the moment I think it was and is worth it. But talk to me in five years, see if I'm being paid to direct.

ASA: I'm obedient to the process, and the fact is that my parents paid for this experience. My alternatives would certainly have been different if it were not so, and I'm not sure my answer would be the same if I had to carry around thousands of dollars in loans. Practically, did I find a community of speakers? Yes. Did I learn the language? I believe so. I have met a collaborator, who I believe is the most important relationship of my life apart from my wife. Those things are real attainments. Whether they become the realization of a dream of winning the Cannes Film Festival, I don't know. I'm not sure that kind of a dream is what the whole film school experience is all about ultimately.

JL: The investment is in the process that you want to undergo, and who knows what financial upside there might be to that?

OM: And where do you go from here?

ASA: Home.

JL: Brooklyn.

OM: Seriously.

ASA: Seriously, I'm trying to remain open. I'm trying to write a feature script with Tom, we'll find the right people, and I hope we'll make the film. But I'm remaining realistic.

CM: I hope to make films for a living. I hope I can translate everything I've learned into making something on a professional level.

JL: For me it's not just about producing films, but about producing a certain *kind* of film. And without that I don't have a reason to remain in the film business. I would love films to get back to something aesthetically and politically more disruptive. And if that can't be done, it's probably time to do something else.

Michael Spiller

Michael Spiller: Cinematographer
Oren Moverman: Screenwriter

Michael Spiller graduated from State University of New York, Purchase, NY. He has shot all of Hal Hartley's films, including No Such Thing *(2001),* Henry Fool *(1997),* Flirt *(1995),* Amateur *(1994),* Trust *(1990) and* The Unbelievable Truth *(1989); as well as* Drop Dead Gorgeous *(1999),* The House of Yes *(1997),* Niagara, Niagara *(1997) and many other features, music videos, commercials and documentaries around the world. He is currently lensing and directing episodes for the HBO series* Sex and the City.

Oren Moverman graduated from City University of New York, at Brooklyn College. He co-wrote Alison Maclean's Jesus' Son *(1999) and Bertha Bay-Sa Pan's upcoming feature* Face. *He also wrote* William Burroughs' Queer *for actor–director Steve Buscemi and is currently working on the adaptation of A. L. Kennedy's* Original Bliss.

OM: People tend to refer to NYU and Columbia, both undergraduate and graduate, as the places to go to for film on the East Coast. They have fame, celebrity graduates, a solid reputation and high tuition fees. You and I came out of very different systems. I graduated from Brooklyn College of the City University of New York, you from Purchase, a New York State University. Why did you end up there?

MS: First and foremost, because they accepted me. The fact that they had a film program was a large part of the reason I went there, even though I wasn't completely certain I wanted to major in film. I took a couple of theory classes in high school and I got very excited. I had always been a huge fan of watching films, but hadn't got into the sort of analysis one gets into in a film class, the sort of layered reading of a film where every element has meaning, where the aesthetics is central to what the film is about. I started making movies when I was 12. I saved up money from my daily newspaper route and bought a Super-8 camera and made these little monster movies and detective stories in my neighbourhood, so I had a little bit of hands-on experience. When I went to Purchase as a Liberal Arts major, I took a few film classes and really got turned on. There was a professor there named Tom Gunning*

---

* Author of D. W. Griffith and the Origins of American Narrative Film (University of Illinois Press, 1991).

who was just brilliant, who really inspired me. The first class I took with him at Purchase was on *film noir* and I knew, 'This is it, I have to major in film.'

OM: Listening to him in a theory class suddenly defined your own attraction to film?
MS: His passion was so clear, and he showed the depth to which you could read a film. We had analytical projectors and we could look at scenes again and again in slow motion. He would have these simple exercises where the whole class would clap whenever there was a cut on screen, to make the edits completely visible. And he would also get more intense, with serious Freudian analysis of films, things that would open your eyes to characters or plot elements that created such clarity in the way you watched a film. It was so much fun just listening to him, being active in learning. Then I got into production, which was a whole other thing.

OM: Going into production classes, were you thinking about getting more training in how films are made, or were you thinking, 'I want to be a director'?
MS: At the time I don't really know what I was thinking!

OM: Ah, the joys of youth . . .
MS: I think things have changed, though. But at that time it never really occurred to me that I would be a film-maker, or someone who works on films. I don't even know that I considered it a career. When you're 18 years old and in school, you're thinking it's great to watch a lot of movies – you're still just a kid enjoying yourself. Purchase provided a film production education that is rare for undergraduate school: 80 per cent film classes and 20 per cent liberal arts, so it was a true major. But I didn't really have an objective. Nevertheless, people started to respond more and more to my cinematography work – films I shot both for myself and for other people. But even then I never thought it was how I was going to earn my living.

OM: It just snowballed?
MS: Yeah, and you know Purchase is a state college, tuition was low, it was really a working-class program and people were struggling, working a couple of jobs to buy film stock, which brought a unique energy and drive to the school. And we were really lucky to have fellow students and faculty who were constantly inspiring and pushing everyone, so all the planets were aligned at that particular moment in time for people to come out of that program as working film-makers. I don't know how it was for you at Brooklyn.

OM: Well, it was also very much working-class, and also completely multicultural, sometimes funky. But it was a somewhat different type of program, very small, and your film work was just one part of your academic requirements. You had your major and you needed a certain amount of credits to earn your degree, but you also needed to fulfil school requirements, which were demanding and diverse and had nothing obvious to do with film. It was far from 80 per cent geared toward film production or studies – more like 35 per cent.

MS: Well, I think going to Purchase was really like going to a conservatory. Of course, I've never been to a conservatory, so I may be way off base, but you have to admit it sounds good! And on one level it was a bit of a limitation being so immersed in film, because you find there are lots of classic books you haven't read, there's a lot of knowledge in other disciplines you were never exposed to. In a way it was like a graduate program without the benefit of four years as an undergraduate, so it was a bit myopic. Your program at Brooklyn, I guess, was more of an attempt to get the best of two worlds, which is what liberal arts programs offer.

OM: Sometimes in such an attempt you simply get too little of the two worlds, you're left with just a hint of what film-making is and with only a general overview of other academic subjects. It could be neither here nor there, and it can also be, as I feel in my case, that a single class in Genetics or a seminar on the Middle East can shape some of your perspective on film-making. To tell you the truth, I don't know how much our faculty trusted us to become working film-makers. The feeling within that academic structure in the early 1990s was more like, 'Get a well-rounded education because you never know what you're going to end up doing.' How was your program structured?

MS: In the first year, everyone made their own films on Super-8. We wrote, directed and shot them with a minimal crew. In the second year, we started shooting 16mm. We had a documentary track too, which was really great. After the sophomore year, you would decide on a sub-major within film – documentary or narrative. But you would still be writing, directing and shooting your own projects. You would also be taking writing and acting classes as well as drama classes, the history of drama, *et cetera*. By the junior year everyone would direct their own short film with a full crew, and you would therefore crew for other people in other roles. Also in the sophomore year – or is it junior? I can't recall – you would make a film together as a class, with a working director and a working DP, and the whole class would function as various crew members. The idea was to get a real experience as to what it is like to work on a film; you didn't have to discover it all yourself. People would get assigned to crew positions, boom operators, gaffers, assistant cameramen, and the definition of those positions would be laid out for them on a day-by-day basis. And sometimes the fit was wrong, you got a guy who has sound-mixer written all over his forehead and you assign him to work the lights, so it's not going to work. And so you learn about performing your job on a film set responsibly, and you also find your own professional niche, getting some experience in that niche that you can take into the real world.

OM: What do you mean when you say a 'working director' would work with you?
MS: I mean one of the directing teachers, not an outsider. Our teachers were working professionals, which is not as unusual as one thinks it is in the state or city schools. They were people who made films and had film experience on various levels. We would pick a film 20 or 30 minutes long and work on it as a unit.

OM: Sort of basic training?
MS: Yes. It was incredible. I think I was a camera assistant on our class film, and I really bonded with the guy who shot it, a Russian cinematographer named Yuri Nayman.

OM: He shot Slava Tsukerman's cult classic *Liquid Sky*.
MS: Exactly. They instituted a cinematography class that year, taught by Yuri. I really thrived in that class. They basically invented it as we went along, Cinematography 2, Cinematography 3, and so for a year and a half I took classes that specialized in cinematography, which was unusual. We basically learned by doing, but also through analysis of the work. The classes were equally scientific and aesthetic, which is what the job is. You have to know the science to manipulate the craft to suit your aesthetic ends.

OM: What was the feeling amongst the students as all this work was going on?
MS: It was not much different from what it's like working in the field now. There's a certain amount of competition, because there is always the year-end review and maybe not everyone is going to be asked back. But at the same time there were loads and loads of support. You couldn't expect someone to crew for you on your film unless you were willing to crew for them. But it goes beyond that – you need people's critical eyes, you would look at other students' rushes and read their scripts and give notes. We were all living in the same place too, so we were all living and breathing film, sometimes to a fault. But people needed to be collaborative in order to make the program work, much like in the world of film. Whatever personal feelings exist between crew members, if they are not going to work together they won't be able to do their individual jobs well. I'm sure it was the same for you.

OM: Completely. People were honestly supportive and encouraging, they would watch your back, cheer you on and work with you. But it also had to do with a certain underdog feeling, we had good equipment but little of it, we had no money to invest in our work – this was before the digital revolution – and no one had heard of us at that time as a place to study film. That's changed somewhat, it's a bigger and stronger program, and video saved the day financially. What's your take on the 'To film school or to film?' dilemma of the digital era?

MS: One argument I have in support of film schools in any era is that you can end up having immensely productive creative relationships with your school-mates.

OM: It doesn't happen all the time, but I can think of director/DP teams that met at film school, like Wim Wenders and Robby Müller or Emir Kusturica and Vilko Filac. How did your relationship with Hal Hartley come about?

MS: Hal and I were friends before we were collaborators, although as class-mates we critiqued each other's work and discussed the merits of our projects over many beers! In our junior year, when we made our individual films with other people shooting, Hal asked me to be his DP. He said that my stills and the movies I shot for other people as well as for myself were the same pictures he would have made, only different. He liked that. And I guess that's one of the keys to a good collaboration, seeing things the same way but keeping it some-how different. That's pretty much half the battle right there. When a director doesn't have to sit and describe every detail and nuance in the film to a DP, you have a shorthand method of working, which is a great advantage. The first film I shot for him went very well and he asked me to shoot his senior project, his thesis film, and that also went really well.

OM: By that time did you see yourself emerging exclusively as a cinematographer?

MS: Yeah, I think I shot a record number of thesis films and I graduated in essence as a DP, because I never really completed my own thesis film to an answer print. But I think I shot five other projects, and the faculty recognized that was my strength, that I was gravitating in that direction. But even at the time I never imagined that Hal and I would be shooting features and travel-ling the world, doing all this stuff. It didn't click. It was only in my senior year, when a friend of mine who had graduated a year before got an assistant to the editing assistant job, or something like that, on *Broadway Danny Rose* (dir. Woody Allen, 1984) that I realized it was possible, that you can earn a living doing film work. It finally dawned on me that this was going to be my career.

OM: People like you who I knew at school were really shocked upon entering the industry to realize the cruel reality that no one considers them cinematographers, no matter how great their reel is.

MS: I know, so I just began crewing on different things for very little money, and it simply took off from the moment Hal raised some money and asked me to do *The Unbelievable Truth*. So, I guess the people you meet at film school and the connections you make can prove to be very valuable in the long run. In a sense, going to film school is like being on a film shoot for four years, where the people always stay together on set and off.

OM: Where tight bonds form in the trenches . . .

MS: Absolutely. Of course, it's great if you can pull it together and just make your own film without going to film school, but it's not just about writing something, shooting it and assembling it to completion. It's also about the critique you get and the feedback from the faculty and your peers that guides you in a certain direction as a creative film-maker. Sure, with digital video you can go out and shoot something in no time, and cut it on your iMac, download it back and play it on your TV, which is very exciting. But it also opens the door to a lot of crap. It doesn't make you a film-maker. Being able to push the 'Record' button doesn't mean you have anything to say on film. So I'm afraid there will be a lot of bad film produced and also a few really great things that will find an audience, on the Internet or whatever venue they can get.

OM: Let's face it, most film students want to be directors. And more and more people go to film school. Whether you want to call it a dream factory or a playground for the rich, the reality is that they are being sold an illusion to a certain extent. You can't really go out into the world saying, 'I went to NYU, Spike went there too, here is my short, my profession is directing, when do I start?'

MS: It's very rare that you walk out of film school with your diploma and your thesis film and a three-picture deal. I'm sure it does happen, and some films really catch the eye of people who give money to film-makers out of film school. But not everybody emerges as a director. Most of the people I went to school with are working professionally in the field, few are directors, some are cinematographers, camera assistants, gaffers, sound mixers, editors or people who move around – like editors who also direct. And I guess you have to be flexible and realize there are a lot of great, satisfying ways to work in film. And that's something that film schools are not totally comfortable saying. They can be great training grounds for many jobs in film, but they tend to generally emphasize the writer/director track, because that's the path that attracts most people to film schools. But you can figure this out while you're there, if you open yourself up to the situation around you. I saw the path to cinematography opening up for me at Purchase at that particular time; you saw a path to screenwriting at Brooklyn and you took it. Ultimately, it's about a private journey through an institution that could be great or lousy, and it's what you make of it.

OM: What about the tuition business? SUNY and CUNY are not free, but they are considerably cheaper options next to the big schools. It's easy to criticize NYU and Columbia for their absurd tuition and general expenses, but they have the market cornered. When I tell people I went to Brooklyn, I get the benefit of having gone to a school in a borough that is now artistically hip, but I am also always asked, 'Do they have a film department?'
MS: Yeah, that's the reality. But I wouldn't limit it to film school. Whether you choose to criticize higher education for not being free in America, or embrace its competitive nature, it's the same for every discipline. The major universities are also businesses. My experiences, and yours I believe, are different in that respect: it's not about the money. As far as I am concerned, it's a luxury to go to college in the first place, and it's a luxury to be able to get out of college with no great debts that force you to take jobs outside the field you've studied. A smaller, cheaper college provides you with that luxury.

OM: What about growth of the human being in school? It's not all job training?
MS: The growth is what happens when you are not looking. You don't sit there and think, 'Gee, I'm really *growing*.'

OM: Did you have any professors who cared about your personal growth and not just about having you graduate from Purchase and move on?
MS: SUNY Purchase had this phenomenal faculty who really were like counsellors as well as educators. They were mostly very talented people who were making films or who had made films. You didn't get the sense of 'Those who can't do, teach'. We also had really small classes, only about 13 people. And the SUNY Purchase documentary class was only composed of three people in the years I was there, yet no one ever thought about cancelling that track – they were concerned about those three people. And the faculty did care about the emotional wellbeing of students, especially when people were making their thesis projects and selling their comic-book collections, working three jobs or borrowing money from their parents to make their film. There was a lot of pressure, people felt like they were mortgaging their future, and the faculty were very attuned to that, very caring. It helped that it was a small program.

OM: Did where you went to school make a difference in the professional world?
MS: No. In fact, it didn't make a difference that I went to film school at all, in terms of name. What made a difference was what they got when they hired me.

They got someone who had one line in his résumé, but had worked on 20 films already in every capacity. So the first few projects I worked on as a Production Assistant, I could load mags and help the gaffer, because I knew how to do all that stuff. So I very quickly moved up the ladder and could work in a number of job categories. I worked as a gaffer, grip and camera assistant. But my education was still continuing after school. I was still a sponge, just taking it all in. I had a diploma, but my film education continued.

OM: On the flip side of that, I met someone yesterday, a screenwriting teacher at one of the bigger schools on the East Coast, whose work has never been produced, who admitted to struggling to finish every screenplay he starts to write, completing none. He was baffled about how films get made. So I was wondering about him as a teacher. Did you feel that because your professors were working film-makers, you got more out of them?
MS: It's a difficult line to walk. I've taught these little seminars at Purchase and other places, and have found that it is really hard to get someone who is regularly working in the field to commit to one or two days a week for a semester. As you know, the business is uncertain and you have no idea of your schedule. But at the same time, whoever does teach has to be committed to be there, plan a curriculum, work outside their teaching hours providing time for counselling and office hours on campus. So you don't just want to go for the prestige of having big names teaching your students if they are not going to be there for the students. A working professor's list of film credits does the student no good; it may help the school raise contributions, but that's not what it should be about. It's not going to benefit the students. So what you sometimes get is someone who wants to take a break from the uncertainty of the freelance lifestyle and wants to be secure, and so he teaches. Or someone who feels it's important to impart their knowledge to the next generation of film-makers. And yes, sometimes you get those who do nothing professionally, but who knows, at the level they teach they can be great at certain things students really need.

OM: I found that those teachers who never worked regularly in film, or did so only in the distant past, gave the students much less of a sense that they could get out of film school and work in the industry. It just wasn't their world. And maybe that's not a criticism, but in a system like City or State University that is suffering from lack of resources and an inferiority complex to begin with, it's not much of a confidence-builder for students. Did you have the confidence that you would be working in the industry after film school?
MS: I did, and in fact my cinematography teacher got me a job, one day a week, working on a movie he was shooting. That was great, that taste of a professional film set. Other professors would leave for a semester to make a movie and

when people left to direct or shoot or write, you realized it was part of the trade-off, that there was something to do at the end of all this schoolwork, a film world in which you make a living.

OM: What was your impression of the students when you went back to teach?
MS: I love film students; I love their passion. That's why I enjoyed working in the non-union world. It's a very tough business to work in, and you have to love it because you are not going to make money in the first couple of years. You never know if you're going to work again after a job is done. There's lots of fear to live with in this business. You have to love it to stay in it. And it's a great feeling when you go to work surrounded by people who love their jobs. That isn't the case with most professions. It's rare to smile as much as we do at work. And when I stood in front of 15 Purchase students as a teacher of sorts, a working professional coming back to his school to talk, I saw the desire to learn in their wide eyes, and it was really exciting. I could see how it could be a huge turn-on for an instructor, something that can be immensely satisfying.

Nicholas Ray, Greenwich Village 1970. © Chris Reguis

Nicholas Ray: Director, Teacher/Master, Harpur College, State University of New York, Binghamton
Danny Fisher: Producer/Graduate, Harpur College

Nicholas Ray was one of Hollywood's most distinctive directors, thanks to such legendary films as They Live By Night *(1949),* In a Lonely Place *(1951),* Johnny Guitar *(1954),* Bigger Than Life *(1956) and, of course,* Rebel without a Cause *(1955). In 1971 he came to teach at Harpur College where, along with his students, he made a film entitled* We Can't Go Home Again. *His death in 1979 was immortalized by Wim Wenders'* Lightning Over Water/Nick's Film *(1980).*

Danny Fisher is the president and creative director of City Lights Media Group. He served as editor and executive producer of the documentary A Generation Apart, *and as producer on* Unforgotten: Twenty-Five Years After Willowbrook *(1997) and the feature film* Torn Apart *(1990). Danny is currently producing* Interrupted, *a feature film about the life of Nicholas Ray, based on a screenplay he has co-written.*

Oren Moverman: You're developing a project about Nicholas Ray, but you are also a former student and a teacher's assistant of his. I don't know of any story about a film teacher that is wilder and more extraordinary than the Nick Ray story. It is the most extreme form of what a film teacher could be and how he can affect the lives of his students. Tell me about how you came to study with Ray at Harpur College.

DF: I actually wasn't a film major, but I was really interested in the arts at high school. I was inspired by my brother Joe, who's a painter, but it was frowned upon by my parents who were Holocaust survivors and wanted something practical for me. I felt pressure to do anything non-artistic, so I became a psychology major when I went to Harpur. Before I got there I picked up my father's 8mm camera and one of those 'How-to' books on film-making and brought them back to school. I started shooting stuff with my girlfriend at the time. I began to feel that film was something I could get into. It was an art that bridged science and math, things I was good at. Then in my freshman or sophomore year of college I heard there was this really cool guy who was making a film on campus and it sounded interesting, so I showed up.

OM: Nick Ray was hired to teach film. How did the course go from him teaching to actually making a film on campus?

DF: The film department at Harpur was experimental, drawing on the avant-garde philosophies of people like Larry Gottheim, Ken Jacobs and Ernie Gehr. So it was very controversial the way this experimental film department brought in Nick Ray, the former Hollywood big shot. They thought they were bringing in this great Hollywood outcast director who was a rebel and a new advocate of the avant-garde, but when he came in he was shocked to discover that the students didn't know how to load a 16mm camera. Students were making what he considered to be masturbatory 8mm films and didn't know how to work with each other. He thought that the film department was just full of people doing their own indulgent exercises and they were never really going to learn anything. For him, film was about being with a crew and to some extent the commercial Hollywood process was the tried and true way of making films. So he wanted to change the thinking at Harpur and the only way for him to teach film was by doing film. He just thought, 'To hell with these classes, let's just make a film and you'll learn everything there is to know.' And the faculty really resented him, either out of envy or because of artistic differences. And also because he had an alcohol and drug problem which he would openly share with the students. He wasn't your typical university professor.

OM: What was his approach with the students?
DF: He was always the director, but he rotated crew. He taught film in the sense that we were all on a set, working and watching him run it. There were call sheets, which got the experimental film-makers very upset. While he was anti-Hollywood intellectually and emotionally, he was forming his own little studio there, he was looking for his system.

OM: What were some of his unorthodox methods?
DF: Nick tended to work at night, so some of the classes would start at around midnight. And there were never any classrooms. The classes would go on for ten hours. And so there I was shooting little 8mm films, thinking that was cool, starting to like these experimental films, and I hear about this wild guy with long white hair, an eye-patch and outrageous approach. The first time I encountered Nick Ray was the middle of the night and he was shooting in a basement. He was the most charismatic guy! He was shooting a scene in which a girl called Leslie, who came from the theatre department to become the female lead, gets tomatoes thrown at her. I walk in and see the lights all over the place and the professional-looking camera. And I see Nick Ray acting as key grip and pulling the dolly as well as calling action. Her monologue was this really brutal confession about getting the clap from this man she knew, and at the end of the monologue Nick orders the students to throw the tomatoes at her. And I saw Nick take Leslie off to the corner of the room for half an hour when he wasn't satisfied with her performance. I don't know what he was saying to her, but it was

Nicholas Ray and Danny Fisher at Harpur College.

very deep and appeared very seductive. I looked at all that and thought, 'Fuck everything else, this is it!' This wasn't just film school, it was life experience, and movie experience. And I was just observing, standing there. Nick didn't know me. I went up to him and said I wanted to be there. He asked me if I had Cinema 101 credits and I told him that, frankly, I wasn't even a cinema major. But I told him how much I wanted to do it and he said, 'Just come aboard.' And I never signed up or got credits for it. He was never technically my teacher, and I was so struck by him and the way he immediately made me a part of the family. I don't know why, but Nick Ray always seemed to have this respect for students. I think that he really respected those who were always asking questions. He didn't believe in hierarchy, he was obsessed with film-making and with life, he was genuinely interested in people in a way that few teachers can express honestly. He was wide open, always teaching, manipulating like hell.

OM: But he was also the director of 20 Hollywood films, many of them classics. At one point he was the highest paid director in Hollywood, or so he claimed. He was a Howard Hughes favourite, he studied with Frank Lloyd Wright, he slept with movie stars, and he lived a director's mythical life. What was he doing teaching there and making essentially the student film *We Can't Go Home Again*?

DF: I would have to answer that from two perspectives: from my perspective as a student at the time and from what I learned subsequently. From the first perspective, I don't think I really thought about his films and I hadn't even seen all of them. Most students didn't know any of them. For me it was all about the here and now and I didn't think, 'Here is this great director.' I just thought, 'Here is this incredible artist and great teacher.' Not 'Here is a washed-up artist, what is he doing here?' The first film of his I saw was *They Live By Night* and at first I thought it was just another American genre film, but then he talked a little about it and I began to really love it. He showed us *Bigger Than Life* in his bedroom on a sheet stuck to the wall . . .

What I know now about him is that he needed a job and that none of the projects after *55 Days at Peking* really got off the ground. He collapsed on that film, and had a premonition that he would never make another film again – since he technically sold out and did it just for the money. But he was never bitter about it, you never got the sense that he wanted to be somewhere else. And later on when we started working at Lee Strasberg together, he told me that teaching had been more rewarding than his entire directing career. I thought he was kidding. But he felt that when he was teaching he was still working as an artist, still growing. At Harpur the attitude was more like, 'If I am going to teach film I'm going to make one goddamn kick-ass of a film that would break all the rules.' He experimented with multiple images and video in its infancy and the synthesizer that had just been developed by the video artist Nam June Paik. He was, in a sense, already an avant-garde film-maker, but the way he would work on the film was more traditional, at least in structuring the crew work.

OM: There seems to be a very romantic aspect to his classes.
DF: Nick Ray's classes were never classes. They were the antithesis of film school. They were about life and about art. So, yeah, there was something romantic about the notion. He would teach about the concept of action and motives. He would also say certain things over and over, like, 'Content determines form, form conditions content'. He would also go nuts when someone didn't respect the actor. He would go into a tirade and say, 'The camera services the actor, the actor does not service the camera.' These were things we would hear over and over again. He had ways of working, but he never sat by a blackboard. You can see a lot of that in the book Susan Ray edited from his later writings, it's a great learning tool in itself, just sharing some of his ideas about acting and film: the concept of action, 'The melody is in the eyes' – which he learned from Charles Laughton. We are basing our film about Nick on Susan's book, so this may come off as a shameless plug, but I've heard of film students who have read it and were truly inspired.

OM: **When I read Susan's *I Was Interrupted*, and the great introduction she wrote, I thought that this guy couldn't help but teach, he surrounded himself with young people because he did not respect his own generation and he shared his amazing experiences and knowledge with them.**

DF: We all became family, although I was probably an outsider because I was strait-laced at college. We would all drink together, but I never did drugs with him, like some of the others. He was very giving that way! He would shoot up and his line was that amphetamines were his vitamins, and I accepted that. We were like a commune, all sleeping and breakfasting at his house. I thought, 'Is this a film school?'

OM: **It officially started as school and it became a production with your teacher?**

DF: Very much so. In the last few months we decided to finish the film in Hollywood, because we were invited to the Cannes Film Festival. And I hitched there with Tom Farrell, one of the leads, who became an actor and has worked with Wim Wenders over the years. And I think Nick wanted to re-live some of his Hollywood experience in the making of *We Can't Go Home Again*. So there I was, not getting school credit for the film, and I wasn't even on campus. From the point of view of the film department, it was like a runaway train. We were spending tens of thousands of dollars on sound recording *et cetera*. He put his pay cheque into it and of course, nobody got paid and we were spending money we didn't have, just accumulating debt.

OM: **The making of the film turned into an adventure that lasted a few years.**

DF: Yeah, he was a teacher that taught by doing, and then it became a movie about teaching. *We Can't Go Home Again* was very prophetic in being able to show what was going on around the country at the time, but it was also a lot about self-discovery, for example in the scenes of Nick's death. So he crossed the line from being a teacher to being a film-maker and an actor working with students. But as a film student, I couldn't think of a deeper experience. I learned a lot about making a movie, but on a greater level I got immeasurable inspiration. Here was a guy for whom art was more meaningful than anything else, which was kind of the scary part of him. If you're going to take your art so seriously, are you going to have to sacrifice your entire life? If I looked at the Nick Ray model, I would say you have to give it all up. He was a role model as an artist and a teacher, but not as a father or husband in his personal life. He was sort of a father figure and a guru to the students, yet he was approachable. You could suggest changes. And it takes a certain sort of brilliance to be *interested* in the way he was, he was always interested. And we all

Nicholas Ray (in Santa outfit) directs *We Can't Go Home Again*.

believed as students that the movie would change the world and make waves. I still believe it. Once it is reconstructed and released, I believe it will have an impact.

OM: Many students have special relationships with their teachers, and some of the people I've talked to remember certain professors as influences. But it sounds like his effect on his students' lives was not something they are going to be able to shake off.
DF: He had a strong intellectual side, but there was little required reading for the students: Camus' essay on *The Myth of Sisyphus* and Bergson's essay on laughter, that's it. And he sometimes posed the question, 'When you write your biography, will it read "The Art In My Life" or "My Life In Art"?' And, as I said, I'm still not sure what the correct answer was, but the theme was, 'What's more important?' For Nick Ray it was art and film, and anyone who wanted to join that was going to be touched by it for ever. Now, that may sound overly dramatic, but it happens to be true. Thirty years later, we are still talking about it.

OM: At what point in your relationship with Nick did you realize that film was going to be your calling?
DF: Within the first five minutes of meeting Nick Ray. I never signed up for anything because it never seemed relevant. It wasn't school, it was an experience. I became part of the devoted group of fanatical acolytes. There were others who came and went, and some who could call me brainwashed and thought the whole thing was too intense. But about 50 people were affected by him. And a lot of people became successful after the Nick Ray experience. I have a feeling that a high percentage of students wound up working in film – certainly Jim Jarmusch did, from the sober NYU years, not the Harpur years. But Nick was never a conventional teacher. I learned a lot technically, but what I did I had to teach myself by doing. In Hollywood Nick had this idea that we were going to be able to do everything professionally because we happened to be in a fancy mixing studio or somewhere, working with Hollywood professionals, but it was often really a fiasco. Our tracks were out of synch and the splices were falling apart. Nick was not a technical teacher, you had to teach yourself and you made mistakes.

OM: At one point he left Harpur but the film went on?
DF: I think he was there for two years. And when he left, that experience ended for me. Then I had the experimental experience. That was traditional film school, you know, classes. There was tremendous resentment toward the chaos Nick created at Harpur. One teacher, who is still there 30 years later, still can't hear his name.

OM: What happened to *We Can't Go Home Again*?
DF: Nick continued to edit it, but I kind of lost touch, although I still saw him from time to time to show him my short films. We would meet in New York and he would be very gracious. In terms of *We Can't Go Home Again*, I didn't participate directly after the Cannes Film Festival and after he left Harpur, but I understand he travelled between New York and LA and San Francisco, borrowing cutting rooms until he wore out his welcome. He would pick up new acolytes and devotees along the way. He continued working on it, and on a second version with his wife Susan Ray several years later. I became involved again much later when he started working with Wim Wenders on *Lightning Over Water*. Wenders became intrigued with *We Can't Go Home Again* and was convinced that there was a great movie in there. I was hired by Wenders to organize the film and complete it. We all knew, though, that Nick was going to die of cancer by then, and that the film wasn't going to be completed. But I organized the materials. In the last few days before he died, I met with Nick and talked about the completion of the film. And I really saw that this was his vision and I didn't really know how to complete the film without him. Even in its uncompleted stage, I believe that *We Can't Go Home Again* is a hidden masterpiece.

OM: What are we talking about technically? It isn't just a narrative film in the conventional sense?
DF: Well, it is a narrative film, and not an avant-garde film in the Stan Brakhage sense – you know, visual poems. Yet there are purely visual passages. Nick had this dream, where he envisaged a cinema where you can take a 600-page novel and tell it in 90 minutes, and he had been fascinated with multiple images for a long time. In fact he had tried to incorporate multiple images in his last commercial film, *55 Days at Peking*, but apparently the producers didn't go that way. He wanted to shatter the rectangular convention of the movie screen, where you see one frame at a time. He wanted to make it a work of art where scenes could be played simultaneously and could complement each other or be in counterpoint to each other together with several frames on the screen at the same time. So it's shot in various formats, 35mm, 16mm, Super-8, video and synthesized video. And almost all of the film consists of multiple images where you see more than one scene at a time, sometimes as many as five, six, seven images all at once. Sometimes it's only two scenes, but they are two major scenes playing at once, chronologically unrelated but playing against each other thematically. I don't think it's ever really been done in the way he envisioned. There's documentary footage in it as well, scenes from the 1972 political conventions and the Chicago riots. He also had some plans for animation, something I only recently found out about. I saw Mike Figgis's film *Time Code*,

which does have the split-screen quadrant. But Nick was trying to do a different type of thing, a painting and a symphony at the same time, really trying to treat the screen as a canvas upon which you paint emotionally and in terms of narrative. On the other hand, it wasn't pure avant-garde with only visuals. There were real actors, students, and there was story, although it drifted. There are themes, and the overriding one is the students and Nick searching for themselves, what Nick called 'self-image'. They want to know who they are, and retreat from the counter-culture world of the 60s. They want to know who they are and why they are there. In a sense, he was exploring the 'Me Generation' very early on.

OM: You mentioned that you were invited to be Nick's assistant when he taught at NYU and the Lee Strasberg school. How was he different as a sober teacher than the addict teacher?

DF: On the one hand, he was a completely different personality, and on the other, he was the exact same. He was lucid, and was more like a professor. Even there it started out fairly conventionally but it changed. He didn't like the students sitting and the teacher standing at the front of the class, so he got rid of all the chairs and we sat on apple boxes. On day one, he wanted to get away from the teacher label. And while it was more formal, he started to have strange improvisations, which I would film – some students didn't get it, others did. All of a sudden it was a bit like the making of *We Can't Go Home Again*. Maybe because of his sobriety and illness it didn't have the same reckless abandon, but it was still different. Lee Strasberg was a great teacher, but with him you would always know who was the giver and who was the receiver. Nick Ray's class was much more freestyle. He would always let you come up with the ideas he had in mind for you; he had this way of making you work, answering questions that led you to a conclusion he already arrived at. It was very empowering. And he could also insult you, make you feel small, but he never ended it there, he had a way of apologizing and drawing you back in. And when he went to NYU he was shooting improvisations with much less structure and was much more interested in creating experience. In so doing, he also created a lot of confusion among the students, which he wanted. I think he believed that confusion was more interesting than looking at textbooks. If someone was confused they were forced to deal with it, make art out of it. It was kind of wild, a once-in-a-lifetime experience.

DIRECTORS

Walter Salles. © Paula Prandini

An interview with Walter Salles
by Peter Stephan Jungk

An accomplished maker of both documentary and fiction films, Brazilian direc-
tor Walter Salles has centred his work on the themes of exile and the search for
identity. His first feature, Terra Estrangeira/Foreign Land *(1995, co-directed by*
Daniela Thomas) was crucial to a renaissance of Brazilian cinema, travelling to
many festivals, winning several prizes, and enjoying great success in Brazil
before its US release in 1997. With his next feature, Central do Brazil/Central
Station *(1998), Salles sealed his international reputation, winning the Golden*
Bear at Berlin. His latest work Abril Despedaçado/Behind the Sun *was unveiled*
at Venice in September 2001.

Peter Stephan Jungk is a novelist and screenwriter. Born in Los Angeles in 1952
to émigré parents, he studied at the American Film Institute. He now lives in
Paris. His books include Stechpalmenwald *(1978), a collection of short stories*
set in Hollywood; the biography Franz Werfel: A Life Torn by History *(1990);*
and the novel Tigor *(1991, published in English as* The Snowflake Constant*).*
His most recent novel, published in German, is King of America *(2001), a fic-*
tional biography of Walt Disney's last months.

Peter Stephan Jungk: Let's start in the very beginning – if you agree?
Walter Salles: I was born in Rio de Janeiro in 1956, but three years later, 1959,
I left Brazil when my father became a diplomat. He was appointed twice or
three times on a mission to the United States. We lived in Washington DC. for
four years, from 1959 to 1963. One of the first images I recall clearly is a
Wendersian image of the back window of a car leaving the tunnel of
Washington behind as we are heading towards the freeway to go to another city.
The idea of leaving, and the idea of that oval back window was already a frame
in itself. It's a *leitmotiv* that comes back again and again. I remember very
clearly being in the States in 1963 because of the shock of the Kennedy assas-
sination – how shocked my parents, how shocked everybody was. Television
still being in the pre-CNN era, it wasn't *live*, so communication was heralded
from person to person, and this remains with me vividly, very much so, even
today. We left right after that; my father was again appointed, to France this
time, and we lived there for six years.

PSJ: What schools did you go to in France?
WS: I went to several schools in Paris. I never felt totally at ease in the French school system. Yet I continued to study in the French school system until I was 17 – as we were going back and forth between countries, I went to the Lycée Français wherever we lived and did the Baccalauréat de Philosophie, which explains why I'm bilingual. I remember very vividly the events of May 1968, in Paris, just before we left. I went to school on my bike every morning, and back home in the afternoon, and I remember observing everything from the bicycle level.

PSJ: A dolly perspective.
WS: A gentle Mizoguchi-perspective of constant travelling. I remember seeing Daniel Cohn-Bendit reaching the Odéon theatre. Ten years ago, he came to Brazil, doing a series called *Nous qui avons tant aimé la révolution*. I had done a series of documentaries on the re-democratization of Brazil, so we lent him some footage for his own series. I told him, 'I remember you so vividly from those days in May 68.' And I thanked him for making life so much more interesting at that point, because the only other interest I had in that specific period of my life was cinema. Living in Paris, I didn't like the city at all.

PSJ: Did you watch films in the movie houses or on television?
WS: In the movie houses, the *salles*. We lived near the Avenue de la Grande Armée, which leads from Arc de Triomphe to the Porte Maillot, and there was a cinema on that avenue called Studio Grande Armée, if I'm not mistaken, that only showed double features. It doesn't exist any more. I was so sad to walk by there a few years ago and discover it had become a—

PSJ: McDonald's?
WS: No, a motorcycle shop.

PSJ: How did you get in at the age of 11 or 12?
WS: Well, I just did! Another cinema, the MacMahon, wasn't far off either. And they showed retrospectives that were incredibly interesting. I saw most of John Ford then and there. At that time, in Paris, in early adolescence, I started writing stories – not really short stories, longer stories, in those Clairefontaine copybooks, and every story filled one of them. The story was told on the left. And on the right were drawings that depicted the scenes on the left.

PSJ: You were storyboarding?
WS: I was storyboarding, yes. I remember drawing, and I remember developing the stories. They were mostly adventures. I loved Kipling, but also

Conrad, very early on. I always invented stories that took place in strange, distant latitudes.

PSJ: Did you keep those Clairefontaine booklets?
WS: I would love to go through my mother's belongings that have been put into huge boxes after she passed away. I could probably fill half a room with my writings and other things like that.

PSJ: The school you visited in Paris was private?
WS: Yes. There was no school on certain afternoons, like Wednesdays, and weekends, of course. I told Cohn-Bendit that one of the best things that happened in 1968 was that you could go to the movies more often – the teachers were on strike! The first films I saw were by Chaplin, obviously.

PSJ: And then a lot of Westerns?
WS: Yes, but Chaplin's films I saw when I was very young, six or seven or eight. I still remember my astonishment that other films I was seeing weren't as good as Chaplin's; because obviously very few films are comparable to *Gold Rush* or *City Lights* or *Modern Times*.

PSJ: Often films you see when you're very young are so impressive, and nothing ever matches them thereafter.
WS: That's true. What was your first film?

PSJ: I was five and still living in Los Angeles. It was a short French film called *The Red Balloon*.
WS: A wonderful film.

PSJ: Years later, I found a book with all the pictures from the film. It made me understand my love for Paris. It originates from that very first film I ever saw.
WS: It was a very effective film, I remember it very well.

PSJ: Your jumping back and forth between different countries reminds me of my own childhood. I was born in Los Angeles, but during my first five years my parents couldn't decide where to settle. They lived in London, in Munich, in Paris, and in between they returned to LA – by ship, because my mother had a fear of flying. We finally settled in Vienna. And when I was 16, we left for Berlin, in 1968. I believe that being 'déraciné', as a child, gives you a very special kind of energy . . .
WS: Sometimes, when I settle somewhere, I almost miss that feeling of being lost.

PSJ: But you hardly ever settle.
WS: Well, even when I stay in a place for a while, like for four or five months per year, I miss the idea of movement. Also, symptomatically, I sometimes sleep better in hotel rooms than in my own apartment in Rio. And I feel totally at home in airports . . .

PSJ: You have two brothers?
WS: I have three brothers. One of them is a documentary film-maker.

PSJ: Are they all older?
WS: One is older. He writes for the theatre, part-time.

PSJ: Then there is the publisher?
WS: In fact, he's the same one.

PSJ: Did all of you go on those trips with your parents?
WS: Not my older brother, the publisher, who is my half-brother. He's ten years older than I am, from the first marriage of my father. We became best friends a bit later in life. Our paths didn't cross in the very beginning. In the Washington DC. period, he was still with his mother. I really only met him when I was 12 or 13, that was when we really started to see each other. And I was 15 or 16 when I started living with him. Which is also something that is very determining. Discovering a brother when you are that age is really an important gift.

PSJ: Like in *Central Station*, when the boy realizes that he has a brother?
WS: Yes. There is a direct link. I actually never thought of it. Must be because you grew up in Vienna . . .

PSJ: I can tell you why I immediately jump on that link. In my work, in my writing, to include autobiographical elements is no shame. On the contrary . . .
WS: I don't think that one could do otherwise. Yet I admire those who leave autobiography out of their work completely. Though I don't believe that you can really escape your own history. Even authors who re-create, or have the capacity to re-create a different form of reality – I am thinking of Fellini, for instance – always include their own history, their own experiences. When you see *Amarcord*, you can see how important those early impressions of childhood were for him. The same is true about Almodóvar, his *All About My Mother*, which represents the complete opposite direction of what I do in cinema. I think my experiences as a documentary film-maker shaped my fictional work . . .

PSJ: How would you position yourself altogether? As a European film-maker? As a Latin-American?

WS: I sometimes get the impression that European cinema seems to have abandoned epic storytelling. European film-makers are basically interested in developing what Jacques Rancière in *Cahiers du Cinéma* has called 'infra-fiction' – tidbits of fiction, looking at 'smaller' events that become representative of a larger canvas. It's an impressionistic approach. As opposed to story telling in American cinema which is basically about the larger context, what they call the 'supra-structure', or 'supra-fiction'. I think that part of Almodóvar's strength derives from the fact that he escapes the 'infra-fiction'. He manages, as a European film-maker, to create some kind of epic quality. The European answer to something that Scorsese or Coppola have managed to do with their epic outlook that can be seen in *The Godfather* or *Raging Bull* or *Casino* or whatever. So the fascination with Almodóvar has to do with the fact that he is one of the few *auteurs* from Europe who can overcome this actual trend in European cinema. But getting back to Brazilian cinema: I think our strength, but also our weakness, lies in our desire to tell stories that have a continental quality, to embrace a whole country that is almost a continent. Even the smaller Brazilian films, like the ones I have made, show the ambition to encompass all the main structures prevalent in that specific part of the world. You can see the same trend in Latin-American literature. And I am not only talking about Gabriel Garcia Márquez and his *Hundred Years of Solitude*; I mean also Cortázar and Borges. And in Brazil there are some wonderful writers too.

PSJ: Although Brazilian literature is very little known outside Brazil, if I am not mistaken. Comparing the two main currents we talked about, the European mainstream and the American one, Scorsese, Coppola, et al, where would you place Cinema Novo?

WS: Cinema Novo was certainly the point of convergence of different vectors. On the one hand, of neo-realism and the possibility to create not only a new cinematographic aesthetic, taking the camera to the streets, but also a new cinematic ethic. Neo-realism put the faces of an entire nation, a *people*, on the screen for the very first time . . .

PSJ: They hadn't seen themselves in cinema up to that moment.

WS: Exactly. So that was one of the vectors, but there were others too: the sudden urgency to tell stories, influenced by the French *nouvelle vague*.

PSJ: Both movements started more or less at the same time?

WS: They dialogued. But before all that, there was the Eisensteinian influence on Glauber Rocha, in particular. Don't forget that Glauber was extremely affected by

Eisenstein's montage technique, and very much influenced by Eisenstein's desire to interfere with reality, to change reality to a certain degree. At that time in Brazil, in the late 1950s, beginning of the 60s, before the *coup d'état* of 1964, there was the general impression that a new country could be created from scratch.

PSJ: As we see with the city of Brasília.
WS: This is when a new capital blossoms in the middle of nowhere, Brasília. This is when Bossa Nova, the new trend in music, emerges, and this is when Cinema Novo appears.

PSJ: All more or less at the same time?
WS: Exactly at the same time. Before the revolution. Under the democratic government of Juscelino Kubitschek. The revolution of 1964, and then the second *coup d'état* within the *coup d'état*, in 1968, just blocked all possibilities of the development of those new movements. There was such a creative upsurge that it became impossible to block it totally. But several of the Cinema Novo directors had already gone into exile. Among them Rocha who went to Africa, to Spain and Portugal. He actually shot films in Africa and Spain. He fell ill in Portugal and returned to Brazil only to die, when he was 43 years old.

PSJ: Did you ever meet him?
WS: I saw him two or three times, but I never had the chance to speak to him. But Nelson Pereira dos Santos is a close friend of mine – and he really was the originator, the initiator of the Brazilian Cinema Novo. I admire him tremendously. In 1955 he made a film called *Rio 40 Degrees*, long before Cinema Novo started. Yet the film must be considered a forerunner, it announces the arrival of something, although it's not considered the film that ignited the movement. *Rio 40 Degrees* was prohibited by the political police of the time, based on the assumption that in Rio the temperature never rises to 40 degrees Celsius! They said it distorted reality.

PSJ: That reminds me of the regimes in Eastern Europe, before 1989.
WS: In fact, the film showed life in the *favelas*, in the slums of Brazil, for the very first time. Again, what the film tried to do, following the tradition of neo-realism, was to put the face of a whole country on the screen. But even that film with such popular qualities could not find a large audience when it was finally authorized – months after it was first banned. It just reached two or three screens and stayed there for two or three weeks, and then it was taken out.

PSJ: Are they now revived and shown, those films?
WS: Yes, you can often see them on television . . .

PSJ: Pereira dos Santos is now in his late 60s?
WS: He turned 73 this year. He is preparing a new film, he is still very creative.

PSJ: Was he a teacher too?
WS: He was a teacher and one of the founders of the cinema school of the University of Rio.

PSJ: Did you go to film school yourself?
WS: No, I didn't. I first went to university, in Rio, studying the History of Economics, for four years. I was possibly one of the worst economy students in the history of that university. Several Brazilian film directors went to that school too – so every time I'm asked, 'What's the best film school in Rio?' I say it is the History of Economics Faculty . . . But the other 'film school' that has an interesting historical tradition in Brazil is the architectural department of the Federal University, and also its law department. Several masters from the Cinema Novo studied there! Later, I left for Los Angeles and studied Communications at the Annenberg School of Communication at the University of Southern California. I have friends who learned cinema in film schools. For many reasons, I chose a different route. I also had the chance to make my own films in Super-8 very early on, before turning 15. As a result, I feel self-educated more than anything else.

PSJ: The Annenberg School was within the USC campus, in downtown LA?
WS: Yes. But I left before reaching the end of the course, because that was exactly the moment when a certain democratization started in Brazil. Television channels suddenly multiplied, and I was offered the chance to do my first documentaries. So I started shooting my first film three months before getting my master's degree. I opted to return to my country. It was interesting on many different levels: I got nearer to a reality I wanted to plunge into, which was that of my own country. On the other hand, I could also do documentaries, which was what I was aiming to do since I was 17, but I'd never really had the possibility until then.

PSJ: You arrived in Brazil and immediately had the chance to shoot documentaries?
WS: At that time, in 1983, there was a certain policy of laissez-faire that allowed the arrival of new television stations. The regime accepted the idea of a limited diversity. That is when I started to do a series of documentaries for television. The initial one was a series about Brazilian society called *The Brazilians*, a ten-hour series that I produced but didn't direct; and an 11-hour series on the Xingu Indians, an indigenous nation in the Amazon region. Also, this was the time

when I started to direct a series of profiles of film-makers and artists, such as Fellini or Kurosawa, writers like Borges and Garcia Márquez, but also politicians, like Fidel Castro, who was seen on Brazilian television for the first time in decades, or the Spanish prime minister Felipe Gonzales. That was a specifically important program, because for one hour, prime time, Gonzales talked about the necessity of re-democratization – in a country where a dictatorship was still alive.

PSJ: Did you do the interviews?
WS: No, I directed them. We won many prizes with this program in Brazil. We did between 30 and 35 such hour-long programs that were presented monthly, for three years.

PSJ: Allow me to return to your personal story . . .
WS: Let me just add something regarding the films of the Cinema Novo movement first. They were films about the larger canvas in general. To give you a few examples: Glauber Rocha's *Black God, White Devil*, shot in 1964, was about the structure of the land in Brazil, and the relationship between the classes that exploit the land. Like all major works of art, it's a film that talks about a lot of topics – not least about the racial and cultural roots of Brazil, about how they oppose and complement each other. A film shot in 1966, *Sao Paolo S.A.*, by a very interesting director called Luiz Sérgio Person, is about the industrialization of Brazil on one side, and the disintegration of personal relationships on the other – how one is personally affected by the pressure of the larger political situation. It is also about the beginning of the endemic corruption in Brazil. So you see that most of the Cinema Novo doesn't fit into what Jacques Rancière calls the 'infra-fiction'. It is closer to the tradition of *Rome – Open City*, or of the cinema of Eisenstein.

PSJ: If I'm not mistaken, I think I detected an Eisensteinian moment in your second feature film, *Foreign Land* – the lovemaking scene, which I adored by the way. Because normally, one sees such unbearable love scenes in cinema!
WS: I'm a total fan of Eisenstein and most specifically of films of his that are less known, like *The General Line*, later entitled *Old and New*, in which there are two montage sequences that count among the two most impressive sequences in the history of cinema for me. One being a procession of a group of peasants who believe their prayers may bring about rainfall – going into a scene that I find so indescribably beautiful and powerful, the terrible disappointment of these same peasants as they realize that the rain isn't coming. Their feelings of doubt become visible, tangible. Suddenly the sacred, religious truth is put into question. And the second sequence is the one in which they produce butter and

cream. That amazing moment of utter joy – set in stark contrast to the first sequence of despair. I believe what fascinates people about Eisenstein has less to do with his montage technique, and more with questions regarding the realm of desire. I read a brilliant dissertation on Eisenstein and Brecht recently, written by Hans-Joachim Schlegel, one of the members of the Berlin Film Festival. He speaks Russian fluently and has published books on Eisenstein. He talks about the two sequences I just mentioned, and develops the concept that Eisenstein felt there had to be, in the construction of a film, orgiastic moments, moments that could in fact organically link all the elements of a film together – in a moment of extreme joy. During one of his trips to Japan, Eisenstein saw pornographic and erotic drawings that were stained by blood. He asked where they came from, and was told: When the Samurais went to battle, they carried those drawings with them. And when they were wounded, they looked at them to get well quickly, to be able to return to the battlefield as quickly as possible. So that gave Eisenstein the idea to try something similar in his films. If you remember the scene in *Battleship Potemkin* where the knocking noises of the ship's engines can be heard, the chunking of the cylinders – this can be associated with slowly growing sexual arousal, and that sequence explodes in the moment on the steps in Odessa. Eisenstein wrote about his theory to Carl Jung, and Jung saw *Potemkin* and wrote back to Eisenstein: 'Mr Eisenstein, we definitely have to work together.' But, finally, they didn't. You can find a lot of Eisenstein's influence in Glauber Rocha's films. He really studied him.

PSJ: As you yourself did.
WS: I'm a great admirer of Eisenstein. But getting back to my own personal experience, my film *Foreign Land* is really about all possible forms of exile. It's a film about homelessness, rootlessness and exile – three states of mind that are interconnected and superimposed. States of mind that are not only my own, but also those of my collaborator, Daniela Thomas. She is the co-writer and co-director, and a very dear and close friend. She comes from a similar background, lived in London, then in New York, she studied history and worked in the theatre before doing cinema. I gave her equal credit, so *Foreign Land* is a film *realisado por* Walter Salles and Daniela Thomas. I normally don't like to see 'A Film by', because I feel a film is really a collective work and enterprise. It always shocks me a little when something is signed by one person only, as though we were painters or writers.

PSJ: Was Daniela involved with *Central Station*?
WS: No. But she did a project for the German/ French television station ARTE with me, the film that takes place on 31 December 1999, called *Minuit/The First*

Terra Estrangeira/Foreign Land. © Walter Carvalho

Day. That particular project was much more Daniela's than mine. But *Foreign Land* was my initial idea . . .

PSJ: You almost work like the brothers Taviani, the two of you.
WS (*Laughs*): In *Foreign Land* we wanted to tell a story that would be directly linked to a moment we had experienced in Brazil. A very specific moment in the history of our nation, a moment when the country came to a halt, when the cultural production of Brazil came to a total standstill. We just had this desire to talk about all that had happened, and with a sense of urgency.

PSJ: Was the script written by the two of you?
WS: Yes, with the collaboration of a young law student called Marcos Bernstein, who later became one of the writers for *Central Station*. At that point he was an intern in our production house, but he added so many good ideas to the screenplay that we decided to give him a writer's credit.

PSJ: When you say 'we', do you mean the company you founded with your brother?
WS: Exactly. My younger brother, João, the one who makes documentaries, and myself, we founded Videofilmes. It's a very small production company that does

one feature and maybe two or three documentaries per year. But getting back to *Foreign Land*: again, it is not 'infra-fiction' – it's a film about a country in a specific moment of its history. Perhaps it tries to talk about too many things at the same time. In *Foreign Land* you find several genres that intermingle. You have a certain reference to neo-realism, you find elements of Wenders' *Alice in the Cities* and *Kings of the Road*, and certainly of *Dans La Ville Blanche* by Alain Tanner, and of Antonioni's *The Passenger*. And you also have a reference to certain John Huston films, in the film noir tradition, like *Asphalt Jungle*. The end is certainly reminiscent of *The Treasure of the Sierra Madre*. It has the qualities and the shortcomings of a first film.

PSJ: There are a number of moments that don't work. But what's more important to me is its overall impression, which I find very intense. It has so much atmosphere, and depicts this very acute moment in Brazilian history so very convincingly.
WS: What was so interesting in that specific time is that a whole generation that was turning 20 was just as lost as the country itself. There was an identity crisis that encompassed every moment of everybody's life, creating a sense of collective despair. This glued us together and eventually created the ability to overcome chaos.

PSJ: How strange that all this happened after you had finally got rid of the generals! Instead of an improvement, it got worse than it was before!
WS: And for the first time in 500 years, the country became a country of emigration instead of immigration. More than one million Brazilians left the country at that time. The official number being 700,000, the unofficial 1.5 or 1.6 million, so the true figure must be somewhere in the middle.

PSJ: And you were among those who left.
WS: We left, and I started working in France, doing documentaries for French television.

PSJ: Can you give me one or two examples?
WS: We did, for instance, right in the middle of the crisis, a documentary called *Chico Buarque, ou Le pays de la délicatesse perdue* – 'the country that has lost its delicate quality'. A 90-minute film about Brazil, visualized by the lyrics of Chico Buarque's music. I shot it in Brazil for France 3. A little bit later, we did a documentary about Bossa Nova for ARTE/La Sept. We really started to work on a constant basis during that period for French TV.

PSJ: When was your company founded?
WS: In 1986, before the crisis. And believe me, everything, the whole country,

came to a halt. In the history of our nation, nothing could ever be compared to that moment. All saving accounts were blocked. It was a moment of total absurdity. So *Foreign Land* really coincided with the identity crisis of a whole country. What we experienced as Brazilians at that specific time can be compared to what many other young people may have experienced at the same time, and people who came from different parts of the Third World were also experiencing in Europe.

PSJ: It precedes something that is now very much a *sujet* – people who are not Europeans by birth face the greatest difficulties to stay here.
WS: When we finished *Foreign Land*, we had in a way discovered what we wanted to talk about, both Daniela and myself, and *Central Station* is in fact the complementary half of *Foreign Land*, '*par opposition*'. Because it goes to the heart of identity, the heart of the country, where the Brazilian identity hasn't yet been totally spoiled by the actual cultural submission we all live under. There is a certain innocence that is still possible in *Central Station*. That's why two films that are so different belong so closely together.

PSJ: I found that *Minuit/The First Day* had certain ties to both features too.
WS: Well, it talks about two characters who are in exile. They seem to come from different origins, but both understand that the only way out might be through the discovery of a certain affection and solidarity amongst themselves. This is the common denominator of *Foreign Land*, *Central Station*, and *Minuit/ The First Day*, it's what ties them together: the belief that you can create something starting from a newly found relationship and unity. And that you can eventually overcome the limitations of your present situation. You can transcend them.

PSJ: Allow me to go back almost to where we started, that moment in time when you watched the May '68 revolution in Paris.
WS: I was 12 at that time.

PSJ: How long was your father stationed in Paris?
WS: Until 1969, so I returned to Brazil when I was 13, and it was really a revelation. It was almost like a foreign land. More than that, it was really like re-discovering where I came from.

PSJ: You had rarely been back in between?
WS: I had been there two months every year, and always missed it tremendously, without being able to define why. I felt a constant malaise living in Europe. I was constantly sick. I remember having rheumatic fevers all the time. I couldn't

Minuit/The First Day

live without pain. The only 'womb' for me at that time, really, was the movie house, *la salle de cinéma*, the only place where I felt totally safe and where I liked to be. Never would I have imagined that would be my profession in later years, being a film-maker. Cinema meant too much of a sacred universe to me. It was such a sacred territory that I didn't think I could be part of it except as a spectator – I profoundly worshipped the films I saw in those cathedrals called movie houses. When I was 12 or 13, I wanted to become a photographer. I was very impressed and influenced by the work of Cartier-Bresson and of André Kertesz. A tradition that leads up to Sebastião Salgado, whom I admire tremendously. That was what I really aimed to be.

PSJ: What drew you closer to the world of cinema?
WS: The first time someone had doubts that something I had written was the truth. I'll never forget. In school, in Paris, during Easter vacation, my parents were travelling and left us money to go to amusement parks, but obviously I went to the movies instead, continually. Back in school ten days later, one of the teachers asked us to put in writing what we had done. For instance, if somebody had seen a theatre play or a film, he should say so in that paper. So I listed all the films that I had seen. And the teacher said: 'You're a liar. This cannot be!' I replied, 'I beg your pardon. I *did* see all those films.' He still didn't believe me.

It was a Jesuit school, and the teacher was a Jesuit priest. Of course it went against the rules to go to the cinema at all! All the Godards and Truffauts. During Easter! Totally unacceptable.

PSJ: Moments like that are what makes writers, artists . . .
WS: What is your first memory? What do you remember from childhood?

PSJ: Ships crossing the Atlantic. Going back and forth. But it's not so much an image, more an atmosphere of leaving, and of returning. And a closeness to my parents who were always very much at the centre of my interest. I was an only child.
WS: But the fact that this is more an impressionistic memory is perhaps typical for a writer's background. What I remember are glimpses of very specific images. Always in movement, constantly travelling.

PSJ: That reminds me of a still frame, in Hollywood, when I was three or four: a rainbow, something very rare in Southern California. And for a child a rainbow is something particularly special – now that I myself have a child, I realize what a big event a rainbow can be. That's one of my very first images.
WS: What is your first memory of death?

PSJ: I must have been ten years old. I watched myself thinking that death is part of life. My parents tried to keep everything away from me that had anything to do with sadness, darkness, death in any way. But when I reached the age of ten, these things became suddenly known to me within a matter of days. Not before.
WS: I remember two very specific incidents. One of them was an accident in a car that ran over a motorcycle. I was in that car. The person didn't die, but he was injured. I remember how the discovery of the pain and the idea of death was, at that time, shocking to me. I must have been about seven or eight. The second one happened in a film. I don't remember the title, I saw it at the Grande Armée. It was an old film from the Cold War era, people trying to escape a city that had been hit by a nuclear bomb. It was certainly a B-picture, with horrible scenes of death, crude and raw. Those two moments gave me a sense of tremendous pain. Both events, the fictional one and the real one, conveyed a sense of terrible inner pain. Perhaps, also, because the fictional one wasn't aestheticized.

PSJ: I would never have been allowed to see such a film before the age of 16 or 17.
WS: This is why I have such a hard time accepting a scene like in Quentin Tarantino's *Pulp Fiction*, where the Travolta character shoots the guy in the

back of the car, and they start laughing about it. The problem really stops being an ethical one and becomes a cosmetic one, like, 'How can we clean the car?' I do not want to judge Tarantino, of course, but it just departs so much from my beliefs of what one should show or not show in a film. That moment was really striking for me. Two years ago, I was in a jury with Thomas Vinterberg, who directed the great film *Festen*. He told me of a seminar with Paul Schrader, who talked about that specific moment. Schrader was very moved, in a very sad way. He said, 'After that scene from *Pulp Fiction*, one can show anything.' Including, for example, a cradle being run over by a bus, just to show that the bus was speeding. That suddenly becomes acceptable. I think he's right. On the other hand, it makes me very optimistic when I see films done by young film-makers who are still in film school. They often have a humanistic quality and an ethical approach that departs totally from this trend of cynicism that we saw in films of the early 1990s. The idea of unjustified violence makes little sense to me. Perhaps this has to do with the films I was lucky enough to see while growing up, in a totally random manner.

PSJ: In 1969, approximately, your father was asked to come back to Brazil. Considering the fact that he was the main representative of his country – first in Washington, then in Paris – it must mean that he felt in accordance with the regimes in power?
WS: No, he was an ambassador *before* the generals.

PSJ: Wasn't there also a kind of dictatorship then?
WS: No, not at all. After the military took over, on 21 March, 1964, he was never appointed again. One of the reasons why we stayed in Paris after the *coup d'état* was that he didn't want to go back. We only left Paris five years later, in 1969. We all returned to Brazil at that time. And then I stayed there continuously without going back to Europe.

PSJ: And you went to a French school in Rio?
WS: I did. That was the only way not to miss a whole year of school – school there doesn't start at the same time of the year. It starts in Spring instead of September. It was a bilingual school, the Lycée Franco-Brésilien. It gave us the possibility to study in Portuguese and French at the same time. It was an ideal situation.

PSJ: The *nouvelle vague* films from France entered Brazil approximately at that time?
WS: Some of them did.

PSJ: Does that mean the regime wasn't such a harsh dictatorship after all? You wouldn't have seen films from France in Eastern Europe in the 1960s ...
WS: Maybe the generals weren't smart enough to be able to pinpoint what the films meant. Or they were too smart and knew that such films would never reach a large audience. But little by little they stopped letting films into the country that were more blatantly of a political nature, like Costa-Gavras's *Z*. On the other hand, they saw no reason to block the distribution of any of the Truffauts or most of the Godards. For instance *A bout de souffle*, *Masculin, Féminin*, even the famous *Le Mépris*, with Bardot. What they were very moralistic about was *L'Empire des Sens*, for instance, or Kubrick's *A Clockwork Orange*, those films they really censored. And sometimes they were even more stupid than you can imagine. For instance, they banned Stendhal's novel *Le Rouge et le Noir* because they found it politically unacceptable!

PSJ: Returning to Rio, did you find a comparable 'womb', a cinema you loved as much as the Grande Armée?
WS: Less than the Studio Grande Armée, but there were two or three cinemas in Rio that were quite interesting. You could find projections of independent films from Europe, Asia and America there.

PSJ: How did you experience your homecoming?
WS: First of all, that period was one of constant discovery: discovery of the country, and an in-depth understanding of the social imbalances and injustices. At the same time, a more in-depth discovery of the richness and polyphonic quality of Brazilian culture and society – and the way those roots were translated into popular culture. Discovery, for instance, of certain samba composers such as Cartola. There is an *hommage* to him in *Central Station*, to his music: he sings the music that closes the film, during the end credits. But the most interesting part was the discovery of the local, original culture, of the originality of that specific part of the world.

PSJ: Perhaps you saw everything with more open and curious eyes? Looking in from the outside?
WS: I agree. It was like coming to a city I had never seen. I looked at it with total innocence and a desire to learn and to understand. I fell in love with it, almost immediately, and in a growing manner.

PSJ: I had a similar experience with Los Angeles. I went back to study there at the age of 22, and I had this fascination with a city not my own, yet my roots are there, to a certain degree. I started looking for a city that was inside me.

WS: Did you have the impression that you had already been to certain places when you visited them?

PSJ: I had been there only twice in between, but I felt completely different when I actually moved there. It was like a revelation. And I was enamoured by the city.
WS: What did you study?

PSJ: I went to film school. I studied screenwriting at the American Film Institute. The directors John McTiernan, Edward Zwick, and the producers Marshall Herskovitz and Stuart Cornfield were among my classmates. It was a good school, I must say. I'm glad I went there. But I turned into a fiction writer nevertheless.
WS: Although you write scripts too?

PSJ: I do, yes. From time to time . . .
WS: When Renoir lived in Los Angeles, he was asked once whether he felt completely at home in this specific place in this specific moment of his life. He pointed to the sole of his shoes and said: '*Jeune homme, la poussière du pays ne quitte jamais les semelles de nos chaussures!*' 'The dirt of one's home country never leaves the soles of one's shoes.'

PSJ: I never felt completely at home anywhere. You at least have Brazil!
WS: One doesn't come from somewhere by obligation, I believe, but by option. Hector Babenco, for instance, is Argentine-born, but he is one of the most Brazilian directors I can think of. He's intrinsically Brazilian.

PSJ: Does he speak the language perfectly?
WS: He speaks perfect Portuguese. And I think that he understands the country in its huge complexity. I find it almost unbelievable how a director like Billy Wilder managed to arrive in Los Angeles without speaking English, and a few years later he could jump from genre to genre with total ease.

PSJ: But he is one of the great exceptions, like Fritz Lang or Otto Preminger.
WS: Or Jean Negulesco, the Romanian director.

PSJ: Or Murnau. But when Wenders first moved to LA to do *Hammett*, that was not a good film.
WS: *Hammett* was certainly very theatrical, very different from what you would expect from him. I believe that 90 per cent of the time it is a trap to do the move towards America, but in the 1930s, 40s and 50s, for some directors it was not.

PSJ: One cannot see into the future, as we both know – *que sera sera* – but do you think that one day you will be considered a Brazilian director, or a director who is working everywhere in the world who happens to have Brazilian roots?

WS: I think that the only choices that you make as a storyteller have to be defined by the closeness you feel toward certain themes. Your own interests, your desires, your angst, are the determining factors. You must keep your integrity. I could never see myself doing *Batman 5*, or any industrial project or studio product not related to my own passions. More specifically, I would say that the great majority of what I develop or what I am interested in are themes linked to Brazil. Since I was exposed to so many different cultures and influences when I grew up, I also relate directly to storytellers who are not Brazilian. For instance, Cormac McCarthy's stories touch upon themes that are similar to the ones that interest me.

PSJ: Did you ever do commercials?

WS: Yes, I did, during the 1980s, when most of my documentaries were made. We needed sponsors for those films, so one of the agencies we contacted said, 'Okay but we want you to direct the commercials that will accompany the programme.' And this is how I ended up doing documentaries and commercials at the same time, for six years, between 1986 and 1992. But if I hadn't worked primarily in documentaries I would have lost my sanity in the process.

PSJ: What will your next film be?

WS: I have just completed a film inspired by an Albanian writer I admire immensely, Ismael Kadaré. I think he is one of the major living writers of our time, and this specific book, called *Broken April*, was given to me by my brother João. The whole atavistic question of violence, and how to overcome it and how to explain it, are described in the most acute and convincing manner. It's the story of a vendetta, and how ridiculous this never-ending cycle of killing really is. Paradoxically, the book helped me to understand a specific situation in Brazil, regarding the vendettas you find in north-eastern Brazil.

PSJ: So you transplanted an Albanian story to Brazil?

WS: That is correct. It will be called *Behind the Sun*. I live in a country where the presence of violence is more and more palpable, and this gave me an urgent desire to approach the theme. I found it more interesting to talk about the genesis of violence than to reproduce what you see on the news of every single television channel in my country. You see, blood feuds and fratricidal struggles for power defined the boundaries of several territories in the Brazilian north-east. Through the protagonist in *Behind the Sun* one understands – like through Orestes, or Hamlet – how crime engenders crime.

Abril Despedaçado/Behind the Sun. © Christian Cravo

Abril Despedaçado/Behind the Sun. © Christian Cravo

PSJ: Did you try something out, artistically, that you hadn't done before?
WS: I tried to think of each shot as an expression of everything that had happened previously in the film, as well as everything that would happen afterwards. I tried to think of the film more in terms of its cinematographic pace than its visual rhythm. 'Visual' is what is seen by the physical eyes, the world of appearance, while 'cinematographic' is the pace of seeing, understood by the eyes of the spirit, beyond the world of image and appearance. Closer to poetry than prose . . . Eisenstein used this overlapping of elements in the two sequences I mentioned earlier from *The General Line*.

PSJ: Are you satisfied with the final result?
WS: To start with, I am never satisfied with the final result of anything. We're still in the middle of post-production and I haven't developed the necessary distance to evaluate what the film truly represents.

PSJ: You must be under terrible pressure, after the huge international success of *Central Station*. Everybody around you is waiting for your next step.
WS: I am basically trying to respond to my inner voice. I never develop only one project at a time, but two or three, because I found out that one project nurtures the other ones in a strange way.

PSJ: Who produced your new film?
WS: I have always seen film as a collaborative process, and I believe that a creative producer is a crucial part of this equation. I have been working with Arthur Cohn, producer of *The Garden of the Finzi-Continis* and several other Vittorio de Sica films (among many others) for the last two projects. Arthur Cohn is a producer who belongs to the humanist tradition in film. He has an innate, intuitive capacity to judge projects and to help them evolve. He is also a perfectionist, who believes that a film is never finished until it is polished in its finest details. I empathize with this perspective and have learned a great deal from him.

PSJ: Was Kadaré involved in the screenwriting process of *Behind the Sun*?
WS: No, he has the intelligence to understand that there is a distance between the book and the film. When we met, in Paris, he said: 'I never give my opinion on a screenplay or on a project that was adapted, so that I won't ever have to say what some writers tend to say, you know, "My work has been betrayed!"'

PSJ: Interestingly enough you chose an author who himself is constantly travelling and who is not at home in the country where he lives. He is also someone who is '*déraciné*'.

WS: Kadaré, I think, is extremely proud to be Albanian, and I can understand why. It is the same feeling I have in regards to Brazil, and yet – with the blessing of Tolstoy – we could say that what is of a very specific local nature can sometimes become universal. This is certainly the case here.

PSJ: Do your screenplays change a lot while you're shooting?
WS: Well, if you had seen the screenplay of *Central Station* and the final screenplay, the two are very different indeed, although the film had won a screenplay contest at Sundance. We did more than ten drafts, but through the process of working with the actors, the option of working with amateurs, and after the screenplay had been rehearsed like a play for three to four weeks, it just kept changing and changing. What at first seemed perfect on the page asked for very specific changes when it was played out.

PSJ: I believe a screenwriter should always keep that in mind. And remain open, very open.
WS: Being a documentarist at heart, I need to develop the fiction on paper, because otherwise, I would feel too attracted to what can be found on the spot and in the moment. So I need to have a very solid, almost Cartesian approach on the one hand, to be able to pursue and explore what is totally improvisational. To discover what only the unexpected encounter with the real world can bring you.

PSJ: Coincidences that fall upon a bed that is prepared shine much brighter. They have more strength.
WS: I agree.

PSJ: I am a deep believer in invisible links. Often we do not realize the large amount of coincidences that accompany our lives – only sometimes do they surface.
WS: That's interesting, as I stand on the opposite side of the 'belief circle'. I abhor everything that has mythical, mystical undertones. I always believed in '*le jeu de dés mallarmésiens*' – the fact that life is deeply illogical. But I must admit that I am constantly confronted with so-called coincidences that start to make me doubt my theories more and more.

PSJ: How do you deal with believability in film? Some stories cannot be told without allowing the screenplay at least one or two moments that are difficult to believe.
WS: I once tried for years to adapt a novel, *The Manhunt*, by Alejo Carpentier. I worked with wonderful screenwriters, but never managed to come up with a

perfect adaptation. Carpentier is a precursor of magical realism in Latin America. He's from Cuba. The story is very simple. A young man escapes from prison, in the 1930s, and the only place where he finds shelter is the Municipal Theatre of Havana. He enters it at the same moment a conductor from a foreign country starts to play Beethoven's *Third Symphony*: the Eroica, symphony of the revolution – betrayed by Napoleon. The fugitive knows that until silence reigns again, he will live. And silence will mean death. Louis Malle had the rights to this screenplay for 15 years. I once met the screenwriter Jean-Claude Carrière, I admire him tremendously, and he told me that he had tried to develop this material, and that he and Malle had finally given up.

PSJ: Was believability the central problem?
WS: Yes. I couldn't solve the problems relating to believability in several different parts of the screenplay. The book is very impressionistic, and once we would fill in the gaps, bringing in a part of the story that was not in the book, that insert would appear artificial. I often get the impression, in other people's adaptations, that things have been added to a structure that is intentionally left with gaps and abysses. One shouldn't force something upon a story that doesn't belong to that specific structure. I abandoned the Carpentier project after seven or eight years. I really hope that wonderful novel will one day reach the screen. It truly deserves it.

PSJ: Do you work with new collaborators on each project?
WS: No, there is a group that has been working as a family team with me for a long time. It includes the director of photography, Walter Carvalho.

PSJ: He shot *Central Station, Foreign Land, Minuit/The First Day* and *Behind the Sun*?
WS: Yes. And I worked with him on documentaries for 15 years. As a logical step, we started doing feature films together.

PSJ: The very first fiction film you ever did, in 1989: is that one you prefer not to talk about?
WS: I don't mind talking about it, because it's interesting to analyse its shortcomings and why it was premature to do it. It was called *Exposure* in the US, and *A High Art* in the rest of the world. It was based on a novel written by a Brazilian novelist, Rubem Fonseca. Although he is known as a roman noir writer, Fonseca is in fact closer to the Dostoyevskian tradition than anything else. And there is a pathos in the characters that becomes emblematic of the whole malaise of society. I was very attracted to this book. I had invited Rubem to write the screenplay for *The Manhunt*. It was such a pleasure to work with

him and to learn from him. And when we didn't manage to find the solution for the adaptation or the financing for that project, we turned to the possibility of adapting one of his own novels. That's how *Exposure* came about.

PSJ: Was it done with American money?
WS: No, not at all. The producer is from São Paolo, Paulo Brito. He has been faithful to all my films since this first one, although it wasn't a success. He financed it entirely. But as we got close to production, the internal market in Brazil collapsed. The only solution to get the film made was to transform the central character, who was a lawyer in Brazil, into an American photographer, who would be travelling to Brazil. In a way we were following the same path that Hector Babenco had explored so brilliantly in *Kiss of the Spiderwoman*.

PSJ: So it was shot in Brazil, after all?
WS: Yes. English, Portuguese and Spanish are all spoken in the film, because there is a part that takes place in Bolivia. This is actually the part I feel closest to in the film. Since the whole family of actors and crew only got together a few days before the start, there was no possibility to dive into the atmosphere, to really prepare the whole production carefully. I think that had it been possible to keep the project in its original form, we would have managed to translate the novel's qualities onto the screen. I was certainly not equipped to write a film in three different languages, shot in two different countries, with its production complexity. Still, the film was picked up by Miramax for distribution in the US, and then led a life of its own. I remember several moments of it fondly, although I feel estranged from other parts of it today. But I would certainly never shoot a film spoken in English in Brazil again, even if it is justified by the fact that the main character is American.

PSJ: As always – I would like to return to your biographical roots. What was your father's profession after he stopped being a diplomat?
WS: Even before being appointed, he had founded a bank with my grandfather and two friends, called Unibanco. He came from the financial world and got back into it. But the time in life he really preferred was that period when he joined the diplomatic corps. That he really loved: to be on a mission. He was not an office man.

PSJ: And your mother – was she more the classic mother who did not have her own profession?
WS: She accompanied him most of the time. That deprived her of the autonomy that she had intellectually, but never managed to develop in a specific profession. She died in a deep state of depression.

PSJ: How old were you when she passed away?
WS: It happened in December 1988. I was 32. And my father died just recently, in 2001.

PSJ: Do you believe your artistic vision has something to do with your fore-fathers and foremothers, or do you believe it all comes from your own development?
WS: Well, there is no case of writers or musicians or artists of any sort in the family, at least that I know of. Both families were from rural areas. My father was born in a town of less than 500 people, in the interior of Brazil. My grand-father had a very small store where he sold hats, toothbrushes and barbed wire for farms. He had enough money to educate one son, so the eldest one was cho-sen to go to São Paolo to be educated, and that was my father. He was the only one of his family to be given this chance, among five brothers. So he always thought he had to do well, and to prove to the family that he merited this huge chance. He arrived in São Paolo in the beginning of the 1930s, in a moment when the country was in a chaotic state because of the 1929 stock market crash and its effect on the Brazilian economy. But he also had the chance to arrive there at a time where the São Paolo University was being built up with the help of a number of French structuralists. So he studied with Claude Lévy-Strauss, for instance, and several other professors, guests of the structuralists. That explains how a young man who came from a very underprivileged background such as his could go so far on one of the last frontiers that Brazil still was. Similarly, my mother also comes from a very small town, and they both migrated to Rio de Janeiro, where they met.

PSJ: Is there a documentary film you made which you consider the most achieved of all?
WS: I believe it is *Socorro Nobre*, about a woman who was in prison, in Brazil, yet loved the art of a sculptor so much that she started writing letters to him, from prison, without knowing him personally at all.

PSJ: How come she knew about him?
WS: She found an old magazine, in prison, with an article about a 73-year-old sculptor, Frans Krajcberg, born in Poland, who went to the Amazon, picked up pieces of burned wood and reshaped them. Somehow, his work touched her soul. He happens to be one of my best friends.

PSJ: I always wondered how you managed to film inside the women's prison?
WS: We asked for the authorization and it took us a month to get it. We had no personal contacts at all, but the woman that ran the prison was quite an

unusual and wonderful character. She was clearly hoping that the film could help Socorro. And she understood that Socorro was a very sensitive, gifted, intelligent individual. She wanted to give her a chance. So we were allowed to shoot during three days. The first day, we didn't film. That I learned from Sebastião Salgado: 'Look first.' We opted not to film, not only in order not to be intrusive but also to offer the inmates the option to become part of our film or not. I didn't know Socorro when I got there. We had no clue of what she looked like, or what she was like.

PSJ: And Frans Krajcberg didn't possess a photograph of her. She had only sent him letters.

WS: She had sent him a letter with an envelope that only stated: 'To Franz Carlsberg' – it wasn't even spelled correctly – 'who lives near the town of' – and the name of the town near his village. And the letter miraculously reached him. He was so shattered by it that he showed it to me, so we sent her a letter asking her whether she would agree that we do a documentary on the exchange of those letters. At that time, she was still looking at a very long prison term, 20 years.

PSJ: You didn't want to mention in the film why she was in prison?

WS: What I aimed at was to show that Krajcberg's sculptures gave her the desire to survive in prison. It is a much more radical look at art than the one people normally have in museums. Normally they have a very superficial, contemplative understanding of art. But here is a woman whose soul was literally touched, who was viscerally moved by an artist. Ultimately his oeuvre changed her life. I was more than happy when she accepted the idea of participating in the film.

PSJ: She certainly had nothing to lose!

WS: You are looking into the rear-view mirror. It's easy enough to say that now. But we could have been journalists working for one of the scandal TV stations. Yet she accepted us, and I think that we were as moved by the experience as she was. In the end, when Krajcberg meets Socorro, it was a moment in which the emotional voltage was so uncontrollable that not only Socorro and Krajcberg were utterly moved, but also the other women of the prison. They were crying as well, and so were we behind the camera. '*Par pudeur*', I eliminated the sound in those last two or three minutes of the film, in order not to intrude in a moment that had been unforgettable, but whose emotion was almost too much to bear. I remember coming back to Rio on the plane, how shattered I was by that experience. Also by the fact that we, the film crew, left and those who had become our friends, somehow, were abandoned, remained behind bars. Weeks later we were still discussing what we had lived through. It took me almost one year before I edited the film. I normally edit what I do immediately, but here I did the opposite, to keep a Brechtian distance. And yet the documentary possesses an emotional quality that I had always refused before. That documentary is a turning point for me. After that, I completely changed my attitude towards writing a scene, a sequence: I no longer refused to allow emotions to surface if they flourished in a natural, convincing, organic manner.

PSJ: I cannot not ask you this: what was Socorro's crime?
WS: Her crime was one committed by several members of the family. When her parents died, a fight broke out in that family – for the inheritance. The conflict ended with the death of one brother. Socorro and several of her siblings were judged and given the harshest possible sentence. They weren't properly defended, as they had no means to pay for a private lawyer.

PSJ: But was she involved in the killing?
WS: She wasn't there when it happened. But she had taken part in the discussions when it was decided one would have to go to the brother armed, because a fight may break out – so she was considered a collaborator. Now, why didn't I want to go into that? Because it would have been a film about that specific case and about guilt and about punishment, but I wanted to do a film about the possibility of healing and about a person that grants herself a second chance. Much in the same way that Dora does, in *Central Station*, in the end of her journey. She discovers her love for Josué, and consequently her ability for affection and solidarity.

PSJ: Would you say that *Socorro Nobre* is a kind of missing link? The moment in which you thought: 'Documentaries? Fine, important, interesting. But I want to go into fiction also'?
WS: *Socorro Nobre* was made in 1994. After *Exposure*, and before *Foreign Land*. But *Socorro Nobre* was a turning point for me, nevertheless. I think that the end of *Foreign Land*, where the character of Alex sings a song to Paco who is dying and who is lying on her lap in the car, is a total improvisation that derives from the experience with Socorro Nobre. I would have resisted that turn of events, had *Socorro Nobre* not occurred before. And, in *Central Station*, it obviously doesn't happen by accident that the first person appearing on screen is Socorro Nobre herself. The whole concept of *Central Station* derives from the experience of *Socorro Nobre*.

PSJ: She's in tears in that first image, isn't she?
WS: Yes, and it is a real letter that she dictates to the letter writer. To somebody she has left behind in prison. For me the possibility to visualize a story is really

what triggers the desire to tell it. I could see *Central Station* in its pivotal points before I started writing it. In the same vein, what triggered *Foreign Land* was an image I woke up with one day: an image of a couple in dismay, sitting on a totally deserted beach, and a boat sunk into that beach. Then a few months later, walking in Paris, I saw a book by a French photographer called Favreau, a book about the Capeverde Islands – and there was the image of the ruined ship I had dreamed of.

PSJ: Quite a coincidence, wouldn't you say?
WS: This is when I realized that the film was going to exist.

PSJ: In *Foreign Land* and in *Central Station*, the mothers die at approximately the same minute of the film. In the twelfth minute, or something like that. Ever since we talked about the fact that you had no 'esoteric' feelings, I've been curious about your relationship to religion.
WS: Whenever people ask me whether *Central Station* is primarily a political film, I tend to say, 'Well, you have political overtones there.' I wanted to talk about social injustice, yet the film leaves the decision about how to decode it to the spectator. It neither aims to be patronizing in a political manner, nor to impose a specific religious vision of the world. The idea that makes more and more sense to me is one of tolerance in regards to religion. I hate the idea of sectarianism. The possibility of intolerance is something I abhor. Being raised in Jesuit schools at specific moments of my life created in me over many years a total refusal of that way of life. I became very anti-clerical. But little by little, I have come to respect the idea of all religious options.

PSJ: Apart from Christianity.
WS: Definitely. As I become older, the only thing I am certain of is my immense insignificance. In a way that is what nurtures my desire to reflect upon my times and my country. Basically, I am a sceptical person, but I am not Cioran-esque. I don't believe in the inevitability of a gloomy future, nor in suicide as the only possible solution – although I have cases of suicide so close to me in my own history, in my own family.

PSJ: I found that *Central Station* had rather strong Christian over- and undertones.
WS: Interestingly enough, most of what could be characterized as religious themes or scenes in the film were non-existent in the beginning, in the initial draft of the script. But the fact that we encountered those pilgrims on our way, and those Christian names as we were doing our research in the areas where we filmed, influenced us, and almost obliged us to incorporate what we had seen.

Central do Brasil/Central Station. © Paula Prandini

Central do Brasil/Central Station. © Walter Carvalho

PSJ: The power of coincidence?

WS: No, I don't think it is coincidence, it has to do with a respect for reality and the need, much in the documentarian tradition, to propose a reflection of your time, to put into a frame what you have seen. Borges used to say that one of the greatest pleasures of literature was to name what has not yet been named. In going into the very interior of Brazil, we sometimes had the impression that we were seeing what had not been seen before.

PSJ: You even went beyond the north-eastern Brazilian tradition that Glauber Rocha and the others had filmed?

WS: No, I think they went far beyond what I could see; because they came from that specific reality, and had a much more in-depth vision of it. I did try to be truthful to what I saw, and I had the impression that many things had not been seen in that way before. Many of those scenes are totally improvised and came as we were moving along with the crew. I didn't try to impose anything, nor did I start the film with the intention of conveying a specific religious message. Even in *Foreign Land* there are no religious over- or undertones.

PSJ: I insist: *Central Station* has a religious core.

WS: The more deprived a society is, the more dependent on a saviour it becomes. For the simple reason that the local authorities do absolutely nothing to solve the real problems of that specific population. And as we were venturing into that part of the country, we could not give a distorted image of what we were seeing. It may be that our way of seeing is biased by our previous history, our cultural upbringing, *et cetera*.

PSJ: Searching for a father equals searching for God – don't you agree?

WS: Yes, but that's also a very Latin-American theme indeed.

PSJ: In Judaism, for instance, this Father-concept of God doesn't exist . . .

WS: I understand what you mean, but you see, the search for the father has historical and political meanings in our reality. For the simple reason that we are a continent that was colonized by the founding fathers, who later abandoned us. Obviously we hated them, and our countries are the soiled mothers from whom everything was taken. The precious stones, the wood, even the tree that gave origin to the country name 'Brazil', can't be found anymore, because our founding fathers took everything back to Portugal.

PSJ: Not only did they soil the mothers—

WS: They raped the mothers. So, this idea of the missing father goes far beyond the question of Christianity in Latin America. It is rooted in the foundation of our countries and our societies. This is why Paco's search in *Foreign Land* is an impossible one. Paco is a fatherless son, we never hear about the father, he is never even mentioned. And he is a fatherless child who returns to the country where his mother and father came from. He returns only to die, and only to find that relationships with the ones that have created him is a mirage. Paco's voyage is an impossible one. There cannot be a happy end. The only element that saves him is finding Alex who allows him to cling to life, to transcend his existence.

PSJ: In one of my novels, *The Snowflake Constant*, the main character goes through a similar process. In the end he understands that it was actually his own death that pulled him through all the adventures he encountered. And I think Paco is in a similar situation. Death is the magnet that pulled him, although of course he doesn't know it.

WS (*Laughs*): Do you really think that you come from a different religious upbringing than I do?

PSJ: Mine was very areligious.

WS: So was mine, after a certain time. But do you really believe that your upbringing shapes you in any way? Or shapes the literature or the themes that you develop?

PSJ: Definitely.

WS: Or is your upbringing just the fuel, with which you can look at the world, but still have the distance to separate from it in order to create something of a new order, with a fresh quality?

PSJ: To regard one's upbringing as a 'fuel', as you put it, would be ideal; to be able to look at things from all points of view. I think there's a tremendous danger that our upbringing overshadows us and pushes us only into one direction. I'm a sentimental character in many ways, but I have a longing to be less sentimental. I think sentimentality is a magnet in the wrong direction. It keeps you glued to certain truths that you believe you must stay true to. A feeling you can't deceive your ancestors . . .

WS: I totally understand what you mean.

PSJ: Sometimes, I wish I were more courageous to leave everything behind. Some of my characters manage – the one I mentioned, his name is Tigor – to leave everything behind. But he is much more courageous than I am. And I remember my father reading that book ten years ago, saying, 'Oh my goodness, I hope you are not like him!'

WS: That means he reacted to a character that was well fleshed-out, otherwise he would not have made that remark. Do you feel that a character becomes interesting when in the writing process you don't predetermine everything that he will say and do? That he starts escaping your original intentions?

PSJ: That's really why I started writing, because of that adventure: what happens when you have only a very faint idea of something and you decide to sit down with a feeling, or atmosphere and a general idea of who your main characters are, and then suddenly everything starts to move. To me, writing is the highest form of art conceivable. I think of it as an almost God-like action.

WS: My brother did a documentary with the Brazilian writer Jorge Amado, for France 3, within the series *Un siècle des écrivains*. And Jorge talked about a very popular character of his, called Theresa Batista. He said that slowly, but irrevocably, she started to have a life of her own. He suddenly looked at the page that he had just written and he started talking to her: 'Gosh, Theresa, I didn't know you were such a bitch!'

PSJ: What was your very first documentary? Do you remember?

WS: My very first one was with Marcello Mastroianni. It was lovely, really lovely. The second one was on Mick Jagger, interviewed by Caetano Veloso. The third was Gabriel Garcia Márquez. And the next one was with Kenneth Galbraith. We wanted to do something that would be understood as an influence against the tidal current of that time, in Brazil. And last, but not least, I did a portrait of Chagall, in 1984, just one year before he died. He still had paintings in his *atelier* that dated from the 1920s and 30s, from the period in Vitebsk, paintings that he had not finished, because he didn't know how to finish them, they were only partly done. That shows you that we are not the only ones who don't know how to solve problems sometimes.

PSJ: That's a beautiful final word, but I do have a last question: how did Nelson Pereira dos Santos react to *Central Station*?

WS: In a very generous and wonderful manner. When journalists interviewed him for the newspapers and for television, he said that this is the film that 25 years after Cinema Novo returns to the same ethical principles of the movement whose leader he was. That kind of blessing was very important to me, for the simple fact that I have the highest respect for him.

Pawel Pawlikowski. © Clive Postlethwaite

An interview with Pawel Pawlikowski
by Andrew Pulver

With Last Resort, *his first released feature film, Pawel Pawlikowski was immediately catapulted into the front rank of British film-making, winning the Michael Powell Award for Best New British Feature at the Edinburgh International Film Festival 2000. Its thematic topicality – the indignities suffered by asylum-seeking refugees in the thinly-disguised entry-port town of Margate – and the apparently effortless skill of its faux-documentary camerawork meant that* Last Resort *struck a socio-political nerve as well as taking its place in the pantheon of contemporary British realist cinema.*

But Pawlikowski is a complex figure: not the least because, as his name indicates, he was born and grew up in Poland. He then lived and worked in a number of European countries before establishing a career in the UK. As such, he is well placed to record the travails of the modern immigrant in Britain; but his cosmopolitan background has always found its way into his work. For almost a decade before Last Resort, *Pawlikowski has been one of British television's most successful documentarists, winning multiple awards for a string of films that focus primarily on literary and political figures from eastern and central Europe. Pawlikowski found a home at the BBC's* Bookmark *strand, and from there made highly formalized and deliberately non-objective documentaries about subjects such as Václav Havel (in his dissident days), Radovan Karadzic (while the battle for Sarajevo was actually in progress in 1992) and Vladimir Zhirinovsky (when he represented a serious threat to the Russian government).*

In retrospect, Pawlikowski's documentary work anticipated the 1990s habit of ironizing its subjects: despite the obvious difference in thematic content, documentaries like Dostoyevsky's Travels *(in which Pawlikowski records the novelist's descendant's frantic attempts to buy a car in Germany) are forerunners to the contemporary school of straight-faced documentary satire exemplified by* Louis Theroux's Weird Weekend, Molly Dineen's Geri, *and the like. Along with Nick Broomfield, Pawlikowski can count himself as one of the most influential practitioners of the medium.*

The one skeleton in Pawlikowski's closet is The Stringer, *his first attempt to move into fiction film-making. Drawing liberally on* Tripping with Zhirinovsky, *a documentary he'd made a little earlier, his story about a young news cameraman drawn fatally into the orbit of a maverick Russian politician was an embarrassing fiasco, and was never released theatrically.* Last Resort, *as this interview reveals, was made in a spirit of complete opposition to his experience on* The Stringer, *with Pawlikowski taking great pains to replicate the conditions of his documentary-making in a fictional context. The acclaim with which it was greeted is ample proof of his success.*

Andrew Pulver: You had a very peripatetic early life – how did you end up in Britain?

Pawel Pawlikowski: I was born in Warsaw, and I first came to Britain with my mother, when she married an English guy – a bit like in *Last Resort.* I was 15, and I didn't get on at all. I was sent to a school for Polish exiles' children, the Divine Mercy college, in Henley-on-Thames, but I didn't last long; they threw me out. But by then my father had escaped to the West as well, and he ended up living in Germany. So I went there for three years, to be with him; then I went to live in Italy for a while. Then I came back to London in the late 70s, and it was there that I felt at home. I had a whole European experience, and then I came here and did my studies here.

AP: What sort of film education did you have?

PP: I didn't go to film school. Never mastered the art at all. I did my postgraduate thesis at Oxford, about the Austrian expressionist poet Georg Trakl, a very interesting guy. But I got really bored with my PhD, so while I was in Oxford I started making films. There was a film workshop there, Super-8 and 16mm, and that got me really interested in film. So I got a job in a company that was preparing a film Peter Greenaway was supposed to do in Poland about Polish composers: that was my way into the industry. I was a researcher, helping to invent the film, basically. Then Greenaway got another movie off the ground, so he didn't make it our one. At the same time I also used to write about films – there was a film magazine called *Stills* that a friend of mine started, and I used to write about European cinema. For about three years I was their European film correspondent. I used to go to film festivals, stay in cheap hotels and cover them. That was my film education really, watching those movies.

AP: How did you actually get behind a camera?

PP: After the Greenaway thing, I went to the BBC, and strayed into a strange area called the Community Programme Unit. It was a separate entity, very left wing, full of very angry people. This must have been 1986. The CPU had a programme, *Open Space,* where people were supposed to write in and request films to be made about some burning issue – it was completely not my scene, but it was a job, you know? What happened was that I read somewhere about a priest in Lancashire who was fighting against local satanists, and I suggested to him he request a programme about the threat of Satanism in Lancashire. He had this huge plan to put a 20-metre cross on the top of Pendle Hill and claim it for Christianity! A good story, a good film to be made. It became quite a funny film. But in the end the priest didn't get permission to put the cross up – the local council didn't agree. The cross would have constituted a new development, so there was no payoff to the film – and my main scene went missing.

AP: How random an occurrence was it that you began making films in Britain? Do you have any special affinity with this country?
PP: There is a definite reason I ended up here. I've noticed one thing about Polish refugees – from the intelligentsia at least – they either choose Paris or London, according to temperament. I always found Britain more mysterious, more interesting; it always meant more, too, partly because of rock music and stuff that I was into when I was younger, but also because there's a kind of mystery here. I still love that you can get on a bus and arrive somewhere weird and unknown, and that the town is a playground where you discover all sorts of nooks and crannies and all these separate civilizations. Mystery always existed for me in London, but not in Paris . . . London doesn't offer itself to the outsider. There's a paradox there, though: because of all these strange codes between people, and also because people are so secretive, they're not very generous. Society is very complex here, complicated and pointlessly so.

AP: In an interview you once described Britain as a 'spiritual wasteland' – do you still feel that way?
PP: Now I'm older, I find it frightening and interesting that the world is losing any sense of spirituality – or even urge for meaning. Britain is, quite possibly, in the forefront of this development! Because it was so fucked over by the Industrial Revolution so long ago. There's still some rural Britain, but it's a very suspect place. The way I see it, in an industrial society you get a complex, multi-layered social situation, a progressive automation of humans, where people are plugged into a certain part of society and they know their place – unless they become rock musicians or footballers, and leap over the barriers. But after observing the British – because I'm trying to invent stories in Britain, looking for English heroes for films – I realized that people give up here very early on. They give up yearning for . . . something more.

AP: Are you saying that Britain has lost its sense of the picturesque?
PP: Not exactly. Britain does have a look to it, it's not hopeless. The Thames estuary, for example, is a landscape I'm currently obsessed with. I'm trying to come up with a story for that area. It's *Heart of Darkness* territory, the idea of this gateway to the empire that is actually a complete wilderness, on the doorstep of a huge metropolis – a bleak, derelict landscape.

AP: All this notwithstanding, your first significant documentary took you back to eastern Europe, with your film about Václav Havel.

PP: For me, at the time, it was a really major epic. The finished film I think is a bit boring, but it was incredibly exciting to make – real cloak and dagger stuff. Czechoslovakia was still under Communism, and officially we were making a film about theatre life in Prague. Every now and then I'd slip into Havel's house and interview him, and film bits and pieces.

I had a lucky break to get the project going. I had a couple of film ideas, and I was walking through the BBC building at Kensington House – a real clapped- out place – where the most interesting bits of the BBC were. The BBC was interesting until about ten years ago: there was a real culture of eccentric commissioning editors, people who were their own masters. Some of them are still going, but they've been kicked into touch, as they say . . . Anyway, I walked through the door of Nigel Williams, who was running a literary strand called *Bookmark*. He was a playwright and I'd seen a play of his I really liked, *The Class Enemy*, so I thought I'd go and see him. He had just had one of these famous BBC lunches – which of course have been stamped out now – and he was a bit drunk; I told him my ideas, and he said, 'Yeah, great.' We got on very well. So I made my film about Havel – he was a man I really admired at the time, and because it was a literary programme it had officially to be about theatre or something, but of course I was trying to make it about him. While I was making it he got arrested, which was an 'interesting' experience. The film has some highlights, but I was so in love with my subject and so excited – we outwitted the police, we were smuggling cassettes out of the country, diplomatic bags on my body – that I made a kind of boring, incoherent film. But it was still an event.

The funniest thing was that it was the *only* film of Havel, so that when the Velvet Revolution happened, I went back and did a small film of my own of Havel – in its way, it's one of the most interesting things I ever did. Just the adventure in itself, but it was also the three days that changed Czech history. All the world's media was there, but I was the only one who Havel knew so I got to film things as they were happening to him. Then when the revolution succeeded, he rang me up to tell me he was going to run for President, and could he borrow the *Bookmark* tape and put it out on Czech TV, because no one knew what he looked like. I rang up Nigel and got the tape to Prague. The film got shown on prime time in Czechoslovakia as propaganda for Havel, because it made him look very good. So I contributed to Havel's election!

AP: So making the Havel film taught you early on how to subvert the system?

PP: Yes, the BBC was an ideal playground for that, because it was literally a big machine with a lot of loose money and some eccentric guys, and bosses who went with it. Now there's only bosses, there are no eccentrics left. But from my point of view, I was using the experience to make films about the world I left behind. In fact, Hans Magnus Enzensberger, the German poet and essayist who championed my films, said that my films were like different versions of myself. There's something in that: hypothetical versions of the life I might have had. But I avoided Poland: I felt very inhibited there. I made one *Bookmark* there, called *Life in a Palace*, about a Polish writer. Poland has become unrecognizable from the way I remember it.

AP: So how *do* you remember Poland?

PP: Of course, the most intense things in my life happened there. When I left, I didn't know we were leaving for good, so I left everything unfinished, including my first girlfriend, and I couldn't go back until five years later when I got the right papers. I always had a sense of guilt that I left: it wasn't my decision of course, but going there is always embarrassing because I was one of the people who went away. In the 80s, I started going back: a certain kind of milieu existed there, film-makers, writers, certain of my family were very impressive individuals, and it became my spiritual home. Though I lived in Britain, my idea of right and wrong and moral behaviour was formed by my contact with these people. This was before Solidarity, I should point out; Havel's crowd, the dissidents of Charter 77, seemed incredibly impressive people at the time too. In the West, I saw people chasing pointless aims. Also, because nobody's really protesting, you don't really know who's who in Britain: people have attitudes, they espouse causes, they adopt ideas, but no one has sacrificed anything. The worst that could happen here is that you lose your job; that is a big thing of course, but hardly on the scale of eastern Europe.

I also discovered the Polish documentary movement, which was very impressive at the time – films made from the mid-70s onward, by Kieslowski and his contemporaries. They were not doing the British thing of simply following people around, but were actually imposing a metaphorical way of seeing, and finding forms to match the content. Treating the documentary as a medium of social analysis, but also as an artistic medium. They shot on 35mm with real thought about how you were doing things. Most of these documentaries were on the shelf: they weren't screened, but you could get hold of them. They were a real eye-opener: how you could look at the world and see it in a metaphorical or synthetic way. Of course, in Communism it was easy: there was a situation there, and everything signified the situation. If you made a film about, say, a cook, it would immediately be very metaphorical! So in a way it was a limited art form, but premised on the nature of society.

AP: Did these films directly inspire your development of an aestheticized documentary style?

PP: Partly, for sure. But also it stemmed from my literary background, and my love of adventures, and my love of exposing myself to interesting situations. Suddenly what you look at has a literary shape, a formal shape to it. I've got this mythicizing brain anyway. My film *Dostoyevsky's Travels*, for example, was a kind of Gogol exercise. When I came across him, his story was a way of seeing literature in the real world, or a fictitious situation at the heart of reality. You get this good hero, this good basic paradox and joke, where everything starts working for you.

AP: *Dostoyevsky's Travels*, for those who don't know it, follows the novelist's great grandson, a tram-driver in St Petersburg, on a seriocomic quest to make some money out of his family name in the West, and buy a Mercedes. Was it your explicit intention to create such a character-driven, dramatic film?
PP: It happened like that, because it was a story with a concrete hero with an aim, which is the basis of all good drama. This is how it was set up. I was snooping around another film in St Petersburg and came across him: he was the real thing, the great-grandson of Dostoyevsky, and I spent an evening with him talking and drinking. He was a very funny guy, with very bizarre ideas of the West. He had these little drawings, for example, and he was convinced he could flog them. He wanted to know how to buy cars. He also had this bizarre notion that, in Hollywood, Warner Bros have a script written by his granny about Dostoyevsky's life, and he wanted to cash in on that. Basically, he wanted to make money, come hell or high water. And he was talking like mad, about everything and nothing. After that evening, I thought it was so rich; in him I had a guy who was determined to reach his aim of buying a car, which was also this great metaphor, and a good key to look under the skin of western society.

I did a screen test of him, a bit of filming, and he was great. I directed him a bit – I'd say, 'Can you stop making faces at this point?' – but he had his own way of doing things, his own body language, and a very straight face. So then I visited him when he'd got to Germany – he had been invited by the Dostoyevsky Society, he was living with this German woman in her house. He was dreaming of doing some moonlighting and raising some money, and she wouldn't let him. She was a very law-abiding German aristocrat and couldn't bear the fact that Dostoyevsky's descendant would stoop to such things. So he was stuck there: she was a vegetarian, so he was starving; he couldn't smoke, so he had to smoke in the toilet. I went there to see if the situation was promising, and I thought – I don't know where this situation is going to take us, but it was a great premise. So I rang up Nigel – I said, 'Give me some money, even if it's not exactly literature,' and Nigel said, 'Great.' I hired a camera and started shooting off my own bat.

AP: How much of the film was staged?

PP: I eventually got a DP and crew over, and then we shot stuff as it happened. There was a bit of manipulation here and there. Then a funny thing happened. I thought we should go to Baden Baden to try Dostoyevsky's roulette method. When we got there, the casino got very excited; then the local media came, saw us filming him, and there was an avalanche effect. He became a personality suddenly; it was a self-fulfilling prophecy.

AP: But some of the sequences look like they've had some careful camera and lighting. How does that affect your relationship with your subject?

PP: It was a fairly hybrid technique. I just set things up, even lit them a bit. Some things – like an embassy party where he approached a businessman for money – happened on their own, and all we needed to do was frame them right. But other things are clearly staged – I was just busking it. I would do it differently today.

AP: In an interview he did later, Dostoyevsky complained that he thought you had tricked him, or ripped him off somehow. How would you characterize your relationship with him?

PP: That was all stupid journalist stuff. What we did was make a film with no money, and he had no money either; so I said, 'We'll give you a grand and we'll see what happens.' So he said he'd do anything – literally – he said, 'I'll be your whore.' Great. He's an obsessive guy, didn't wash, didn't sleep, he was completely focused on his thing. Wouldn't spend a penny on anything except the car. At the same time I was feeling a little bad: it's a horrible thing to do to manipulate a man, but he knew exactly what I was doing. He said to me, 'I wouldn't do such things in Russia, but here I'm abroad, I'm on a mission.' In a more modern type of documentary, I would have used these moments where he turned to me, and showed that we have a relationship. What I was doing instead was to pretend this was objectively happening, and it wasn't. So the film has major flaws. I wouldn't say they were moral ones, exactly, but it would have had more layers had I done it today: possibly more about me, but the truth was I was making a film not so much about him but the world he enters. But I was really finding my way. To be really honest, I really didn't like the film when I watched it: it was satirical, filled with cheap pathos. I like films that have different textures in them and work on more levels. For a long time I was expecting him to rebel against the whole thing – not so much against me, but the whole situation – and I could use it dramatically in the film, but he never did. He was a complete automaton. The Germans he tortured – he was living on people's floors, refusing to leave, being a real pain in the neck. The Germans would say, 'No wonder we couldn't win against the Red Army, this guy's unstoppable.' I was never satisfied with the film, because I'm a big fan of Dostoyevsky and I was hoping for another layer to the whole thing which I couldn't invent – it wouldn't be something I could make him do. That's how these films are made.

AP: Was *From Moscow to Pietuskhia* – a *Bookmark* you made earlier about the Russian samizdat writer Yerofeyev and his classic *Moscow Stations* – more satisfying?
PP: I was in love with the whole thing, the book, the man . . . *Moscow Stations* was a little classic in translation in the Polish underground in the 70s. It was a wonderful piece of literature, as well as being very funny. It was my father's favourite novel, but it was difficult to get hold of, since it was samizdat, so we'd steal it from each other. Then my father died, and I thought to make a film about his favourite book. The problem with Yerofeyev was that there was a rumour he didn't really exist, that it was the pen name of a well-known writer who was scared to write this anarchic stuff – not very Soviet. But he did exist: people knew him, but it was very hard to find him, he had no papers, and he'd been living rough for 30 years. By the time I found him he was already with this woman who looked after him, his second wife. He died immediately after the film. It was a real artistic challenge for me to take this book which worked on so many levels: as a satire, as a romantic, poetic journey of a tortured soul, as poetry, and which was saturated with Russian literature. The London edition had footnotes as long as the text explaining all the allusions, because he was magnificently well read in a very unpretentious way – quoting everyone from Kant to Hegel to Pushkin to Yevtushenko. I was trying to do justice to the literature, to do justice to him; but also trying to show the Russian alcoholic culture – a kind of counterculture – as both tragic, which of course it is, but also show its appeal, its glamour. It's a sad phenomenon, but how do you convey this brilliant mind with this wreck of a body? It was a real labour of love, despite its flaws – it's very heartfelt. I like the tone, which is partly from his novel, and which has influenced all my work, really. There's a mixture of anarchic humour, and a literary intent, a romantic yearning . . .

AP: It seems amazing that anyone would commission it.
PP: At that point Yerofeyev had not been published in the West, he was a nobody. To get a film off the ground about somebody no one's read nowadays would be impossible – but Nigel was great like that. Then, thank God, the film did very well critically, it got a fantastic response – it even got an Emmy. Then Faber translated his poetry, and he was put on the map a bit.

AP: After *Dostoyevsky's Travels* you made what's probably your best-known documentary, *Serbian Epics*, about the oral poetry tradition in Serbia and its

connection with Radovan Karadzic's nationalist ideology. How did you fix on this cultural phenomenon?

PP: I'd spent a lot of time in the Balkans after the Serb-Croat war, and I got terribly interested in the way it was being represented in the media. Then when the Bosnian war broke out, I started wondering about making a film. I didn't know how to tackle it: I didn't want to do something about victims and oppressors – mostly because the media was full of it already. I was looking for a key to the whole thing, the Balkan syndrome, so I contacted the Slavonic department in London University, and I talked to scholars there. From them I discovered these oral epics which were the basis on which the modern Serb state was founded. They had had no statehood for 500 years, not even historiography or an intellectual elite that kept things going. The Serbs had lost everything, apart from the churches and these oral epics. The whole country found its identity through these songs, which were collected by Vuk Karadzic, an itinerant poet-balladeer type, who went from village to village in the early nineteenth century writing them down. He even had to reinvent the Cyrillic alphabet for the Serbs, because there was no written culture as such. I soon realized that there was something very interesting here if you could see that the whole self-image of the Serbs is rooted in this selective and mythomanic view of history. The key epic, for example, was about the battle of Kosovo, and king Lazar's decision to die rather than surrender to the Turks.

I went out to do some more research as the war was beginning in Bosnia and I realized people really know them well, and Karadzic was well known among Serbs who live in the villages, and that these epics were being revived by the nationalists. What also struck me was the general euphoria for the war, which also reminded me of the mood of the oral epics, where people go to war in a euphoric state. I had a distinct feeling that the Serbs had no sense of reality, that no one was going to allow them to do this after the end of the Cold War. So I started the film with the premise that the Serbs were going to lose, just like they lost all the battles before, and that they were expressing a self-destructive death wish. Everything that happened since has confirmed my theory.

I went to Bosnia with this idea, and to my surprise the front-line troops were using these oral epics to keep themselves going. People told me there were *guzla* [single-string violin] players in the front lines, and I went hoping to find what I was interested in. To get permission to film I had to go through the Serb press office, which was a very amateurish, chaotic outfit. You realize why the image of the war was so one-sided, because they couldn't create anything positive at all. The Bosnian government in Sarajevo were much more media aware. But the Serbs were completely ignorant, they had no idea how to handle the media at all – sometimes very authoritarian, sometimes letting people film stuff they should have never let anyone near. The Serbs were stupid.

But I couldn't get any way of filming interesting things, especially if I couldn't get to Karadzic, who I'd heard was from the same oral epic family. But in charge of the press office was a failed poet, who was really into the French symbolists. We discussed Paul Valéry into the night, and he was very happy. So through him I got to the Serb government. They were pleased that some guy from the BBC in the middle of the war wanted to make a film about oral epics – at least, they thought, he'll show us as having some kind of culture. So I got to Karadzic and so on. And because I wasn't a proper journalist, and I was very interested in the culture, I got quite far into the political situation. The scene in the war cabinet, for example: I thought, why are they letting me film this, this is going clearly wrong. The funny thing in that scene was I put a battery light on and it was blinking like mad, and creating an interesting lighting effect. But I was really on thin ice here, because here's Karadzic, Mladic, the whole elite, and I'm messing around with a light! And then there was the moment when Karadzic falls out with Mladic . . .

It was another case of following my nose – but I had a strong formal sense, I was very interested in images, in tableaux, sound and picture, not interested in war as such. It was right next to us, but we didn't film it at all.

AP: Your documentaries, including *Serbian Epics*, are marked by their idiosyncratic framing – do you have any system for establishing camera position?
PP: I have a very un-modern approach: I feel there's only one good angle for everything. You find the right spot, put the right lens on, and you can milk a scene brilliantly; it comes to life like an animation sequence. Under pressure you can think very quickly, but the main thing is not to put it up their nostrils. Just move around and follow the action. I have a whole ideology of shooting things against the grain – this is what it looks like when you shoot it head on, but this is what it looks like when you shoot from a certain angle. That applies to the very idea of the film, the way the war looks from a certain angle.

AP: In effect then, it's a war against cliché?
PP: Absolutely. Media is my main bugbear. The media is one long cliché. What I wanted to do was a film that was ironic against the Serbs, but not simply dismissive. There was a sense of pathos about the whole thing, because I felt they really were plunging into catastrophe. They're idiots, living in some kind of bubble, and it's going to end very badly. Which explains the final sequence, which not too many people understood. It was symbolic: some black and white footage from the First World War where everything falls apart. It was a really interesting film, and the one I'm most proud of, because I was vindicated afterwards, the one film I can watch today. It hasn't aged very much.

AP: You were accused of being seduced to a certain extent by the Serbs, and criticized for not including footage of the atrocities that were being carried out. How do you feel about that now?

PP: Atrocity was on the box every day, there was nothing but atrocity, as if the war was about committing atrocity. There were so many levels on which you could have dealt with the war. But TV journalists are all idiots. The film was shown in Sarajevo during the siege and the Bosnians loved it. Most western films are totally off target; once you understand the Balkans even a little bit, you realize what a quicksand it is. Also, there's a kind of pornography of atrocity, dwelling on it all the time – women raped and men hanged – so the moral stance that many in the media took was, for me, often deeply immoral, simplifying things to the point they were lying, and not corresponding to the complexities of the war.

AP: Was your Zhirinovsky documentary an attempt to retread the success of *Serbian Epics*?

PP: Not as such. I was a bit stuck for things to do after *Epics*, and I thought Zhirinovsky was a kind of Gogol character. Then I thought, 'Fuck, everyone's interested in Zhirinovsky, I'm not going to make a film about him.' But a friend of mine said he was going on a boat trip, so – here I come! *This* is a film, now I see how to do it. So I went on the boat with them, but it was very heavy going because they didn't trust us at all, it was a very difficult situation to manipulate. But it was a good metaphor for something too.

AP: Why did a boat trip appeal to you?

PP: It was a whole visual thing. Plus, there's a tradition in Russia of demagogues and rebels going down the Volga. There are echoes. But it was disappointing – the film was a kind of farce, nothing more to it. It showed what a petty, shabby crowd they are, but I didn't have the access to establish a narrative. And I didn't actually like Zhirinovsky, so I wasn't prepared to make friends with him. I always wanted to get out of his presence, so I never got close to him. It would have made a nice short film, but because it was for Fine Cut it had to be extended. My first idea was to follow him to Iraq. But in the end it became such a political hassle, getting permissions – basically they're all bandits – so it collapsed.

AP: Is it fair to say that *The Stringer* took a lot from it?

PP: While I was with Zhirinovsky, I met a boy who was a bit like the kid in *The Stringer*. I was hanging around filming Zhirinovsky every day; the boy was like part of the family and created Zhirinovsky's image – whatever Zhirinovsky did, he filmed it, then flogged it to various TV stations and media. That was the starting point.

AP: Now that your reputation is secure after *Last Resort*, can you look back at *The Stringer* and say why it turned out so badly?

PP: I learned a lot from it. It was a very sharp lesson in what to avoid. First thing was: it was a thing I should have done on the hop, very few actors, not a big deal. But BBC Drama insisted we needed a proper script, and so I wrote and wrote and wrote. I ended up writing a genre thriller, where the kid ends up finding out more than is good for him, and then his life is threatened. What I ended up with was a thriller – not what you see on the screen. It was full of clichés, to get from A to B, like most films are. When I got to Moscow to shoot it, none of these things rang true in terms of the people that I knew or the actors I could get. I was really embarrassed to ask Russian actors to do the stuff I'd written; there was no depth to it. There was a functional structure and plot.

Secondly, by that time in 1997, Zhirinovsky's threat, and the whole demonic nature of Russian politics, was not there any more. I had written it earlier, but by the time the BBC was interested it was too late. So it was ridiculous: the premise of the thriller was that this guy was actually an influential politician who could change the fate of Russia, and this kid holds the key to the future of the nation. But I knew too much about Russia to take it seriously. So as I was there setting it up I started rewriting it like mad. Plus we didn't have the money. Russian actors will do something if they know it's idiotic, like James Bond or The Saint, for serious money. They would only work on this film if they believed in the characters. So I changed the Zhirinovsky character from someone who is about to seize power, to one who's long lost it, a no-hoper, who needs the media to go on existing.

That got me interested again. But then the third thing came along. The money from British Screen that came in was contingent on a British star, and on paper the female character was totally underdeveloped. No English star would do it apart from Anna Friel, and she was sort of bankable, but had a very limited range. I could have rescued it, I think, if I had done the same job as on *Last Resort* or *Twockers*, and really controlled it. But with Anna Friel, who was the star and paid a lot of money, the whole film schedule was structured around her availability. The Russians, much better actors, were paid peanuts. It was mad, because the script didn't really add up, so there was a complete idiocy at the heart of the whole thing.

Next, the kid who I wanted to do the lead decided he didn't want to do it, and Bodrov was a last-minute replacement. I really liked the original kid, he had lots of soul, you really believed him. With Bodrov – he's a good actor, but there's no soul there, you don't even believe he likes her. A week before filming started I was walking the streets of Moscow looking for my hero. And the script wasn't ready, either. And the guy who was going to play the politician had a heart attack, so I had to get another late replacement. I was in a situation where I was in debt, so I couldn't pull out. Also the Russian crew and English crew didn't get on; so the situation was so chaotic that lots of scenes didn't get done.

AP: One thing that's clear is that *The Stringer* seems so thoroughly conventional a film, compared to both your earlier documentaries and your later fiction films. Was that something to do with it being your first attempt to make a feature, and being uncertain how to proceed?
PP: Yes, I was running behind the film, you know? I literally didn't know where I was, so I ended up playing by numbers. I would shoot a scene, I didn't know where it fitted any more because the script was all over the place; and yet I didn't have the freedom to shoot chronologically, or the flexibility to change things around. It was a nightmare, every possible mistake was made: starting without a script but having no freedom; starting without the actors you want; disrupting the organic set-up by having some being paid much more than others; and shooting a film about one culture for the benefit of another culture. That was the basic original sin. I often plunge into things and busk my way out of it, but it didn't work. It was really embarrassing. The funny thing was it got into Cannes, in the Director's Fortnight.

AP: Did its failure damage your career?
PP: No, some people loved it. In Cannes it went down very well. On the big screen it has some atmosphere, here and there. And in Russia it did well, they saw something in it. It didn't hurt me at all – thank God it wasn't distributed.

AP: *Twockers* – your 40-minute film about a bunch of car-thief teens – looks like a deliberate antidote to *The Stringer*. Was that the case?
PP: First of all, I made a conscious decision to work with friends. On *The Stringer* there was no community. *Twockers* was a conscious effort to move away from that. I did it with Ian Duncan, a really decent guy: someone with whom you can invent things, and someone who pulls the thing along. It means I'm not the only one who's doing the pulling. Small crew, shot chronologically, documentary set-up, we didn't start filming till we found the perfect kid for the lead, and we were tweaking the script all the time as we went along. And we had a break in the middle, which is a great thing to do. Two weeks of editing in the middle, where you can see if the thing is working. So the scriptwriting and film-making is part of the same process. And above all, there was a community spirit, we all lived in the same house, and had a great time. There was a sense of purpose, which was so liberating.

And *Last Resort* was a step further: where I handpicked the actors with no compromise about who I cast; where the script was an outline; where I took time to find the right people; where I find the right landscape and I don't have to build anything with crappy designers who are full of themselves; and I can use my documentary eye for finding atmospheric angles and interesting compositions; and with a cameraman whose half a documentary camera man who doesn't need gadgetry to see things.

AP: Speaking of *Last Resort*, did you ever think you'd blown your chance at features after *The Stringer*?
PP: No, no. I thought, I'm going to survive it because I now know what to do and what to avoid.

AP: Had it always been your ambition to continue making fiction?
PP: Not necessarily. Basically, I came to the end of the road with documentaries, because a certain kind of documentary film-making died around that time – it was all replaced by docu-soap. My documentaries didn't really find huge audiences because they were quite oblique and needed a bit of effort to follow them – and that became anathema. The funny thing was I could still get money to make them, because I was a bit of a star in documentary terms. But I thought it's not worth it. If a normal audience doesn't like what I do, why should I do it? I thought this is the end of the road for a certain type of film-making, so I must reinvent where I lie. And just as my first two documentaries were, to be honest, a bit off target, a mess, and it took me two films to fuck up before I discovered what I like doing . . . the same with feature films. I plunged into it, and it was the best film school you could ever go to.

AP: Can you account for *Last Resort*'s success?
PP: I don't know. I know what *I* like about it. I love films where the actors practically coincide with the characters, where they bring a lot of themselves in – like De Niro in *Taxi Driver* – and are almost documentary in the way the character comes in. The story was always there, but once I found Dina it changed somehow. I went through a lot of actresses who had their own kids, who knew what it was like to have a kid, but when I saw Dina, I thought, 'This is it, she's fantastic.' She's a deep and interesting woman, and a bit mad too. I tweaked the character to suit her. It's not really her, but a lot of it comes from her. And we did a lot of work-shopping scenes before we finalise the dialogue – or even after that, right before you shoot it, you throw it up in the air again to make it fresh. Often the stuff you make in workshop doesn't feel right any more. What I'm good at is living the moment, just feeling my way into the moment, and if I'm allowed to do it, to sculpt the thing with good materials, then I know it will be interesting.

Last Resort: Artyom Strelnikov (Artyom) and Dina Korzun (Tanya).

Tanya and Artyom take flight with Alfie (Paddy Considine).

AP: Paddy Considine did a very good job opposite her.

PP: He was amazing. It was interesting, we didn't know who his character was for a third of the film. I left him very ambiguous at the beginning, I don't know whether you notice. He could be a very sinister guy, because we genuinely didn't know. We had all sorts of plot devices to make him more disreputable, more manipulative and nasty. But then there were a few days during the shoot when I developed a real rhythm in the filming, and I realized we could generate real warmth between them. It depends so much in creating the right set-up, the right atmosphere. It's very difficult in Britain because the actors are all doing their own thing, and if they are any good they go straight to Hollywood.

AP: Again, in the past you've often criticized the production system in Britain. Can you expand on that?

PP: In Britain there are very few people who can cut the bullshit, very few people with real intuition. But the real problem is there are no writers to write with. Most writers are fought over – and, let's face it, they're not very good writers – because there's all this money to make films with and all this machinery to feed, and not enough scripts or ideas. So every little writer is built up by their agents as some genius. There is no tradition of writers working for directors. Here writers all work for producers, and then directors are brought in at some point later.

AP: Where do you go from here?

PP: My big passion now is to immortalize interesting people; immortalize the last humans that I can identify among actors and non-actors. There are people out there who are like artefacts, and it is good to create stories for them. But the awful thing about great cinema – the movie where the actor coincides with the character, the landscape is right, and all that – is that they exploit it to the full, and can't do it again. It's like Trevor in *Twockers*: he's a great kid, but that's more or less it. The film wasn't a career move for him; he's got a job in an upholstery factory now. I put him in touch with some agents, but he wasn't interested. In the end, feature films are like documentaries – they hit the right time and the right place, the right group of people, and the right person to put it all together. And that's frightening if you want to make film-making your career. What you have to do is generate certain conditions, and that's very often an accident.

François Ozon

An interview with François Ozon
by Ryan Gilbey

The films of François Ozon provide a good reason to get excited about cinema, and to stay excited. Although he only made his first feature four years ago, the body of work which he has amassed, not to mention the richness of that work, would be impressive coming from a film-maker considerably older than his 34 years. His presence was announced in the mid-90s by some succulent short films. There were sunny sex comedies: in A Summer Dress/Une robe d'été (1996), the erotic focus is cleverly transferred onto a dress with which the three characters – two squabbling gay teenagers and a beachfront floozy – come into contact, while Bed Scenes/Scènes de lit (1997) is a collection of vignettes set before and after sex. There were elliptical dramas: A Little Death/La petite mort (1995) traces a son's efforts to settle old scores with his dying father, and the bite-sized x2000 (1998) imagines the serene, surreal morning after the millennium before.

Most astonishing was See the Sea/Regarde la mer (1997), a psychological thriller about a young mother in a French coastal town who befriends a sinister female backpacker. See the Sea attracted comparisons with Chabrol, Polanski and Clouzot. It is beautifully shot, full of alluring images of tranquillity, each of which is systematically contaminated with menace. After a shocking denouement, the film seems to seal shut over the horrors it has revealed, leaving the surface as pristine and inviting as it first appeared. That's some trick. Only David Lynch, another master excavator, has so comprehensively covered his tracks after an expedition into the unsavoury unknown.

Ozon made his full-length debut with Sitcom (1998). This camp comedy, about a bourgeois family whose inhibitions collapse after the arrival of a pet rat, paid affectionate homage to John Waters and Luis Buñuel. Ozon's attitude toward sexual experimentation was as cheerfully blasé as ever: group sex, sadomasochism and incest all passed before the camera's unblinking eye like groceries at a supermarket checkout. The frivolity of Sitcom was unexpected after See the Sea, but then unpredictability is one of the qualities to be treasured in Ozon's choice of styles and subjects. He goes where his inspiration takes him, regardless of jarring switches in tone or genre, with the result that one film can be, superficially, strikingly different from another. Who ever held that against Powell and Pressburger?

I first met François Ozon in London in 1998, when he was promoting Sitcom, *and I was struck, as many interviewers were, by how his appearance didn't quite match his movies (unlike, say, his countryman and contemporary Gaspar Noe, who looks perfectly capable of making films as feral as* Carné *and* Seul Contre Tous). *Ozon was polite, clean-cut, spick-and-span, where his films were mischievous, transgressive and provocative. How could you reconcile this fellow, who would charm your grandmother, with his films, which might give her a heart attack? And why should our creative impulses and desires be reflected in our physical appearance anyway? What did I expect him to turn up in –thigh-length boots and a harness? It might be a subject for a François Ozon short. When we meet again in summer 2001, it is in Paris, at the offices of Fidélité Productions, with whom Ozon has been collaborating since his 1994 short* Truth or Dare/Actionvérité. *The walls are crowded with posters advertising his movies, including the three features which quickly followed* Sitcom. *First came* Criminal Lovers/Les amants criminels (1998), *which begins as a thriller about two teenagers who murder a classmate but gradually warps into a macabre, homoerotic take on* Hansel and Gretel. *Like its heroes, the movie strayed far from the beaten track, without leaving a trail of breadcrumbs for its audience; it mixed contradictory flavours to alarming effect, but undeservedly found little favour (it was not released in Britain).*

Before Criminal Lovers *opened, Ozon had already begun shooting* Water Drops on Burning Rocks/Gouttes d'eau sur pierres brûlantes (1999), *an adaptation of the obscure Fassbinder play* Tropfen auf heisse Steine. *Rather than opening up the action, as some adaptations do, Ozon deliberately closes it in, making the set design and compositions as theatrical as possible, and never departing from the cramped apartment where two men, teenage Franz and his bullying middle-aged lover Leopold, are self-destructing. But Ozon's finest work to date is* Under the Sand/Sous le sable (2000), *a moving study of grief and isolation starring Charlotte Rampling as Marie, a woman who retreats into fantasy when she is unable to accept her husband's disappearance. The film's chilly beauty never feels cosmetic: each shot, each frame, pulls us into this widow's solitude, until the last moment, when Ozon abruptly severs our ties with her. The shattering final shot leaves Marie to wade deeper into her delusions.*

Ozon took a break from editing his new picture, Eight Women, *to meet me. Although his English transpired to be more than adequate, I had brought along a translator, and Ozon greeted us enthusiastically at the door, like a child whose chums have come round to play. We began by discussing his latest project.*

RG: What can you tell me about *Eight Women*?
FO: It's a very strange film. I started editing it two weeks ago. It is a murder mystery with eight women and one man.

RG: It's an impressive cast list: Catherine Deneuve, Isabelle Huppert . . .
FO: Yes, and also Fanny Ardant, Emmanuelle Béart, Virginie Ledoyen . . .

RG: Everyone . . .
FO: No, not quite everyone. Isabelle Adjani and Sophie Marceau are not in it. (*Laughs.*)

RG: Is it true that it's influenced by Agatha Christie?
FO: A little. I know that to sell it in England we are calling it 'a bitchy who-dunnit'.

RG: What about visually?
FO: Visually it will be very stylized. It's set in the 50s, and I think you will sense the influence of American comedies, American films, like the work of Vincente Minnelli, George Cukor, those kind of films. The 50s were important because it was a great time for the way women looked – the shape of the clothes, their style and colour. Christian Dior was very important. And also a lot of directors that I like were doing some of their best work in the 50s – Douglas Sirk, Fritz Lang, Michael Powell.

RG: Will audiences be expected to take the murder part of *Eight Women* seriously?
FO: (*Feigning alarm*): But murder is always serious!

RG: Not always in films.
FO: When we were shooting, the film felt quite dramatic, almost tragic, and now as I'm editing it is becoming more of a comedy. I find that as I am working on something, it can gradually change its shape, its tone.

RG: I heard that *Criminal Lovers* changed a lot in the editing room.
FO: Yes, there were no flashbacks originally. But I'm going to put together a different version of that film for when it is released on DVD. I'm going to try something new with it. People really didn't like that film in France. It was very unpopular. *Sitcom* had been a success but neither the critics nor the public liked *Criminal Lovers*.

RG: Why do you think people reacted so badly to it?

FO: It was a big change. After *See the Sea* and *Sitcom*, suddenly this movie was very different and perhaps difficult; a lot of people were disconcerted by it. Often films that are based on real-life tragic events, true crime, don't seem to work in France; the new film by Cédric Kahn [*Roberto Succo*, the true story of an Italian killer] seems to have suffered the same fate.

RG: But there isn't much of the real-life case in your film – I'm sure the scene where Alice and Luc have sex in the forest while all those Disney-style woodland animals gather round them isn't taken from life.
FO: It could happen!

RG: One of the common complaints among those who are hostile to *Criminal Lovers* is that you treated Alice, one of the killers, so cruelly.
FO: But she's cruel. It's a sadistic film, and in a film you have the right, or the freedom, to be sadistic, because it is just a film.

RG: But Alice's boyfriend, Luc, he—
FO: He's a masochist.

RG: Sure, but he gets off much more lightly than Alice, who is shot and then besieged by dogs.
FO: On that movie I wanted to show two different characters with two different approaches. Luc realizes that he has to accept reality and the law. Alice refuses to accept that. For her, there is only pleasure. Freud talks about the reality principle and the pleasure principle, and if you want to become an adult you have to admit reality into your life. Alice isn't prepared to do that. She would rather live all the time in dreams, and so she also dies that way at the end, denying reality. For me it was not the case that one is good and the other is bad. It's two choices. I love Alice and I love Luc, but people thought I didn't like Alice. But I like her. And I like it when she is in the cellar. It's like her jail. She is a murderer, after all.

RG: What changes will you make in the re-edited version?
FO: The murder comes too soon in the original version. And I would like to show before the murder more of the relationships between Saïd [the murder victim] and Alice, and Luc and Alice. It was too disturbing for the audience to watch that movie because after five minutes there is this horrible murder that makes it hard to identify with the heroes. If you have more time with the characters before the murder, you can have empathy and go with them in their travels. I think the way I showed it in the film was very ruthless, very merciless, toward the audience. I know now with more experience that if you want to tell

the audience something difficult, you have to seduce them, and in *Criminal Lovers* there is no seduction. For me, there is seduction, but not for everybody, so a lot of people rejected the film.

RG: **The murder itself is very hard to watch.**
FO: It was important for me to show that the murder was very violent, and not turn it into an aesthetic experience. I showed the murder twice, the first time in a realistic style, and the second with Alice looking back on it, dreaming about it as something aesthetic. The second time, it's exactly the same shot as the first but slowed down, with just the sound of Alice reading a poem. I wanted to give the same images, the same shot, a different significance, to show that one incident can have different interpretations.

RG: **You began *Sitcom* with something much stranger – a flash-forward to a man massacring his family, which is later revealed to have been a dream or fantasy. Why did you structure the film that way?**
FO: Usually flashbacks are very psychological: they're used to explain things, and in this context I wanted to use it for the opposite purpose, to disorientate the audience and make them feel like they were in a dream. Buñuel did a similar thing in *The Discreet Charm of the Bourgeoisie*, where the characters are having dinner and they realize they're on stage.

RG: **The use of space in your films is very striking. In *Sitcom*, *Water Drops on Burning Rocks*, and even *See the Sea*, which is largely exterior and in sunlight, there is a strong feeling of claustrophobia.**
FO: With *Sitcom* it was a matter of having only a month to make a film, and thinking to myself: it has to be set in one place. That meant a house or a prison. And I didn't want to spend a month in a prison. But most of the time I don't like to change sets. I like to be in the same set for most of the film – to use actors like rats in a laboratory. My father is a scientist. He did experiments with frogs and lizards and as a child I loved to be in a laboratory with him, watching as he did these dissections.

RG: **Maybe you did follow in his footsteps after all.**
FO: Yes. But my father's main area of work is in reproduction. And in my films there is a lot of sex but no reproduction.

RG: **If your actors are like laboratory rats, which sounds quite clinical, how do you feel toward your characters? Do you empathize with them?**
FO: I want to keep a distance from the characters, because that's the way to respect the audience. I don't want everything to be indicated or explained in the

Regarde la mer / See the Sea

Regarde la mer / See the Sea

films. And usually I don't like to judge; I want to give the freedom to the audience to think what they want about the characters. But sometimes you have to show empathy to your characters, and other times you must be sadistic. Because I'm not an angel, you know.

RG: So would there be things about, say, the father in *Sitcom*, who is the symbol of what is wrong with the family, with which you could empathize or identify?
FO: Yes. He has a lot of distance himself and a lot of humour. He talks in proverbs. He sees what's going on in the house and he keeps his distance. But he doesn't want to have any emotions, and that makes the rest of the family suffer.

RG: Isn't there a serious point in *Sitcom* about how fathers can be a destructive influence?
FO: I never intended to make sociological observations about families but if there is a problem in that house, it's because of the father: he's there and somehow not there at the same time. Maybe if he was not there at all it would be better for everyone.

RG: I do notice a series of absent or irresponsible fathers and father figures in your films. In *Sitcom* and *A Little Death*, the father is inadequate, while in *See the Sea* he is absent altogether. Is this a conscious theme?
FO: That's interesting. Of course in *Under the Sand* too he is not there either. Very often the narrative comes from the fact that someone is missing. I mean, not just someone, but the father. In *Eight Women* it is the same: there is one man and he is murdered in the first minute! I think one day I will have to make a film about a father in which he is there for the whole film. But not for the moment. For the moment, I prefer the father away. Or dead.

RG: Can you talk a bit about your time at film school?
FO: I left university with a master's degree in Cinema. I had made about 30 Super-8 movies with my parents, my family and friends. Some of them would just be footage of my grandmother sleeping, or my sister's bottom. After that I came to La FEMIS and began to make real short films – among them *Victor* (1993) and *A Rose Between Us/Une rose entre nous* (1994).

RG: And that's where you met Claudine Bouché?
FO: Yes. She was a kind of teacher there. At La FEMIS, a lot of people working in movies come just for two weeks to work with the students. She came first of all to talk about her editing and her work with François Truffaut on *Jules and Jim* and *Shoot the Pianist*. We became friends. I loved the way she was talking

A Summer Dress

about movies – how to edit a film, how you sometimes have to cut very fast, or not keep the first minute of a scene, but to begin a scene at the end or in the middle, always moving things around. She's an old woman – she's 70 years old – but she's very modern in her ideas on editing. We worked together at the school, and after school I phoned up to ask if she would come and see something I was working on because I was having problems. She loves my work and what she says is very helpful, because often during the editing you see nothing, you think it's awful, so you need to have an objective viewpoint, someone outside the mess. Each time I make a film, she comes during the editing to help me. She's a good friend now.

RG: Can you remember a specific occasion where she helped you during editing?
FO: In *A Summer Dress* there is a scene where the boy and girl return to the beach and everything has been stolen and the boy is nude. The girl says, 'I can give you my dress', and the boy says, 'No'. The scene was shot from the girl's point of view and then at the end the boy was shown putting on the dress. It was very sexy to see him putting it on. And then the next shot was the boy walking along wearing the dress. Claudine said that it might be better not to see him putting on the dress – that the scene would be stronger if the audience had the surprise of suddenly seeing him wearing it. The idea was to show him saying,

'No, I don't want to', and then straight after he's said that, we cut to him in the dress. And everyone in the audience always laughs, of course. At first, I said no, because I thought the shot of him putting the dress on was so sexy. But when I saw that it was funny the way Claudine suggested, then that was more important. Sometimes you don't have to show everything. You can build an effect instead. And with those things she is very helpful.

RG: Is it Claudine's influence that makes your films so lean?
FO: No, that's just my taste. No fat. The audience have to make the movie themselves in a way. You don't have to give them everything.

RG: What do you miss about making short films?
FO: The speed of working. But in a way they are all the same movie. The difference between *Eight Women* and the previous movies is that there was no Catherine Deneuve before. That's the only difference. Other than that, it's all the same work.

RG: Can you describe the pressure of moving from shorts to features?
FO: I didn't feel any pressure. I had made a lot of short films, and I really wasn't in a hurry to make a full-length film. When I started *Sitcom*, we didn't have much money, so the conditions weren't very different from making a short. All my films are very low budget. *Eight Women* is the exception but that's because of the cast.

RG: What about pressure in terms of sustaining narrative or mood?
FO: It's often more complicated to tell a story in six minutes than in 90. The fact that there's no fat on my movies may be something left over from making short films, where you have very little time to say things. Usually my long feature films are very short anyway, compared to other people's. *See the Sea* was only 52 minutes. But it was enough.

RG: Was that economy learned in film school?
FO: You don't learn a lot of things at La FEMIS, but you just work – you have the opportunity to keep working constantly. I learned the most when I was shooting Super-8 movies because without sound you have to tell the story only in images.

RG: You tend to collaborate regularly with the same people – Yorick le Saux was your cinematographer from *Truth or Dare* through to *Sitcom*, and now Jeanne Lapoirie has taken over that role. Do you prefer to keep the same personnel on each film where possible?

FO: As I work very fast it's easier for me to work with the same people because I don't have to spend time explaining what I want. They know me so they can propose things before I need to explain. I met Yorick at film school. He wanted to be a director so he worked with me first as cameraman and now he has gone on to directing, which is why we don't work together. Jeanne had worked with André Téchiné on *Wild Reeds/Les roseaux savages*. We have a very good feeling together; we don't have to talk too much about the work because we understand.

RG: Was it daunting taking on a Fassbinder play in *Water Drops on Burning Rocks*?
FO: I just tried not to make a Fassbinder movie. When Kenneth Branagh makes a movie based on a Shakespeare play people see it as a Kenneth Branagh film. But that's not a very good example because I hate Kenneth Branagh! I wanted to give my own version of the Fassbinder play: to get inside his world but to give my own interpretation. What I liked was that it is not a complete play, it's not a perfect play, but it has elements that would be developed later in his work. It's better to work with a book or a play that is not completely formed or accomplished, so you can bring some perfection to it. I prefer to adapt something like *Eight Women*, which is a bad play – a very bad play. Better to adapt that than Proust, which is an accomplished work already. With *Eight Women* I kept the plot and that's all. But with *Water Drops* . . . I tried to show what I like about Fassbinder's movies. When I first saw the play I found it very funny and very cruel but always realistic. I think when you are 16, 17, when you discover love and sexuality, you have a lot of idealism, and you always end up suffering very badly, like Franz in the film. I recognized myself at that age, and then I thought: perhaps now I'm Leopold.

RG: Oh no.
FO: Maybe not exactly. But I think when you are young you are very naive about love, and then after the cruelty of reality hits you, you become like Leopold.

RG: Do you think the film is a warning against living together?
FO: No. I love to share my life with somebody. I just think it's not possible for a couple like Franz and Leopold because Leopold has no taste for life. And Franz is a masochist, and very idealistic. So together it doesn't work.

RG: Was Leopold once like Franz?
FO: Yes, I'm sure of that. It's a cycle. What I liked about the play was that it showed the mechanics, the inner workings of the relationship, like clockwork –

there's somebody with power, and someone suffering, and it goes on like that, and that's how things can seem when you're in love and you're hurting. Life can always be like that if you want to live in a sadomasochistic relationship, but it doesn't have to be. I think it was the view of Fassbinder because he wrote the play when he was only 19, and it was autobiographical – he was Franz. His perspective never really changed. Just before his death, he was still thinking that relationships between people are always power struggles. But Fassbinder was born during the war and throughout his childhood in Germany there was a lot of guilt. That might be why he had such a dark, black vision of life. I was born in the 60s so for me it's not the same story.

RG: For Fassbinder, there was another level of power because he had emotional relationships with his actors, like Gunther Kaufmann, who was the lead actor in *Whity*.
FO: Yes, they were lovers. Fassbinder liked to mix his life with his films. I do not do that so much. To make movies was a way for him to have love. I don't use my director's life for my private life. I try to really separate them, though sometimes they mix.

RG: What did you respond to when you first saw a Fassbinder film?
FO: I liked the combination between the stylized and the realistic. Film theory is very important in France for movie lovers – people like to know for certain whether a film is realistic or stylized – and I think Fassbinder mixes up those distinctions, which is what made his films interesting and daring for me.

RG: Why did you begin *Water Drops . . .* with those picture postcards of Germany?
FO: I knew the audience would be stuck in the apartment for the whole film, so I said: let's give them some beautiful shots of Germany before it is time to go inside!

RG: Can you talk about why you incorporated the transsexual from Fassbinder's film *In a Year of 13 Moons* into the character of Vera in *Water Drops . . .*?
FO: The original play was very misogynistic. You got the feeling that Fassbinder didn't like women, because at that age I don't think he really knew them. He was in love with a man. So the women were there only for the story, they had no personality. I tried to give them more depth. For the young woman, Anna, it was easy because she is like the female equivalent of Franz. But for Vera, she only came in at the end. I wanted to give her an identity. I was watching all my favourite Fassbinder movies; I love *In a Year of 13 Moons*, and I thought it

would be interesting to put this character into *Water Drops* ... as Vera. In his relationship with Leopold, Franz loses his identity and so I wanted him to meet someone who has no identity anymore, because Vera is not a man or a woman, she's a transsexual. Meeting her is like being in front of a mirror for Franz. This is what he will become if he stays with Leopold: he will change his sex, he will become what Leopold wants, and for him the only way to escape is suicide.

RG: Many of your films feature characters who only seem complete after having sex with both men and women – the boy in *A Summer Dress* who has sex with the girl at the beach, and then finds that his relationship with his boyfriend is better; Luc in *Criminal Lovers*, who can only make love to Alice after he has had sex with a man; Franz and Leopold in *Water Drops* ... are both bisexual; then there are pretty much all the characters in *Sitcom*!
FO: Usually my films are about young people discovering sexuality. When you are young, you try lots of things, and that's why my characters try with men and with women. They can choose. In *Under the Sand*, there was no homosexuality. Marie could have become a lesbian. It was a possibility but I didn't pursue it because I think she knows what she likes at this stage. What I like about young characters is that they are like a blank page – anything can happen, they are open.

RG: Do you mind your films being classified as gay films?
FO: For me it's not a problem. *Water Drops* ... won a lot of gay prizes – at Berlin it won the Teddy Bear. My most loyal audience has been gay people. My first successes came from gay festivals and gay audiences, and I'm pleased for that recognition. But I know that when *Water Drops* ... received the gay prize at Berlin, the French press were not happy because they felt it was stupid to say it's only a gay film. But I don't care. No, the film is not only gay, and it would not be interesting for me to make a film that is only gay, with exclusively gay ideas and politics. I know that *A Summer Dress* was used as a gay political weapon or symbol. In all the gay festivals, that film was like a flag. I was surprised because I didn't think of it in this way. I wanted to make a fairy-tale without guilt. I made it at a time when Aids was on everybody's mind and everybody used condoms and there was so much guilt in the gay community. The film was like a dream, a fantasy, because in it we said you can have sex as you want, but just use condoms – you can try men and women, you can have pleasure, you don't have to feel guilty. In the film, the boy feels guilty at first. Then after, when he's wearing the dress, everything is OK. All the gay viewers after the film said, 'I want to buy a dress and then everything will be OK!' So I think the gay community was very happy that a film was saying, yes, there is Aids, but you can go and have sex, why not?

RG: I read an interesting quote from you in which you said, 'People in France think I'm making too many films. People think I'm a spoiled child.'

FO: Yes, but I think it's wrong, because I have worked very hard. It's hard to get into La FEMIS. And now I only make one film a year. It's not too much. I would be able to make two films a year but it's not possible with the release dates and so on. I realize now that as a director I have a lot of promotional work to do once I've made a film. When I began making movies I didn't think that would become such an important part because it's not what I like to do. I like to make movies, work with the actors, to edit. But if I want to work on another film, I have to do the promotion. I think now with the success of *Under the Sand* in France, and with *Eight Women* coming up, I can stop doing that so much. The first year it's very nice because you do lots of travelling, but then you realize it's always the same; when you are travelling you don't have the same relationship with people. I would like to travel again just as a tourist and not as a director always visiting the best hotels, the film festivals. But I don't mean to complain.

RG: Did the success of *Under the Sand* in France make it harder for you when it came to starting *Eight Women*?

FO: A little bit. It's easy to go on after a failure. If you make a movie that everyone hates, you say: I have to go on and make something better. After a success, you can feel everyone waiting for your next move. *Under the Sand* did very well, and Charlotte Rampling was loved in the movie. In France she had a lot of press; she made the covers of all the big movie magazines. All the actresses were very surprised and jealous. They said, 'We want to work with him now!'

RG: *Under the Sand* came from childhood – you remembered a woman on holiday whose husband had vanished – but in a few of your films the idea of a vacation, a beach, is something to be feared rather than enjoyed. Is that also a feeling from childhood?

FO: Well, *See the Sea* was not from childhood. That came from an English friend, Sasha Hails, who is the actress in the film. She had a baby and she had a very strange way of speaking about her maternity, and that inspired me to write the film. With *Under the Sand*, I was trying to recapture a sensation rather than an event. I wanted to try to understand the details of this woman losing her husband – what it means to her in a physical, material way. So the beach is important. When you go to a beach sometimes, especially if it's empty, then it can be very beautiful, but it can also create anxiety. You can feel like you're on another planet, and that's the feeling I was trying to recreate in *Under the Sand*. It's like being there at the beginning of the world – there's nothing, it's new and pure, but you also have to confront the savagery of the world.

Sous le sable / Under the Sand: Charlotte Rampling as Marie.

RG: Had you thought for a long time about using that sensation as a starting point for *Under the Sand*?

FO: When I'm working I don't tend to think consciously about where an idea has come from; if I want to tell a story then I just write it. It's your job to take it from there. But on the DVD there will be a film of my parents and it's very much like *Under the Sand*. Not exactly the same story, but my parents are there during summer, and there is some of the same feeling. I didn't think about it while I was making *Under the Sand*, but it was strange to come back to it and discover that there was real continuity. There will be some other short films on there that I made with my family. Sometimes I'm not sure it's a good idea! Not all of them, only the most watchable ones. Some of them were not that bad, I wasn't too ashamed when I was watching them again. Some of them are really pornographic.

RG: You had a six-month break between shooting the first section of *Under the Sand*, in which Marie's husband vanishes on holiday, and the rest of the movie, which finds her back in Paris alone. Was that break an artistic decision or a financial one?

FO: First it was artistic, then it was financial. It was supposed to be a three-month gap, but then we had no money, so we had to wait six months. There was a lot of anguish, because I didn't know if we would finish the film. We had to complete it in 16mm, whereas the first part is in 35mm.

RG: Do you think that the film ultimately benefited?

FO: Now I can say yes. (*Laughs.*) When I was working I thought it was terrible, a nightmare, because when you begin something and then can't finish it, it's awful, you feel like something has been amputated. And it was terrible for Charlotte too because of the waiting. It was hard, but now I see that it was good for the film, because in that six months I had more time to work and think about the main goals. We had only five weeks to finish the rest of the film, which is not long, so I had to know exactly what I wanted to do because sometimes I don't know exactly. I thought it was a good economic and artistic idea to begin the film without knowing where it was going to go, but it didn't always feel so good. I shot the first 20 minutes, then showed it to the television people and said, 'Look at this 20 minutes, and if you want to see what happens next, give me the money!' Everyone said, 'Oh it's so sad, and the cast is so boring, Charlotte Rampling and Bruno Cremer are so old-fashioned, nobody wants to see old people like this, we don't care for these characters.' I gave them the script, but nothing happens in the second part – it's just a woman living with a ghost. They said, 'Nothing happens'.

I said, 'Trust me, you'll see, something will happen in Charlotte Rampling's face.' But it was not enough for them. Nobody wanted to give us any money. We got money from Italy, Japan, Switzerland, and finished the film. And because people were so closed off, it gave us more determination, to prove that they were wrong – that it was a good story, that Charlotte Rampling is a great actress. In my mind, I didn't understand why we were getting rejected, because when I was making the movie I had the feeling that it was a universal story. So I was very happy when it became successful.

RG: Presumably that made *Eight Women* easier to finance.
FO (*Clicks fingers*): Like that! Very easy.

RG: Do you think you're an outsider in French cinema?
FO: I don't feel like I belong to any particular group or establishment. Maybe I feel a connection with young film-makers, but then I have made five films already, so I'm not that young. I don't know where my place is. I don't think I have a place.

RG: That's a good thing, isn't it?
FO: Yes, certainly. I don't want to have a place, I don't want to be like Bertrand Tavernier. For a lot of people, I'm an iconoclast; they don't know exactly where I am. That's why I disturb sometimes. After each film, people don't know what to expect. After *Water Drops . . .* , *Under the Sand* was very surprising, and with *Eight Women* it will be different again.

RG: What are your feelings about French cinema in general at the moment?
FO: French movies have become successful again recently. It's a good thing for our economy. Artistically I'm not sure. I am waiting. In France, we are always trying to take lessons from America, trying to make some kind of French block-buster. This year, French blockbusters have had a lot of success – for example, *Brotherhood of the Wolf/Le pacte des loups*. So that's good for the economy, because the money trickles down, and it becomes easier for directors making their first films. And at the same time that these blockbusters were being suc-cessful, *Under the Sand* became a success too, a smaller success, so people were very happy – they saw that a big popular film and a difficult, arty one can both do well. These two kinds of cinema can co-exist. That's the strength of French cinema.

RG: Has Bruno Dumont made his English-language film yet?
FO: I don't know if he's done it. I know he wanted to make a film in America.

RG: Could you see yourself doing that?
FO: First I have to learn enough English to direct actors. I have a project that

I would like to make in England. I don't want to do it in America; I prefer working with European money. If you use American money, you don't have control. I want to keep my freedom. But this English project, it has to happen in England. It's that kind of story – typically English.

RG: Do you have any sense of where you're heading?
FO: No. I follow my pleasure, that's all.

Bruno Dumont

Bruno Dumont on Bruno Dumont
by Kaleem Aftab

With only two features to his name, 43-year-old French director Bruno Dumont has already won more international prizes than most auteurs *could hope for in a lifetime's work. And yet jeers greeted Dumont as he collected the coveted Grand Prix du Jury at Cannes in 1999. Critics from around the world decried the 'monstrous approval' bestowed by David Cronenberg's jury upon* L'Humanité, *Dumont's yarn about a murder investigation set in the northern French town of Bailleul. In fact the carping had started even earlier with the announcements of the jury's awards of Best Actor and Actress to Dumont's two leads, Severine Caneele and Emmanuelle Schotte. (Intriguingly, as the pair picked up their prizes they appeared to share the same unusual mannerisms exhibited by their screen characters, Pharaon and Domino.)*

Criticism of Dumont's film did not stop at Cannes. So unsure was Sight and Sound *of what side of the fence it would be most expedient to sit upon that it took the ultimate editorial cop-out and commissioned two articles about* L'Humanité *for its UK release, one for the film and another against. But Dumont had already simplified the argument for the defence by his reaction to those boos at Cannes. He simply turned his back on the audience and took each of the jury members by the hand, signalling perhaps that he was only concerned with the views of those willing to understand what he was trying to achieve. One might be reminded of Jean Cocteau's quip upon being told after a screening that no one had liked his film: 'You're wrong. The only "one" was the audience.'*

The widespread hatred of L'Humanité *should be set in context with the near-universal acclaim that greeted Dumont's debut film* La Vie de Jesus *(1997), a work that earned him the Prix Jean Vigo at Cannes, the Sutherland Trophy at the London Film Festival and the European Discovery of the Year prize at the European Film Awards. Though far less ambitious than its successor,* La Vie de Jesus *shares several stylistic characteristics. It too is set in the small town of Bailleul, and follows a teenager called Freddy (David Douche) as he grows up with little prospect of employment. Beset by epileptic fits, Freddy's emotions boil over when his girlfriend Marie (Marjorie Cottreel) is clumsily courted by an Algerian youth Kader (Kader Chaatouf).*

L'Humanité, *though, is much less plausible on the surface. Pharaon de Winter is a simple man put in charge of a murder investigation. The film opens as Pharaon runs across a sparse landscape, seemingly fleeing from the violated corpse of an 11-year-old girl. (The image Dumont shows us of the girl's wound-ed sex recalls a famous painting by the French realist Gustave Courbet, L'Origine du monde. Up on a cinema screen, the image is as shocking as Courbet's picture must have seemed in Paris in 1866.) Pharaon's subsequent investigation is hampered by his desire for his neighbour Domino; also by the fact that he seems to be mentally slow. Yet we are asked to believe that this man will solve this most heinous of crimes. In short, it soon becomes apparent that this is no ordinary policier. In fact Dumont delights in rejecting not only the sta-ples of genre, but also most of the attendant clichés of contemporary cinema. The cast are all non-professionals, the 'dramatic' moments lack any tension, music is conspicuous by its absence, and there are no fancy shots, but rather a passionate interest in landscapes of the kind rarely demonstrated outside of Parisian galleries.*

Dumont's method would appear to invite ready-made comparisons with the work of Robert Bresson, of whom he is a devoted fan. Yet Dumont is less inter-ested in cinema than in philosophy and art history, whence many of his influ-ences derive. Given the nature of Dumont's first two films, it's almost shocking to report that he is now working on an English-language film to be set in the United States, provisionally entitled The End. *It seems that for Dumont, like Godard before him, the lure of an American project is simply too great. Nevertheless, at the time of writing Dumont is also at work on another film based in Bailleul, which is liable to be shot before* The End.

Kaleem Aftab: You studied philosophy before you turned to film-making. Did those studies influence the way you approached film?
Bruno Dumont: I studied philosophy because it demands an intellectual out-look on the world. I was 20 at the time, and it made me look inside myself, to find answers to questions about my own life. But I soon discovered that philosophy was too subjective: it lacks heart, it's over-intellectual, and I found that it made me cut myself off from the everyday. I made lots of short films around that time, and they were very intellectual, formal and aesthetic. They were out of touch with reality, too thought out. So when I wrote *La Vie de Jesus*, it was a kind of reaction against my former instincts: a journey back to real life. And to shoot the film, I returned to the town where I was born. It was a difficult journey for me – it weighed on me for a long time. But I saw that the road I had taken previously was a bad one. For me, cinema is pri-marily *physical* – and it's only after you've succeeded in putting the physical onto film that you can begin to consider the spiritual. What concerns me now, more than anything else in film, is creating a sense of rhythm and har-mony.

KA: *La Vie de Jesus* and *L'Humanité* have certain similarities. They both take place in Bailleul; they both focus on a misfit central character. Is there a general formula by which you construct your films?

BD: You need a core figure, a centre of attention – there's always a hero. And I view my films as a relationship between the audience and this central figure. He has to be a magnetic force – sufficiently open so that the audience can identify with him, and yet also embodying the ambiguity that surrounds us in life. And this magnetic figure is a vehicle for the ideas of the film. I do think it's necessary to have a story, or a subject matter, but really it's the least important aspect of the film. What's most important is how the characters behave. The story is just a pretext by which people meet and speak. I think there are too many films – even great films – that completely lose the essence of their characters by the need to wrap us up in a story.

KA: By not giving your audience an obvious storyline, you're asking them to do more work while they watch, as readers do.

BD: The beauty of literature is that there is a certain equilibrium between the author and the reader, but in cinema this equilibrium doesn't exist at all. And if you think about most American films, they're made to be 'universal'. As a result of that, American cinema is aristocratic – it treats the viewer like an idiot and gives him nothing to do. But I think it's politically necessary to make the viewer equal to the director in deciding what happens in a film. It makes for a kind of democracy, and that's important.

KA: You often leave the audience guessing about the 'back stories' of your characters. For instance, both Freddy in *La Vie de Jesus* and Pharaon in *L'Humanité* live at home with their mothers. But in neither film is there any mention of a father.

BD: I don't know why that is. Obviously the absence of the father means an absence of authority. But then, that's not really important to the events that are occurring on screen, in the film's present. With *L'Humanité*, I wanted the audience to be aware that Pharaon is not just an old boy who lives with his mum. He is an adult. He has had a life, with a wife and a kid. But something happened to them – we don't know what. Now he's left with his mother. And he's trying to escape something.

KA: Clearly you pay close attention to 'real life' in your films. But the result is not exactly realism.

BD: No, I'm definitely not a director of 'social realism'. At most, it's a kind of mirage inside my films – that's definitely the case with *L'Humanité*. But even in *La Vie de Jesus*, there are so many aspects of real life that aren't shown. For instance, the youths in the film don't drink or smoke, you don't see them hanging about on the streets and so on. My desire is to modify reality into film. On its own, reality is not interesting.

KA: What then do you want to show with the film image, if not reality?
BD: I prefer to see myself as a painter – a good impressionist or expressionist, someone who's able to reconstruct the real, from the depths of the heart rather than the eye. I'm more interested in how a painter speaks to me than a *cinéaste*. I find that *cinéastes* bore me. But I adore paintings. What interests me especially is the technique that the artist uses in order to speak of his subject.

KA: Which films and film-makers do you feel are working from the depths of the heart?
BD: I love the cinema of the 1970s and 1980s, directors such as Fellini, Resnais, Godard, Kubrick, Bresson. I love it when cinema is a tool used to express something other than what one can see on the screen – when the scenario is a ploy, so that another message can be conveyed. Undoubtedly there are good films that simply show us exactly what it is they want to say. But for myself, I love cinema when it's mysterious – when I don't understand exactly what I've seen, when I'm forced to go away and reflect. When I have everything set out in front of me, all dictated and fixed – that doesn't seem much like life to me. Television is the perfect example of this. Everything is explained to the viewer. There are no conundrums behind the television screen.

KA: Your interest in painting is indicated in *L'Humanité* by the way that you cite the artist Pharaon de Winter and his work. Where did that influence come from?
BD: I discovered Pharaon at an exhibition in Bailleul. There's a plaque in his honour there, like the one we see at the start of the film. And the idea for the picture of the little girl came from a painting by Pharaon. There is an intense reaction between my Pharaon and that painting, similar to the kind that occurs in the cinema between the film and the audience. The painting speaks to Pharaon, it tells him shocking things about his work and the crime that's been committed.

I've been influenced by many artists, such as Lucien Freud, and Courbet. The realism of *L'Origine du monde* is astonishing for the nineteeth century, it's so strong. The first time that we see the sex of the dead girl in *L'Humanité* is an *hommage* to that painting. From the vagina stems the extreme possibilities of the world: sex, and also childbirth. So there are two meanings to that image. One is the end of the world, absolute horror; the second is the possibility of bringing life onto the earth.

I try to emulate painting by not moving the camera. I want to minimalize things as much as possible – to make everything extraneous disappear. To not move the camera is to lose its presence, or make it impassive. What matters are the ingredients on screen, not me or the camera.

KA: Is your love of painting the reason why landscape is so important to your films?
BD: Landscape has such a strong presence for us, because we have a primitive tie with nature. Landscape is the first expression of nature – it's the surface-truth. In *L'Humanité*, whenever Pharaon is happy or sad he always returns to the countryside, and he looks at the sky. I enjoy associating the human form with nature because there is an attraction of the body towards nature that expresses the spiritual. It's the condition of man on earth. In the scenes where Pharaon is in the allotment – it's as though it's the earth that understands what he's doing. The relationship between them becomes mystical. And the mystery arises from setting this rather simple image within a complex relationship, one that develops its own character. Pharaon is uncomfortable when he is in the city, when he goes to London as part of the investigation. It's because of the architecture. We see him interviewing witnesses in a high-rise building, and he looks out of the window and sees a fight in the car park down below. He's unable to react because he's stuck in a building, he's too high up. The building disables him.

KA: In neither of your first two features do you use a music score. Why?
BD: Because I think that film music tries to express immediately the kind of sentiment that ought to arise over time. Cinema creates emotions that require further contemplation. But music interrupts this process by spoon-feeding the audience. Cinematically, it's a poor tool. If I layered music over the image, it would be too simple for the audience to know how to react to the characters. I prefer to allow the audience that time to reflect. It's better to show them something that at first seems like nothing, but then after a few days keeps on gnawing at them, crying out for further reflection. It's like when people take long walks in the countryside – what's important isn't the walk itself, but the memory one has of the event. We're all made up of such memories. And these moments are important. When you go to see a film, it's not the two hours in the cinema that are important. What matters is the memory of the event: that's what you retain for the rest of your life.

KA: In *L'Humanité*'s many street scenes, you regularly show people just sitting on their doorsteps, watching the world go by. Are they engaged in the process you've just described – capturing memories that they'll reflect upon later?

BD: From the moment you step outside your home and escape the confines of
the house, you enter the community. And there's always something going on
that creates conversation, but these events are nearly always banal – like a
passing lorry. I don't like to make comments about 'life' in general. I'm just concerned with everyday events, and I feel as though I can describe them far more
effectively than the kind of events that are considered 'profound'. I believe that
the visible aspects of ordinary life are an expression of the extraordinary.
Ordinary life is the most profound state of being, emotionally and intellectually
– you have to watch it so carefully. I don't like film characters who sit around
talking about profound things. It annoys me. It's far better for characters to do
than to say. Cinema is a way to enlighten audiences, to engage an audience is to
be on the same wavelength and rhythm. This process is slow. It's the mundane
that creates this. It is not found in a didactic that has characters making high-
brow statements to engage the audience, which is how a lot of directors in
France operate. That's not my sensibility. In the same way, I choose not to cast
actors who'll give me a lot of very choice, well-delivered phrases – that infuri-
ates me.

KA: So you use non-professionals?
BD: Yes. And the working environment is a bit rougher that way. But it means
that the actors in the film are always expressing something from the heart – be
it the highs of love or the depths of despair. And it's not the intellect that delivers those emotions.

KA: Do you think that if you cast actors then you would be changing the essence
of your characters?
BD: Yes, I would have great difficulty working with professional actors.
Professional actors want to invent something – it's in their nature. But I want the
person I cast to *be* the character, in effect. This will help them to add something
strong to the film, rather than making for something that's empty. A lot of actors
are often artificial – and the worst thing about cinema is the artificial.

KA: Whereabouts do you find the kind of people you cast?
BD: I look around in shops, and in the kind of public places where I can build
up a photographic dossier. I can't go looking in cafés and bars, partly because
the management in those places won't allow it. But also it's a matter of social
convention – the women I approach would think that I'm trying to get into bed
with them. (*Chuckles.*) And I prefer to find people in their natural environments.
I'm not doing anything very out of the ordinary. I'm really just like any old
employer – someone who provides work for people. And in fact, I find I'm more
likely to cast people who are themselves out of work. I think the unemployed

are actors. I pick people on the strength of their faces, and then I talk to them for five or ten minutes, just trying to assess their characters. That's the time when I decide whether to audition them. Then I like to see them two or three times, so that they can overcome the fear of the camera. And in the end I cast those who are most akin to the vision I have of the character. For example, after a year of this process with *L'Humanité*, I had three Dominos and Pharaons in mind before I made my final choice. I did screen tests to see who could act. Of course some people are afraid, shy of the camera – they just can't do it.

KA: Do you see yourself always working with non-actors?
BD: No, it depends on the particular film and its subject matter, what the characters are like. My next project is set in America, and I'll be using professional actors – because the characters don't exist in reality, so it's necessary to create them. Whereas I felt that the characters in *La Vie de Jesus* and *L'Humanité* existed already, so I searched for people who could fill out the roles, almost like decoration.

KA: Freddy in *La Vie de Jesus* and Pharaon in *L'Humanité* are not characters you would immediately identify as 'normal'.
BD: No, they're not ordinary people – in fact, they're extraordinary. I think of them as being a bit like the sculptures of Rodin. I felt I was using some of the art of the expressionists in constructing these characters. I don't think that anything can be learned in art by trying to make exact reproductions of life. But by accentuating the form a little, something can be learned, as long as it's not too grand a change. So I like to alter people a little. One of my own favourite aspects of *L'Humanité* is the way that Pharaon speaks – very slow, very strange. But I'm fond of this, because it obliges us to re-hear everything he says. Like the way Pharaon says 'Salut' – it echoes in our minds. It has a rather deferential sound to it . . .

KA: This has been taken by some viewers as evidence that Pharaon is a little simple-minded.
BD: He isn't, not at all. But I wanted to achieve a certain feel by using a man who is somewhat constrained by physical limitations. He's not what you'd expect a police detective to be. You could say that *L'Humanité* is a traditional film, in that it's a 'police film', one in which an unsolved crime is a central feature. But policemen in films are traditionally cold and insensitive. We have never seen a policeman like Pharaon. His status is indicated at the outset of the film simply by his driving a police car. But police in general are the inverse of what he is.

KA: Why did you place such particular images on the wall of the police station?
Like the photo of Chirac, and the posters proclaiming that the police are 'on the
side of youth'?

BD: I put the photo of Chirac there to amuse myself – because he's smiling in
that ridiculous manner of his. I think there's something ridiculous in the idea of
French democracy, and European democracy in general. The politicians treat
the public like infants – they tell us how to live, how to act. So those posters in
L'Humanité are a kind of comic reflection of reality, and of the distortions of
real-life politics. The politicians are absurd and *L'Humanité* is a film that tries to
highlight the acceptance of the absurd in life, so that it can be destroyed. I wanted to take an academic genre, in this case 'the crime film', and explode it. All of
the situations in *L'Humanité* we've seen a thousand times before. But each of
them is unravelled and rendered ridiculous, by the way that the characters
behave.

KA: Because of this contradiction, *L'Humanité* has been read by some critics as
a fantasy. In other words, the situation is too absurd to be real. Is everything that
passes not just inside the head of Pharaon – like the dream of a simple man?

BD: I think that the events of the film are sufficiently close to reality to have
occurred. But then there is something of the imagination locked inside it. We
don't know what Pharaon is running away from at the start of the film. It
could be something within Pharaon – or possibly the film itself! But Pharaon
doesn't have the capacity to dream. It's the spectators in the audience who
dream.

KA: Don't the final shots suggest that the film might be a reverie?

BD: *L'Humanité* is a very 'open' work. It's true, there are people who think that
Pharaon is the murderer. There's not one single meaning that's concretely
evinced by the film. And that's part of the ambiguity that resides within guilt.
But I don't think that you can take some bits of the film as real and others as a
dream. I haven't said anything conclusive on this. But I would say that there's no
'hidden meaning' to the film.

KA: In 1996 there was a notorious rape and murder of an English schoolgirl,
Caroline Dickinson, in the north of France. The subsequent police investigation
was widely condemned both in England and France. Did this influence the plot
of *L'Humanité* in any way?

BD: That case, and the Belgian paedophilia case, were very much in the forefront of my mind. The rape of a child is the worst thing that can happen. It's
an absolute horror. And the characters in *L'Humanité* have to confront that
horror – in the face of which, all the powers of the police amount to nothing.

But the crime itself is not at the centre of the film. Pharaon's reaction to it, rather than his investigation of it, is what interests me most.

KA: Pharaon is so sensitive to the needs of others that he seems to take the guilt of others upon himself. What were you trying to express there about the theme of guilt?
BD: I wanted to say that in life there's always the possibility for us to be bastards. So it's necessary for us to be on guard at all times. When I consider things that I've seen in newspapers, all the crimes that I've read about, it makes me believe that it would be possible for me to commit such a crime. Within us, everything is possible. Our fascination with serial killers stems from our sense that it's possible for us to behave that way, and it scares us. But man makes a choice in life. Along with guilt, there's the possibility of happiness. I tried to make the audience conscious of this as they watch.

KA: Guilt is also crucial to *La Vie de Jesus*, when Freddy is accused of killing Kader. He flees the police station, but the police seem to let him go.
BD: That's because, even though it's the job of the police to protect the public, they're actually incapable.

KA: But Freddy displays no sign of guilt over the crime.
BD: When Freddy is asked if he's guilty of the killing, he has to flee – because the policeman has posed a question that is intellectual. And Freddy doesn't care for ideas about the moral intellect, so he runs away. It is a flight from self-reflection – a plague on scruples, on the whole question of 'Am I this or am I that? Is what I did good or bad?'

KA: Why did you call the film *La Vie de Jesus*?
BD: I had been wondering if my child who is ten years old would come up to me one day and ask me if the story of Christ is true, or just a joke. I thought it was necessary to give an example that wasn't from the Bible, one that could identify the things that make up the beliefs of man. The life of Freddy is parallel to the life of Jesus: they're both stories about people who *rise*. Even if the actual similarities are small, they are parallel in that they both try to escape their reality and better themselves. I saw the title as a way to function like a painter – where the title of the painting is far removed from what's on the canvas. There are many paintings, especially abstract ones that are all in one colour, that have a title which forces you to think. It's also true of a sculpture such as 'Je suis Belle' by Rodin, a man carrying a woman. All the poetry is in the void between the title and the work itself.

KA: **The women in both of your films sometimes seem to overpower the men, emotionally. And they're not just prey to male desires.**

BD: I think that sex in my films is confined to a meeting-place. The object of desire is always the same – the end is always copulation. There's a need for two people to join together, and sex seems to be the way of doing this. But when Marie offers to sleep with Kader in *La Vie de Jesus*, or Domino with Pharaon in *L'Humanité* – all the joy of courtship is then lost. It moves direct-ly to the end of things, it shows up the baseness of desire. It is a definitive statement, leaving no room for argument. And both Kader and Pharaon react in the same way. To be asked to give up their bodies so easily – it surprises them, because they want to conquer the woman. Otherwise there's no satis-faction – it's all over, finished.

KA: **When you depict sex, it's seen as an emotionless act.**

BD: It's completely animal. I present the lowest animal instinct – I don't try to show the romantic identification between the characters. The purpose of it is to demonstrate forcibly that, whatever the desire between two people, it's impossi-ble for them to achieve fusion. I take it for granted that a cinema audience is sexually sophisticated, so I don't have to make these scenes too finished, too civilized. And I need to show the savagery of it. The cruelty and the violence in the sex scenes are aspects of a relationship that are normally hidden, but I need to throw a piece of raw meat into the equation. Then it's the audience that has to do the work. And, as I say, I adore that relationship with the spectator. The crude sex and violence are aspects of relationships that are normally hidden.

KA: **Towards the end of *L'Humanité*, why does Pharaon kiss Joseph when they're alone in the police station?**

BD: He kisses him, and then he rejects him. It's not erotic in any way. It's just that Pharaon wants contact. He's like a vampire at that moment – it's a vampiric gesture. Even if Joseph is a bastard, Pharaon still wants to embrace humanity, he wants to attach himself to it physically. I often have that impulse myself when I see a criminal – I want to embrace that person, because there is someone who's in need of aid. Pharaon does the same with the drug dealer. Humanity attracts humanity.

KA: **In the next scene, we see Domino in close-up, crying, clearly having heard the news. You hold that shot for some moments before we see that she's with Pharaon, and he embraces her.**

BD: I wanted to see the horror on Domino's face, to see her fear of the crime. Joseph is her man; and her face is horrible when she cries like that. For her to then receive a gesture of sympathy from Pharaon, one that has no sexual significance – that's something that ties them together emotionally. It's a physical reaction. When someone is having such a bad time, there's nothing left to say.

KA: How did you feel about the booing that greeted the awards given to *L'Humanité* at Cannes?
BD: I thought the booing was very good – very desirable. That jury gave the prizes to the films that they preferred, and it's important that those films were inventive and tried to move cinema forward. If the jury had just rewarded the media favourites, the event would have lost the kind of spontaneity that cinema ought to have. Cinema is not about rewarding people at certain stages of their career. The majority of people hate that so much, they want to see a change in cinema – it's boring to see the same directors and actors win. The jury didn't care about the etiquette of these things. Plus, it was a blow for international cinema. Who cares if the Americans were furious? What was especially pleasing was that the critics who booed were essentially supporters of mainstream cinema.

KA: You've said that you're a fan of Robert Bresson. Is it true that you once wrote to him, expressing your admiration?
BD: Yes, I wrote him a letter in which I described him as a great man, a great director who really made cinema. There aren't too many people like Bresson. He considered cinema as art, and he used cinema as a poet would, to describe the truth. He really investigates his subject, he makes it beautiful, and he truly interacts with his audience.

KA: Do you think you've learned how to make films from studying Bresson?
BD: I'd say that the best school for making a film is life, not cinema. The worst films are made by people coming out of film schools. They tend to be preoccupied by *Cahiers du Cinema* and the *nouvelle vague*, and they make films that are clones of this. They copy those styles of cinematography and directing, they make 'art films' full of references to film history – films that are like 'the cinema of cinema'. I don't care about film history. I respect it as necessary, but to me a *cinéaste* is someone who watches people and shows life. I think there's a kind of Parisian cinema that is enclosed by its own boundaries. It includes the children of the *nouvelle vague*, directors like André Téchiné, who work inside a closed system. So they don't have the possibility to move on. But I think that directors such as François Ozon and myself come from elsewhere, and we don't refer back to that kind of cinema. Film-makers search for an aesthetic, dogma and discipline. For myself, every film has a different theory – I don't have a global vision of cinema.

KA: Given what you've said about American cinema and its dominance, why are you going to make your next film in America, and in the English language?

BD: The American cinema is so strong. So I feel like I want to add my bit to the equation. It will be interesting – I expect that it'll change my sensibility. Godard always did things in this way: he renewed himself by going off to work in different surroundings. I love to listen to English, there is a music to the language. So I'm going to make a film in English for my own ears, whereby the language is an instrument of sound. When that's finished I'll have a break, and after that I'll make one more film in Bailleul. There's another story, another subject, that I want to take on in Flanders.

ACTORS

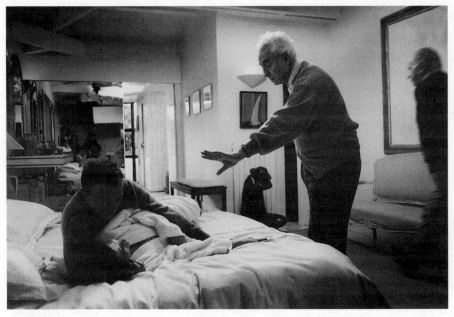

Beyond the Clouds: Peter Weller and Fanny Ardant, under the direction of Michelangelo Antonioni.

Days with the Maestro: My time with Michelangelo Antonioni and Italian Cinema in the making of *Beyond the Clouds* by Peter Weller

Prelude

I had never seen pubic hair in a film until Michelangelo Antonioni's *Blow-Up*. I had hardly seen pubic hair at all, to tell the truth. I was 18 years old, had only just lost my virginity, old by today's standards. But there it was . . . in a film . . . long before the 1980s boom in visual marital aids. Two models, one whose name I do not recall, the other – the English actress now living in France, Jane Birkin. Both of them rolling and tumbling in the photo studio of David Hemmings. And if that wasn't thrilling enough, a brilliant and beautifully statuesque Vanessa Redgrave (whom I'd seen the year previous as Ann Boleyn in *A Man for All Seasons*), strolling through same studio, lithesome arms crossed over bare breasts. The cherry on the *gelatto* was Hemmings crashing a London party, while behind him my then favourite band, the Yardbirds – featuring both Jeff Beck and Jimmy Page resembling high-school flunkies – made wonderful noise. The movie had my attention. Possibly for all the wrong reasons.

Alas, I was simply an aspiring young jazz musician, and several hipster friends had told me this movie was geometrically hip. But it 'cut no ice' that I was watching a film by Michelangelo Antonioni, a gifted exponent of modern artic-ulation, whose themes of the shifting realities in love and life of a listless Italian post-war bourgeoisie had been heralded as the *expression nouveau* in cinema. Some years later – after I'd given up jazz as a profession (realizing I would never be Miles Davis) – I began anew with the films of Antonioni. Having finished act-ing school in 1972, I'd begun working in Joe Papp's New York Shakespeare Festival/ Public Theatre while continuing professional studies with the distin-guished actress and acting teacher, Uta Hagen.

Around this time the Jack Nicholson opus, *The Passenger*, was released. It also starred that beauty, Maria Schneider, who'd recently appeared in *Last Tango in Paris*, a brilliant movie that baffled me at 23. Lord knows, 23-year-olds, particularly actors, endorse immortality so – Brando or no – I had as diffi-cult a time relating to the terror of middle age as I had had with Hemmings' reality problems in *Blow-Up*. But *The Passenger* – a story of a guy so sick of his life that he changes places with another guy who's dead – hooked me immedi-ately. As did the beautiful paradox: the dead guy's life, assumed by Nicholson, is even more hideous and perilous than Nicholson's own.

Those being the days before videos, *The Passenger* sent me searching for more Antonioni movies in the re-run art movie houses of New York. And I subsequently discovered that virtually everyone in every Antonioni movie was also on a search. But for *what*?

In *L'Eclisse*, what, in this life or the next, do Alain Delon and Monica Vitti *want* from one another? Why does their dance of dialogue take them only to the *edge* of what they really want to say? And do they get together in the end or not, after promising to meet at 8pm? And where's that girlfriend, Lea Massari, who disappears and whom everyone is trying to find in *L'Avventura*? And why did she split in the first place? What's that *fog* in Red Desert, into which Richard Harris and Monica Vitti wander? And why is everyone *lost* in it?

Where, why and what? The American film experience always *answered* the dramatic questions. I looked forward to that American device of the mallet over the head; the music, close-ups and a thousand words banging me again and again lest I did not get the point that I was meant to laugh! Or cry. But now? After this first dip into Antonioni, I left the theatre, with my head spinning. But not with answers or catharsis, only enquiries. Yet it was a new and wonderful bewilderment.

In the summer of 1992, I'd been invited to a film festival in Taormina, Sicily, a beautiful medieval village on the island's eastern coast. I'd been asked to stand on the stage of a breathtaking fourth-century BC Greek amphitheatre over the sea, with volcanic Mount Etna adorning the horizon, and introduce the David Cronenberg film of William Burroughs' classic satirical hallucination, *Naked Lunch*, in which I'd performed with Judy Davis.

I'd intended to fly from Los Angeles, stopping by New York for a day to allay some of the expected jet lag from the long flight east. Two days before I departed, I was jogging with my friend Brian Hamill, a noted motion picture still and poster photographer (*Annie Hall, Raging Bull*). Brian asked me if I'd ever been to Sicily. As an arrogant Italiophile who speaks the language, studies the history and collects the coinage of first-century ancient Rome, I was ashamed to admit I'd never been. The only thing I'd ever seen of Sicily was the landscape of what I considered to be a *bad* early 1960s film, *Il Gattopardo* (*The Leopard*). Based upon Lampedusa's renowned novel of the same name, it is the story of Sicily's last king and his family. Set in the 1860s, it follows the king's life in the final weeks before Garibaldi's revolution ended the monarchies of Sicily and Naples for ever, uniting them to the rest of the cities of Italy, thus creating the country as we know it now. In spite of the fact that *Il Gattopardo* was directed by another tremendous Italian post-war talent, Luchino Visconti, I thought the film 90 minutes of horrendous, indecipherable dreck. It surely didn't approach the brilliance of the masterpieces of his oeuvre, like *Rocco and his Brothers* or *Death in Venice*.

'Funny you should say it's "dreck",' my bud Brian retorts while jogging. '*The Leopard* is one of Scorsese's very favourite films.'

Now Hamill has known Martin Scorsese for years, having shot the production photos and subsequently won the world wire services award for best film poster of the 80s for Robert De Niro's sweating head in *Raging Bull*. But, I figure, Hamill is mixed up as to what film Scorsese was referring. Because Martin Scorsese is, as many will attest, a walking tutorial on the history of the motion picture. And not just on folks like Griffith, Eisenstein, Renoir, Kazan, Bergman and David Lean. I'll take a short bet that Scorsese has seen every piece of moving celluloid yet developed, from the Lumiere Brothers' invention of the medium, inclusive of Third World cinema, to *I Was a Teenage Frankenstein*. But, based on the thing I saw, I cannot believe that *The Leopard* is one of Scorsese's very favourites. Did Hamill mistake the word 'very' for 'least'? What have I missed here?

On Saturday, exactly two days after this conversation with Hamill, I hop the plane to New York and *that night* I open the *Sunday Times* to a miracle – a full-page ad for the American premiere of the recently restored director's cut of *Il Gattopardo*. Showing at the Newman Theatre in the New York Shakespeare Festival/Public Theatre complex on Lafayette street. One night only. Sunday. Tomorrow! Completely repaired to Visconti's original version of 3 hours and 45 minutes, including a digitally reproduced score. Sponsored by several Italian/American cultural societies, the presentation comes straight from two previous showings only; the first in Rome, introduced by the film's female star, Claudia Cardinale, the second in Paris, introduced by its male romantic lead, Alain Delon. The *Times'* advertisement for this restored cut has 'SOLD OUT' stamped across the page. A sold-out, black-tie event – invitation only. But the venue for the viewing is the Public Theatre. And happily the Public Theatre's founder, Joe Papp – God bless him – gave me, as I've stated, my first of many subsequent gigs as an actor. I make a call.

The American screening was to be introduced by Burt Lancaster, the headliner star of the film. Instead of another Hollywood vehicle, Lancaster chose to appear in Visconti's epic soon after he'd won an Oscar for *Elmer Gantry*. But Lancaster (who has since passed away) is incapacitated at the time of this presentation, and can't make it. An assistant Production Designer whose name escapes me, stands on stage to introduce the film. He describes the restoration work we will see of the *1 hour and 40 minute* wedding sequence that climaxes the film. (In the US version the wedding sequence is 15 minutes.) He tells us that it took three hours each morning to prepare and light all of the candles for the ballroom in this sequence, in order that the continuity of the burning candles corresponded to the passage of time, i.e. from dusk until dawn.

The film, subtitled in English, is staggering, moving, opulent, panoramic, overwhelming . . . brilliant. Vistas of majestic Sicilian aridity. Of palm trees counter-pointing the peeling paint of yellow and *pompeiio rosso* (southern Italian red) on ageing pillared villas, amidst broken sculptures of Roman emperors long gone. The acting is stunning, the women gorgeous: Lancaster at his best; a young, ebullient, charming Delon; and Cardinale . . . what can one say about Cardinale? A mesmerizing spirit of beauty, and an extraordinary actress as well. The elegance of the production is underscored by perhaps the most inventive of filmdom's costume designers, Piero Tosi (Fellini's *Satyricon*, Visconti's *Death in Venice*).

Luchino Visconti is dead. He never had the satisfaction of seeing this, *his* cut, released. Every single distributor in every single country who exhibited the film sliced it up according to their desired 'commercial' length. For shame. Because after seeing this mind-blowing epoch of sensuality about an antiquated society forced by time to leave their dying world behind, it is evident that if Scorsese heralded the film a favourite, he must have been referring to this, Visconti's own cut of *The Leopard*.

Armed with this indelible impression of Sicily from Visconti, the very next day I leave for the festival in the village of Taormina.

Taormina

Sicily actually has very little to do with Italy other than language. The civil and religious architecture is primarily Gothic, due to the long Norman and Spanish influence. There is a Greek/Moorish feel to the island, rather than the Italo-Medieval/Renaissance vibe that Joe Tourist is wont to encounter on the Italian peninsula. Taormina is an enchanting medieval village in the northeast, sitting on a cliff high above the Ionian Sea at the foot of Mount Etna.

I check into the San Domenico Hotel, an old monastery of long corridors, small but elegant rooms with vaulted ceilings. It is shrouded by bougainvillaea, palm trees, terracotta, a rustic swimming pool and endless sunshine.

Naked Lunch isn't in competition, but will be shown to promote the release of the film in Italy. For this celebration, I've invited an old friend from Rome, Francesca, to meet me in Taormina. The night of arrival we attend a party on a terrace of the hotel, where I notice an elderly gentleman alone at a corner table. An occasional somebody or other walks up to him. The gentleman returns only a nod, never so much as opening his mouth. Francesca informs me that the gentleman is one of the last great living masters of post-war cinema, Michelangelo Antonioni. Despite having seen all of his films by this time (save for his last, *Identification of a Woman*, never released in the US), I had no idea what he looked like. I had heard rumours that Antonioni was dead, almost dead, or brain-dead. Francesca whispers that an aneurysm ten years earlier has left the maestro with difficulties in speech and movement, though still completely lucid. And there he is, sitting alone, gazing about.

Legit admiration is usually met with courtesy, so I walk over, introduce myself, confess myself a fan from my young jazz days when I first viewed *Blow-Up*. His lovely multilingual wife, Enrica, joins us, says that she and the maestro will be present when I introduce *Naked Lunch* the next evening. Barely speaking, but nonetheless attentive, Antonioni listens as I blather my impressions of *L'Avventura* – the barren landscape of Sicily in general, and the village of Taormina in particular as a poignant visual metaphor on the modern emotional void separating men and women; that the film is a timeless commentary on romance; that seeing it now or one hundred years from now, it will have lost nothing, and probably gained anthropological significance about late twentieth-century Western behaviour. As I begin to hear myself sound like an over-zealous pedant – worse yet, a film critic – Enrica reveals to us that this very monastery/hotel was the precise location for the finale of the film. We all say good night, and Francesca and I walk away buzzed to have met the man in the very setting of his *capo lavoro*.

Italy birthed many great film-makers after the war: Vittorio De Sica, Roberto Rossellini, Visconti, Dino Risi, Maurizio Bolignini, the maverick poet-essayist-director Pier Paolo Pasolini, master of masters Federico Fellini, to name only a few of the better known. The combined body of their work is mammoth and penetrating. The films of these and other Italian directors in the three decades after the war were fortuitous for the medium, simply because Italy was pitched into an economic and cultural evolution far ahead of the rest of the western world. Responsible for the war, yet more or less forgiven because of its last-minute aid to the Allies and its indictment of Mussolini, Italy had been morally let off the hook. But it was not allowed to play in the world market – a slap on its hand by the US, France and England for being in bed with Germany. So by the 1950s, Italy, through dubious banking, the stock market and an influx of tourism, had a self-inflated economy. Money by the bag for a burgeoning upper middle class was offset by a persistent post-war poverty for the rest. All of this was long before the big 1970s export boom of that country's fashion and automobile exports. In the 50s Italy exported nothing. Except wonderful films about its predicament.

But with all Italy's new money, there was no vision, no possibility or venue in which to invest or spend . . . except itself. The bourgeoisie of Rome and other cities found themselves, at the end of the 50s, literally all dressed up with no place to go: Fellini's *La Dolce Vita*, Bolognini's *Il Bell'Antonio*. This decadence was counter-pointed by the poor getting poorer, all dressed down and barely a place to live: Rossellini's *Open City*, Pasolini's *Accatone, Mama Roma*, Visconti's *Rocco and his Brothers*.

Thus, with no vision outside of its own survival, Italy, rich or poor, was more or less only marking time. Whatever the disparities in social strata, ennui begot the demise of love's old story. The catholic (universal) notion of love and romance was blown open. No more was the modern conflict a discord of 'I don't love you anymore, Rosanna. I love Anna'. The dilemma was now 'Yes, I love you Rosanna, but it's 3am, the casino's closed, the TV's off the air, we've been to the same clubs for the last week, the new car is no fun, and our friends are all having affairs. So what should we do to keep the attention off how lost we are?'

The new drama wasn't so much the dilemma of *whom* but *why* and, anyway, *so what*? Perhaps, in the jargon of the 1990s, Italy gave us the first 'fear of intimacy' films. That is: the failed expectation of Love to change, to lift, to fulfil in a day when the speed of money and diversion had begun to make it easier and easier to relax, to coast, to float, to *avoid*. Now these themes may seem over-cooked to us, because in the last decade of the millennium they have been thrown around every week in *Seinfeld* and other sitcoms. But the themes were birthed in the sociology of Italy 40 years ago. (I digress to say that I had the pleasure of making a remarkable film, again with Judy Davis, entitled *The New Age*, written and directed by Michael Tolkin (*The Player*). *The New Age* is an Antonioni-influenced opus about moral bankruptcy in 1990s LA. When asked by a reputable French critic at the festival at Deauville what this film had to do with Paris, Tolkin replied, 'Let's talk again when you have one hundred cable stations.')

Italy had no cable stations in the 50s, but the country was awash in self-obsessed diversion. And this was a malady that inspired a generation of Italian moviemakers, each of whom brought a unique visual story to a decadent society. The personal interpretation of this problem, the inquiry into the inertia, the frontier separating a single modern couple, was never more acutely visualized than in the films of Antonioni. And his work is non-ephemeral, more applicable even at the relationship-conscious end of the twentieth century.

Thus, in Taormina I spend a few days with Michelangelo and Enrica Antonioni. The maestro gives me a newly published book of his own sketches – he was an artist before a film-maker – and on the frontispiece draws a small portrait of me as 'Bill Lee', my character in *Naked Lunch*. On the afternoon of departure he and Enrica walk me to a terrace outside the monastery-hotel San Domenico. In the distance is Mount Etna. He asks me if I know where we are. I don't. Without the scaffolding on the wall that was so asymmetrically present in the very last shot of *L'Avventura*, I do not recognize that we are on the terrace where Monica Vitti puts her forgiving arm around Gabrielle Ferzetti, as the volcano looms before them.

Antonioni turns to me, and says he will be making a film soon. And would like me to appear in it. I am ragged between the honour of the invitation and the sorrow I feel, knowing that no company will insure a man (no matter his talent) into his eighties, impaired of health, *sans* the energy required for the gruelling schedule of directing any film. I am sure his film is not to be. And thus I depart, soon to be reminded of the words of God's formidable sage, Yogi Berra of the New York Yankees: 'It ain't over till it's over . . .'

Los Angeles

Six months later, Michelangelo comes to LA. I have dinner with him in an elegant Chinese restaurant and invite two friends, screenwriter Mel Bordeaux and film director Mike Figgis. The communication is difficult, Michelangelo attended by an assistant and interpreter. He is in LA for a special UCLA screening of *The Passenger*, introduced by its star, Jack Nicholson, who owns the film. I can see Michelangelo is exhausted and looks far more fatigued than he did in Taormina. Figgis and I ask him many questions about *L'Eclisse*, the last of Antonioni's trilogy of modern love stories (including the aforementioned *L'Avventura* and an opus with Marcello Mastroianni and Jeanne Moreau entitled *La Notte*).

L'Eclisse is a beautiful excursion through the distracting relationship of a lovely upper-middle-class girl, once again Monica Vitti, and a stockbroker on-the-drive, a gallant-looking Alain Delon in my favourite of his performances. The opening sequence of *L'Eclisse* is a *tour de force* on the end of a romance. The camera focuses on a lamp inside an apartment in the suburb of early 1960s Rome. There sits a handsome man in his thirties (not Delon) in a white shirt, black slacks, the remnants of evening wear. On the sofa is Vitti, gorgeous blonde tresses falling about shoulders and a black dress. They sit in stillborn silence. She meanders as he watches her. Five minutes without so much as a word. But this is not midnight. As she parts the curtains we realize this is dawn. They've been up all night. And they have said what they have to say. And this is the end. Finally she says she must go, and he asks her to stay a bit longer. But they have nothing more to say. And all of us who have ever put toothpicks in our eyes until 4am to 'get to the bottom of it' with a significant other *know* there *is* nothing more to say. Yet we do not want to approach that threshold of 'Adios'.

Vitti first meets Delon in the stock exchange in Rome. The stock exchange is a maddening sequence where Vitti has gone to retrieve her mother from the miasma of frantic inflated post-war gambling, when the populace was allowed *into* the exchange to scream at their respective brokers, like a Wall Street horse race. Delon, a stockbroker, and Vitti go through the 'Come here, go away' of new love set against an opera of racism, the Bomb, and the growing assault of media. The lovers court, both aware of something missing, but *what*? They live in, but are unaware of, the barrage of everyday distractions. Is the romance worth the trouble? In the end they make a plan to meet at a street corner where they first romanced. They speak this plan to one another in one of the most touching exchanges of lovers' dialogue I've yet seen or heard. They part. The afternoon passes. Images of the old and new Rome. A man gets off a bus with a newspaper headlining nuclear testing. A horse-drawn cart clip-clops down a modern boulevard. The camera moves to the street corner, to an old water barrel where the lovers had their first rendezvous. Night comes and the streetlights illuminate, but no one comes. And the film ends. Do they get together? This is the eternal film-school question of *L'Eclisse*. And Mike Figgis and I want an answer.

Michelangelo smiles and shrugs. 'Non so.' ('I don't know.') And it's not that he isn't telling. He says it because he does not *know*. And he'd like someone to tell *him* what happened! Figgis and I look at each other. Damn. Later on, in Paris, I will ask him, 'What happened to Lea Massari?' – the missing girlfriend for whom Monica Vitti and Gabriella Ferzetti spend the entire movie searching in *L'Avventura*. He will shrug again. 'Non so.' At this dinner in LA in 1993, I don't reprise the Taormina discussion of his future film. It seems further from reality than ever.

But in the summer of 1994, I am contacted by Enrica Antonioni to appear in Michelangelo's new film, to be shot in Portofino, Italy; Aix-en-Provence, France; Ferrara, Italy (Antonioni's hometown); and Paris. I am asked to act in one of four short stories, all penned by Michelangelo, and adapted by Tonino Guerra, author of the dialogue in most of Michelangelo's films. Enrica says the salary is only 20 grand, US. 'You mean that's all you have to pay him?' quips Michael Tolkin. Yes, I would pay Antonioni to work with him. I am to play a writer against Sophie Marceau's shopkeeper in Portofino. And I'm thrilled.

But two weeks go by and I receive no script. My manager calls the production office. He is told the film is having money troubles. A week later my manager is told they cannot cast an American in this role. A well-followed lesson in the making of films is: 'Don't get your hopes up until the camera's turned, the film is "burned" [shot], edited, released, released on video, cable, then re-released in a theatre as an "art" exhibit, and finally some cheerless chubby from Iowa walks up and asks you to autograph the DVD case for his zit-faced brother, Buster, raving, "We all loved you in . . ."' Only then, looking at that plastic box before you, thinking, 'Gee, I made that movie?', should you feel assured that the film is a reality.

The disappointments and rejection in every department of film-making can be a legion of horrors with no end – no matter the height of one's success. And one must be in love with this existential crap-shoot, as well as the work process (and one must *adore* the work process) to survive on any level in motion picture-making. My constant advice to aspiring film luminaries: 'Don't.' If you're asking, 'Should I?', you're already outta here. So I read between the lines at Enrica's stall on the offer and blow off Michelangelo's flick. It takes thick skin to let the near-miss roll off. I had a couple of jollies with him, but his new film is of no further concern to me.

Kyoto

Two months later, in the fall of 1994, I am invited to be a judge at the Film Festival of Japan in Kyoto. I will be joined by Jeanne Moreau, Vittorio Storaro, producer Mike Medavoy (head of Phoenix Films, one-time head of Orion Studios with whom I made *Robocop*) and the composer for one of cinema's most compelling directors, Akira Kurosawa – a lovely Japanese gentleman named Masaru Satô. I bring to Japan my personal assistant, Michelle Mundy (now a television producer), a lovely and serene young woman who travelled the world with me, organizing my professional life on location. The day we arrive at the hotel, our Japanese hosts treat us to a lavish lunch. Sitting at the lunch, I hear a snip of a conversation across the table, between Jeanne Moreau and one of the jurors in the secondary competition, Gabriella Cristiani, editor for Bernardo Bertolucci. They speak about Antonioni's 'new film', which has indeed commenced, I overhear, 'with *John Malkovich* as the writer opposite Sophie Marceau . . . and isn't it wonderful!!' No. It is not wonderful.

John Malkovich is a friend of some years, but at this point, I'm of an opinion that Gore Vidal once described like so: 'Whenever I hear of the success of one of my friends, a little something inside me dies.' Particularly when the s.o.b. has my part. Truth out, I'm happy for Antonioni directing again. But hearing this conversation, I wish a pox on the film, Malkovich *and* Antonioni, aneurysm or no. Antonioni hung a carrot in front of me, then yanked it. Screw him.

I and my judicial brethren watch two movies a day. The hosts are cordial and supportive, but the films are – save a Japanese Samurai epic and a magnificent human elegy by Ho Yim, a young Hong Kong director – tedious, overdone or amateurish.

We give the prize to Ho Yim for *The Day the Sun Turned Cold*, a fictional account of the true story of a woman in Hunan who, with her lover, murdered her husband and was turned in by her son. A vibrantly acted tale about guilt and absolution, the movie finds its real power in that it makes no one wrong, not even the brutal husband, such that the audience has no easy place to spoon-feed blame or responsibility. We are forced to feel every one of the characters' fears and needs, even the cop who arrests this woman whom we hope will be exonerated. The film is all the more poignant because the real woman *was* executed in Hunan the very Saturday before the Tuesday we viewed it. This, a tragedy compounded by the fact that the young director didn't even know this horrible news until it was imparted to him the day we awarded him his prize. Hard reality always throws around a little perspective. My Antonioni impasse seems blasé now.

Paris

After the final festivities, I immediately depart Kyoto to join an amateur golf tournament with a bunch of rich American geriatrics in Paris. Thus I leave the temples of heavenly rest for golf with the overly dressed. The day after the golf concludes, I am on my way out the door of the Paris hotel, headed for my favourite haunt on the Amalfi coast of Italy, when the phone rings. It is Woody Allen's office asking me to join him in his latest comedy about love, set in New York and – of all places – Taormina, Sicily. To add, I get a second call from Brian Hamill, Woody's still photographer and the same pal who started this escapade with the chat-while-jogging about *Il Gattopardo*. Brian clarifies that the character, the lover of Woody's wife, played by Helena Bonham-Carter, had originally been cast as a younger man, but Woody now thinks it a mistake. It's only five scenes, and he's in a jam. Can you do it? 'When do I shoot?' I now ask a production secretary. 'Tomorrow,' she almost screams. 'Your Concorde ticket will be waiting at Air France.'

That night, before I leave Paris, I go see the great jazz singer Shirley Horn with a pal, actress Valerie Kaprisky. After the show, we sip hot chocolate at the Café Deux Magot.

'Who are you playing in Woody's film?' she queries.

'The love interest,' I respond.

'You mean, "the jerk",' she corrects.

'No. The lover of Helena, the love interest,' I defend.

'Woody's the love interest, Peter. You're the jerk,' she parries.

'I'm the romantic foil,' I espouse.

'Who gets the girl?' she ripostes.

'I do,' I assure her.

'In the *end*?'

Pause.

'Woody does.'

'Precisely. You're the jerk.' And Valerie goes about sipping her chocolate.

Next morning off I jump to New York to play the jerk in *Mighty Aphrodite*.

I've known Woody, albeit casually, for some time. Familiarity disarms idolatry. It is an honour, nonetheless, to work with a film-maker in the same cut as Antonioni. Woody, whether one is a fan or not, is a discerning individual. He writes his own stories and shoots them in *his* style at a time when movies are

looking more and more homogenized. Contrary to what he may consider himself, I found Woody an incisive actors' director. I'm guessing that Woody ducks
the 'actors' director' moniker because he's never been schooled in any particular
acting process. Hence, he doesn't dig the lingo. But the vernacular is only just
that: jargon. I found Woody to say just enough. If the scene wasn't working, he
had a succinct path to make it happen: 'No' or 'Yes'. It was great fun working
with him.

And he's more of a hipster than I ever imagined. As a mediocre bebop trum-
pet player, I'm usually listening to jazz tapes on a Walkman around the set of a
film. One day in Montauk, when cloud cover had us delayed, I'm sitting on a
sofa while the rest of the crew is mulling around the beach mansion, rented for
the shoot. Some of the crew lounges on the furniture in this, the living room,
where I sit in my private reverie. Someone taps me on the back from behind the
sofa, and I look up to see Woody.

'What are you listening to?'

'Charles Mingus,' I respond.

Now Woody plays Dixieland and has an affinity for great American standards
of the 30s, 40s and 50s. But Mingus can be fairly far-out jazz, particularly when
he incorporated the talent of an alto sax player named Eric Dolphy who blew
remarkably complex stuff, only to die at a young age in Paris. It is the purest of
jazz enthusiasts who would know Dolphy's music, much less dig it.

'What album?' Woody enquires further. Now I've got the earphones off,
startled that he might actually be familiar with heavy Mingus.

'*Three or Four Shades of Blue*,' I respond.

Without a beat, Woody comes back with, 'Oh, yeah. I used to front for Eric
Dolphy.'

I'm startled he even knows who Dolphy is, much less could make the leap
from the mere mention of the album title.

'"Front" for him?'

'I was the house comedian for the Village Gate for years. I fronted for many
of the post-Miles guys.' (By this he meant the modern, freeform jazz artists,
like Ornette Coleman and Dolphy.) And indeed, most of us forget that Woody
was a stand-up comedian, as well as a television writer long before he was a
movie-maker. He goes on to describe the experience of fronting for John
Coltrane and Ornette, and many other of the more sophisticated musicians of
the 60s. He describes one of Ornette's very first gigs in New York, and a concert toward the end of Coltrane's life in Carnegie Hall where, afterward,
Woody was so knocked out by the music he didn't want to hear anything else
for three days.

'Woody,' I respond, 'I *was* a musician then, but I didn't comprehend what
Coltrane was doing in those final days.'

Peter Weller with Woody Allen, at work on *Mighty Aphrodite* © Brian Hamill

'Oh, the level of musicianship was superb. Eric Dolphy, Ornette, later Coltrane . . . remarkable music.'

'I never saw Coltrane live,' I lament. 'The only other thing I would envy that even comes close is seeing Stravinsky conduct.'

'I saw Stravinsky conduct,' he shoots back.

'Now I'm pissed,' I laugh. And I realize we've been talking for about 30 minutes, and Woody has the rapt attention of everyone in the room, most of whom are crew with whom he's worked for two decades but wouldn't know John Coltrane from Horowitz. Yet they're enthralled by this mini-music seminar, delivered by the guy famous for being extraordinarily terse. When I've passed this yarn on to many friends who play jazz for a living, I'm usually met with, 'I knew the cat played good Dixieland clarinet, but I didn't know he was *hip!*'

Nearing the last day with Woody, I hear that Malkovich has finished shooting with Antonioni in Portofino. My part! Coveting, coveting . . . Would I have missed the Woody film if I'd done the Antonioni? Yes. Would I have chosen the Antonioni over the Woody film? Who knows? Ahhh . . . so what? My glass is half-full. John's a good guy. Known him a long time. Got me to do a live fashion show for Comme des Garçons in Paris once. I wish him well, yessir. And I'm working with Woody. So who cares about Italian cinema anymore? They only shoot female body parts now anyway. The Italian cinema is nowhere, man. Dead. Don't believe it? Go see *Cinema Paradiso*.

The phone in New York rings.

Antonioni wants me to star in the last of the four short stories, shooting in Paris immediately after the Woody gig . . . I love Italian movies.

I get the script for *Beyond the Clouds*. My segment is entitled 'Nole me Tangere'/'Don't Touch Me'. Christ's statement to Mary Magdalene, the first person to see him resurrected. It is about a married man who meets a young woman in a cafe in Paris, strikes up an affair, but can't leave his wife for the lover, or the lover for the wife. Finally the wife leaves *him*. A young actress, Chiara Caselli, will play the spitfire. She looks like Ellen Barkin. Fanny Ardant – on whom I've had a crush since I saw her in her late companion François Truffaut's swan song *The Woman Next Door* – will play the wife.

Paris – Take 2
Day 1 – Thursday
I arrive back in Paris on 23 February. I've also heard that Irene Jacob (*The Double Life of Veronique*, *Three Colours: Red*) is in one of the segments of Antonioni's film. Coincidence – because I've decided to pursue her for the lead in *Incognito*, a thriller about art forgery that I've developed and am set to direct in early 1996. I stow my gear at the Royal Monceau and am driven to a high-rise office building in Montparnasse. The building, all glass and steel, serves as production office for the Parisian episode. It will also serve as the location for the end of my episode when Fanny Ardant leaves me and rents an empty hi-tech apartment from a guy whose wife has left *him*, played by French actor Jean Reno.

As I enter the building, I see Jean. He looks discombobulated and solemn. He sees me, smiles, takes my hand and whispers, 'Enchanté.' Looking around, I notice an area nearby where a crew is preparing to shoot a scene with Fanny. Indeed, cameras are whirring. Everyone is looking in my direction waiting for something to happen. I'm not working this day, so they can't be waiting for me. But whoever it is they are waiting for has not appeared . . . because it seems someone else is standing in front of that someone upon whom this entire crew is twiddling its thumbs. Yes, they are waiting for . . . Jean Reno to make an entrance! And yes, that someone else holding up the scene . . . is shaking his hand right now, saying 'Hello'! I move the hell on.

I go upstairs and meet the production team of Germans, Italians and French, including an eccentric line producer named Bernard Grenet. Bernard is a bespectacled cigar-smoking sweetheart of a guy with whom I will form a good friendship. The costume designer has a few ideas, asks that I try on a few things, and points to an empty office. I am pulling on some pants when in walks Wim Wenders. And here I am without my pants.

Wim has given up a year of his life to be the signatory for the insurance policy for the film, i.e. the guy who will take the reins should Michelangelo be unable to finish. But so far, says Wim, Michelangelo has orchestrated and driven, every camera move, every piece of physical life by himself. Wim has taken stills and assisted with script problems. That's all. Wim will also make three short connecting films, the glue between Michelangelo's four stories. We collapse in chairs in his office where he happily confesses he's been helping to clear up any incongruities between the actors and Tonino Guerra's script. As there are three languages spoken, Wim is sort of the sieve into which all the versions are poured.

I run an idea by Wim that's been brewing since I read the script. I know that Malkovich spoke English in his story with Sophie Marceau. I also know that Fanny Ardant doesn't speak English that well. What if I played an American journalist working in Paris, perhaps a writer who's married to a French woman? I would speak the dialogue in *French* throughout. Then, when angry in two scenes, lapse back into the mother tongue of English. Wim thinks it's a good idea, but can I handle the French easily enough so that the acting isn't self-conscious? I've never acted in a foreign language, and my French is good, not great. I began studying French in 1986 with an actor named Daniel Lambert, then living in New York, now living in Paris, so I call Daniel, tell him what I need.

In the afternoon, I shop for costumes with a very sexy German wardrobe coordinator who 'vants me in ezzzattly ze rrright clodes fur der maestro'. That night Daniel and I rendezvous at the Café Deux Magot. I lay out my scenes in the story, and we begin diction work. Daniel and I have ended many a day, after strolling one of the tours in the green/historical Michelin Guide of Paris, always retiring to the Deux for café au laits and unanswerable polemics on women. For all we know about that subject, neither of us ever married, so draw your own conclusions.

Day 2 – Friday
The next day, I shop at Armani with my German. We buy more conservative goodies, but in truth, no one has a clue about what Michelangelo really wants – regarding my costume or anything else. As will be shown time and again, the maestro has a thousand and one ideas, only elucidated on the day they are executed, and then conveyed with the abstract expression of an ancient man hindered by the fallout of physical handicap.

I arrive, once again in the empty high-tech building in Montparnasse for an afternoon wardrobe look with Michelangelo. As I take the glass-walled elevator up to the production floor, I can see down the sides of the building. Glass and steel throwing back reflections of old Paris. I wonder if they've picked this building because it resembles *La Notte*. That film, the second part of Antonioni's famous trilogy, takes place in the day and night of a man and wife played by a much younger Marcello Mastroianni and Jeanne Moreau. A successful couple in their thirties, we first see them drifting apart on a sea of success, infidelity and apathy. After a mutual search (once again) for some kind of *bump* in their marriage, the film climaxes at a party where the decay of modern Rome spins round them. They end up at dawn in a field where she reads him an enduring love letter that so touches him, he's moved to ask her the author. The author is indeed Mastroianni himself, having long since forgotten he'd written it when they first met, having long since buried the innocence that brought him to love and marriage. The credit sequence of *La Notte*, a series of reflections of old Rome off the glass of a corporate sky scraper, once again serves Antonioni's theme of the classical dissembling in the face of the modern. And here I am, riding up a steel and glass building, watching the reflection of the surrounding Hausman's Paris bounce off the windows. Perfect Antonioni. I exit the elevator to an awaiting Enrica, all smiles, happy that I am doing the movie. The smile seems a little duplicitous, given that she firstly sent me an offer and later reneged. With her is an intellectual and overqualified male assistant named Andrea, an eloquent and charming sort, who speaks whatever language anyone else is speaking, and who hovers around Michelangelo like Pollux around Castor. Antonioni joins us, and for the first time I notice, behind the small grin, an extraordinarily handsome man. He twinkles, offers his only good hand, we kiss cheeks, and I decide right then and there to let the casting quandary of six months ago pass. It's my usual M.O. to confront on the spot whatever the hell is bugging me. Guiltless anger, I say. And I've gotten myself into dicey moments in so doing, but I've lived a life of less baggage because of it. Alas, here in this building in Paris, the point is moot; the Malkovich stuff is shot and gone. And I am happy to be here.

I change into an outfit, walk into a small room crammed with two wardrobe people, a production designer, Antonioni, Enrica, Andrea. People sitting on the divan arm, the floor. Everyone likes the outfit; Michelangelo hates it. I make jokes about his obsessive taste, and he laughs. But it's physically difficult for him to laugh, and I fear he will choke. I try on another pair of slacks, sweater. Everyone loves this too. I like it. He hates it. I try another. Amidst warm greetings and expressions of gratitude to be working together, he hates every costume. They are all either too cool, or severe. 'Mix them all up', he motions. He's tired and must go home now. I'm amazed at how Michelangelo looks, but I wonder how in hell he's made it this far through the film. Vibrant, happy, he's actually speaking more than he did in Taormina or LA. Enrica tells me it's as if he's become younger each day of the shoot.

Before he walks out, I suggest my idea about the character's speaking French throughout, except when I segue into anger. He mulls. He likes it. I can see the doubt on the faces of everyone else. Alas, if I've learned anything in film, it's that any good idea is signalled by unique support of the director and collective doubt from everyone else. It's almost a guarantee of a good idea. It also shows a director who trusts himself in the face of fear. But if most of the crew and other actors laugh at a funny scene or uniformly love an idea – watch out. It's usually doomed.

After the costume fiasco, I go next door to change back into street clothes, and *va-voom*, in struts the vamp who's to play my lover. Chiara Casselli isn't a woman one might exactly regard as 'beautiful'. 'Captivating' is more like it. To be precise, she's a veritable sensual tornado, cocked with physical energy, opinions, and insecurity the length of the Seine. Not unlike many of the early Actor's Studio banshees like Kim Stanley, Janice Rule, Shelley Winters, Chiara's 23 years old and a whirling dervish of a starlet-talent combo I've seen only rarely. While I have my hair trimmed, Chiara, in a sort of salacious challenge, proceeds to try on dresses, disappearing into one of the offices, only to reappear in a different skirt, each time revealing more and more of a set of extraordinary gams. With each entrance she fires little questions at me in French and Italian, cutting her space with me, letting me know she's a serious actress and not to be toyed with. By the time I've finished my haircut, I feel as if I've been married to her for 20 years and divorced for ten. She's exhausted me, and I've spoken a total of 12 words. I'm thinking she'll be terrific in this film.

Day 3 – Saturday

The scene is Chiara and myself in a first-time encounter in the café at the Hotel Lutece. I meet the first assistant director. If you've never experienced the ordered chaos of a movie set, the first assistant director is a combination drill sergeant and diplomat. It is he who orders about the worker bees – camera crew and equipment, electrical crew and equipment, rigging, production assistants and actors – into the assembly that allows the director space and time to shoot a movie . . . a sort of pit boss. The first AD's name is Beatrice Bonfi. She's Italian-Swiss, speaks eight or so languages fluently, and worked for years with Pier Paolo Pasolini as well as Visconti. Half the crew is Italian. Half are French. Approaching a vivacious and lovely 60 years, Beatrice runs it all, wearing Chanel pants suits, Hermès scarves and Reeboks.

The day is delayed because Michelangelo is reported to be not feeling well. Perhaps we won't shoot this day. Then at noon, he appears, orchestrates me to a booth, Chiara to another. In the scene she sees me reading a paper, comes over, introduces herself and asks me to shed some light on a *National Geographic* article she's perusing about an expedition in the Andes. And the article is this:

> A group of American scientists on a forced march up one of the mountains are stalled halfway because the Inca porters have stopped and refused to move or explain why. At the point of giving up on the porters, the scientists are confronted by the chief porter who informs the scientists that they may now resume and to please pardon the delay. The scientists are perplexed, and the chief porter explains that the Indians simply needed to pause to allow their *souls* to catch up to them, because the scientists were travelling up the mountain too fast.

This is definitely an apotheosis of Antonioni's themes, a kind of an Antonioni theme within the theme: mankind out-running its own soul. My character Roberto responds to this story with a laconic riposte, more interested in the girl than her parable. At this juncture Chiara's character and mine begin a love affair that lasts for three years, and for which I get chastised soundly and eventually left by my enduring wife, Fanny Ardant. I assume we will be at the Hotel Lutece all day because we're so late in starting. But Michelangelo is working with two cameras, and wants only four shots. He shoots me in two sizes (lens focal lengths). He shoots Chiara. That's it.

While we shoot, two lovely individuals show up to say hello to Antonioni. The aforementioned Irene Jacob has already shot her segment in Aix-en-Provence with Vincent Perez. We make a plan to have coffee and discuss *Incognito*. Then, just before my first take, in strolls Marcello Mastroianni, one of the most brilliant comedians on film or off, as was proven to me almost 20 years ago in New York when eight young actors and myself had dinner with him on two consecutive scorching evenings in July. All of us in T-shirts at the Upper West Side, ever-infamous Café Central on Amsterdam and 75th, Marcello arrived both of those nights in black suit, black shirt, black coat draped about his shoulders, black hat, tinted glasses, drinking bottled Campari, for which the proprietor canvassed all New York. Marcello kept us bewitched with stories about Fellini and De Sica the entire first night. The second night, Peter Riegert, a friend and very gifted actor who'd missed the first evening, arrived late. Without so much as an introduction, Peter proceeded to slide into a seat and commence blathering on at Mastroianni for ten minutes in gibberish Italian. Riegert doesn't speak Italian, or any foreign language for that matter. But he is a comic master at dialect blabber, having appeared in an hysterical Oscar-nominated short film called *The Interview* wherein he posed as a fictitious Italian film *auteur* during a phony interview, speaking a concoction from which one could only discern an occasional 'mozzarella', 'provolone' or 'pomodoro'. During Riegert's remarkable two-minute deadpan, nonsensical

Italian gobbledygook, all the while flipping cigarettes and calling for waiters, the entire sidewalk was in hysterics. But Mastroianni simply watched, jaw agape. As Riegert finished, Marcello extended a perfect pause, squinted at Riegert, leaned into him, seemingly dumbfounded at the incredible horseshit he just heard, and shrugged, 'You-ah must-ah beee from da South!'

So now, on to the Paris set, through the closed-off street door of the Café Lutece strolls Marcello, hunch-backed from age, silver hair askew, with eternal sunglasses, carrying a rumpled trench coat. He kisses Michelangelo, murmurs something which only four people can hear. They burst out laughing, and Marcello, knowing a good exit line, turns on his heels and rumbles out as fast as he entered, just as Beatrice is calling for the cameras to roll.

Chiara is fantastic, a mass of sex and neurosis reminiscent of Tuesday Weld. My stuff feels unconnected. In four hours it is over. I walk to the Café Deux Magots, smoke a cigar and continue writing a screenplay about Paris and jazz until Daniel arrives to drill me on the correct pronunciation of 'amour'.

Day 4 – Sunday

That afternoon, at the Deux Magots, I meet Julie Delpy, the young star of Kieslowski's *Three Colours: White*. The producers of the aforementioned *Incognito* have insisted that I at least meet her for the lead, despite the fact I've already set my sights on Irene Jacob, who stars, coincidentally, in the third part of Kieslowski's trilogy, *Red*. Julie is far too young for the role in *Incognito*, in spite of the fact she is extraordinarily bright. She turns out to be a mutually avid fan of the playwright/ actor Stephen Berkoff, whom I'm also pursuing to play the antagonist in *Incognito*, and we fill a wonderful evening with banter about the state of the theatre and literature in France. She comes from theatrical parents. I know very little of the French theatre at present, having only seen one dreary play at the Comédie Française wherein all the actors spoke in a low-key monotone. This phony style of naturalism, into which French film acting fell in the 60s, was the self-conscious fallout from the powerful New Wave movement, after which, save for a few performances, I found to be dreary stuff. Bring back Jean Gabin, Yves Montand or Alain Delon – who's still around, matter of fact!

Day 5 – Monday

The following day I'm driven to an elegant apartment in a suburb in the south of Paris, complete with Louis XIV park and walking garden behind. I meet Fanny Ardant in a small nearby hotel room, converted for makeup. Contrary to the roles she usually plays, Fanny has all the charm and disport of a precocious five-year-old. She is one of the instantly adorable human beings on God's Earth, and almost everything she says has irony, chaperoned by a gorgeous smile. She likes the idea of my speaking French in the film. She wants to burst forth with

English at one point. She attempts to speak it. She has absolutely the single worst accent for the Queen's English I've yet heard on four continents. She laughs, 'Terrible, no? I'm going to do a love scene for Sydney Pollack in *Sabrina*, and I don't know what to do.'

She asks if I mind if she smokes. I don't. I ask how old she is. She says in English, 'Fifty, and I smoke. And I like it.' I'm enchanted. She asks why I speak French. I reveal that, once upon a time, I lived with a beautiful, supremely intelligent and charming woman named Ali MacGraw, and it was Ali who inspired me to learn everything from languages to art. 'Oh, I *love* Ali MacGraw!' exclaims Fanny. 'She is the same age as me and she is so poised and elegant and bright and classy . . .' And on and on . . . I assure her I will pass this on, which I later do, rejoined by mutual homage from Ali.

Fanny and I begin the work with a short scene. Michelangelo wants me to enter our huge apartment where Fanny confronts me about the love affair with Chiara. At this point the affair has been going on long enough for any dysfunctional marriage in the psychology-hip America of the 90s to start looking for lawyers. Alas, we are making a 'European' film where divorce isn't so facile, where couples will hang on 'for better or for worse', and the issue isn't so much whether one is sleeping around, but how long one can extend the drama that defines being alive.

Michelangelo choreographs my entrance, standing in the middle of the room, confronted by Fanny. In real life, nobody comes in and stands in the middle of a room to be confronted by his wife. That confrontation usually brings a retreat to the bathroom, door slamming, dish-washing, or some other physical affair in which to bury one's self. So I suggest all sorts of physical ideas, like opening the door with keys, reading mail, dropping overcoats, *et cetera*, such that I am 'caught' by Fanny rather than standing around like a self-conscious goon anticipating an actress saying words. Maestro doesn't care. He just wants me in the middle of that room for that confrontation.

We eat lunch after shooting one take. The crew takes seats at long tables in the back of a truck/kitchen affair. The kitchen serves great steaks, good espresso, all catered as you sit and schmooze. Very civilized. In the States, the crew must wait in line at the mobile kitchen for the tray of the usual slop (unless you're lucky enough to get one of the three or four good caterers) always served at picnic tables set up in a parking lot or some such place. No booze, which is the only good part because, unlike the Americans, or even worse, the English, the French can come back to the set after wine at lunch, and get a passable afternoon's work done.

After lunch, Fanny walks to a window, demands I stop seeing the girl, I follow, drop the mail. I ask Michelangelo for more rehearsal. I begin feeling more secure in my French, looser in the scene. We do four takes of two camera positions and are finished by five o'clock. The wife of the owner of the apartment gives me a huge Havana Hoya de Monterey double-corona from her husband's stash. These are expensive cigars, even in Paris, and she looks gleefully vindictive as she steals it out of the humidor, insisting I take a second. If this gets her even with her old man, so be it. I pocket the cigars, take a jog in the sprawling Louis XIV park and smoke one of the stogies back in the city at the Café Deux Magots where I meet Daniel and practise a correct pronunciation of 'detest'.

Day 6 – Tuesday

The scene says this: I walk into a bedroom. My wife (Fanny) holds a vase. I ask what is the matter. She looks at the vase and asks back, 'What does a vase make you think of? Vase – flowers. Flowers – beauty. Beauty – that 23-year-old bitch you've been seeing for three years?' She breaks the vase. I tell her it makes me sad to see her behaving like this, drunk and sick. Then I kiss her and tell her I want to make love with her. She demands that I give up Chiara, which I promise to do. End of scene. That's what's written. Alas, none of this is on Antonioni's agenda.

First thing – he wants her to break the vase. 'With me watching?' I enquire, as does Fanny, Beatrice, Alfio the cinematographer and Enrica. 'Dio mio' ('My God'), the maestro growls. Everyone loves it when he growls. It is only his frustration with his own communication skills. We love it because this is an 84-year-old man, whom everyone had given up for dead, bursting forth like a shot in the ass for all of us. So we all shut up and listen. Yes, contrary to the script, he wants her to break the vase first, without me there. He gets up. He mimes for her to break the vase, then he walks her back into the bathroom and mimes for her to get into the shower in her slip. He wants her to sing in the shower. *Then* he mimes for me to come in and see the broken glass, kick it aside and find her in the shower, then *kiss* her.

'You want me to get into the shower with her, Maestro?' He smiles. He mimes for me to kiss her through the glass. Did he just make that up? Now I'm wondering when all this dialogue about vases and beauty begins. Michelangelo then asks her to walk past me out of the shower, for me to follow her out of the bathroom, back into the bedroom where he wants her to sit down on a stool, look at the broken vase, and begin to speak.

So: I go downstairs and wait for them to shoot the beginning with Fanny breaking the vase. I wait. I wait. At one point I noodle some Bach on a piano in the foyer. 'Si!', I hear from above. Figuring they're ready to shoot upstairs, I quit playing. Beatrice jumps out the door and yells down to me, 'Peter, Michelangelo wants to move the camera out here and shoot you playing the piano as if that's what you do when you come home.' Okay. The guy uses everything, including my terrible piano. He shoots me playing the Bach as a kind of 'Honey I'm home' motif.

'She presses her voluptuous lips to the glass': Fanny Ardant and Peter Weller.

We move upstairs to shoot the meat of what he just showed us. And what was, on the page, a turgid, heavy scene from the get-go, now becomes a sort of a loony flirtation between married folks. Fanny breaks the vase. Goes into the bathroom, steps into the shower, begins to croon. I walk in after no response to my piano, see the broken vase, hear the singing from the shower, and, expecting to find a naked wife, walk to the bathroom. I pass the broken vase, wondering what went down here, kick the larger pieces away, and low and behold, find a wife in a slip in the shower. She presses her voluptuous lips to the glass. I start laughing as I kiss her back and she opens the shower door and pushes past me through my first line, 'Qu'est-ce qu'il passe?' She chuckles, goes into the boudoir and sits down. I follow, enjoying this goofy stuff, and she starts with her indictment of me with the vase speech. Which only now has turned the expectation of marital fun and frolic into a confrontation of lies.

Thus Michelangelo has extracted a subtle yet wonderful reversal. What was a one-note heavy scene now starts off as a whimsical event, transforming into a foreboding one. We finish the second beat of the scene, me kneeling in front of Fanny as she weeps, finally pushing me away. I fall backwards and accidentally cut myself on the broken vase. She throws herself on the bed. I follow her there, kiss her foot and bite her on the ass. She bites my bleeding hand, tells me in

French to go fuck myself, which prompts me to beg her to make love with me. I promise never to see Chiara again. She rolls on top of me, we kiss. Cut.

Acting is beginning to rejuvenate me. I don't know where I'm going in this flick, but I must completely trust an octogenarian speech-impaired, cane-walking romantic. For only Michelangelo knows the vision and the outcome of this density. It is *his* canvas, in which I am an image. I doubt if I could work in every film like this, as it isn't my bailiwick to always be led by the hand. And I revere an experience like *Naked Lunch*, wherein David Cronenberg and I spent months in pre-production and time every morning, before shooting, aligning on the intention of a scene. But Antonioni is a different horse.

Day 7 – Wednesday
I'm driven to the location of the final confrontation with the brazen Chiara Casselli. Set in an apartment in Montmartre, it is a bohemian's dream, a stone's throw away from La Coupole, Le Select and Le Dome where Ernest Hemingway drank through his 'Moveable Feast' rendezvous with F. Scott Fitzgerald, James Joyce and Ezra Pound.

The apartment is a small, non-renovated one-bedroom affair with a closet-size bathroom. It's a place I would have kissed its filthy floorboards to have when I was a young actor in New York. Twenty-four hours in that joint now, I'd stick pencils in my ears. Its one big attraction, and the reason why Michelangelo loves it, is the ancient turret window, wrapping around the petite living room, offering a view all the way down the boulevard to Montparnasse Tower.

There are two scenes to shoot. The first takes place in movie-time directly after the first scene with Fanny where she asks me to dump Chiara. I've arrived at Chiara's apartment to break it off. This scene calls for me to come in and to start an explanation of the sayonara which is brought to an abrupt halt by Chiara kissing me, implication being, of course . . . I knock on the door, Chiara opens it, and before I've said a 'Bonjour', Chiara grabs me, pulls me against the wall and puts a kiss on me wild enough to send me back to confession in a Catholic Church. We move into the apartment, she hikes up her skirt, climbs on my lap. As I begin to explain why I must break off with her, she kisses me again. Cut.

Michelangelo, on his cane, waves his good hand at Alfio, his director of photography since *Zabriskie Point*. (His DP in the 60s was Carlo Di Palma, Woody's DP on *Mighty Aphrodite*.) He wants the camera to move slower. Every single camera move, every piece of physical life from every actor, every light, sound, shadow, is sifted through his eye. The actor can invent within his visual parameters, but Michelangelo's vision, *his* frame, *his* camera, is the priority. It's a style that might not only jam up but also piss off many American actors in their need for 'freedom'.

A certain method of directing actors, and one that I prefer (*à la* Sydney Lumet, David Cronenberg, Mike Nichols), is not simply to 'block' the scene, but to rehearse the hell out of it until its physical and emotional life have been completely discovered and sometimes redefined. Lumet does this for four weeks in a rehearsal room *before* he shoots. Thus he's shooting what amounts to be a well-crafted stage piece. A rehearsal this extensive will permit the director to design the shots around the events unfolding with the actors. There will, of course, be the occasional predetermined shot with this mould of director, but, by and large, the design of the film and the thrust, the *event* of each scene, is discovered in the physical rehearsal with the actors. A director like this must be strong and extraordinarily patient and adoring of actors, because he's controlling his sheep by giving them a large pasture. He trusts the event of the scene to be executed precisely as he expects, yet he's allowing that most sensitive of birds, the actor, to cut a path to that event.

This rehearsal process is most liberating if the actor developed his craft on the stage. The theatre gives the opportunity for the life of a scene to be discovered and deepened in rehearsal after rehearsal. And that very repetition can bring one to freedom. Many film directors are foreign to the process of rehearsing actors, hence they fear it and want to shoot immediately, under the guise of keeping the performance 'fresh'. Some actors get worse with rehearsal. They have charisma, but no craft. I've not worked with many of them. There isn't a scene I've ever encountered, as actor or director, that didn't improve with rehearsal.

Michelangelo uses little rehearsal. He stages, designs and shoots after one or two passes. So the actor must be on his game. Antonioni wants all the mistakes and whatever is happening to be shot right now. This velocity is facilitated by the sparseness of the dialogue. But the thing is, he takes so long to stage these shots that I feel I've rehearsed the scene for days. He dozes between set-ups, but is up out of his chair like an ageing tiger sniffing meat the moment Beatrice is ready for him. He rehearses, blocks, choreographs for the camera, changes dialogue, and spies the two video monitors (for the two cameras) like a stamp collector through glass.

Michelangelo shoots the rehearsal with Chiara and myself. Shoots two more takes. That's it. Lunch. The line producer Bernard Grenet gives me a great cigar, so I forgo eating and take a hike up the boulevard Montparnasse, ducking into the three Hemingway hangouts for a trio of espressos.

After lunch, we block the second scene in this location, the final showdown between Chiara and myself, in movie time, following the vase-breaking fight with Fanny. I'm already in the room staring out the turret window, looking down the boulevard. Chiara, leaning against the door jamb of the kitchen, asks me if I still make love with my wife. I lie, in French, 'No, not in three years.'

Chiara pins me on the lie, says she can tell I'm lying because she can smell my wife on me (racy stuff, these European movies). I walk past her, into the kitchen, down the hall, taking off my jacket, raving at her in English to get off my back. She follows, raving back in French and Italian. She smacks me, I turn, smack her back, and we kiss. Cut.

Again this was what was on the page.

I go to my dressing room in a hotel next door to the set, change into my wardrobe. The drab shirt they have for me is not the one discussed for the scene, and contrary to the elegance of the character. I walk up to the set to tell the maestro that I hate the shirt. Before I open my mouth, he says he hates the shirt. 'What else do they have?' he queries. Nothing, because the shirt I was supposed to wear was already used in a scene with Fanny. Michelangelo tells the costume dresser to go out and buy a shirt in blue. The dresser responds that it may be difficult, as there aren't many classy shops in the neighbourhood. Michelangelo will wait. At this point the young German producer pipes up that we'll 'lose the day' (not finish on time, or have to quit before finished). Michelangelo shrugs nonchalantly, throws a look, implying, 'What're you gonna do, ruin my career?'

Antonioni is respectful of a budget, but, having shot almost all the film, he doesn't really give a damn about someone else's schedule. He hates the shirt so we'll all just wait until the dresser comes back with a better one. The German producer looks at me, as if I've started this. Wim Wenders and the French/Italian producers say nothing. Wim knows it comes with the territory. A director must be an obsessive about production design, right down to a single shirt in a four-minute scene.

We wait for an hour. Certain stores are closed. The German producer leaves, comes back 30 minutes later with a couple of Cohiba Robustos and a cigar clip for me as a peace offering. 'There was no need,' I thank him. He smiles. We rehearse again while we wait. After rehearsal I come out of the bedroom without my shirt and there in the living room is Claudia Cardinale – Visconti's angel of *Il Gattopardo*, 30-something years later. It all comes full circle. Lithesome, elegant in black pants suit, anyone's vision of beauty even at 60, she and that film are the spirits who took me to Sicily and, thence, to this very spot. Enrica introduces me. I tell her I've dug her ever since *Big Deal on Madonna Street*, *Bell'Antonio* and, of course, *Il Gattopardo*.

She only brightens at the mention of *Bell'Antonio*. She considers it one of her better performances and is flattered that an American knows it, as most Americans only know her from her American movies (*The Professionals*, *The Pink Panther et cetera*). The arrival of my shirt interrupts the schmooze, sadly. We kiss cheeks and say 'Adios'. Ahhh . . . La Cardinale leaves, and we shoot.

What follows, some may consider a vilification of the sanctity of a movie set. An actor or director should never "rat" on events of a provocative nature – it's bad form. It is an unspoken code, because, as tricky as the vibe may be on a set, there is an unsung loyalty to the process, no matter how bizarre the events. But the following happened under the auspices of an ancient innovator, so I've no compulsion about relating the mad inspiration of it all.

As I said, the scene as written has Chiara standing by the door jamb of the kitchen, chastizing me for sleeping with Fanny and lying about it. I walk by her, taking off my jacket, yelling back in English that Fanny's my *wife* and I'll do what I want. Chiara follows me down the hall, both of us led by a Steadicam operator. We reach the bedroom, Chiara smacks me, I smack her back, and we kiss. Cut.

The bedroom is too small for anyone other than the camera operator and we two actors. So we rehearse it, while Antonioni watches in the monitor. Antonioni hobbles down the hall. After Chiara smacks me he wants me to shove her down on the bed in a sitting position, then begin to kiss her body such that I end up kneeling in front of her. Now he stands above us. I'm on my knees in front of Chiara. He motions for me to pull her slip over her head. I do. Chiara is half-naked. Then he motions for me to pull off her panties.

'Cosa?' she demands in Italian.

'Tutta nuda!' ('Totally naked!') Antonioni demands.

'Se io dovrai essere tutta nuda, lui dovrebbe essere tutto nudo!' she demands. ('If I must be totally naked, he must be totally naked.')

I step in with an abrupt, 'No tutto nudo here, Maestro.'

He laughs. 'Solo la camicia.' ('Only the shirt.')

I relax. Chiara is pissed off. We get ready to shoot and she departs for the hall outside. I follow her out. She's like a wild horse now, and I think her desire to completely please the maestro is running counter to an anxiety about this panty-removing bit. 'Look, tell him you don't want to have your panties off,' I help out. 'He won't make you do it, if you don't want to do it.' She's crying. 'It isn't that,' she insists. 'I don't care about the underwear. It's my top. My breasts aren't big. I don't want to show them.'

This is a new one on me in the actress nude-scene-freak-out milieu. I, for one, feel that nudity is gratuitous in film. I've never seen a film that wouldn't have been just as good without it, as much as the world since Antiquity has appreciated a beautiful woman naked. However, except for Jane Fonda and John Voigt in *Coming Home*, I'm hard-pressed to remember a goddamn intrinsic bonus in the quality of filmic storytelling that nudity has ever added. As if the two seconds of what's-her-name's breasts are really going to pack that many more voyeurs into the theatres, or get that extra weirdo to rent the video. Besides, Paul Verhoeven made breasts forever passé at one fell swoop in *Basic Instinct*. But would the film have been a hit without the Sharon Stone leg-crossing? I think so. As good as her performance was, would *Sharon Stone* herself have been as large a world-wide sensation without it? Hmmm . . .

So Chiara is worried about her breasts. I'm damned. Her breasts are beautiful. If she were French, she would have no problem with the breast thing, as the natural look of intermediate size breasts is not only considered erotic, but a feminine attribute *preferré* in France. Alas, Chiara is from Italy, a country, like the US, with a mindset that sends up mammary obsession like the national flag. If an actress possesses anything less than the she-wolf of Romulus and Remus, she might as well sell shoes.

So we rehearse once again. I suggest to Michelangelo taking off my shirt first, then taking off Chiara's panties before her top might be more erotic. He agrees. This also gives Chiara's breasts less screen time, as her top will be the last thing removed before I begin to kiss her. When I remove her top, however, she hunches over, trying to hide her breasts with her shoulders. 'Nooo!' comes the cry from the other room where Michelangelo watches on the video. On comes the sound of his cane rapping the floor as he hustles back into the bedroom, insisting she looks like she is trying to cover her breasts. She exclaims she doesn't want to show them, but he has no compassion. Almost everyone somewhere in this film (and many of his other films) has been naked, including Malkovich and Marceau. Antonioni wants the nudity to be complete and casual. He walks away. Chiara sulks. I take another shot. 'Your breasts are absolutely lovely,' I say, 'but you're not going to believe me. So believe this. If you bend over you'll not only look like a woman trying to cover your breasts, but they really *will* look small, because their appearance will be diminished by this high camera angle. But if you stretch out and lean back like he wants, your torso will elongate. And your form will resemble a beautiful sculpture.' Plus which, leaning back like that is very erotic and enticing, and it doesn't take a dummy to figure out that's what Michelangelo's after. She looks at me like I'm holding 51 cards, but rolls with it on sheer velocity alone.

We rehearse again. After I take off her top, I'm to start kissing her body, which I discreetly mime for the rehearsal. Finally Chiara feels up to it, we shoot. In the first take I walk past her, she chastizes me. I walk down the hall, she follows me, the both of us yelling at one another. Whereupon she bops me on the back, I turn around, slap her, she tries to hit me again, I grab her wrists, pitch her onto the bed, pull off my shirt, pull her underwear down off her feet, then over the head with her slip. I begin to kiss her. Face, neck, breasts, stomach. I stop, figuring that's as far as propriety will take it, and figuring I haven't heard a 'Cut' because everyone's too far away or riveted to the monitor.

'Nooo!' Here he comes, down the hall on his cane, the final stage of the riddle of the sphinx. He strides into the room, looks at her. She covers up. Both of us haven't a clue as to what's wrong. He looks down at me, on my knees before her.

'Tutto il corpo,' he insists. ('The whole body.')

'Lo bacio?' ('I kiss it?')

'Sì.'

Now at this point, I'm not quite sure what else to kiss in the realm of discretion. Because I *was* at her stomach, and figured that was close enough for movie purposes – at least, the movies *I* have in mind. But I ain't quite sure what the Maestro has in mind. So I'm looking up at Chiara for some help here. And she's looking down at me . . . bewildered. 'Don't worry,' I say to her. 'I've an idea I know what he wants.' She isn't buying any of it, my Lochinvar rap now sounding like a carny act.

We begin again. I walk past her, she cheap-shots my wife. I yell over my shoulder, she following me down the hall to the bedroom yelling back. She whacks me harder on the back, I turn, slap her, and she *whacks* me again. Gee, this isn't written. And the second whack hurts too! I grab her now, sit her down, off with the threads, kiss, kiss, kiss, down the body. I'm below her navel, her back is arched in movie ecstasy, and I'm thinking – any further and the vice cops will come in and shut us down. I stop. This is as far as it gets, and as far as I'm going.

'Nooo!' Here he comes again, and I'm lost. First problem is the breasts. The fight is getting torrid too fast. Sit her down slowly. Pull off the clothes with the same passion, but the kissing should also slow down, particularly when I come to her breasts. 'Dolce, dolce' ('Sweetly, sweetly'). 'Piano, piano' ('Gently, gently'). And Michelangelo closes his eyes and starts to kiss the air as if the Venus di Milo were a living thing before him. I'm on my knees with no shirt, in front of a totally naked woman on a bed, both of us looking up at an 80-something-year survivor of a brain haemorrhage who's leaning on a cane with his eyes closed, kissing the air. We watch this man in a reverie, reliving some moment-gone-by of the best that life can give a man . . . a beautiful woman. I'm looking up at the inspiration and abandon in which he pretends, and I'm wondering where – at this precise moment in his long past – he is. And I have an epiphany – a gift from the universe. This is hope for all Mankind: for if a man in his eighties can give up this kind of juice . . . it's never *over*.

And why should it ever be over for someone with so particular, so lean and clear a message as Michelangelo? We are moving too fast for our souls, and that is why we have lost 'intimacy'. And for that lost intimacy – so needed, so much sought after, here at the beginning of our century – for that image of Plato's – of two halves separated, forever searching for the salvation of love – what must we do? Pause on the mountain until our soul catches up to us? And what if what Ingmar Bergman said is true: that the real sorrow of living isn't *betrayal* or even

Beyond the Clouds: Chiara Casselli, Peter Weller.

the approaching of *death*, the vestiges of which – age and change in all its forms – we in the West do everything to run from or stave off. Nor is it *loss*, because loss has always a resolution of gain somewhere else. But what if it is truly *separation* that is life's most harrowing horror: that is, the terrible suspicion that we belong nowhere and to no one; that those we need are indifferent and unavailable, and that each of us is unattached, dissimilar and alone – if *this* is the terror and ultimate sorrow of living, then the converse is obvious. The joy of living is *belonging* – the experience of being beholden, not just to the empirical humanity, but to some other *one*. But even in the presence of that someone, how do we end this separateness, this longing? For many times it is a deeper separation we feel in the presence of a loved one than in solitude. Wim Wenders' trapeze artist says it best in *Wings of Desire*: 'Only with you, whom I love, can I truly feel lonely.' So how do we fill this hole, this need, particularly when the 'someone' to whom we ostensibly belong is right in front of us, and we have nothing to say?

Michelangelo's films unveil the dilemma, yet bestow no answer. And now Michelangelo stands right above me, an old man, kissing Nothing as if it were Aphrodite, and maybe that is *his* answer – just lay out the devotion whenever you can, baby. Even if it's thin air.

We run the scene again. It's great. Chiara is now smacking me hard enough where, if we were in Hollywood, someone would have called in a stunt coordinator. I ward off a second blow, spin her onto the bed, pull off her clothes, and begin the consummation, she moaning in Italian. I'm right where I left off when I believe I hear 'Cut' and I stop. 'Noooo!' It seems I didn't hear 'Cut' after all. He arrives on his cane, I look up at him. 'Maestro, cosa vuoi?' ('What do you want?') 'Que io mangio la sua fica?' (For this translation, use your imagination and just assume I wouldn't actually do what I was asking anyway.) In response to my query, I hear the Italian and French crew break into hysteria in the other room, while the two female powers present – Beatrice and Enrica – arrive, yelling, 'Peter, noooo!' Of course, 'No' to what I *think* he wants. But for the life of me, I can't figure out what he really wants, so I'm just laying all the cards on the table. Because I've gotten so close to her crotch on so many takes, Chiara has become absolutely blasé about all this. Meanwhile Michelangelo is chuckling away at my question. 'Continua,' he orders, and gives Beatrice and Enrica a 'Dio Mio' as he herds them back to the other room.

We begin again, and this time the punch almost sends me into the wall. I'm too far away from Chiara as a result of the force of her blow, my slap goes wild and lands on her jaw with a crunch which, for a split second, scares the hell out of me. But then she comes at me full speed, which only allows my rejoinder of pitching her on the bed, holding her hands behind her, kissing her neck with a voracity to which she responds in whisper 'Piano, piano'. I continue downward and, at the point of no return – in a flash – realize that Michelangelo wants me to continue in *some* fashion so that he has time for a cut. I kiss Chiara's abdomen for another 15 seconds, without embarrassing her, the film or, most importantly, my mother, should she see this movie. Beatrice finally yells, 'Cut.'

Now all of this sexy mumbo jumbo may make the civilian think, 'Gee, what an erotic place to be, a movie set – nudity, sex, kissing problems!' Nothing could be more the contrary, as most any actor who has performed in a love scene would tell you. The crew, the technical banter, the endless talk, the endless repetition, and the self-consciousness of film-making altogether combine to make the love scene one of the dreariest experiences of a shoot. (This scene in the finished film, by the way, is quite tame.)

Michelangelo is happy, but the German producer wants an 'American' version that will have me descending Chiara's body out of shot, while the camera stays on Chiara's head and neck. Michelangelo detests this idea, but, alas, the guy hasn't made a film in a decade, and these are the new days of television sales. Arms and legs blown off – no worries. The kissing of an abdomen will bring vilification. Are you laughing somewhere, Lenny Bruce?

Bernard Grenet lays a couple of great cigars on me. I buy champagne for the crew. Michelangelo wraps his film. He weeps. I'm poured a thin beaker of bubbly. I never drink the stuff. But the champagne has no effect on me whatsoever, and it is the second time since I can remember that I've imbibed something I hate. The first was with the reformed heroin addict, now deceased, William Burroughs, a great writer who became a dear friend from our association in *Naked Lunch*. Burroughs offered me a toke off the weakest marijuana ever, in a mutual celebration of this same order. It was like taking the pipe with the Commanche. I did, and I'm happy I did. Yes I inhaled. No, I didn't get high. Darn . . .

I bid everyone 'adieu'. I go to my dressing room at the hotel next door, knock on Chiara's door, the room next to mine. 'You're the only woman with whom I've ever made love who had to fake pleasure,' I tease. 'It was getting to a point where the acting wasn't necessary,' she flatters me. We laugh. We hug. I'm gone.

New York – Take 2

I walk around Paris for two days, before I'm to leave for England to recce for *Incognito*. The evening before I depart, I'm called to return to New York immediately, to re-shoot a scene with Woody and Helena Bonham Carter.

'When?' I ask.

'Tomorrow. Your Concorde ticket is waiting at Air France . . .'

Woody budgets for re-shooting, as he'll sometimes rewrite a scene while editing the film, if he thinks the scene, as shot, doesn't work. So I'm on the Concorde the next day, a Sunday, then shuffled immediately out to Montauk, Long Island to shoot the rewrite wherein I, as the jerk, make a pass at Helena. Then into Manhattan, where we shoot a rewrite with Helena and me (yet again, kissing), realizing that our extramarital affair isn't going to do either one of us any good, much less her husband, Woody.

In the midst of this re-shoot I realize the irony. I'm playing two characters, both of whom are buried up to their ass in a swamp of infidelity; Michelangelo's Roberto betrays his wife with another woman, while Woody's Jerry Bender (lest the significance of *that* name go unnoticed) betrays his friend (Woody) with that friend's wife. I've never been married, yet I've played the 'other guy' in both Alan Parker's *Shoot the Moon* and Sydney Lumet's *Just Tell Me What You Want*.

And so, during a break in shooting during this Sunday in New York, I impart to Woody, Brian Hamill and Woody's director of photography, Carlo Di Palma, the parallels of these two characters and my experience of the joyous weeks I've just passed with Michelangelo. Both Woody and Carlo are inquisitive of Michelangelo's health and his process, considering his age. Antonioni is surely an incisive influence on Woody, just as he must be on any film-maker who has attempted the personal story in the modern age. And Carlo is concerned for the

Maestro, having been Michelangelo's camera operator and director of photography from *L'Avventura* to *Red Desert*. (Carlo was also, coincidentally, married to Michelangelo's ex-companion, Monica Vitti.) At one point, while explaining to them the confusion in the passionate scene between myself and Chiara, Helena walks over, having overheard my reference to 'kissing her abdomen' and my mimicry of Michelangelo's 'Nooo!' She asks what in hell I'm talking about. 'Well,' I heave, realizing that restarting will make the context of the conversation cumbersome. Getting me off the hook, Woody quickly interrupts with, 'Peter was just explaining a very bizarre dream he had.'

Los Angeles

A few months later, Michelangelo receives the special Oscar for Life Achievement. I am sitting in the apartment of a friend. The roll call of folk present (all of whom gather every year at my friend's house to watch the Oscars) represents a cross-generational 'Who's Who' in movies and music.

Early in the evening I witness a very moving moment. Kirk Douglas sits very close to one of the many TVs blaring away among the loud chitchat that only settles down when one of the big six awards are presented. He watches the obituary tribute to the great entertainers who have passed away during the year. Burt Lancaster's picture comes up. Kirk, unobserved amid the chatter, stands and raises his drink to his long-time friend for the entire obit. They made great movies together, the best of which is one of my favourite films ever, *Gunfight at the OK Corral*, scripted by Leon Uris (*Exodus, Mila 18*), scored by Dimitri Tiomkin and directed by John Sturges (*The Magnificent Seven*). And Douglas's portrayal of a tubercular, vitriolic, alternately raging and charming Doc Holliday is one of his very best, in my opinion. His quiet toast to his friend went unseen by most in the room, but I shall never forget it. And as I watched him raise his glass to the television image of Lancaster, I wondered if Douglas had ever seen Lancaster in *Il Gattopardo*.

Halfway through the Oscars, Jack Nicholson appears on screen to present the award to Michelangelo. Through a montage of scenes from *Il Grido*, *Red Desert*, *L'Avventura*, *L'Eclisse*, *The Passenger* and *Zabriskie Point*, Nicholson narrates a concise and accurate précis of Michelangelo's unique contribution. He speaks of the space, the undefined void between men and women, the place and time where speech is meaningless, where words dissolve and no longer heal, where the modern age has devoured passion, love, hope, joy, like the Pac-Man of excess. I sit next to Sophia Loren, herself next to her husband, Carlo Ponti, a quiet and erudite man, and a master producer of an immense cinema legacy. As each film clip appears, I mutter the name of the film to myself.

'Tell me,' asks Sophia. 'How do you know these films?'

'I've seen them all. I just worked with him.'

'No!' I detect jealousy.

'Yes.'

'My husband produced two of his films.'

'Yes, *Zabriskie Point* and *The Passenger*.'

'I never had the pleasure of working with him,' she mourns.

'It was splendour,' I say.

She smiles. 'You are fortunate.'

She introduces me to her husband. Ponti is charming and articulate. In person it is easy to see why they've been together so long. She is definitely La Loren. She rocks a room, while he is obviously a demure source of power and support.

The following night the Italian Cultural Institute throws a party for Michelangelo and Enrica. Loren and Ponti are there. There are 2000 people, and one table. I arrive late, push through the multitude and sit at the table with Michelangelo. I tell him I miss him. I point out a beautiful girl, and ask him what he thinks. He laughs and puts his forefingers and thumb together, shakes his hand in the great and typical offering of Italian approval. I kiss him on both cheeks, leave the party. The next day he leaves LA.

Baltimore, Maryland / Venice, Italy

The spring of 1995 passes developing *Incognito* with Irene Jacob. She hasn't committed. But, while on a location scout, I visit her in London where she is rehearsing for *Othello*. In the fall, I embark for Baltimore to direct an episode of Barry Levinson's television show, *Homicide – Life on the Street*, against the strong advice of my *Incognito* producer. ('Don't besmirch your future in film direction by directing television.')

Before I leave, I am told that *Beyond the Clouds* will be at the Venice Film Festival. So will *Mighty Aphrodite*. I receive an invitation from Miramax, the distributor of Woody's film, and Cecchi Gori Productions, the Italian distributor of both *Aphrodite* and *Clouds*, to attend Venice for the purposes of promoting both films on two different nights. This excursion will demand three days of my time, coinciding with pre-production of *Homicide*. The line producer of *Homicide* happens to be Jimmy Finnerty, with whom I worked on the second job I ever had in feature films, Lumet's *Just Tell Me What You Want*. Jimmy tells me that there is a long Labor Day weekend that first week, and, being that I plan to return Monday night, it's no problem going to Venice. I finish a location scout in Baltimore on Thursday, and a very hospitable driver named Rick drives me the 40-odd miles to Washington to catch the non-stop to Rome, and thence to Venice.

I'd never been to the festival, but Venice is an old friend.

I arrive at the airport on a fresh September day and am greeted by a lovely redheaded representative of Cecchi Gori Productions, awaiting me with a boat taxi. As we coast across the back lagoons toward the canals and skyline of enchantment, I feel as though Visconti has brought me full circle again to this, the location of his brilliant film of Thomas Mann's magnum opus of beauty and solitude, *Death in Venice*.

I dump my bag, take a shower at the Danielli, and we proceed to the island of the Lido, a long strip that lies between the lagoon and the Adriatic sea, and which, unlike the main islands of Venice proper, has cars and buses. While most of the American glitz stays at the Excelsior, most of the hip Europeans stay at the Grande Hotel du Bains, the setting of *Death in Venice*. But the Excelsior is where the madness of the film festival awaits. I am shovelled off the *vaporetto* into the hotel, up the stairs to the lobby, amok with tourists, autograph hounds, producers, directors, publicists, bimbos, studs, hangers-on, up more stairs to a terrace where the photographic publicity of *Mighty Aphrodite* is in progress. Also present are Mira Sorvino (who would go on to win an Oscar for her performance), F. Murray Abraham and Michael Rappaport, an enchanting lout who has never been to a film festival and who's actually a stand-up comic from the Bronx. Three minutes of *paparazzi* is enough to cure anyone anywhere of his hunger for Warhol's full 15. Head turning-to-the-flash enough to give one lateral whiplash, I hate the stuff, as do most who've gotten over their first smell of fame. But I'm here to help the two movies do well, and one doesn't come to a film festival to play coy.

The actors, distributors and publicists from Miramax and Cecchi Gori meet in the lobby of the Excelsior for the walk over to the grand theatre for the premiere of *Mighty Aphrodite*. We will march a hundred yards down the road, followed by a rush of paparazzi. At this point, I have yet to see the film. The four of us actors are seated on the front row of the mezzanine next to Cecchi Gori and Gillo Pontecorvo, head of the festival and director of *The Battle of Algiers* and *Quemada* (*Burn!*), masterful dramas of violent social/racial revolutions, the latter starring Marlon Brando. The Italian audience goes nuts for Woody's film. (It would go on to make more money in Italy than any other Woody opus.) Afterward we all walk to a large outdoor stage in front of live TV while hordes of fans yell and misbehave.

The next day, Saturday, I'm ferried from the Danielli, over to the Excelsior once again, to do press for the film. At lunch I go back to Venice proper, meet two friends from Rome, and eat the first white truffles of the season at Harry's Bar. (The original Harry's, and *nothing* to do with anything else in the world called 'Harry's Bar'.) The rest of the day is free, and I've yet to see Antonioni, as *Beyond the Clouds* premieres the following day, Sunday. But I run into Cecchi Gori who asks me if my evening is open. Yes, I say. His wife has produced a film on the murder of Pier Paolo Pasolini, film-maker and poet – and homosexual.

Pasolini made no secrecy in that regard. He was brutally beaten to death and run over by his own car in the mid-60s, near a poor outskirts of Rome. Subsequently a young man, far too diminutive to have perpetrated the murder alone, was arrested. The court maintained that the boy could not have acted alone, as Pasolini was far too agile and strong to receive a beating so ferocious that it destroyed his face and much of his torso. It was a beating that went on for hours, as heard and reported to the police by impoverished residents around the vacant lot in which it took place.

The higher federal courts overturned the lower court ruling, claiming that Pasolini was indeed murdered by the single hand of the boy; thus the case was closed. Protests resounded throughout the film and literary worlds. And Pasolini became a martyr, not only to the artistic community worldwide, but to the lower and middle classes of Italy who felt they'd been dealt their own death knell by the fixed banking and the crushing taxes going into the pockets of crooked businessmen and the politically privileged few. Pasolini had been attacking this corruption vociferously in the press for years.

His murder was proclaimed a cover-up on the part of the courts who were probably just as pissed off at Pasolini as just about every political faction in Italy. With articles, essays and films claiming that the government and the financial community had been in bed with corruption ever since the war, he raved that the true victims of Italy's gross mismanagement were the working people. And his sentiments were always worn on the sleeve of his artistry. The outrage that Pasolini so personally and articulately voiced for almost 25 years has had a rebirth. The recent overhaul and purging of the Italian government, and the trials and testimonies of politicians, bankers and Mafiosi, have revealed a vice so deep and tenacious that the entire political and financial infrastructure of Italy is only now beginning to leave behind its world reputation as a joke.

As Pasolini said in his last poem (the only tape extant of his voice), his greatest sorrow was that he would not live to see the wrongs – perpetrated upon the common folk of Italy by the collection of bandits and thieves posing as politicians – righted. Indeed he didn't. Homosexual toughs or homophobic heterosexual toughs executed Pasolini; or, as suggested by many, government thugs or Mafiosi made it *look* like homosexual or anti-homosexual aggression. Whatever the case, the courts of Italy deafened his posthumous voice in Italy.

The guy was a maverick without parallel. *The Gospel According to Saint Matthew*, a savage film depicting, for the first time, Christ as a pissed-off Messiah, was once desecrated by the Vatican but is now on its list of preferred films for Catholics. As rough as his films were, no one of his time or this had the balls or energy to match him. Many movie-makers have the poetry, but, in my opinion, of the directors burning film today, few have the guts of Pasolini. His films stand as a hallmark in the evolution of entertainment and art.

So, on Saturday night I attend the premiere of this docu-drama on Pasolini. I go with Cecchi Gori, his wife Rita, and producer Lawrence Bender (*Pulp Fiction, Fresh*).

The film is of television quality. Not much in the way of film-making, but the actual footage of interviews with Pasolini and those who knew him, including a young Bertolucci, is powerful. The drama of the film centres around the murder and the cover-up, including the firing of an internal affairs cop who was on the threshold of a link between government cops and the toughs who probably killed the man. The film ends with a still of Pier Paolo, who, along with Jean Genet and William Burroughs, was one of the very few high-profile, give-a-damn-who-knows gays, before any social movement protected the culture. We hear Pasolini's voice over the frame, reciting his last poem, wishing for the righting of wrongs perpetrated on the people of Italy by their own so-called protectors, and predicting his own imminent death. At the film's end I'm weeping. Lawrence Bender is weeping. Much of the audience sobs. I was recently told that the film's impact re-opened the investigation into Pasolini's death. Praise be.

I go to the ceremonial dinner for the Pasolini film at the ballroom in the Grand Hotel Des Bains. There I see Bernardo Bertolucci and Jeremy Thomas, producer of Bertolucci's recent films and of *Naked Lunch*. Neither he nor Bertolucci had time to see the film, but I dine with them and ask Bernardo a hundred questions about Pasolini, all of which he is happy to answer. He feels Pasolini, more than anyone else, was his mentor, brother and friend. Bernardo tells me he remembers the day, as a young man, still in film school, working as a typist and assistant to Pasolini, that Pier Paolo came to him with the news that he had obtained minimal funding for *Accatone*. Bernardo says that Pier Paolo invited him to be the first assistant director. Bernardo protested, claiming he had no experience, no power to control a professional film set, much less any knowledge of the particulars of physical production. 'That's all right,' Pasolini responded. 'I don't either . . . but we'll learn together.' And so they did.

The final day for me at the festival begins with a reunion with Antonioni and all the actors in *Beyond the Clouds* in the press conference room in the Excelsior. Antonioni is smiling. Wim Wenders acts as moderator. How he tirelessly fields the endless stream of film intellectualism – the abstract questions about Michelangelo's deeper meanings, the excursions into the symbolic power of Michelangelo's process, and the interpretations of his style – is beyond me. The forum almost throws me into vicarious valium O.D. as I sit on the dais, listening to the droning of one high-brow journalist after another demanding long, significant interpretations of the movie. Malkovich is asked nothing whatsoever in this tirade of snore-dom, as he is absent, shooting in Rome. All of us on the dais embody Brando's definition of an actor – 'Anyone who, if you ain't talking about him, he ain't listening'. I repeat the photo-op from the Woody round, and it is amazing how much less verve a man's very own country has for its own maestro than for the barrage of movie Americana.

That night for the third time on the Lido, I make the march with Cecchi Gori over to the theatre for a premiere. All the actors, including that glamorous wonder Fanny Ardant – plus the German, French, Italian producers and their wives – are seated in the first two rows of the open mezzanine. We're all introduced, then on goes the film.

At first look, *Beyond the Clouds* is slow, uneventful. About 15 minutes into it, I have to reawaken to the fact that this is Antonioni. His movements, his vision, his films are like cool jazz, like the city of Venice itself – always seductive but never imposing. We, the modern movie audience, have become so used to being strapped in for an assault from special effects akin to the fall of Saigon, that films like Michelangelo's tend to subvert our expectations at first. You must *go* to Michelangelo's movies, you must *watch* them. The movie will not come to you. Like the difference between New York and Venice. Venice is a city that you must go *into*, walk through, move through, spend time in. It doesn't come *at* you with its power. Its energy is feminine, elusive and sublime. If you get away from the tourist bullshit, Venice will wrap its arms around you and seduce you into a serenity and reverie like no other city in the world. The same is true for jazz. It is a music in which you, the listener, must invest, must surrender. It doesn't come at you like Beethoven or the Stones. *You* must go to *it*.

This is most true in the first – and my favourite – segment of *Beyond the Clouds*. A young Italian man meets a young Spanish woman in a small hotel in Ferrara, Italy. They almost make love, but don't. Then, as Malkovich the narrator intones, they never see each other again. But they do. And the man's adoration of the woman is such that he balks again in the final moment before consummation. Then they part. The space between them, the eternal and inexplicable between a man and woman, is never more evident than in this piece, the most haunting of the four. Most critics, of all nationalities, have praised the third story, the most realistic of the conflicts posed in this film, the story in which I star with Fanny, Chiara and Jean Reno. It is this story in which Michelangelo began with the least interest, but in which, Enrica tells me, he ended up with the most; perhaps because it was closest to the reality of his own life. But the first of the four, in my opinion, is the most beautiful, the most lyrical, and the most truly Antonioni.

I part company with the Maestro at the party after the screening. The film had a reverent but unspectacular reception, no more. For such a film at a festival with the glitz of Venice, what can one expect?

Epilogue

In February 1996, *Beyond the Clouds* was premiered by the American Film Institute at the Motion Picture Academy's screening room. It was once again critically well received, as it has been all over Europe, where it had made money. Jack Nicholson threw Michelangelo and Enrica a dinner afterward. He sat across from Michelangelo, teasing the Maestro about doing another film with him – only this time Jack would get to write the script. Michelangelo winked. Nicholson asked me how I found working with him. 'Rejuvenating,' I responded. Nicholson concurred.

Michelangelo and Enrica left LA. I prepared and shot the film with Irene Jacob for a few joyous weeks in Paris, Amsterdam and Brussels. Then I had 'creative' differences with the company, and left. The rest of the fall I spent in Las Vegas acting in a film with Dennis Hopper entitled *Top of the World*. One day Dennis stands in a dressing room with me, bemoaning the universal sin that an Antonioni film such as *Beyond the Clouds* could have no American distributor, despite its worldwide reception.

Clouds went on to the New York Film Festival (which I could not attend, as I was on a location scout in Florida, preparing to direct a film of Elmore Leonard's *Gold Coast* for Paramount/Showtime; a happy and profitable experience.) The *New Yorker* published a great review and a homage to Antonioni in the context of the festival. The meat of the article hinged on the accurate observation that, in a day when the *style* of movies seems interchangeable from one to the next, with an Antonioni film one is watching an individual, an artist whose focus and personal stamp on communication is unique and unmistakable.

I did not see Michelangelo Antonioni in almost a year. I called him in the fall of 1996, on my way through Rome, to say hello. Of course Michelangelo cannot speak well on the phone, so I spoke with Enrica, who happily exclaimed that they were in pre-production for yet another movie. I commenced the editing at Paramount for *Gold Coast* in the spring of 1997. In March I attended a party in Los Angeles for Michelangelo, who was attempting to raise funds for his new movie. He screened *Beyond the Clouds* at my agency, CAA. Sophia Loren and Carlo Ponti arrived; but no one else of note from the community of film in Los Angeles attended. I went to the reception but did not stay for the film. I was melancholy. *Beyond the Clouds* was now behind me.

The applicable knowledge I've accrued from my 20-odd years in this carnival called motion pictures is a legacy of mad people who have dreamed up stories to exalt some dilemma, or some ensuing conflict, or even some *resolution* of what it is to live with one another on this planet. But my time with Antonioni was one of a kind. The beauty and distinction of Michelangelo's artistry has left a formidable impression, one that gives no escapist's answer, no resolution. He only delivers unto us remarkable dramas of separation, conveyed in a chorus of images. What is *it* that is never resolved between two people who love one another? And why is this missing *it*, this unfulfilled space, the real stuff of being human? He serves us this question over and over again, in stunning and provocative pictures on film of women and men in a timeless search for the evidence of love.

If I were banished to a desert island with only 20 movies, half of these would be from the Italy of 1945 to 1970. Four of them would be Michelangelo's.

I am fortunate to know him, blessed to have worked with him. And I will treasure my time with him always.

Peter Weller

April 1997/Los Angeles, CA

12 March , 2001/ Florence, Italy

Pissing in the Tall Grass with the Big Dogs
Fiction by Ethan Hawke

It's 6.58pm. You are sitting on a blueish-grey chair in the living room. The chair, the couch, the carpet and the three framed prints on the walls all match exactly. The lights are off in the room and you are watching the last remnants of sun fade as shadows twist into darkness. You have to go to the theatre soon and wonder how only four hours of work can fill a whole day. Perhaps there will be a transcendent sign that you will be brilliant tonight. You know you won't be. But maybe . . . You recite lines in your head. Somewhere in the middle of a monologue you get bored and notice how beautiful the room looks. It is purple and everything, even your hands, looks far away like a grainy photograph.

It's 7.14. You've got to go to the theatre now. You try to find a song to exit on – maybe a loud rock 'n' roll song to break the mood. But you don't want to break the mood – it's sad, but you like it. You like the silence. You gather up your shit, throw cough suppressants, aspirins and a book you will never read into a tatty leather bag and wonder if the people at the theatre notice that you don't change your clothes.

Walking out of your mirrored elevator into the lobby, you think to yourself just how reminiscent this building is of a huge gerbil cage. You have spent your life in buildings like this, transient housing. Oh, what the hell, check the mail again. It's the fourth time you've done it today. To your surprise there's something in your little cubby box – one of those coupon envelopes addressed to 'current resident'.

You walk out of your building and there is that dark-haired lady with the two little dogs, Scooter and Muffy. Those dogs pee more often than you do – which is a lot, considering the way you've been downing liquids. The flu is almost gone, but so are the antibiotics – and you're scared. You know if you could stop being scared, you would stop being sick – but this happens every time you do a play.

You get in your car. It stalls out three times before you can do the eight-point turn required to get out of the parking space. Your car is cool. It has nice curves and looks fast without drawing attention to itself. It's from the 70s and weighs a lot. Sometimes you can see its reflection in glass buildings as you drive and think, 'There goes a pretty cool guy.' You're glad it's autumn because you have broken out your leather jacket. Between the jacket and the car, for about three and a half minutes, you're feeling a little sexy. The feeling fades, however, when you hit traffic and turn on the AM radio. 'Dusty Radio,' the woman says in a languid bedroom voice. You like the station and for some reason the phrase 'dusty radio' gets under your skin.

The woman on the air speaks with a thick urban black accent but you suspect she's white. She's rambling about a local scandal-laced trial and how the jury is finally in deliberation. You turn off the radio and continue driving through the projects. You see that far off, one basketball rim still has a net, but all the rest of the playground is shot to hell. Your teeth hurt – something about the way your mouth has been closing lately hasn't been right. You busted your lip a couple of nights ago. (You did it on stage. Everyone said it was your best show. 'You should try to hurt yourself every night. Ha, ha, ha.' They think they're kidding.) It's a steady throbbing pain that you don't really notice until you begin pulling on your teeth.

Oh, shit. You pass a clock that alternates time and temperature. 7.31. You're definitely late. You quickly play through a scenario where you walk into the theatre and the director screams, 'Wouldn't you know it, the worst one in the show is late.' You work yourself into a mild panic, pull into the parking lot, back into a chain-link fence, jerk on the emergency brake, turn off the ignition, lock the door, grab your junk and hop out in one quick gesture. Once you're out, you notice it: Chicago smells like chocolate-chip cookies.

You walk in the theatre and downstairs into the dressing rooms, passing some early theatregoers who notice in whispers that you are you. No one seems to notice you're late. Cool.

The guy you share your dressing room with seems like a good enough guy. He was released from prison in 1974 and discovered acting as part of rehabil-itation therapy. He is very good. The two of you have had a couple of laughs talking about pussy before, but for the most part he's real quiet, especially before the show. You sit in your chair, take off your shirt and look at yourself in the mirror. There is an electric current of expectation vibrating through the air of the theatre. You like this part of the day. You straighten up your area and wonder whether to shave or not. You decide it can wait till tomorrow. Your roommate says something about hoping he doesn't pull any stupid bull-shit tricks like he did last night. You know what he means, but you secretly think he's brilliant and don't know why he insists on being so hard on himself. 'If you were half as good as he is,' you think, 'you'd just relax and have a good time.'

You get dressed. You dig your costume. (When the play is over, you hope you can steal it – particularly the cowboy boots.) The belt you wear is a belt you brought from New York. You've owned it since you were five, the buckle any-way. Your father gave it to you. You thought it would be appropriate for the play because the play is all about fathers – at least it is for you.

You're dressed now and it's time to warm up your voice – something you normally never do. It always seemed faggy, but the director is paying for this 'expert' woman to come in before the play and warm up your voice. Your character has to scream a lot in the show, and in the second performance you ripped your vocal cords to shreds, so you suppose this lame-brain exercise is a good idea, but you still find it mildly humiliating. The woman is pleasant, though, with giant breasts that she heaves up and down trying to prove the benefits of breathing from the diaphragm. She makes you do tongue exercises. Up, down, all around. Up, down, all around. You wonder if she is thinking about oral sex – you are.

By the time you are warmed up, the play is ten minutes underway. You're not in the first act, so there is still plenty of time. 'How are they?' you ask the gaggle of understudies and techies hanging out in the green-room watching the monitor. You are referring to the audience. 'Quiet,' someone says. 'Well I'll get 'em,' you say, trying to manufacture some confidence. 'Give 'em hell,' someone cheers. 'Have a good show,' your voice coach says. You ignore her and walk back to your dressing room. Over the monitor you can hear your roommate onstage. 'God, that guy is good,' you think to yourself. The audience is laughing all over themselves. It makes you smile.

You put on a large suede jacket. It's tough. It weighs a lot, like your car. Then the last little touch – the sunglasses. You reach into your jacket pocket only to find they're broken. Fuck. You run to wardrobe. They give you a different pair of shades, but you know the whole evening is ruined. These shades suck. 'Buck up,' you tell yourself. The play is not called *Sunglasses*. You're staring at yourself again, only this time you see the scrap of paper you pinned to the mirror – a note from the director: BRING THE AUDIENCE TO YOU. DON'T ACT WELL, DON'T PERFORM WELL, JUST LIVE. You like the director. He's a prick, but he's talented and you know he's right. Fuck. You wish those sunglasses weren't broken.

There's a knock on the dressing room door. It's her. Your co-star, the ingénue, your leading lady, whatever she is. You hate her. She's spouting all her fantastic ideas in regard to the local trial with an unbearable preachy tone of voice. You love her. You want her to sit on your lap, sometimes she does, but you don't want to appear too lecherous. You wonder what she would do if you asked as politely as possible if you could please suckle her titties.

She does, hooray – she sits on your lap. You place your hand on the small of her back. Her shirt is midriff and you actually touch her delicate skin. It makes your heart beat faster. Now she is talking about today's notes from Herr Director. You are wondering what her pussy looks like, how soft it must be, how wonderfully pink and wet. Ohh. You make her get off your lap. Then she says something like, 'I just think everyone in this cast is wonderful.' You hate her. It's okay, you remind yourself, let it out on stage.

Act I is over. The two of you are next. You are not nervous. She is. She always is. You hold her hand as you run lines and walk toward 'places'. You stand backstage, impatient, fiddling with the crappy new sunglasses, listening to the crowd file back in after intermission. While waiting you joke and goof around with 'Missy Thing', because you know it's helpful if you are playful. 'You're a nice guy,' you think. You know you're a liar.

The music starts.

The crowd quiets down.

The cue light comes on.

Your eyes are fixed on it.

The music stops.

The sound of mechanical rain takes over.

The cue light goes off.

She laughs.

You walk onstage.

For the first few lines you are self-conscious. Trying to project, aware of how you are moving your arms. She is very funny and looking you in the eyes. 'She is a good actress' is the last thing you remember thinking until you walk offstage 35 minutes later and blow your nose. You always get so worked up in the scene, your nose starts to run. You think it went well, but you can't remember anything – you think that's a good sign.

Act III is next. That's the tough one: back to the dressing room. You pour water all over yourself. You do three sets of 33 push-ups. You sit in the bathroom and turn off the lights. Someone walks in. You apologize and walk out.

You try to feel drunk, tripping yourself on purpose as you stumble through the green-room on your way back to the stage. Someone says, 'Tear it up.' You're walking fast. A stagehand tells you to hurry, you're late. But it's all right. You're focused. You get all your props, try to hyperventilate yourself. Boom – your cue. You run onstage, break down the door and pour whiskey all over yourself. Hot damn, you're flyin' – till you reach a minor glitch where you catch yourself imitating what you did the night before: 'Shake it off, live it.'

The end of the play is near. You're three-fourths of the way through your big monologue. It's not boring – even you are interested. You're talking about your father. You can feel yourself, you can feel the text. In the glare of the lights, you can see your father's disapproving eyes staring back at you – mean, lonely and angry. Three seconds before it's over, you screw it all up. You think to yourself, 'Boy, this is going well', and you're out of it – the power is gone. You know it.

The final lighting cues are called, music thunders through the audience and they ooh and aah at the director's skill. He is good. The curtain goes down. You get in position. The curtain goes back up and everyone slowly applauds. The cast joins hands and bows. About half the house rises to its feet, cheering. You smile.

You wonder if the director will come backstage and tell you that you were brilliant – or does he know that you choked in the last moment? But it was still better, you know that. You tell your roommate that you think you actually had a good show. He only nods. You think that he hates your performance. Well, fuck him. The director doesn't materialize.

You get dressed and go to the bar across the street. People, mostly girls, stop you and ask for your autograph. They tell you the show was 'really, really . . . I mean, it was really good'. You say thanks and hurry on over to the bar. You'd forgotten it was Friday. The bar is packed. You buy your roommate a beer and hope that when he arrives, you'll get an honest compliment about the show. He sits down, says thanks for the beer, but never does mention the evening's per-formance. You say that you liked the show. He agrees.

You sneak out of the bar without saying goodbye to anyone and wonder what has happened to your social skills and why you never hang out anymore. Loneliness perpetuates itself, you decide, as you drive around the city streets pulling on your teeth again. Meandering your way through the traffic of the posh districts, watching people waiting outside ritzy bars dressed up in their new outfits, you continue on into more depressed neighbourhoods, looking for the Taco Bell you were at the night before. Finally, you find it, but you forgot just what a lousy part of town this is. You notice once again that Chicago smells like chocolate-chip cookies. You want to mention this to someone, anyone, a stranger, but you don't. You walk into Taco Bell and sit up on the purple railing you're supposed to wait behind. The manager, a large black guy with a long braid running down his back, yells at you to 'get off that'. You look at him. 'Hey, tough guy,' he says, 'relax, I just don't want you to fall over and split your head open.'

You hadn't meant to be a tough guy. You order – two soft tacos, a nachos supreme and a medium Dr Pepper.

Some 20-something kid with a striped shirt and a brand-new haircut has been staring at you since the manager yelled at you. He tells you that you look a lot like yourself. You nod. 'Do people tell you that all the time?' he asks. 'You wouldn't believe it,' you say. 'You're his spitting image,' he says. You shrug him away. The manager yells at you again. 'Can't you read? That ice machine is broke. Use the one over there.'

'Okay,' you say.

'It must not be your day,' he says.

You sit down across from a beautiful black woman and her daughter. You like them because they look downtrodden. You've never rooted for a winning sports team. You wonder if that means you're a loser.

You wonder how many hours of your life you've spent in Mexican restaurants.

You overhear the woman talking to the manager. He has sat down next to her with a bag of Dunkin Donuts. You realize that she is a prostitute. 'My daughter knows what I do. I want her to. She know I do it for her, so we can buy things. I mean, I ain't no Bloomingdale's shopper, you know, but if I see something I want, I want to be able to own it.' Her daughter is fat. She stares off into the Taco Bell wallpaper.

'I only have to work four hours a day,' she says, 'and that includes travel time.' You realize that you and she work the same number of hours a day. You wonder if those measly four hours take over her whole day, too.

As the woman and her daughter stand up to leave, the manager says to the girl that next time, he will buy her some Taco Bell. The mother says, 'Bullshit. You don't even eat here.'

'Well they ain't serve no real meat.' The three of them walk out, and you look down at your taco. This place gave you a stomach ache last night. And you're back.

Driving home, you pass through an area with lots of beautiful women in tight red sweaters and blue jeans that outline their behinds. You stare at them till you realize you're in the wrong lane and about to die.

Quickly you recover. You pass a Porsche with what appears to be engine trouble, but in fact some guy and his little cutie coed are just going through their CD collections. That depresses you. You turn on Dusty Radio.

It's your favourite song.

You can't believe your luck. You park your car outside your building and listen to the whole thing. When it's over, you turn off the car and walk back toward the building. Realizing you should wait till you get upstairs, but knowing the elevator ride would be unbearable, you pause by a small tree and take a quick piss in the bushes. You are reminded of Scooter and Muffy. The air still smells like cookies. You think about what your agent said when he told you that you'd been offered this play: 'Congratulations! Hey, man, you're pissing in the tall grass with the big dogs.'

DIGITAL CINEMA

The New Frontier?
Richard Linklater's *Waking Life*

Richard Linklater's latest film *Waking Life* is a unique and revolutionary fusion of the cinematic possibilities enabled by digital video cameras and computers. It is the fruit of a close collaboration between writer–director Linklater and computer animation savants Bob Sabiston and Tommy Palotta, creators of the unique 'interpolated rotoscoping' computer software.

Linklater originally shot and edited live-action digital video footage, which was subsequently 'painted' over on computer, frame by frame, by a team of over 30 artists working in Austin, Texas, under the supervision of Sabiston and Palotta. '*Waking Life* is not animated in the truest sense of the word,' Palotta has insisted. 'It is a composite of wildly different, re-imagined video scenes drawn in cartoon style.' The artists were able to select specific moving designs from the video footage, whereupon interpolation tools were used to take a hand-drawn stroke and stretch it smoothly across a series of frames. Each artist worked on only one character throughout the entire production process, and each minute of film required 250 hours of animation work.

The feeling created by the completed film is that of an Impressionist painting, breathing with cinematic life. Its protagonist (Wiley Wiggins) travels through a series of encounters and observations in a world that may or may not be reality. It is this surreal existence, flourishing with endless ideas and possibilities, that ultimately brings him to the question, 'Are we sleep-walking through our waking state or wake-walking through our dreams?'

It is a measure of the film-makers' achievement that in September 2001 *Waking Life* became the first animated piece to compete for the Golden Lion at the Venice Film Festival. 'We have no prejudices on this type of cinema,' festival director Alberto Barbera told the Italian daily *Il Sole 24 Ore*. He further proclaimed digital image-making to be 'the new aesthetic frontier'.

The images across the following pages are a tribute to *Waking Life*, albeit of a more simple illustrative nature than the frames of Linklater's film, drawn as they are from the limited-edition *Waking Life Colouring Book*. **Readers must provide their own crayons.**

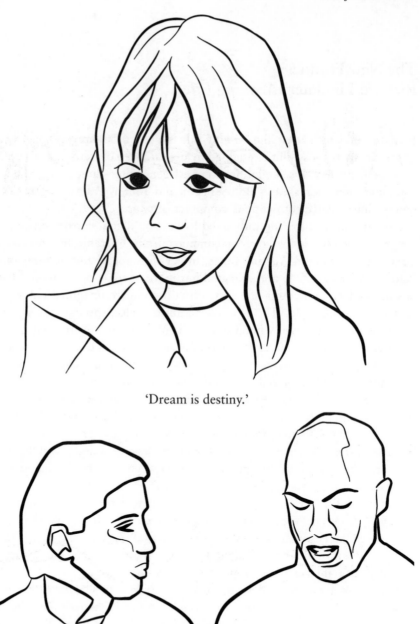

'Dream is destiny.'

'You haven't met yourself yet. But the advantage to meeting others in the
meantime is that one of them may present you to yourself.'

'He's all action and no theory. We're all theory and no action.'

'It's like there's this whole telepathic thing going on that we're all part of whether we're conscious of it or not.'

'It seems like everyone is sleep-walking through their waking state or wake-walking through their dreams. Either way, they're not going to get much out of it.'

'The story is singular, but in fact it is story after story.'

IN MEMORIAM

Wim Wenders, Peter Falk (seated) and Henri Alekan on the set of *Wings of Desire* (1987).

Wings of Desire (1987): Bruno Ganz and Solveig Dommartin.

A Tribute to Henri Alekan
by Wim Wenders

Dear Henri.

If someone would ask me
which professional collaboration
I have cherished the most,
during the 20 films or so that I have done,
or what I'd be most proud of, in hindsight,
I wouldn't hesitate for a second to answer:
The two films
I had the privilege of shooting with you.

I have learned from you all that I know
about lights and shadows,
that's for sure,
but much more than that.
You showed me something very precious,
some sort of principle
that nobody would dare to pronounce,
let alone teach,
but in my book
it's still the most beautiful lesson of cinema:
'Every shot done without love,
for its subjects and for film itself,
isn't worth a red nickel.'

You taught me that,
but probably without being aware of it.
You were the living proof yourself
that each and every gesture on the set,
every use of the camera,
every movement of a crane or dolly,
in short, every little act of our craft,
could be done with tenderness and care,
with curiosity
and a never-ending eagerness to learn.

I still see you
standing next to the camera,
always beaming with enthusiasm,
with either a smile on your face,
or that slight concern
that meant
you were about to change something.

I see your bushy eyes,
full of all that experience,
yet those of a big kid's . . .

I see you putting your heads together,
you and your marvellous gaffer friend,
Louis Cochet,
with whom you worked together for sixty years!
You didn't even have to talk about the light!
Just a few indications with your hands,
a couple of nods,
and off he went running,
eighty years old,
but younger than all the other electricians on the set
with their age of thirty or forty . . .

I see you measure the light
just by squinting your eyes.
You trusted them more than your spot-meter
which you only carried,
as you jokingly said,
to show that you had one
and even knew how to use it.

I see you next to the camera,
your attention always glued to the actors,
never on the operator or the dolly grip.
You would look at me,
when I'd say 'cut',
and I could tell what you thought,
even if you'd always refrain
from expressing an opinion.

I see you
and it all comes back to me:
YOU yourself,
you were that most beautiful lesson of cinema.

Dear Henri.

La Belle et la Bête (1946): Jean Marais and Josette Day.